Introduction	1
Overview of System Operation	2
Signal Description	3
Bus Operation Description	4
Address Translation	5
Instruction Set Processor	6
Protection	7
Breakpoints	8
Coprocessor Interface	9
Access Level Control Interface	10
Operation Timings	11
Electrical Specifications	12
Ordering Information and Mechanical Data	13
Instruction Set	A
Hardware Considerations	B
Software Considerations	C

HANS-JOACHIM MÜSCHENBORN
Münchenlaan 25
B - 2400 MOL / BELGIUM
Phone: 32-14-58 98 93

MC68851

PAGED MEMORY MANAGEMENT UNIT USER'S MANUAL

First Edition

PRENTICE-HALL, Inc., Englewood Cliffs, N.J. 07632

© 1986 by Motorola Inc.

All rights reserved. No part of this book may be
reproduced, in any form or by any means,
without permission in writing from the publisher.

> This document contains information on a new product.
> Specifications and information herein are subject to change
> without notice. Motorola reserves the right to make changes to
> any products herein to improve functioning or design.
> Although the information in this document has been carefully
> reviewed and is believed to be reliable, Motorola does not
> assume any liability arising out of the application or use of any
> product or circuit described herein; neither does it convey any
> license under its patent rights nor the rights of others.

Motorola, Inc. general policy does not recommend the use of its components in life support applications where in a failure or malfunction of the component may directly threaten life or injury. Per Motorola Terms and Conditions of Sale, the user of Motorola components in life support applications assumes all risk of such use and indemnifies Motorola against all damages.

Printed in the United States of America

10 9 8 7 6 5 4 3 2 1

ISBN 0-13-566902-2 025

Prentice-Hall International (UK) Limited, *London*
Prentice-Hall of Australia Pty. Limited, *Sydney*
Prentice-Hall Canada Inc., *Toronto*
Prentice-Hall Hispanoamericana, S.A., *Mexico*
Prentice-Hall of India Private Limited, *New Delhi*
Prentice-Hall of Japan, Inc., *Tokyo*
Prentice-Hall Southeast Asia Pte. Ltd., *Singapore*
Editora Prentice-Hall do Brasil, Ltda., *Rio de Janeiro*

TABLE OF CONTENTS

Paragraph Number	Title	Page Number

Section 1
Introduction

1.1	MC68851 Overview	1-1
1.1.1	Address Translation	1-1
1.1.2	Protection Mechanism	1-2
1.1.3	Breakpoints	1-2
1.1.4	M68000 Family Instruction Set Extensions	1-2
1.1.5	The Coprocessor Concept	1-3
1.2	Hardware Overview	1-4
1.2.1	Coprocessor Interface	1-7
1.2.2	Access Level Control Interface	1-8
1.2.3	Breakpoint Acknowledge Interface	1-8
1.2.4	Bus Operations	1-8

Section 2
Overview of System Operation

2.1	System Configuration	2-1
2.2	Address Translation	2-2
2.2.1	Address Translation Cache	2-2
2.2.2	Address Translation Tables	2-3
2.2.3	Protection Mechanism	2-4

Section 3
Signal Description

3.1	Logical Address Bus (LA8 through LA31)	3-2
3.2	Physical Address Bus (PA8 through PA31)	3-2
3.3	Shared Address Bus (A0 through A7)	3-2
3.4	Function Code (FC0 through FC3)	3-2
3.5	Data Bus (D0 through D31)	3-3
3.6	Transfer Size (SIZ0, SIZ1)	3-3
3.7	Bus Control Signals	3-3
3.7.1	Read-Modify-Write ($\overline{\text{RMC}}$)	3-3
3.7.2	Logical Address Strobe ($\overline{\text{LAS}}$)	3-4
3.7.3	Physical Address Strobe ($\overline{\text{PAS}}$)	3-4
3.7.4	Data Strobe ($\overline{\text{DS}}$)	3-4
3.7.5	Read/Write (R/$\overline{\text{W}}$)	3-4
3.7.6	Data Transfer and Size Acknowledge ($\overline{\text{DSACK0}}$, $\overline{\text{DSACK1}}$)	3-4
3.7.7	Data Buffer Disable (DBDIS)	3-5
3.8	Bus Exception Control Signals	3-5
3.8.1	Reset ($\overline{\text{RESET}}$)	3-5
3.8.2	Halt ($\overline{\text{HALT}}$)	3-5
3.8.3	Bus Error ($\overline{\text{BERR}}$)	3-6

TABLE OF CONTENTS
(Continued)

Paragraph Number	Title	Page Number
3.9	Cache Load Inhibit ($\overline{\text{CLI}}$)	3-6
3.10	Asynchronous Control ($\overline{\text{ASYNC}}$)	3-7
3.11	Clock (CLK)	3-7
3.12	Physical Bus Arbitration	3-7
3.12.1	Physical Bus Request ($\overline{\text{PBR}}$)	3-7
3.12.2	Physical Bus Grant ($\overline{\text{PBG}}$)	3-7
3.12.3	Physical Bus Grant Acknowledge ($\overline{\text{PBGACK}}$)	3-7
3.13	Logical Bus Arbitration	3-8
3.13.1	Logical Bus Request In ($\overline{\text{LBRI}}$)	3-8
3.13.2	Logical Bus Request Out ($\overline{\text{LBRO}}$)	3-8
3.13.3	Logical Bus Grant In ($\overline{\text{LBGI}}$)	3-8
3.13.4	Logical Bus Grant Out ($\overline{\text{LBGO}}$)	3-8
3.13.5	Logical Bus Grant Acknowledge ($\overline{\text{LBGACK}}$)	3-8
3.14	Signal Summary	3-8

Section 4
Bus Operation Description

4.1	Reset Operation	4-2
4.1.1	Initialization of Internal State	4-2
4.1.2	Bus Interface Initialization	4-2
4.1.2.1	D0	4-3
4.1.2.2	Bus Size (D1, D2)	4-3
4.1.2.3	Decision Timeout Delay (D3, D4)	4-3
4.1.2.4	Fast Table Search (D5)	4-3
4.1.2.5	Early Processing Startup (D6)	4-4
4.1.2.6	Assertion Inhibit (D7)	4-5
4.2	Address Translation	4-5
4.2.1	Signal Usage During Address Translation	4-5
4.2.1.1	Address Buses	4-5
4.2.1.2	Address Strobes	4-6
4.2.1.3	Bus Cycle Termination Signals	4-6
4.2.2	Synchronous versus Asynchronous Address Translation	4-7
4.2.2.1	Synchronous Operation	4-7
4.2.2.2	Asynchronous Operation	4-7
4.2.3	Functional Descriptions	4-7
4.2.3.1	Normally Terminated Address Translation (Non-CPU Space)	4-8
4.2.3.2	Address Translation Terminated by Relinquish and Retry Sequence	4-10
4.2.3.3	Address Translation Terminated by Bus Error	4-12
4.2.3.4	CPU Space Access with Relinquish Request	4-13
4.2.3.5	Translation of CPU Space Accesses	4-15
4.2.3.6	CPU Space Access with Relinquish and Retry	4-18
4.3	Table Search Operations	4-20
4.3.1	Operand Transfer Mechanism	4-20
4.3.1.1	Dynamic Bus Sizing	4-20

TABLE OF CONTENTS
(Continued)

Paragraph Number	Title	Page Number
4.3.1.2	Effects of Dynamic Bus Sizing	4-23
4.3.1.3	Address, Size, and Data Bus Relationships	4-23
4.3.2	Physical Bus Operation	4-25
4.3.2.1	Read Cycle	4-27
4.3.2.2	Write Cycle	4-29
4.3.2.3	Read-Modify-Write Cycle	4-29
4.3.2.4	Bus Error and Halt Operation	4-31
4.2.3.4.1	Bus Error Operation	4-31
4.3.2.4.2	Retry Operation	4-34
4.3.2.4.3	Halt Operation	4-35
4.3.2.4.4	The Relationship of $\overline{DSACKx}$, $\overline{BERR}$, and $\overline{HALT}$	4-38
4.3.2.5	Asynchronous versus Synchronous Physical Bus Operation	4-38
4.3.2.5.1	Asynchronous Operation	4-38
4.3.2.5.2	Synchronous Operation	4-40
4.3.3	Bus Cycle Sequence	4-41
4.4	Logical Bus Arbitration	4-41
4.4.1	Requesting the Logical Bus	4-42
4.4.1.1	Alternate Master Requesting the Logical Bus	4-42
4.4.1.2	MC68851 Requesting the Logical Bus	4-45
4.4.2	Receiving the Logical Bus Grant	4-47
4.4.3	Passing the Logical Bus Grant	4-47
4.4.4	Acknowledgement of Logical Bus Mastership	4-48
4.4.5	Read-Modify-Write Cycles	4-48
4.5	Physical Bus Arbitration	4-50
4.5.1	Requesting the Physical Bus	4-53
4.5.2	Receiving the Physical Bus Grant	4-53
4.5.3	Acknowledgement of Physical Bus Mastership	4-53
4.5.4	Physical Bus Arbitration Control	4-54
4.6	Concurrent Dissociate Logical and Physical Bus Activity	4-56
4.7	Bus Operation Examples	4-57
4.7.1	Table Search Operation	4-57
4.7.2	Logical Bus Arbitration	4-57

Section 5
Address Translation

5.1	Address Translation Tables	5-1
5.1.1	General Translation Table Structure	5-2
5.1.2	Variations in Translation Table Structure	5-5
5.1.2.1	Contiguous Memory	5-5
5.1.2.2	Indirection	5-9
5.1.2.3	Table Sharing Between Tasks	5-9
5.1.2.4	Paging of Tables	5-9
5.1.2.5	Dynamic Allocation of Tables	5-9
5.1.3	Functions Controlled by Address Translation Tables	5-13
5.1.3.1	Protection	5-13
5.1.3.2	ATC Management	5-13

TABLE OF CONTENTS
(Continued)

Paragraph Number	Title	Page Number
5.1.3.3	Data Cache Inhibit	5-13
5.1.4	Root Pointers	5-13
5.1.4.1	Root Pointer Format	5-14
5.1.4.1.1	Lower/Upper (L/U)	5-14
5.1.4.1.2	Limit	5-14
5.1.4.1.3	Shared Globally (SG)	5-14
5.1.4.1.4	Descriptor Type (DT)	5-15
5.1.4.1.5	Table Address	5-15
5.1.4.1.6	Unused	5-15
5.1.4.2	Selection of Root Pointer	5-15
5.1.5	Translation Descriptors	5-15
5.1.5.1	Descriptor Formats	5-16
5.1.5.2	Descriptor Types	5-16
5.1.5.2.1	Table Descriptors	5-16
5.1.5.2.2	Type-1 and Type-2 Page Descriptors	5-16
5.1.5.2.3	Indirect Descriptors	5-19
5.1.5.2.4	Invalid Descriptors	5-19
5.1.5.3	Descriptor Field Definitions	5-20
5.1.5.3.1	Lower/Upper (L/U)	5-20
5.1.5.3.2	Limit	5-20
5.1.5.3.3	Read Access Level (RAL)	5-20
5.1.5.3.4	Write Access Level (WAL)	5-20
5.1.5.3.5	Shared Globally (SG)	5-20
5.1.5.3.6	Supervisor (S)	5-20
5.1.5.3.7	Gate (G)	5-20
5.1.5.3.8	Cache Inhibit (C)	5-21
5.1.5.3.9	Lock (L)	5-21
5.1.5.3.10	Modified (M)	5-21
5.1.5.3.11	Unused (U)	5-21
5.1.5.3.12	Write Protect (WP)	5-22
5.1.5.3.13	Descriptor Type (DT)	5-22
5.1.5.3.14	Table Address	5-22
5.1.5.3.15	Page Address	5-22
5.1.5.3.16	Indirect Address	5-22
5.1.5.3.17	Unused	5-22
5.1.6	Protections	5-23
5.2	Address Translation Cache	5-23
5.2.1	Internal Organization	5-23
5.2.1.1	Tag Section	5-23
5.2.1.2	Data Section	5-23
5.2.1.3	Replacement Algorithm	5-24
5.2.2	ATC Operation	5-24
5.2.2.1	Address Translation by the ATC	5-24
5.2.2.2	Translation Modes	5-25
5.3	Root Pointer Table	5-25
5.3.1	Loading the RPT	5-26
5.3.2	Flushing the RPT	5-26
5.4	Detail of Table Search Operations	5-26

TABLE OF CONTENTS
(Continued)

Paragraph Number	Title	Page Number

Section 6
Instruction Set Processor

6.1	Registers..	6-1
6.1.1	Root Pointer Registers	6-1
6.1.1.1	Lower/Upper (L/U)..	6-2
6.1.1.2	Limit	6-2
6.1.1.3	Shared Globally (SG)	6-2
6.1.1.4	Descriptor Type (DT)	6-3
6.1.1.5	Table Address	6-3
6.1.1.6	Unused	6-3
6.1.2	PMMU Cache Status (PCSR)	6-3
6.1.2.1	Task Alias (TA)	6-4
6.1.2.2	Flush (F)	6-4
6.1.2.3	Lock Warning (LW)	6-4
6.1.3	Translation Control (TC)	6-4
6.1.3.1	Enable (E)	6-5
6.1.3.2	Supervisor Root Pointer Enable (SRE)	6-5
6.1.3.3	Function Code Lookup (FCL)	6-5
6.1.3.4	Page Size (PS)	6-5
6.1.3.5	Initial Shift (IS)	6-5
6.1.3.6	Table Index (TIA, TIB, TIC, and TID)	6-6
6.1.4	Current Access Level (CAL)	6-6
6.1.5	Validate Access Level (VAL)	6-6
6.1.6	Stack Change Control (SCC)	6-6
6.1.7	Access Control (AC)	6-7
6.1.7.1	Module Control (MC)	6-7
6.1.7.2	Access Level Control (ALC)	6-7
6.1.7.3	Module Descriptor Size (MDS)	6-7
6.1.8	PMMU Status Register (PSR)	6-8
6.1.8.1	Bus Error (B)	6-8
6.1.8.2	Limit Violation (L)	6-8
6.1.8.3	Supervisor Violation (S)	6-8
6.1.8.4	Access Level Violation (A)	6-8
6.1.8.5	Write Protected (W)	6-8
6.1.8.6	Invalid (I)	6-8
6.1.8.7	Modified (M)	6-9
6.1.8.8	Gate (G)	6-9
6.1.8.9	Globally Shared (C)	6-9
6.1.8.10	Level Number (N)	6-9
6.1.9	Breakpoint Acknowledge Data (BAD0-BAD7)	6-9
6.1.10	Breakpoint Acknowledge Control (BAC0-BAC7)	6-10
6.1.10.1	Breakpoint Enable (BPE)	6-10
6.1.10.2	Skip Count	6-10
6.2	Instructions	6-10
6.2.1	Data Movement (PMOVE)	6-11
6.2.2	Parameter Validation (PVALID)	6-11
6.2.3	Address Attribute Testing (PTEST)	6-11

TABLE OF CONTENTS
(Continued)

Paragraph Number	Title	Page Number
6.2.4	Cache Pre-Loading (PLOAD)	6-11
6.2.5	Cache Flushing	6-12
6.2.5.1	PFLUSH/PFLUSHS	6-12
6.2.5.2	PFLUSHR	6-12
6.2.5.3	PFLUSHA	6-12
6.2.6	Conditionals	6-12
6.2.6.1	Branch Conditionally (PBcc)	6-12
6.2.6.2	Decrement and Branch (PDBcc)	6-12
6.2.6.3	Set Conditionally (PScc)	6-12
6.2.6.4	Trap Conditionally (PTRAPcc)	6-12
6.2.7	State Save and Restore	6-12
6.2.7.1	PSAVE	6-12
6.2.7.2	PRESTORE	6-13
6.2.7.3	State Formats	6-13
6.3	Exceptions	6-14
6.3.1	Bus Error	6-14
6.3.1.1	Bus Error Signaled from Main Memory	6-15
6.3.1.2	Limit Field Exceeded	6-15
6.3.1.3	Attempted User Access of Supervisor Address	6-15
6.3.1.4	Access Level Violation	6-15
6.3.1.5	Write Protection Violation	6-15
6.3.1.6	Invalid Address	6-16
6.3.1.7	Read-Modify-Write (RMW) Cycle	6-16
6.3.2	Coprocessor Interface Exceptions	6-16
6.3.2.1	F-Line Emulation	6-17
6.3.2.2	Protocol Violation	6-17
6.3.2.3	Configuration Error	6-17
6.3.2.4	Illegal Operation Error	6-17
6.3.2.5	Access Violation	6-17

Section 7
Protection

7.1	Protection Using Address Space Encodings	7-1
7.1.1	Supervisor/User and User/Supervisor Protection	7-1
7.1.2	User/User Protection	7-3
7.1.3	Write Protection	7-4
7.1.4	Access (Read and Write) Protection	7-5
7.1.5	Protection Examples	7-7
7.2	Protection Using the Access level Protection Mechanism	7-7
7.2.1	Overview of Operation	7-8
7.2.2	Access Level Protection Mechanism Operation	7-10
7.2.3	Constructing Address Spaces Using Access Levels	7-12
7.2.3.1	Write Protection	7-13
7.2.3.2	Access (Read and Write) Protection	7-14
7.2.4	Transfers Between Access Levels	7-14
7.2.5	Passing Parameters Between Routines at Different Access Levels	7-15

TABLE OF CONTENTS
(Continued)

Paragraph Number	Title	Page Number
7.2.6	Security	7-15
7.2.7	Relationship Between Access Levels and Supervisor Mode	7-16
7.2.8	Considerations for Non-32-Bit Systems	7-16

Section 8
Breakpoints

8.1	Instruction Breakpoint Mechanism	8-1
8.1.1	Breakpoint Acknowledge Data Registers	8-1
8.1.2	Breakpoint Acknowledge Control Registers	8-2
8.2	Breakpoint Usage	8-4

Section 9
Coprocessor Interface

9.1	Coprocessor Interface Signal Connection	9-1
9.1.1	Selecting the MC68851	9-1
9.1.2	Coprocessor Interface Registers	9-2
9.1.2.1	Response CIR ($00)	9-3
9.1.2.2	Control CIR ($02)	9-4
9.1.2.3	Save CIR ($04)	9-4
9.1.2.4	Restore CIR ($06)	9-5
9.1.2.5	Operation Word CIR ($08)	9-5
9.1.2.6	Command CIR ($0A)	9-5
9.1.2.7	Condition CIR ($0E)	9-6
9.1.2.8	Operand CIR ($10)	9-6
9.1.2.9	Register Select CIR ($14)	9-7
9.1.2.10	Instruction Address CIR ($18)	9-7
9.1.2.11	Operand Address CIR ($1C)	9-7
9.1.3	Interprocessor Transfers	9-7
9.2	Coprocessor Instructions	9-7
9.2.1	Instruction Protocol	9-8
9.2.2	Response Primitives	9-9
9.2.2.1	Null Primitive	9-9
9.2.2.2	Evaluate Effective Address and Transfer Data Primitive	9-10
9.2.2.3	Transfer Single Main Processor Register Primitive	9-11
9.2.2.4	Supervisor Check Primitive	9-12
9.2.2.5	Evaluate and Transfer Effective Address Primitive	9-12
9.2.2.6	Transfer Main Processor Control Register Primitive	9-13
9.2.2.7	Take Exception Primitives	9-13
9.2.2.7.1	Take Pre-Instruction Exception Primitive	9-14
9.2.2.7.2	Take Post-Instruction Exception Primtiive	9-14
9.2.2.8	Response Primitive Summary	9-15
9.3	Instruction Dialogs	9-15
9.3.1	General Instructions	9-17
9.3.1.1	PFLUSH Instructions	9-17
9.3.1.2	PLOAD Instructions	9-17
9.3.1.3	PMOVE Instructions	9-19

TABLE OF CONTENTS
(Continued)

Paragraph Number	Title	Page Number
9.3.1.4	PTEST Instructions	9-24
9.3.1.5	PVALID Instructions	9-24
9.3.2	Conditional Instructions	9-24
9.3.3	Context Switch Instructions	9-24
9.3.3.1	PSAVE	9-24
9.3.3.2	PRESTORE	9-28
9.3.4	Exception Processing	9-29
9.3.4.1	Take Pre-Instruction Exception	9-29
9.3.4.2	Take Post-Instruction Exception	9-30
9.3.4.3	F-Line Emulator Exception	9-30
9.3.4.4	Format Exception, PSAVE Instruction	9-30
9.3.4.5	Format Exception, PRESTORE Instruction	9-32

Section 10
Access Level Control Interface

10.1	Access Level Control Interface Signal Connection	10-1
10.1.1	Selecting the MC68851	10-1
10.1.2	Access Level Control Interface Registers	10-2
10.1.2.1	Current Level (CL) ALCR ($00)	10-3
10.1.2.2	Access Status (AS) ALCR ($04)	10-3
10.1.2.3	Increase Access Level (IAL) ALCR ($08)	10-3
10.1.2.4	Decrease Access Level (DAL) ALCR ($0C)	10-4
10.1.2.5	Descriptor Address ALCRS ($40 Through $5C)	10-4
10.2	CALLM and RTM Instructions	10-6
10.2.1	CALLM Instruction	10-6
10.2.2	RTM Instruction	10-7

Section 11
Operation Timings

11.1	Factors Affecting Execution Times	11-1
11.2	Address Translation Table Search Timing	11-1
11.3	Instruction Timing	11-10
11.3.1	Effective Address Calculation	11-11
11.3.2	General Instructions	11-12
11.3.4	PSAVE and PRESTORE Instructions	11-13
11.4	Interrupt Latency	11-13
11.5	Bus Arbitration Latency	11-14

Section 12
Electrical Specifications

12.1	Maximum Ratings	12-1
12.2	Thermal Characteristics — PGA Package	12-1
12.3	Power Considerations	12-1

TABLE OF CONTENTS
(Continued)

Paragraph Number	Title	Page Number
12.4	DC Electrical Characteristics	12-2
12.5	AC Electrical Specifications — Clock Input	12-3
12.6	AC Electrical Specifications — All Bus Operations	12-4
12.7	AC Electrical Specification Definitions	12-10

Section 13
Ordering Information and Mechanical Data

13.1	Standard MC68851 Ordering Information	13-1
13.2	Pin Assignments	13-1
13.3	Mechanical Data	13-2

Appendix A
Instruction Set

A.1	MC68020/MC68851 Addressing Modes	A-1
A.2	Operation Description Definitions	A-2
A.3	Individual Instruction Descriptions	A-2
A.4	Instruction Format Diagrams	A-27

Appendix B
Hardware Considerations

B.1	Simple System Configuration	B-1
B.2	Alternate Logical Bus Masters	B-3
B.3	Logical Address Space Devices	B-6
B.3.1	Logical Address Space Coprocessors	B-6
B.3.2	Other Logical Address Space Devices	B-7
B.4	Access Time Computations	B-9
B.4.1	CPU-to-Memory Access Time Computations	B-9
B.4.2	MC68851-to-Memory Access Time Computations	B-11
B.5	External Caches	B-12
B.5.1	Logical Cache Implementation	B-13
B.5.2	Physical Cache Implementation	B-17
B.5.3	A Note on "Instruction-Only" Cache Implementations	B-17
B.6	Power and Ground Considerations	B-19
B.7	Test Equipment Considerations	B-20

Appendix C
Software Considerations

C.1	Context Save and Restore Considerations	C-1
C.2	Logical DMA Considerations	C-2
C.2.1	Use of the L and SG Bits	C-2
C.2.2	Mapping of DMA Activities	C-2
C.3	CALLM/RTM Programming Example	C-3

TABLE OF CONTENTS
(Concluded)

Paragraph Number	Title	Page Number
C.4	Multiprocessing Considerations	C-4
C.4.1	Sharing of Translation Table Structures	C-4
C.4.2	Globally Shared Data Areas	C-5
C.4.3	Remote Manipulation of MC68851	C-5
C.5	Defining and Using Page Tables in an Operating System	C-6
C.5.1	CPU and Supervisor Root Pointer Registers	C-6
C.5.2	Task Memory Map Definition	C-7
C.5.3	MC68851 Features and Their Impact on Table Definition	C-9
C.5.3.1	Number of Table Levels	C-9
C.5.3.2	Initial Shift Count	C-10
C.5.3.3	Locking Entries in the ATC	C-10
C.5.3.4	Limit Fields	C-10
C.5.3.5	Page Tables at Other than the Lowest Three Level	C-11
C.5.3.6	Indirect Descriptors	C-11
C.5.3.7	Unused Descriptor Bits	C-12
C.6	Example MC68851 Paging System Implementation	C-12
C.6.1	O.S. Allocation Modules for Example System	C-17
C.6.2	O.S. Paging System Bus Error Handler Example	C-20

LIST OF ILLUSTRATIONS

Figure Number	Title	Page Number
1-1	MC68851 Programming Model	1-5
1-2	MC68851 Simplified Block Diagram	1-6
2-1	Simple System Block Diagram	2-1
2-2	MC68851 Memory Managed System Simple Block Diagram	2-2
2-3	MC68851 Address Translation Functional Timing Diagram	2-3
2-4	MC68851 Translation Table Tree Structure	2-4
3-1	Functional Signal Groups	3-1
4-1	Relationship Between External and Internal Signals	4-1
4-2	Input Sample Window	4-2
4-3	Synchronous Mode Translation	4-9
4-4	Synchronous Translation Accessing Logical Cache	4-9
4-5	Asynchronous Mode Translation ($\overline{LAS}$ Meets Input Setup Time)	4-10
4-6	Synchronous Relinquish and Retry	4-12
4-7	Asynchronous Relinquish and Retry ($\overline{LAS}$ Misses Input Setup Time)	4-13
4-8	Synchronous Cycle Terminated by Bus Error	4-14
4-9	Asynchronous Cycle Terminated by Bus Error ($\overline{LAS}$ Meets Input Setup Time)	4-14
4-10	Synchronous CPU Space Cycle Accessing MC68851 Registers Terminated by Relinquish Request	4-16
4-11	Synchronous CPU Space Read Cycle Accessing MC68851 Register	4-17
4-12	Synchronous CPU Space Write Cycle Accessing MC68851 Register	4-18
4-13	Synchronous CPU Space Cycle Accessing Physical Address Space	4-19
4-14	Typical Physical Address Space Strobe and R/$\overline{W}$ Generation	4-19
4-15	MC68851 Interface to Various Port Sizes	4-21
4-16	Example of Long Word Transfer from 16-Bit Port	4-23
4-17	Long Word Operand Read Timing (16-Bit Data Port)	4-24
4-18	Example of Long Word Transfer from Byte Port	4-25
4-19	Long Word Operand Read Timing (8-Bit Data Port)	4-26
4-20	Read Cycle Flowchart	4-27
4-21	Long Word Operand Read Timing (32-Bit Data Port)	4-28
4-22	Write Cycle Flowchart	4-29
4-23	Byte Write Timing Diagram	4-30
4-24	Read-Modify-Write Cycle Flowchart	4-32
4-25	Read-Modify-Write Cycle Timing Diagram (32-Bit Port)	4-33
4-26	Bus Error Timing	4-34
4-27	Delayed Bus Error Timing	4-35
4-28	Bus Cycle Retry Timing	4-36
4-29	Delayed Bus Cycle Retry Timing	4-37
4-30	Halt Operation Timing	4-39
4-31	Logical Bus Arbitration Flowchart for MC68851 Bus Request	4-43

LIST OF ILLUSTRATIONS
(Continued)

Figure Number	Title	Page Number
4-32	Logical Bus Arbitration During Relinquish and Retry Sequence	4-44
4-33	Logical Bus Arbitration Signal Inter-Connection	4-45
4-34	Single Alternate Logical Master Bus Request Conditioning Logic	4-45
4-35	Relinquish and Retry Operation — MC68851 Arbitration for Logical Bus Preempted by Bus Request from Higher Priority Logical Master	4-46
4-36	MC68851 Passes Logical Bus Grant to Alternate Master	4-49
4-37	Physical Bus Arbitration Flowchart for Single Request	4-50
4-38	Physical Bus Arbitration During Address Translation	4-51
4-39	Physical Bus Arbitration During MC68851 Table Search	4-52
4-40	Physical Bus Arbitration State Diagram	4-54
4-41	Physical Bus Arbitration (Bus Inactive)	4-55
4-42	Example of Single Buffering Requirements for Support of Concurrent Logical and Physical Bus Activity	4-59
4-43	Example of Concurrent Logical and Physical Bus Activity	4-60/4-61
4-44	MC68851 Table Search Example (Table Search with Function Code Lookup and Two Levels of Long Format Descriptors)	4-62/4-63
4-45	Page Descriptor U Bit Status Update	4-64
4-46	Table Pointer U Bit or Page Descriptor U and M Bit Status Update	4-65
4-47	MC68851 Table Search Operation Interrupted by Alternate Logical Bus Master	4-66
5-1	Simplified MC68851 Table Search Flowchart	5-3
5-2	Derivation of Table Index Fields	5-4
5-3	Example Translation Table Tree	5-6
5-4	Example Translation Tree Layout in Memory	5-7
5-5	Example Translation Using Contiguous Memory	5-8
5-6	Example Translation Tree Using Indirect Descriptors	5-10
5-7	Example Translation Tree Using Shared Tables	5-11
5-8	Example Translation Tree with Non-Resident Tables	5-12
5-9	Root Pointer Register Format	5-14
5-10	Descriptor Type Determination	5-16
5-11	Example Translation Tree Using Different Format Descriptors	5-17
5-12	Short Format Table Descriptor	5-17
5-13	Long Format Table Descriptor	5-18
5-14	Type-1 and Type-2 Short Format Page Descriptors	5-18
5-15	Type-1 Long Format Page Descriptor	5-18
5-16	Type-2 Long Format Page Descriptor	5-18
5-17	Short Format Indirect Descriptor	5-19
5-18	Long Format Indirect Descriptor	5-19
5-19	Short Format Invalid Descriptor	5-19
5-20	Long Format Invalid Descriptor	5-19
5-21	ATC Tag Entry	5-23
5-22	ATC Data Entry	5-23
5-23	Detailed Flowchart of MC68851 Table Search Operation	5-27
5-24	Table Search Initialization Detail	5-28
5-25	Detail of ATC Entry Creation During Table Search	5-28

LIST OF ILLUSTRATIONS
(Continued)

Figure Number	Title	Page Number
5-26	Detail of Limit Check Procedure	5-29
5-27	Detailed Flowchart of Descriptor Fetch Operation	5-30
6-1	Root Pointer Register (CRP, SRP, DRP) Format	6-1
6-2	Cache Status Register (PCSR) Format	6-4
6-3	Translation Control Register Format	6-4
6-4	CAL and VAL Register Formats	6-6
6-5	Stack Change Control Register Format	6-7
6-6	Access Control Register Format	6-7
6-7	PMMU Status Register Format	6-8
6-8	Breakpoint Acknowledge Data Register Format	6-10
6-9	Breakpoint Acknowledge Control Register	6-10
6-10	Idle Format Frame	6-13
6-11	Mid-Coprocessor Format Frame	6-13
6-12	Breakpoint Enabled Format Frame	6-14
6-13	Reset Format Frame	6-14
7-1	Logical Address Map Using Function Code Lookup	7-2
7-2	Example Translation Tree Using Function Code Lookup	7-3
7-3	Example Logical Address Map with Shared Supervisor and User Spaces	7-4
7-4	Example Translation Tree Using S and WP Bits to Set Protection	7-5
7-5	Example Translation Tree Structure for Two Tasks Sharing a Common Supervisor Table	7-6
7-6	Example of Protection Mechanism Privilege Hierarchy	7-8
7-7	Example Logical Address Map for System Using Access Level Mechanism	7-9
7-8	Translation Table for Example System	7-10
7-9	Logical Address Map Using Access Level Information as Address Information	7-12
7-10	Logical Address Map Using Access Level Information as Control Information Only	7-13
8-1	Breakpoint Acknowledge Cycle Address Encoding	8-1
8-2	MC68851 Breakpoint Registers	8-2
8-3	Breakpoint Acknowledge Data Register Format	8-2
8-4	Breakpoint Acknowledge Control Register Format	8-2
8-5	Instruction Breakpoint Flowchart	8-3
8-6	Breakpoint Acknowledge Cycle – MC68851 Supplies Replacement Opcode	8-4
8-7	Breakpoint Acknowledge Cycle — Bus Error Asserted	8-5
9-1	Coprocessor Interface Address Bus Encoding	9-1
9-2	MC68851 Coprocessor Interface Register Map	9-2
9-3	Control CIR Register	9-4
9-4	Operand CIR Data Alignment	9-6
9-5	Coprocessor Instruction General Format	9-8
9-6	MC68851 Instruction Operation Word	9-8
9-7	M68000 Coprocessor Response Primitive General Format	9-9
9-8	Null Primitive Format	9-10

LIST OF ILLUSTRATIONS
(Continued)

Figure Number	Title	Page Number
9-9	Evaluate Address and Transfer Data Primitive Format	9-10
9-10	Transfer Single Main Processor Register Primtiive	9-12
9-11	Supervisor Check Primitive Format	9-12
9-12	Evaluate and Transfer Effective Address Primitive Format	9-12
9-13	Transfer Main Processor Control Register Primitive Format	9-13
9-14	Take Pre-Instruction Exception Primitive Format	9-14
9-15	Pre-Instruction Exception Stack Frame	9-14
9-16	Take Post-Instruction Exception Primitive Format	9-14
9-17	Post-Instruction Stack Frame	9-15
9-18	PFLUSH and PFLUSHS Instruction Dialog	9-18
9-19	PFLUSHA and PFLUSHR Instruction Dialog	9-19
9-20	PLOAD Instruction Dialog	9-20
9-21	PMOVE PMMUreg,⟨ea⟩ Instruction Dialog	9-21
9-22	PMOVE ⟨ea⟩,PMMUreg (Root Pointer or TC Registers)	9-22
9-23	PMOVE ⟨ea⟩,PMMUreg (CAL, VAL, SCC, AC, PSR, PSCR, BADx, and BACx Registers)	9-23
9-24	PTEST Instruction Dialog	9-25
9-25	PVALID Instruction Dialog	9-26
9-26	Conditional Instruction Dialog	9-27
9-27	PSAVE Instruction Dialog	9-27
9-28	PRESTORE Instruction Dialog	9-28
9-29	Take Pre-Instruction Exception Dialog	9-29
9-30	Take Post-Instruction Exception Dialog (PVALID Example)	9-30
9-31	Take F-Line Emulation Exception Dialog	9-31
9-32	PSAVE Format Exception Dialog	9-31
9-33	PRESTORE Format Exception Dialog	9-32
10-1	Access Level Control Interface Logical Address Bus Encoding	10-1
10-2	MC68851 Access Level Control Interface Register Map	10-2
10-3	CALLM Instruction Dialog Flowchart	10-5
10-4	Access Status Computation Flowchart	10-7
10-5	RTM Instruction Dialog Flowchart	10-8
12-1	Test Loads	12-3
12-2	Clock Input Timing Diagram	12-3
12-3	MC68851 Initiated Read Cycle	Foldout-1
12-4	MC68851 Initiated Write Cycle	Foldout-2
12-5	Synchronous Mode Translation	Foldout-3
12-6	Logical Master Relinquish and Retry Timing Diagram	Foldout-4
12-7	Logical Bus Arbitration by Asynchronous Master Timing Diagram	Foldout-5
12-8	Physical Bus Arbitration Timing Diagram	Foldout-6
12-9	CPU Space Read From MC68851 or From Other Coprocessor ($\overline{\text{CLI}}$ Asserted by MC68851) Timing Diagram	Foldout-7
12-10	CPU Space Write to MC68851 or To Other Coprocessor ($\overline{\text{CLI}}$ Asserted by MC68851) Timing Diagram	Foldout-8
12-11	Reset and Mode Select Timing Diagram	Foldout-9
12-12	Drive Levels and Test Points for AC Specifications	12-11

LIST OF ILLUSTRATIONS
(Concluded)

Figure Number	Title	Page Number
B-1	Example Simple MC68020/MC68851 Hardware Configuration	B-2
B-2	Example MC68020/MC68851 Hardware Configuration with Single Alternate Logical Bus Master (MC68442)	B-4
B-3	Address/Data Bus Demultiplex Logic for Figure B-2	B-5
B-4	Example MC68020/MC68851 Hardware Configuration with Logical Address Space Device (MC68881 FPCP)	B-8
B-5	Access Time Computation Diagram	B-9
B-6	Access Time Compuation Diagram — MC68851 Initiated Accesses	B-11
B-7	Example MC68020/MC68851 Hardware Configuration with Logical Data Cache	B-14
B-8	Example Early-Termination Control Circuit	B-15
B-9	Example MC68020/MC68851 Hardware Configuration with Physical Data Cache	B-18

LIST OF TABLES

Table Number	Title	Page Number
3-1	M68000 Family Function Code Assignments	3-2
3-2	Signal Summary	3-9
4-1	Coprocessor Data Bus Size Specification	4-3
4-2	Additional Decision Timeout Delay	4-3
4-3	DSACK Codes and Results	4-21
4-4	Size Output Encodings	4-22
4-5	Address Offset Encodings	4-22
4-6	MC68851 Internal to External Data Bus Multiplexer	4-22
4-7	Data Bus Activity for Byte, Word, and Long Word Ports	4-25
4-8	DSACK, BERR, and HALT Assertion Results	4-40
9-1	MC68020 CPU Space Type Field Encodings	9-2
9-2	Coprocessor Interface Register Characteristics	9-3
9-3	Null Primtive Encodings	9-10
9-4	Coprocessor Valid Effective Address Codes	9-11
9-5	Evaluate Effective Address and Transfer Data Primitive Encoding	9-11
9-6	MC68851 Vector Numbers	9-13
9-7	MC68851 Primitive Responses	9-16
10-1	Access Level Control Interface Register Characteristics	10-3
10-2	Access Register Status Code	10-4
12-1	AC Electrical Specifications Reference Summary	12-10
A-1	Effective Addressing Mode Categories	A-2
B-1	CPU-to-Memory Access Time Equations	B-10
B-2	Example CPU-to-Memory Access Time Calculations	B-11
B-3	MC68851-to-Memory Access Time Equations	B-12
B-4	Example MC68851-to-Memory Access Time Calculations	B-12
B-5	V_{CC} and GND Pin Assignments	B-19

SECTION 1
INTRODUCTION

The MC68851 is a high-performance paged memory management unit (PMMU) designed to efficiently support a demand paged virtual memory environment with the MC68020 32-bit microprocessor. The MC68851 can also be used as a peripheral with other processors. Implemented using VLSI technology and an HCMOS fabrication process, the MC68851 is optimized to perform very fast logical-to-physical address translations, to provide a comprehensive access control and protection mechanism, and to provide extensive support for paged virtual systems.

Operating as a coprocessor to the MC68020, the MC68851 provides a logical extension to program control and processing abilities of the main processor. It does this by providing a set of translation, protection, and breakpoint registers that control operation of the comprehensive memory management mechanism. These registers are utilized in a manner that is analogous to the use of any internal processor register.

The implementation of a comprehensive memory management system is facilitated by utilizing the following MC68851 features:
- Fast Logical-to-Physical Address Translation
- 32-Bit Logical and Physical Addresses with 4-Bit Function Code
- Eight Available Page Sizes Ranging from 256 to 32K Bytes
- Fully Associative 64-Entry On-Chip Address Translation Cache
- Address Translation Cache Support for Multi-Tasking
- Hardware Maintenance of External Translation Tables and On-Chip Cache
- MC68020 Instruction Set Extension and Instruction-Oriented Communcation Using M68000 Family Coprocessor Interface
- Hierarchical Protection Mechanism with up to Eight Levels of Protection
- Instruction Breakpoints for Software Debug and Program Control
- Support for Logical and/or Physical Data Cache
- Support for Multiple Logical and/or Physical Bus Masters

1.1 MC68851 OVERVIEW

The primary system functions of the MC68851 are to provide logical-to-physical address translation, to monitor and enforce the protection/privilege mechanism, and to support the breakpoint operations. The MC68851 also supports the M68000 Family coprocessor interface in order to simplify processor/coprocessor communication.

1.1.1 Address Translation

Logical-to-physical address translation is the most frequently executed operation of the MC68851 so this task has been optimized and requires minimal processor intervention. The logical address operated on by the MC68851 consists of the 32-bit incoming address and a 4-bit function code.

The MC68851 initiates address translation by searching for the page descriptor corresponding to the logical-to-physical mapping in the on-chip address translation cache (ATC). The ATC is a very fast 64-entry fully-associative cache memory that stores recently used page descriptors. If the descriptor does not reside in the ATC then the bus cycle of the logical bus master is aborted and the MC68851 executes bus cycles to search the translation table in physical memory. The translation table is a data structure in main memory that, at its lowest level, contains the page descriptors controlling the logical-to-physical address translation. After being located, the page descriptor is loaded into the ATC and the logical bus master is allowed to retry its bus cycle, which is then correctly translated.

1.1.2 Protection Mechanism

The MC68851 hierarchical protection mechanism provides cycle-by-cycle examination and enforcement of the access rights of the currently executing process. There may be up to eight distinct levels in the privilege hierarchy and these levels are encoded in the upper three bits of the incoming logical address. Privilege mechanisms of zero, two, or four levels can also be implemented with the MC68851 in which case the access level encoding is contained in the upper zero, one, or two logical address lines, respectively. The MC68851 compares these bits against the current access level and determines whether the bus cycle is requesting a higher privilege than allowed. In the case where a privilege violation is detected, the MC68851 terminates this access as a fault.

The MC68851 completely supports the MC68020 module call and return functions (CALLM/RTM instructions), which include a mechanism to change privilege levels during module operations.

1.1.3 Breakpoints

The MC68851 provides a breakpoint acknowledge facility to support the MC68020 and other processors with on-chip caches. When the MC68020 encounters a breakpoint instruction it executes a breakpoint acknowledge cycle by reading from a predetermined address in the CPU address space. The MC68851 decodes this address and responds by either providing a replacement opcode for the breakpoint opcode and asserting the data transfer and size acknowledge outputs or by asserting bus error to initiate illegal instruction exception processing. The MC68851 can be programmed to signal the illegal instruction exception on every breakpoint or to provide the replacement opcode n times ($1 \leq n \leq 255$) before signaling the exception.

1.1.4 M68000 Family Instruction Set Extensions

The MC68851 implements an extension to the M68000 Family instruction set using the coprocessor interface. These instructions provide control functions for:
- Loading and storing of MMU registers,
- Testing access rights, and conditionals based on the results of this test, and
- MMU control functions.

The instruction set extensions are as follows:

PMOVE Moves data to/from MC68851 register.

PVALID Compares access rights of a logical address against the current access level and traps if address requires a higher privilege than allowed. This instruction can be used by a routine to verify that an address passed to it by a calling routine is a valid address.

PTESTR Searches the translation tables and loads the status and access rights information of a logical address used for a read cycle into the MC68851 status register. This instruction allows the operating system to quickly determine the cause of faults generated by a read cycle from a particular logical address.

PTESTW Searches the translation tables and loads the status and access rights information of a logical address used for a write access into the MC68851 status register. This instruction allows the operating system to quickly determine the cause of faults generated by a write cycle to a particular logical address.

PLOADR Searches translation tables and loads the ATC with a translation for the specified logical address. The history information in the external translation tables is updated to reflect that the physical page corresponding to the logical address has been used.

PLOADW Searches translation tables and loads the ATC with a translation for the specified logical address. The history information in the external translation tables is updated to reflect that the physical page corresponding to the logical address has been modified.

PFLUSH Flushes translation cache entries by logical address, function code, or function code and logical address. The PFLUSH instructions allow the operating system to easily remove entries from the ATC after making modifications to the external translation tables.

PFLUSHA Flushes all entries from the translation cache.

PFLUSHR Flushes root pointer table and translation cache entries by root pointer.

PFLUSHS Flushes globally shared entries from the ATC by logical address and/or function code.

PSAVE Saves the internal state of the MC68851 in order to support fast context switching and MC68020 virtual memory/virtual machine capabilities.

PRESTORE Restores the internal state of the MC68851 stored by the PSAVE instruction.

PBcc Branches conditionally on MC68851 condition. The conditional instructions provide the operating system with a means by which program flow can be controlled by MC68851 conditions.

PDBcc Tests MC68851 condition, decrements a CPU register, and branches.

PScc Sets operand according to MC68851 condition.

PTRAPcc Traps on MC68851 condition.

1.1.5 The Coprocessor Concept

The M68000 Family coprocessor interface is an integral part of the design of the MC68020 and the MC68851. The coprocessor interface allows the execution of special purpose instructions that are not executable by the processor. Each processor in a system has an instruction set that reflects its special function whether it be floating-point math, memory management, etc. These instructions may be executed merely by placing the instruction opcode and parameters in the MC68020 instruction stream. The MC68020 detects the coprocessor instruction, initiates bus communication with the registers of the target coprocessor to pass the instruction, and tests for conditions requiring further action. The MC68020 performs activity to support the execution of the instruction (e.g., address calculation or data transfer) at the request of the coprocessor.

The interchange of information and the division of responsibility between the main processor and the coprocessor are controlled by the coprocessor interface and this process is completely transparent to the user. The addition of a coprocessing unit to an MC68020 system supplements the instruction set executable by the processor. The register set of the coprocessor is perceived, by system programmers, to be a direct extension of the main processor registers.

The MC68851 functions as a coprocessor in systems where the MC68020 is the main processor via the M68000 coprocessor interface. It can function as a peripheral in systems where the main processor is an MC68010, MC68012, or any other processor with virtual memory capabilities.

The MC68851 is a DMA-type coprocessor that uses a subset of the general purpose coprocessor interface supported by the M68000 Family. Features of the interface implemented in the MC68851 are as follows:

- The main processor and the MC68851 communicate via standard bus cycles.
- The main processor and MC68851 communications are not dependent upon the instruction sets of the individual devices (e.g., instruction pipes or caches, addressing modes).
- The main processor and the MC68851 may operate at different clock speeds.
- MC68851 instructions may utilize any addressing modes provided by the main processor; all addresses are calculated by the main processor at the request of the coprocessor.
- All data transfers (except translation table searches in physical memory) are performed by the main processor at the request of the MC68851; thus the memory management mechanism functions as if the MC68851 instructions are executed by the main processor.
- Coprocessor detection of exceptions that require a trap to be taken are serviced by the main processor at the request of the MC68851; thus exception processing functions as if the MC68851 instructions were executed by the main processor.
- Support of virtual machine/virtual memory systems is provided via the PSAVE and PRESTORE instructions.
- Up to eight coprocessors may reside on the same local bus simultaneously, although only one of those may be an MC68851.

1.2 HARDWARE OVERVIEW

The MC68851 is a high-performance paged memory management unit designed to interface to the MC68020 as a coprocessor. This device fully supports the MC68020 virtual machine architecture, and is implemented in HCMOS, a low-power, small geometry process. This process allows both CMOS and HMOS (high density NMOS) gates to be combined on the same device. CMOS structures are used where speed and low power are required, and HMOS structures are used where minimum silicon area is desired. Using this technology enables the MC68851 to be very fast while consuming less power, and having a smaller die size than is feasible with older technologies.

The MC68851 can also be used as a peripheral processor in systems where the MC68020 is not the main processor (e.g., the MC68010 and MC68012). The configuration of the MC68851 as a peripheral processor or coprocessor may be completely transparent to user mode software (i.e., the same user object code may be executed in either configuration with appropriate emulation software for the coprocessor interface).

The architecture of the MC68851 appears to the user as a logical extension of the M68000 Family architecture. Because of the coprocessor interface, the MC68020 programmer can view the MC68851 registers as though the registers were resident in the main processor. Thus, the MC68020/MC68851 device pair appears to be one processor that has registers for data storage, address pointers, general control, translation and protection control, and breakpoint functions.

The MC68851 programming model is shown in Figure 1-1, and consists of the following:
- Three 64-bit root point registers, one each pointing to the root of user, supervisor, and DMA translation tables (CRP, SRP, and DRP).
- A 32-bit translation control register containing configuration information for the MC68851 (TC).
- A 16-bit cache status register that provides information concerning the MC68851 internal translation cache (PCSR).
- A 16-bit status register that contains status and access rights information for a given logical address (PSR).
- Three 8-bit protection control registers used in the privilege checking mechanism (CAL, VAL, and SCC).
- A 16-bit access control register that contains configuration information for the privilege mechanism (access control – AC).

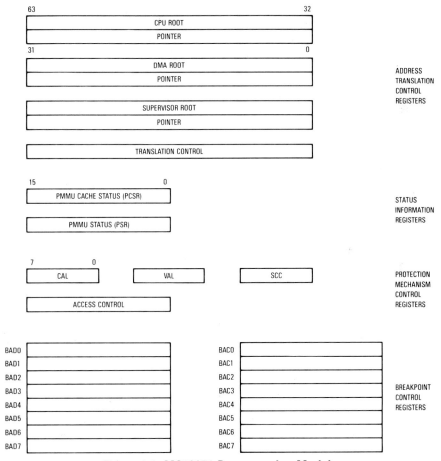

Figure 1-1. MC68851 Programming Model

- Eight 16-bit breakpoint acknowledge data registers that provide replacement opcodes during MC68020 breakpoint acknowledge cycles (BAD0–BAD7).
- Eight 16-bit breakpoint acknowledge control registers that contain enable and count functions for the instruction breakpoint capabilities of the MC68020 and MC68851 (BAC0–BAC7).

As shown in Figure 1-2, the MC68851 can be viewed as being composed of eight major elements: the bus interface (BIU), the address translation cache (ATC), the root pointer table (RPT), the execution unit (EU), the control store, the control logic, the address translation sense circuit, and the register decode logic.

The address translation cache contains 64 recently-used translation descriptors and the control circuitry required to monitor access rights and to create new ATC entries. The ATC itself is composed of three major components: the content-addressable-memory (CAM) containing the logical address and access rights information to be compared against incoming logical addresses, the physical address store that contains the physical address associated with a particular CAM entry, and the control section containing the entry replacement circuitry that implements the replacement algorithm (a variation of the least-recently-used algorithm).

The RPT contains a cache that stores the eight most recently used values of the CPU root pointer and a task alias that is associated with each of the stored values. The root pointer caching and task alias maintenance performed by the RPT allows translation descriptors for multiple tasks to reside in the ATC simultaneously.

The bus interface unit controls the interface to both the logical and physical buses. Included in the BIU are the buffers for both the logical and physical address buses and the hardware necessary to perform bus cycles in the physical address space. Also included in the BIU are the bus arbitration state machines for both the logical and physical buses.

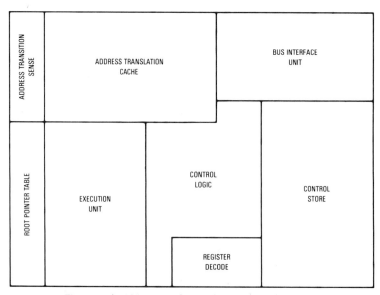

Figure 1-2. MC68851 Simplified Block Diagram

The register decode section contains the logic required to monitor the logical bus for accesses to its register set internally such that no external decoding of addresses is required.

The address transition sense circuitry continuously monitors the logical address bus to detect any transition in one or more of the logical address inputs. When a transition is detected, the ATC and access rights checking circuits in the ATC initiate an address translation. Monitoring for an address transition allows the ATC to begin address translation as soon as an address is presented by the logical bus master rather than waiting for the assertion of one of the logical bus control strobes, thereby optimizing translation performance.

The control store section contains the two-level microcode store of the MC68851 and the address generation circuitry required to correctly sequence the control store during table search operations and execution of the MC68851 instruction set.

The control logic section provides residual decode for the control store and register decode outputs, and it drives control points in the execution unit (EU). The EU performs address calculations for accessing the translation tables, contains the MC68851 register set, and controls table search activities and instruction execution.

1.2.1 Coprocessor Interface

The MC68851 contains eleven coprocessor interface registers (CIRs) that are memory-mapped into the M68000 CPU space. The M68000 Family coprocessor interface is implemented as a protocol of reading and writing these registers by the main processor. The MC68020 implements this general purpose coprocessor interface protocol in hardware and microcode. The MC68851 implements a subset of the general purpose protocol.

When the MC68020 detects an MC68851 instruction, the MC68020 writes the instruction to the appropriate CIR. The register decode section decodes the access from the logical address bus and selects the required register in the EU. The MC68020 then reads the response CIR, which in conjunction with the control store, provides requests for any further action required of the MC68020 on behalf of the MC68851. For example, the response may request that the MC68020 fetch an operand from the evaluated effective address and transfer the operand to the operand CIR.

The only difference between a coprocessor bus transfer and any other bus transfer is that the MC68020 issues a function code and address bus encoding that indicates the CPU address space during the cycle. Thus, the memory-mapped coprocessor interface registers do not infringe upon program and data address spaces. When accessing the MC68851, the MC68020 places a coprocessor ID field of 0 (zero) onto three of the upper address lines in order to distinguish the MC68851 from other coprocessors in the system (refer to **SECTION 9 COPROCESSOR INTERFACE**).

Since the coprocessor interface protocol is based solely on bus transfers, it is easily emulated by software when the MC68851 is used as a peripheral with any processor capable of memory-mapped I/O over an M68000-type bus.

The M68000 Family coprocessor interface is an integral part of the MC68851 and MC68020 design, with the interface tasks shared between the two. The interface is fully compatible with all present and will maintain compatibility with all future M68000 Family products. Functionality required to execute coprocessor instructions is partitioned such that the MC68020 does not have to decode coprocessor instructions, and the MC68851 does not have to duplicate main processor functions such as address calculation for data transfers.

This partitioning provides an extension of the instruction set that permits MC68851 instructions to utilize all MC68020 addressing modes and to generate execution time exception traps. Thus, from the programmer's view, the CPU and coprocessor appear to be integrated onto a single chip. The MC68020 single-step (trace) mode is fully supported by the MC68851 and the M68000 Family coprocessor interface.

The MC68851 initiates bus cycles required to search the translation tables in physical memory in order to load descriptors into the address translation cache, to check privilege information contained in the descriptors, and to maintain descriptor history information. The MC68851 does not initiate bus cycles to fetch instructions or to manipulate any data other than the descriptor operations specified above. The MC68020 is responsible for fetching instructions, transferring them to the MC68851, and performing any other actions related to these instructions with the exception of descriptor manipulation.

1.2.2 Access Level Control Interface

For operations initiated by the MC68020 CALLM and RTM instructions, the MC68851 can be accessed via a set of access level control registers (ALCRs) that participate in the protection mechanism supported by the MC68020 and the MC68851. Similar to the CIRs of the coprocessor interface, the ALCRs are memory-mapped into the M68000 CPU space and accesses to these registers are detected by decode logic in the BIU that selects the appropriate registers and control logic.

Refer to **SECTION 10 ACCESS LEVEL CONTROL INTERFACE** for further details on this interface.

1.2.3 Breakpoint Acknowledge Interface

In response to breakpoint acknowledge cycles, one final method by which the MC68851 can be accessed is via the breakpoint acknowledge interface that supports the instruction breakpoint capabilities of the MC68020. When a breakpoint acknowledge cycle in the CPU space is observed by the register decode section, the appropriate breakpoint acknowledge control and data registers are selected in the EU. The EU, under control from the control store, then provides the correct MC68851 response to the cycle.

For further information on the MC68851 breakpoint operations refer to **SECTION 8 BREAKPOINTS**.

1.2.4 Bus Operations

In addition to controlling access to the MC68851 from the logical bus, the BIU also contains the circuitry required to execute bus cycles in physical memory in order to access mapping information located in the translation tables. The physical bus controller performs accesses in memory following the standard protocol of the M68000 Family bus definition.

The BIU also contains arbiters to control and/or monitor mastership of both the logical and physical buses. The MC68851 allows for multiple logical and/or physical alternate bus masters.

The bus interface of the MC68851 is described in detail in **SECTION 4 BUS OPERATIONS**.

SECTION 2
OVERVIEW OF SYSTEM OPERATION

This section provides a general overview of the MC68851 in a system.

2.1 SYSTEM CONFIGURATION

In a simple microprocessor-based system, the CPU is connected directly to memory, as shown in Figure 2-1. In this system, no memory mapping or protection functions are provided and the addresses generated by the CPU directly identify the physical locations to be accessed. The number of physical devices present in the system uniquely determines the range of the logical address space of the processor that is useable. Any location in the address space that does not contain a device cannot be used by the CPU. This type of system is unsuitable for execution of multiple concurrent tasks since there is no mechanism to protect the memory of one task from corruption by any other task. It is also unsuitable for hosting virtual systems that allow uniform use of an address space that is larger than the address space represented by the devices present, or provide separate unique address spaces for each task in the system.

The MC68851 is designed to provide the mapping and protection facilities needed to construct a multi-tasking, demand-paged virtual system. In order to build such a system, the address bus is divided into two sections separated by the MC68851, as shown in Figure 2-2. The 'logical' address is output by the processor and is monitored by the MC68851 on its logical address inputs. The MC68851 performs translation and privilege checking on the logical address and, if valid, outputs the translated 'physical' value on the physical address bus where it is used to access memory or

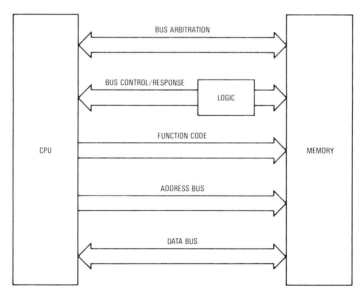

Figure 2-1. Simple System Block Diagram

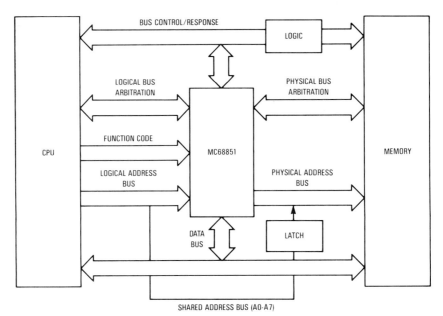

Figure 2-2. MC68851 Memory Managed System Simple Block Diagram

peripheral devices. Using this configuration, all accesses to physical devices are controlled by the MC68851; tasks can be prevented from accessing the resources owned by other tasks, and, under control of an operating system with virtual capabilities, the logical-to-physical mapping functions of the MC68851 allow tasks to utilize the entire address space of the CPU without knowledge of the physical attributes of the system.

2.2 ADDRESS TRANSLATION

The address translation facility of the MC68851 is a comprehensive mechanism that provides logical-to-physical mapping of up to a 4-gigabyte logical address space with no software assistance from the CPU. The address translation mechanism is fully implemented in hardware in order to minimize the system performance penalty for the mapping functions. The address translation mechanism provides full logical-to-physical mapping in less than one clock cycle for a very high percentage of all bus cycles. The functional timing for these translations is shown in Figure 2-3.

2.2.1 Address Translation Cache

In order to perform the translation functions as shown in Figure 2-3, the MC68851 contains a high-speed memory that stores recently used logical-to-physical address translations. This memory, the address translation cache (ATC), is a 64-entry, fully-associative array containing logical addresses and their corresponding physical translations. When a bus cycle is initiated by a logical master, the logical address and function code is input to the ATC where it is compared against all current entries. If one of the ATC entries matches (there is a 'hit'), the ATC drives the stored physical address onto the physical address bus. If the MC68851 detects no exceptional conditions (for example, write violation, . . ., etc.), it then asserts the physical address strobe ($\overline{\text{PAS}}$).

In addition to the address mappings, each entry in the ATC also contains bits that describe the protection information for that mapping, a data cache inhibit indicator, a lock-entry flag, as well as history information used by the MC68851.

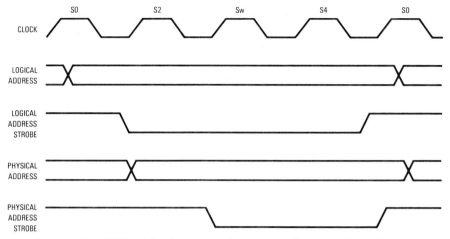

Figure 2-3. MC68851 Address Translation Functional Timing Diagram

In order to improve utilization of the MC68851 address translation cache in a multi-tasking environment, translation descriptors for multiple tasks can reside in the ATC simultaneously. In order to control this, the logical portion of each ATC entry has three additional bits, a 'task alias', that is included in the compare operation to determine if a cache hit has occurred. The task alias identifies one of eight tasks that may have translation descriptors resident in the ATC simultaneously and is used as an extension to the logical address.

The task alias mechanism works in conjunction with the root pointer caching function of the root pointer table (RPT). The CPU root pointer register of the MC68851 contains the address, in physical memory, of the root of the translation table for the currently executing task. The RPT is a table of eight recently-used CPU root pointers. Each entry in the RPT has a unique task alias associated with it. When the operating system initiates a new task, or restarts a suspended one, it writes a value to the CPU root pointer register identifying the location of the translation table for that task. When this value is written, it is compared against entries currently in the RPT. If no match is found, then a new entry is made in the RPT and the task alias associated with that entry is assigned to the current task. If the RPT entry that is written has been previously assigned to another task, the MC68851 automatically flushes all entries in the ATC that are currently identified with this task alias. If the value loaded into the CPU root pointer register is already in the RPT, then the previous task alias is reused and none of the ATC entries are flushed.

2.2.2 Address Translation Tables

When a logical bus master initiates a cycle that does not have a corresponding translation resident in the ATC, the MC68851 performs bus operations to load the mapping for that cycle from the translation tables. To perform this search operation, the MC68851 simultaneously aborts the logical bus cycle, signals the master to retry the operation, and requests mastership of the logical bus. Upon receiving indication that the logical bus is free, the MC68851 completes the arbitration sequence, assumes mastership of the bus, and, after loading the required translation descriptor, returns control of the bus to the logical master which then retries the previous bus cycle.

The translation tables supported by the MC68851 have a tree structure. The root of a translation table tree is pointed to by one of three root pointer registers: CPU, supervisor, or DMA. Table entries at the higher levels of the tree (pointer tables) contain pointers to other tables. Entries at the leaf level (page tables) contain page descriptors. All addresses contained in the translation table entries are physical addresses.

Figure 2-4 illustrates the structure of the MC68851 translation tables. Several determinants of the detailed table structure are software selectable. The first level of lookup in the table normally uses the function codes as an index, but this may be suppressed if desired. The logical address can be between 17 and 32 bits (inclusive). The number of levels in the table indexed by the logical address can be set from one to four, and up to 15 logical address bits can be used as an index at each level.

The first step in a normal table search operation by the MC68851 is to perform an index into the translation table by the function code. The index by function code is performed by adding (unsigned) the function code value generated by the current logical bus master to the value contained in the appropriate root pointer register for that access. The MC68851 uses the sum of this operation as the physical address to read the pointer at the first level of the translation table. The pointer read during this operation is used as the base address for the next table search. Until a page descriptor is encountered, subsequent descriptor fetches by the MC68851 operate similiarly: a table pointer is fetched and a specified field of the logical address (the logical address that caused the table search to be initiated) is added (unsigned) to generate the physical address for the next fetch. When a page descriptor is encountered, an entry is made in the ATC and the table search operation is terminated.

2.2.3 Protection Mechanism

The MC68851 supports a comprehensive protection mechanism that facilitates implementation of fully protected systems. In addition to the option of enforcing the distinction of user and supervisor modes normally found in an M68000 system, the MC68851 also supports a mechanism that provides finer granularity of protection within the user address spaces.

The access level mechanism subdivides the logical address spaces of user mode operations into one, two, four, or eight level(s) of privilege. Routines operating at different access levels can have different privileges to memory and a facility is provided to closely control changes in access level.

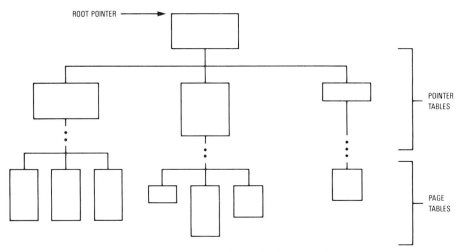

Figure 2-4. MC68851 Translation Table Tree Structure

The access level for a bus cycle is encoded in the highest order (zero, one, two, or three) bits of the logical address generated by the CPU. The access level mechanism, when enabled, compares this value against the current access level as specified in the CAL register. The current access level specifies the highest privilege level that a task may assume at that time. If the privilege level value presented by the bus cycle is greater (less privileged) than the current level allowed, then the cycle is requesting a privilege in excess of its rights and is aborted by the MC68851.

In the MC68851 protection scheme, the privilege associated with a task is specified by its access level. Smaller values for access levels represent higher privilege levels. In a system using eight access levels, level zero is the highest privilege in the hierarchy and level seven is the lowest. The privilege level associated with a particular page is specified by its read access level, write access level, write protect, and supervisor attributes.

In order to access code and/or data that requires a higher level of privilege than is possessed by the current task, the MC68851 supports the MC68020 module call (CALLM) and return (RTM) instructions that allow a less privileged routine to transfer execution control to a module operating at a higher level and to return from that module after completion of the module function. When the MC68020 executes a CALLM instruction that requests an increase in access level, the MC68020 automatically communicates with the MC68851 access level protection mechanism via access level control CPU space cycles, to determine if the requested change is valid. The MC68851 checks the request against a module descriptor for that operation and indicates the validity of that request to the MC68020. The RTM instruction operates similarly except that control is always passed from a higher privileged task to a less privileged one.

SECTION 3
SIGNAL DESCRIPTION

This section is a brief description of the input and output signals of the MC68851 paged memory management unit. The signals are functionally grouped as shown in Figure 3-1. Each signal is explained in a brief paragraph with reference (if applicable) to other sections that contain more detailed information.

NOTE

The terms assertion and negation are used extensively. This is done to avoid confusion when dealing with a mixture of 'active low' and 'active high' signals. The term **assert** and **assertion** is used to indicate that a signal is active or **true**, independent of whether that level is represented by a high or low voltage. The term **negate** or **negation** is used to indicate that a signal is inactive or **false**.

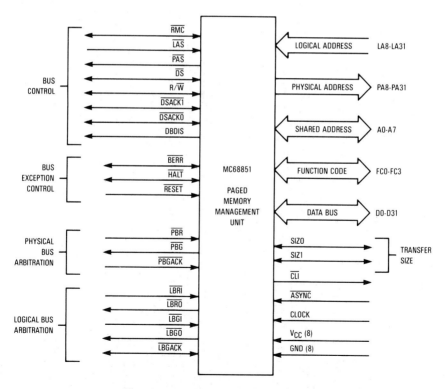

Figure 3-1. Functional Signal Groups

3.1 LOGICAL ADDRESS BUS (LA8 through LA31)

These inputs are the lines on which the MC68851 accepts a logical address for translation or for internal operations. The logical address bus should be connected to the address outputs of all logical bus masters.

If the logical address is less than 32 bits (logical address space $<2^{32}$ bytes) as determined by the translation control register (refer to **6.1.5.5 INITIAL SHIFT**), the unused bits are ignored and should be tied to a constant voltage level (either V_{CC} or ground).

3.2 PHYSICAL ADDRESS BUS (PA8 through PA31)

These three-state outputs provide the physical address for both address translations and MC68851-initiated bus operations.

3.3 SHARED ADDRESS BUS (A0 through A7)

The use of these three-state, bidirectional lines is shared between the functions of the logical and physical buses. When the MC68851 is performing address translations, these signals are input in order that the MC68851 be able to monitor the entire logical address in the event that a CPU space cycle accesses one of its registers. When the MC68851 is the bus master, these pins output the low order eight bits of the physical address. With the inclusion of A0 through A7, both the logical and physical buses have a 32-bit (4 gigabyte) linear addressing range.

3.4 FUNCTION CODE (FC0 through FC3)

These three-state, bidirectional signals indicate the address space of the current bus cycle. When the MC68851 is performing translations, these signals provide the address space being accessed by the current logical bus master. The MC68851 uses the function code associated with a bus cycle as an extension to the logical address when creating entries in the address translation cache. The function code may also be used as an index from the root pointer in the first level of a translation table search.

The 4-bit function code consists of the three function code outputs of the M68000 Family processor and a fourth bit that indicates that a DMA access is in progress. The M68000 address spaces generated by the function codes are shown in Table 3-1.

When the MC68851 is bus master it drives the function code pins as outputs with a constant value of FC3–FC0 = $5, indicating the supervisor data space.

Table 3-1. M68000 Family Function Code Assignments

FC3–FC0	Cycle Type
$0	(Undefined, Reserved for Motorola Use)
$1	User Data Space
$2	User Program Space
$3	(Undefined, Reserved for User Definition)
$4	(Undefined, Reserved for Motorola Use)
$5	Supervisor Data Space
$6	Supervisor Program Space
$7	CPU Space
≥$8	(Alternate Bus Master, Reserved for User Definition)

3.5 DATA BUS (D0 through D31)

These three-state bidirectional signals provide the general purpose data path between the MC68851 and other devices. This bus may be dynamically sized through use of the $\overline{\text{DSACKx}}$ signals, transferring 8, 16, 24, or 32 bits of information during a bus cycle. The most significant byte of the data bus is D24 through D31.

In systems that do not use the MC68020 (or any other 32-bit CPU) as the main processor, the width of the data bus used to communicate between the processor and the MC68851 may be fixed at 16, or 8 bits (refer to **4.1.2.2 BUS SIZE**). In such systems, the dynamic bus sizing mechanism still functions but the maximum amount of data transferred in a single cycle is limited to the bus size. In either case, the processor data bus is aligned towards the high order portion of the MC68851 data bus — that is, an 8-bit master is connected to D24 through D31 and a 16-bit master is connected to D16 through D31.

When the $\overline{\text{RESET}}$ signal is asserted, the MC68851 inputs configuration information from the least significant byte of the data bus (D0–D7). This information determines the bus size for coprocessor operations, sets the 'decision time' for determining whether or not an ATC hit has occurred, determines whether the $\overline{\text{CLI}}$ signal is asserted for all MC68851-initiated bus operations, and sets the timing for $\overline{\text{PAS}}$ assertion. The configuration operation is detailed in **4.1 RESET OPERATION**.

3.6 TRANSFER SIZE (SIZ0, SIZ1)

These three-state, bidirectional signals are used in conjunction with the dynamic bus sizing capabilities of the MC68851. When the MC68851 is the bus master, the SIZE signals are driven as outputs and when accessed as a slave, these signals are inputs. Otherwise, the size signals are ignored. Regardless of the state (input or output) of these signals, they indicate the number of bytes remaining to be transferred during the current operand cycle.

An operand cycle is a bus cycle or sequence of bus cycles required to transfer a complete operand.

The encodings for the SIZE signals are shown in Table 4-4.

3.7 BUS CONTROL SIGNALS

The logical and physical bus control signals are described in the following paragraphs.

3.7.1 Read-Modify-Write ($\overline{\text{RMC}}$)

This three-state, bidirectional signal is used to indicate that the bus cycle in progress is an indivisible read-modify-write cycle. This signal is asserted for the duration of the read-modify-write sequence and should be used as a bus lock to ensure integrity of operation of these cycles.

When the MC68851 is translating addresses, the assertion of $\overline{\text{RMC}}$ by the logical bus master indicates that the master is performing a read-modify-write cycle and that a write operation to the same operand is likely to follow. When $\overline{\text{RMC}}$ is asserted during a read cycle, the MC68851 performs access and privilege checking for that cycle as if it were a write cycle in order that the operation not be aborted after having partially completed the write portion of the cycle. In addition, physical bus arbitration is suspended once the physical bus cycle for the address translation is initiated.

When the MC68851 is bus master, $\overline{\text{RMC}}$ may be asserted to indicate that the operation in progress should not be interrupted by other bus traffic and, hence, all arbitration for the physical bus is suspended by the MC68851 when this signal is asserted.

3.7.2 Logical Address Strobe ($\overline{\text{LAS}}$)

The assertion of this input indicates that the logical bus master has driven the logical address bus, function code, and R/$\overline{\text{W}}$ valid. When the MC68851 is being accessed as a slave, the assertion of $\overline{\text{LAS}}$ also indicates that the SIZE signals are driven valid.

3.7.3 Physical Address Strobe ($\overline{\text{PAS}}$)

This three-state output is asserted when the MC68851 has driven a valid address on the physical address bus. When the MC68851 is master of the logical bus, the assertion of $\overline{\text{PAS}}$ also indicates that the function code, R/$\overline{\text{W}}$, and SIZE signals are valid.

3.7.4 Data Strobe ($\overline{\text{DS}}$)

This bidirectional, three-state signal is used to control the flow of information on the data bus.

When the MC68851 is selected by the CPU, $\overline{\text{DS}}$ is an input that indicates that the MC68851 should drive the data bus on a read cycle, or that the CPU has placed valid data on the bus during a write cycle.

When the MC68851 is the bus master, $\overline{\text{DS}}$ indicates that the slave device should drive the data bus in the case of a read cycle, or that the MC68851 has placed valid data on the bus in the case of a write cycle.

The data strobe is ignored for the purposes of address translation.

3.7.5 Read/Write (R/$\overline{\text{W}}$)

This bidirectional, three-state signal is used to indicate the direction of transfer for a bus cycle.

When the MC68851 is translating addresses, the state of the R/$\overline{\text{W}}$ signal is input in order to support write-protection checking.

When the MC68851 register set is accessed by the CPU for an operation (refer to **4.2.3.5 TRANSLATION OF CPU SPACE ACCESSES**), the R/$\overline{\text{W}}$ output by the CPU determines the direction of data transfer. If this signal is asserted (low) the MC68851 latches data from the data bus at the termation of the cycle. If the signal is negated (high), the MC68851 outputs data on the data bus and signals that the transfer is complete.

When the MC68851 is bus master, the R/$\overline{\text{W}}$ signal is driven as an output. A high level indicates a read from an external device, a low indicates a write to an external device.

3.7.6 Data Transfer and Size Acknowledge ($\overline{\text{DSACK0}}$, $\overline{\text{DSACK1}}$)

These bidirectional, three-state signals, whether used as inputs or outputs, are used to normally terminate a bus cycle and to indicate the **port** size of the responding device.

When the MC68851 register set is accessed by the CPU, the $\overline{\text{DSACKx}}$ signals are output to indicate that valid data has been or will be (see below) placed on the data bus for a read cycle, or that data has been accepted from the data bus for a write cycle. Note that the relationship between $\overline{\text{DSACKx}}$ and data is dependent on the operating mode of the MC68851. When operating in the synchronous mode, the MC68851 drives the data bus on the same clock edge that $\overline{\text{DSACKx}}$ is asserted. Otherwise, the MC68851 drives the data bus two clock periods before asserting the $\overline{\text{DSACKx}}$ signals.

The $\overline{\text{DSACKx}}$ signals are monitored as inputs when the MC68851 arbitrates for the logical bus. After receiving a bus grant from the CPU, the MC68851 waits until $\overline{\text{LBGACK}}$, $\overline{\text{LAS}}$, and both $\overline{\text{DSACKx}}$ signals are negated before asserting logical bus grant acknowledge in order to ensure that the previous slave device has released connection from the bus.

When the MC68851 is executing bus cycles as the physical bus master, the $\overline{\text{DSACKx}}$ signals are inputs to indicate that a data transfer is complete and the port size of the external device being accessed. During a read cycle, when the MC68851 recognizes $\overline{\text{DSACKx}}$, it latches the data and then terminates the bus cycle; during a write cycle, when the MC68851 recognizes $\overline{\text{DSACKx}}$, the bus cycle is terminated. Refer to **4.3.1.1 DYNAMIC BUS SIZING** for further information on $\overline{\text{DSACKx}}$ encodings.

When operating as bus master, the MC68851 synchronizes the $\overline{\text{DSACKx}}$ inputs and allows skew between the two inputs of up to one quarter of a clock.

3.7.7 Data Buffer Disable (DBDIS)

This active-high output provides an enable to external data buffers connected to the MC68851 data bus.

When the logical bus master reads the contents of one of the MC68851 registers, the MC68851 drives the data bus with the required operand. Typical systems directly connect the MC68851 data bus with that of the main processor and the combined bus is buffered before being routed to a large number of physical address space devices. In order to avoid contention, the buffers between the MC68851/CPU bus and the bus driving the physical memory must be disabled when the MC68851 drives the bus. The MC68851 provides the control necessary to perform this function with the DBDIS signal.

In addition, DBDIS performs a function similar to the function of the MC68020 $\overline{\text{DBEN}}$ signal. DBDIS is asserted during table search operations and can be used to control data bus transceivers in order to avoid contention between the transceivers and the MC68851 data bus drivers.

Finally, DBDIS is driven during reset in order to isolate the MC68851 data bus while configuration information is being input (refer to **4.1.1 Initialization of Internal State**).

3.8 BUS EXCEPTION CONTROL SIGNALS

The following paragraphs describe the bus exception control signals for the MC68851.

3.8.1 Reset ($\overline{\text{RESET}}$)

Assertion of this input signals the MC68851 to disable the address translation mechanism, clear all breakpoints, set the internal state to idle, and input configuration information from the data bus. Refer to **4.1 RESET OPERATION** for additional information.

3.8.2 Halt ($\overline{\text{HALT}}$)

$\overline{\text{HALT}}$ is a bidirectional, three-state signal.

When the MC68851 is the logical bus master, $\overline{\text{HALT}}$ is an input and assertion of $\overline{\text{HALT}}$ stops all MC68851 bus activity at the completion of the current bus cycle. When the MC68851 has been halted using this input, all control signals, with the exception of bus arbitration outputs, are placed in their inactive states and the physical address bus remains driven with the value used during the previous bus cycle. Bus arbitration functions normally when the MC68851 is halted.

When the MC68851 is translating addresses, $\overline{\text{HALT}}$ is used as an output in conjunction with $\overline{\text{BERR}}$ and/or $\overline{\text{LBRO}}$ to signal the current logical bus master to perform either a 'relinquish and retry' or a 'relinquish' operation. Refer to **4.2.3.2 ADDRESS TRANSLATION TERMINATED BY REQLINQUISH AND RETRY SEQUENCE** and to **4.2.3.4 CPU SPACE ACCESS WITH RELINQUISH REQUEST**.

During address translation, the assertion of $\overline{\text{HALT}}$ by an external device does not effect translation operations of the MC68851.

3.8.3 Bus Error ($\overline{\text{BERR}}$)

This bidirectional, three-state signal is used to indicate that a bus cycle should be terminated due to abnormal conditions.

When the MC68851 is bus master, $\overline{\text{BERR}}$ is an input and assertion of $\overline{\text{BERR}}$ by an external device signals that there has been some problem with the bus cycle currently being executed. These problems may be the result of:
1) Non-responding devices, or
2) Various other application-dependent errors (for example, parity errors).

When the MC68851 is translating addresses, bus error is used as an output to the logical bus master. Bus error is asserted by the MC68851 for the following conditions:
1) The BERR bit is set in the matched ATC entry,
2) A write or read-modify-write cycle is attempted to a write-protected page,
3) An instruction breakpoint is detected and the associated count register is zero or it is disabled,
4) As a portion of the relinquish and retry operation if:
    a) the required address mapping is not resident in the ATC,
    b) a write operation occurs to a previously unmodified page,
    c) a read from the response CIR causes a suspended PLOAD or PTEST instruction to be restarted,
    d) a module call operation references a descriptor that does not have a corresponding entry in the ATC.
5) An RMC cycle is attempted and a corresponding descriptor with appropriate status is not resident in the ATC,
6) The access level protection mechanism detects an access violation.

The bus error signal interacts with the $\overline{\text{HALT}}$ signal to determine if the current bus cycle should be retried or aborted. Refer to **SECTION 4 BUS OPERATION DESCRIPTION** for additional information.

3.9 CACHE LOAD INHIBIT ($\overline{\text{CLI}}$)

During address translation this output is asserted by the MC68851 if the matched address translation cache entry has its CI (cache inhibit) bit set. Assertion of this output signals to external caches that the data associated with the current bus cycle is non-cacheable. In order to support concurrent dissociated logical and physical bus activity, if a referenced translation descriptor has its CI bit set, $\overline{\text{CLI}}$ is asserted by the MC68851 regardless of whether or not it currently owns the physical bus. Refer to **4.6 CONCURRENT DISSOCIATE LOGICAL AND PHYSICAL BUS ACTIVITY**.

In order to maintain the distinction between CPU space and other address spaces (for example, supervisor program, ..., etc.) the MC68851 does not assert $\overline{\text{PAS}}$ for CPU space cycles. Cache load inhibit is used to generate a CPU space address strobe during CPU space cycles that do not access the MC68851. $\overline{\text{CLI}}$ is asserted on the falling edge of the clock and external qualification of $\overline{\text{CLI}}$ with $\overline{\text{LAS}}$ and a CPU space indicator provides a CPU space address strobe. CPU space cycles that access the MC68851 registers are decoded internally and generate no physical bus activity. Refer to **4.2.3.5 TRANSLATION OF CPU SPACE ACCESSES**. Note that if the MC68851 is not master of the physical bus and a CPU space cycle is executed that does not reference the MC68851 internal registers, $\overline{\text{CLI}}$ is not asserted until ownership of the physical bus is returned to the MC68851. Note also that the operation of the $\overline{\text{CLI}}$ signal during physical bus arbitration is dependent on the operational mode of the $\overline{\text{CLI}}$ signal (i.e., whether it is signaling 'cache inhibit' or 'CPU space cycle').

When the MC68851 is performing table search operations, it continuously asserts $\overline{\text{CLI}}$ in order to prevent caching of translation table information. This function may be suppressed during reset configuration if desired.

3.10 ASYNCHRONOUS CONTROL ($\overline{\text{ASYNC}}$)

When a logical bus master does not present logical bus control signals with the exact timing specifications of the MC68020, this input must be driven, with appropriate setup and hold times, to inform the MC68851 that input synchronization must take place.

Operating in a synchronous mode, the MC68851 utilizes known signal relationships in order to perform faster translations. If the logical bus master does not present signals conforming to these relationships (different control strobe timings and/or different operating frequency), it must assert $\overline{\text{ASYNC}}$ prior to initiating bus activity.

3.11 CLOCK (CLK)

The MC68851 clock input is a TTL-compatible signal that is internally buffered to develop internal clocks for the memory management unit. The clock must conform to minimum and maximum period and pulse width specifications and must be of a constant frequency.

Note that the MC68851 and the logical bus master may operate at different clock frequencies. Refer to **4.2.2.2 ASYNCHRONOUS OPERATION** for further details.

3.12 PHYSICAL BUS ARBITRATION

This section describes the three-wire physical bus arbitration circuitry of the MC68851 used to determine which device in a system is the master of the physical bus.

The MC68851 is the default master of the physical bus and any other devices requiring access to the bus must arbitrate for mastership. Refer to **4.4 Physical Bus Arbitration** for further details.

3.12.1 Physical Bus Request ($\overline{\text{PBR}}$)

This input is the wire-OR of the bus request signals from all potential physical bus masters and indicates that some device other than the MC68851 requires mastership of the physical bus.

3.12.2 Physical Bus Grant ($\overline{\text{PBG}}$)

This output signal indicates to potential bus masters that the MC68851 will release ownership of the physical bus when the current bus cycle is completed.

3.12.3 Physical Bus Grant Acknowledge ($\overline{\text{PBGACK}}$)

This input indicates that some other device has become master of the physical bus. This signal should not be asserted until the following conditions have been met:

1) A physical bus grant ($\overline{PBG}$) has been received through the arbitration process,
2) $\overline{PAS}$ is negated, indicating that neither the MC68851 nor the logical bus master is using the physical bus,
3) $\overline{DSACKx}$ are negated, indicating that no external device is still driving the data bus, and
4) $\overline{PBGACK}$ is negated, indicating that no other device is still claiming bus mastership.

$\overline{PBGACK}$ must remain asserted as long as any device other than the MC68851 is bus master.

3.13 LOGICAL BUS ARBITRATION

The following paragraphs describe the five-wire bus arbitration pins used to determine which device in the system is the master of the logical bus. Refer to **4.4 LOGICAL BUS ARBITRATION**.

3.13.1 Logical Bus Request In ($\overline{LBRI}$)

The $\overline{LBRI}$ input indicates that a device with higher priority than the MC68851 or the current logical bus master requires ownership of the logical bus.

3.13.2 Logical Bus Request Out ($\overline{LBRO}$)

This output is asserted to inform the processor that the MC68851 requires ownership of the logical bus and is used as a portion of the relinquish operation and the relinquish and retry operation.

The request input to the logical bus arbiter (usually the main processor) should consist of wire-OR of requests input to $\overline{LBRI}$ logically ORed with the $\overline{LBRO}$ output of the MC68851.

3.13.3 Logical Bus Grant In ($\overline{LBGI}$)

This input, generated by the MC68020, indicates that the MC68020 will release ownership of the bus at the completion of the current bus cycle, or, if an alternate master is currently the owner of the bus, that the MC68020 will not claim the bus after the alternate master has released it.

3.13.4 Logical Bus Grant Out ($\overline{LBGO}$)

This output indicates that the MC68851 has recognized and synchronized the assertion of $\overline{LBGI}$ by the MC68020, has detected the assertion of $\overline{LBRI}$, and is passing the bus grant to an alternate logical bus master or to arbitration prioritization circuitry.

3.13.5 Logical Bus Grant Acknowledge ($\overline{LBGACK}$)

This bidirectional, three-state signal indicates that a logical bus master, other than the CPU, has taken control of the logical bus.

This signal is asserted by the MC68851 to indicate when it is the current logical bus master. $\overline{LBGACK}$ is also monitored as an input to determine when the MC68851 can become bus master.

3.14 SIGNAL SUMMARY

Table 3-2 provides a summary of the electrical characteristics of the signals discussed in the previous paragraphs.

Table 3-2. Signal Summary

Signal Function	Signal Name	Input/Output	Active State	Three-State	Driven by MC68851 When
Logical Address Bus	LA8–LA31	Input	High	—	—
Physical Address Bus	PA8–PA31	Output	High	Yes	MC68851 Owns Physical Bus
Shared Address Bus	A0–A7	Input/Output	High	Yes	MC68851 Owns Logical and Physical Buses
Function Codes	FC0–FC3	Input/Output	High	Yes	MC68851 Owns Logical and Physical Buses
Data Bus	D0–D31	Input/Output	High	Yes	Read from MC68851 Registers or MC68851 Write Cycle
Size	SIZ0–SIZ1	Input/Output	High	Yes	MC68851 Owns Logical and Physical Buses
Cache Load Inhibit	$\overline{\text{CLI}}$	Output	Low	No	Always
Asynchronous Control	$\overline{\text{ASYNC}}$	Input	Low	—	—
Read-Modify-Write Cycle	$\overline{\text{RMC}}$	Input/Output	Low	Yes	MC68851 Owns Logical and Physical Buses
Logical Address Strobe	$\overline{\text{LAS}}$	Input	Low	—	—
Physical Address Strobe	$\overline{\text{PAS}}$	Output	Low	Yes	MC68851 Owns Physical Bus
Data Strobe	$\overline{\text{DS}}$	Input/Output	Low	Yes	MC68851 Owns Logical and Physical Buses
Read/Write	$\text{R}/\overline{\text{W}}$	Input/Output	High/Low	Yes	MC68851 Owns Logical and Physical Buses
Data Transfer and Size Acknowledge	$\overline{\text{DSACK0}}$–$\overline{\text{DSACK1}}$	Input/Output	Low	Yes	Access to Address Map Occupied by MC68851 Interface Register Set
Data Bus Disable	DBDIS	Output	High	No	Always
Bus Error	$\overline{\text{BERR}}$	Input/Output	Low	Yes	Exceptional Condition is Generated by Address Translation
Halt	$\overline{\text{HALT}}$	Input/Output	Low	Yes	Exceptional Condition is Generated by Address Translation
Reset	$\overline{\text{RESET}}$	Input	Low	—	—
Physical Bus Request	$\overline{\text{PBR}}$	Input	Low	—	—
Physical Bus Grant	$\overline{\text{PBG}}$	Output	Low	No	Always
Physical Bus Grant Acknowledge	$\overline{\text{PBGACK}}$	Input	Low	—	—
Logical Bus Request In	$\overline{\text{LBRI}}$	Input	Low	—	—
Logical Bus Request Out	$\overline{\text{LBRO}}$	Output	Low	No	Always
Logical Bus Grant In	$\overline{\text{LBGI}}$	Input	Low	—	—
Logical Bus Grant Out	$\overline{\text{LBGO}}$	Output	Low	No	Always
Logical Bus Grant Acknowledge	$\overline{\text{LBGACK}}$	Input/Output	Low	Yes	MC68851 Has Assumed Mastership of the Logical Bus
Clock	CLK	Input	—	—	—
Power Supply	V_{CC}	Input	—	—	—
Ground	GND	Input	—	—	—

SECTION 4
BUS OPERATION DESCRIPTION

This section describes the bus operations of the MC68851 during reset, address translation, table search operations, bus arbitration, and accesses to MC68851 internal registers.

NOTE

In paragraphs dealing with bus transfers, a 'port' refers to the width of the external data path to which the slave device for the operation is connected whether that device be the MC68851 or external memory.

During an MC68851-initiated write cycle, all bytes of the data bus are driven regardless of the operand transfer size.

The term 'synchronization' is used repeatedly when discussing bus operation. This delay is the time period required for the MC68851 to sample an external asynchronous signal, determine whether it is high or low, and synchronize the input to its internal clocks. Figure 4-1 shows the relationship between the clock signal, an external input, and its associated internal signal that is typical for all of the asynchronous inputs.

Furthermore, for all inputs, there is a sample window during which the MC68851 latches the level of the input. This window is illustrated in Figure 4-2. In order to guarantee recognition of a certain level on a specific falling edge of the clock, that level must be held stable at the input throughout the sample window. If an input makes transitions during the sample window, the level recognized by the MC68851 is not predictable; however, the MC68851 will always resolve the latched input level to a logical high or low before taking action on it. There are two exceptions to this rule. The first is for the late assertion of $\overline{BERR}$ or $\overline{BERR}$ and $\overline{HALT}$ (refer to **4.3.2.4.1 Bus Error Operation**), where the signal **must** be stable through the window or the MC68851 may exhibit erratic behavior. The second is for the assertion of $\overline{LAS}$ and $\overline{DS}$ when operating in the synchronous translation mode (refer to **4.2.2.1 SYNCHRONOUS OPERATION**) where proper functionality cannot be guaranteed if setup times are not met. In addition to meeting input setup and hold times, all input

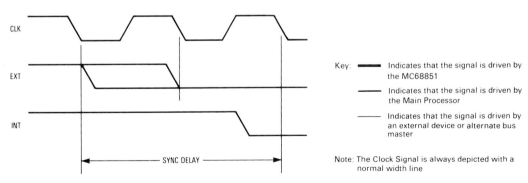

Figure 4-1. Relationship Between External and Internal Signals

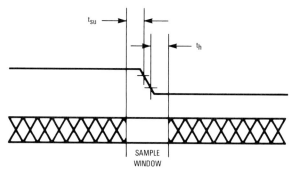

Figure 4-2. Input Sample Window

signals must obey the protocols described later in this section. For example, when the MC68851 is performing a table search and $\overline{\text{DSACKx}}$ is asserted by an external device, it must remain asserted until $\overline{\text{PAS}}$ is negated.

4.1 RESET OPERATION

The following paragraphs describe the operation of the MC68851 in response to an external reset. The timing for the reset operation is detailed in **SECTION 12 ELECTRICAL SPECIFICATIONS**.

4.1.1 Initialization of Internal State

The assertion of the $\overline{\text{RESET}}$ input by an external device initializes the MC68851 to a known, idle state by clearing the enable (E) bits in the translation control register (TC) and in each of the eight breakpoint control registers (BAC0–BAC7), and clearing the ALC field of the AC register.

Clearing of the E bit of the translation control register disables the address translation mechanism of the MC68851 and causes logical addresses LA8 through LA31 to be passed directly through (unmapped) to the physical bus. The physical address strobe is asserted for all non-CPU space translations regardless of the state of the E bit; however, no access right checking is performed when the translation mechanism is disabled.

Clearing the E bit of the breakpoint control registers disables all breakpoint operations. If a breakpoint acknowledge cycle is executed by the CPU while the breakpoint acknowledge functions are disabled, the MC68851 responds by asserting bus error ($\overline{\text{BERR}}$). Clearing the ALC field of the AC register inhibits RAL, WAL, and CAL access level checking.

4.1.2 Bus Interface Initialization

Several characteristics of the bus operations of the MC68851 are system-configurable. The information that determines this configuration is latched from the data bus at the end of the reset sequence (i.e., at the rising edge of the $\overline{\text{RESET}}$ input).

While the $\overline{\text{RESET}}$ input is asserted, the MC68851 asserts the DBDIS output, allowing its data bus to be isolated from all other bus drivers. The condition of both $\overline{\text{RESET}}$ and DBDIS being asserted can be used to gate configuration information onto the MC68851 data bus.

The use of the data bus for MC68851 configuration, as discussed in the following paragraphs, is valid only during reset operation and only the least significant byte of the bus is used. The three higher-order bytes of the data bus are ignored during reset.

4.1.2.1 D0. This input must be either pulled high (logic one) or left floating during the reset sequence.

4.1.2.2 BUS SIZE (D1, D2). D1 and D2 specify the minimum data bus size that connects the MC68851 to any device that may access its internal registers using the coprocessor interface. If multiple logical devices are capable of accessing the MC68851 registers, the maximum size for a single transfer is limited to the size of the smallest of the data buses.

When accessed as a slave device, the MC68851 responds with a $\overline{DSACKx}$ encoding that indicates the port size as specified on D1 and D2 during reset.

Table 4-1 shows the D1, D2 encodings for various bus width configurations. The default value (D2, D1 left in high-impedance state) is 32 bits.

4.1.2.3 DECISION TIMEOUT DELAY (D3, D4). D3 and D4 specify an additional, if any, amount of delay for the MC68851 internal decision-timeout circuitry used to determine when the compare logic of the address translation cache has generated a correct decision. This additional delay is defined from the clock edge on which the bus control signals ($\overline{PAS}$, $\overline{BERR}$, $\overline{HALT}$, and $\overline{LBRO}$) would normally be asserted by the MC68851 in the absence of a timeout delay and results in a delay of the assertion of these signals by an integral number of half-clocks as specified by the encoding of D3, D4. These encodings are shown in Table 4-2.

The additional timeout delay is provided for proper operation of MC68851 devices that have a mismatch between the clock speed and the speed of the address translation cache. If the address translation cache decision logic requires more time to validate an access than is available, as determined by the operating frequency and translation time, it is then necessary to delay the assertion of the bus control signals until that validation can be made. Otherwise, correct functionality of the address translation and protection mechanisms cannot be guaranteed since the bus control strobes may be activated before valid decisions have been made.

The default additional timeout delay is zero and this can be obtained by either forcing both D3 and D4 high (logic one) or by leaving both in the high-impedance state during reset.

4.1.2.4 FAST TABLE SEARCH (D5). During all table search operations, the MC68851 always (except as described below) asserts the physical bus control strobes with the same timing as that of the MC68020. That is, the strobes are asserted on the first falling edge of the clock after initiation of the bus cycle (the falling edge of S1). Normally, during address translations the control strobes

Table 4-1. Coprocessor Data Bus Size Specification

D2	D1	Minimum Coprocessor Data Bus Width
0	0	Unused, Reserved
0	1	8 Bits
1	0	16 Bits
1	1	32 Bits

Table 4-2. Additional Decision Timeout Delay

D4	D3	Additional Timeout Delay	Strobe Assertion Clock Edge
0	0	1 1/2 CLK	Rising
0	1	1 CLK	Falling
1	0	1/2 CLK	Rising
1	1	No Delay	Falling

are also asserted on a falling clock edge; however, the additional decision timeout delay specified on D3 and D4, as described above, may alter this.

In order to facilitate operation in systems that use the control strobes (for example, $\overline{\text{PAS}}$) in a synchronous manner (i.e., the signal relationship to a clock edge is important), the MC68851 can be configured such that the control signals are always asserted on the same clock edge regardless of whether a translation or a table search is taking place. In this type of synchronous system, if the decision timeout delay is set such that the bus control signals are asserted on the rising edge of the clock during address translations, it may be desirable to also have them asserted on the rising clock edge during table search operations.

If D5 is held low (logic zero) during reset, the MC68851 asserts the bus control strobes on the same edge of the system clock during both address translation and table search operations. The edge on which the signals are asserted is determined by the decision time-out delay indicated on D3 and D4. If D5 is driven high (logic one) or left in the high-impedance state during reset, the MC68851 will not delay the assertion of the bus control strobes when performing table search operations and will always assert $\overline{\text{PAS}}$ on the first falling edge of the clock for these bus cycles (bus state S1).

4.1.2.5 EARLY PROCESSING STARTUP (D6). D6 specifies whether the exception processing hardware of the MC68851 is enabled as soon as an exception (any operation by a logical bus master that requires a table search by the MC68851) is detected or delayed until the MC68851 has received control of the logical bus and has asserted logical bus grant acknowledge ($\overline{\text{LBGACK}}$).

There are two factors to be considered when selecting this mode. If the early processing startup is selected, the exception processing hardware is activated as soon as the exception is detected and six clock periods of the startup overhead are overlapped with the termination of the current logical bus cycle and arbitration for the logical bus. However, the early startup poses a potential problem since the MC68851 initiates processing prior to becoming logical bus master.

In order to correctly service an alternate logical bus master, the MC68851 must be ready to perform address translations as soon as that master gains control of the logical bus. In order to perform this service, the exception processing hardware of the MC68851 must be completely idle and ready for the next translation and, for certain exception conditions, eight clock periods are required to bring the exception processing hardware into the idle state. The MC68851 prevents conflicts between logical bus traffic and the exception processing hardware by delaying the assertion of the logical bus grant output ($\overline{\text{LBGO}}$) in response to a logical bus request ($\overline{\text{LBRI}}$), if necessary, by the eight clock periods (maximum) required to idle the exception hardware. If the early startup mode is not enabled, then this delay is not imposed and the worst case arbitration latency for the logical bus is reduced by seven clock periods.

If the early processing startup is enabled, by leaving D6 in the high-impedance state or driving it high (logic one), the normal overhead required for the MC68851 to acquire the logical bus and initiate service for the CPU (for example, table search, . . ., etc.) is reduced by six clock periods. If D6 is pulled low (logic zero), the MC68851 does not initialize its exception processing hardware until it asserts $\overline{\text{LBGACK}}$. In this case, the worst-case $\overline{\text{LBGI}}$ to $\overline{\text{LBGO}}$ delay is reduced by seven clock periods, but the overhead for all MC68851-initiated operations is increased by six clock periods. The system designer must balance the above two criterion when selecting this mode of operation.

It is possible to completely avoid the $\overline{\text{LBGI}}$ to $\overline{\text{LBGO}}$ delay imposed by the MC68851 through the use of external arbitration circuitry. Since the response of the MC68851 to a given arbitration sequence is defined, external logic may be employed to bypass the MC68851 bus grant circuitry such that the bus request-to-bus grant latency is defined by the bus arbitor of the CPU as opposed to the latency of the CPU plus that introduced by the MC68851. Note that this method mandates use of the MC68851 without the early processing startup mode enabled (i.e., D6 must be driven low during reset). This method is not described in detail in this manual; however, the operation of the logical bus arbitration circuitry is explained in detail in **4.4 LOGICAL BUS ARBITRATION**.

4.1.2.6 ASSERTION INHIBIT (D7). D7 specifies whether or not $\overline{\text{CLI}}$ is to be asserted during all MC68851-initiated bus cycles. It is unlikely that external caching of MC68851 initiated accesses would be of value, but this decision is left to the system designer.

If D7 is pulled high (logic one) or left in the high-impedance state, $\overline{\text{CLI}}$ will be asserted for all MC68851-initiated bus cycles. Otherwise, $\overline{\text{CLI}}$ will not be asserted during these bus cycles.

4.2 ADDRESS TRANSLATION

The translation of logical to physical addresses by the MC68851 involves the following signals:
1) Logical Address Bus LA8 through LA31,
2) Physical Address Bus PA8 through PA31,
3) Shared Logical/Physical Address Bus A0 through A7,
4) Logical Bus Control Signals, and
5) Physical Bus Control Signals.

The following paragraphs explain the operation of the above signals during address translation by the MC68851.

4.2.1 Signal Usage During Address Translation

The following paragraphs describe the MC68851 signals that are functional during address translation. Signals not discussed (for example, physical bus arbitration circuitry) are not necessarily inactive, but are not relevant to address translation and are discussed later.

4.2.1.1 ADDRESS BUSES. The MC68851 inputs the logical address to be translated on A0 through A7 and LA8 through LA31. The shared address lines A0 through A7 are always inputs during address translation. Although the least significant eight bits of the logical address never take part in the address translation (the minimum page size being 256 bytes), they are input during each translation in order to supply the register select field should the cycle attempt to access the MC68851 internal registers (refer to **SECTION 9 COPROCESSOR INTERFACE**).

The range of the logical address used is determined by the initial shift (IS) field of the translation control register (TC). This field specifies a number of high-order logical address bits that are to be ignored for the purposes of address translation and table search operations. Up to fifteen bits of the logical address (starting from bit 31) may be discarded, allowing adaptation to systems with logical address buses of 17 to 32 bits. However, regardless of the value specified in the IS field, the MC68851 always monitors at least A0 through LA19 during all CPU space cycles in order to decode accesses to its internal registers.

The page size for which the MC68851 is configured also affects the use of some portions of the logical address for translation purposes. For a page size, N, in a logical address space, M, $LOG_2(M) - LOG_2(N)$ bits of the logical address are used to uniquely identify one of $M \div N$ pages and the remaining $LOG_2(N)$ bits are used as an index into the page. The index into the page does not take any part in the translation processes and, hence, is ignored during address translation. By default, the lower eight bits of the logical address are always ignored ($LOG_2(256) = 8$) and are routed around the MC68851, directly connecting the logical and physical buses. If the page size for which the MC68851 is configured is larger than 256 bytes, additional logical address inputs are ignored during address translation. However, instead of being routed directly to the physical address bus externally, the additional signals are passed through the MC68851 and driven unchanged onto the physical address bus with the same functional timing as the higher order physical address outputs, although somewhat faster (refer to **SECTION 12 ELECTRICAL SPECIFICATIONS**).

The physical address bus (PA8 through PA31) outputs the mapped results of the address translation and remains driven as long as the MC68851 retains ownership of the physical bus. During address translation, the MC68851 always drives the high order 24 bits of the physical address bus and the assertion time always lags that of the logical bus by the MC68851 translation time. Note, however that physical addresses may become invalid very shortly after a transition of the logical address bus (i.e., the delay is not related to the translation time of the MC68851).

4.2.1.2 ADDRESS STROBES. The logical bus master signals to the MC68851 that it has initiated a bus cycle by driving the logical address strobe ($\overline{LAS}$) input low. $\overline{LAS}$ indicates that a valid address has been driven onto the logical address bus and it must remain asserted until the bus master is signaled, by either the MC68851 or an external device, that the bus cycle should be terminated.

After the logical bus master asserts $\overline{LAS}$, the MC68851 responds in one of several manners. If the requested translation is successful and does not access address space seven (the CPU space), the MC68851 asserts the physical address strobe ($\overline{PAS}$), signaling to the physical devices that there is a valid physical address on the bus.

If the logical access is made to the CPU space, but not to the MC68851 (i.e., not a coprocessor, breakpoint acknowledge, or access level control access to the MC68851), the logical address is passed directly through to the physical bus, $\overline{PAS}$ is not asserted, and cache load inhibit ($\overline{CLI}$) is asserted, which, when gated with a CPU space qualifier, can be used to generate a CPU space address strobe.

If the target of the CPU space access is the MC68851, neither $\overline{PAS}$ nor $\overline{CLI}$ is asserted.

4.2.1.3 BUS CYCLE TERMINATION SIGNALS. Attempts to execute bus cycles that the MC68851 cannot immediately translate (for example, translation descriptor not resident in address translation cache) are terminated with the relinquish and retry sequence that involves the simultaneous assertion of bus error ($\overline{BERR}$), halt ($\overline{HALT}$), and logical bus request out ($\overline{LBRO}$) by the MC68851 (refer to **4.2.3.2 ADDRESS TRANSLATION TERMINATED BY RELINQUISH AND RETRY SEQUENCE**).

Bus cycles that the MC68851 cannot allow to complete (for example, a write violation) are terminated by the assertion of $\overline{BERR}$. Certain other accesses to MC68851 internal registers are also terminated with $\overline{BERR}$ (for example, a breakpoint acknowledge cycle executed with breakpoints disabled in the MC68851 (refer to **4.2.3.3 ADDRESS TRANSLATION TERMINATED BY BUS ERROR**).

Finally, bus cycles that access the MC68851 registers can be terminated in one of three ways. If the access does not require execution of table search operations, then the MC68851 drives (during a read cycle) or latches (during a write cycle) the appropriate portions of the data bus (D0 through D31) and asserts one or both of the $\overline{DSACKx}$ outputs (as determined by the bus size for which the MC68851 is configured). If the access does require a table search, the cycle is terminated as above except that $\overline{LBRO}$ and $\overline{HALT}$ are asserted prior to assertion of the $\overline{DSACKx}$ signal(s). If the access causes the MC68851 to restart a table search initiated by a PTEST or PLOAD instruction, or an address is written to the descriptor address ALCR and no corresponding entry is resident in the ATC, the MC68851 asserts the $\overline{\text{BERR}}$, $\overline{\text{HALT}}$, and $\overline{\text{LBRO}}$ outputs to force the CPU to relinquish the bus and retry the cycle after the MC68851 has searched the translation tables and loaded the required mapping into the ATC. Refer to **4.2.3 Functional Descriptions** for further detailed discussion of these operations.

4.2.2 Synchronous versus Asynchronous Address Translation

In order to offer both maximum performance and flexibility, the MC68851 can operate in two different translation modes, as determined by the state of the $\overline{\text{ASYNC}}$ input.

The synchronous mode is intended to provide maximum performance and requires that both the logical bus master and the MC68851 operate in a tightly-coupled manner using the same clock signal and bus timings. The asynchronous mode is provided to allow coupling with logical bus masters that operate at different frequencies, either slower or faster, than the MC68851.

4.2.2.1 SYNCHRONOUS OPERATION. In the synchronous translation mode, the MC68851 is optimized to perform translations for bus masters that present bus timings identical to those of the MC68020. In this mode of operation, the MC68851 operates with the same clock that drives the logical master and uses known timing information concerning address, address strobe, and clock relationships to minimize the delay between the assertions of the logical and physical address strobes. During synchronous translations, $\overline{\text{LAS}}$ is not synchronized by the MC68851 and it is gated through to generate $\overline{\text{PAS}}$ one clock period after the clock edge on which $\overline{\text{LAS}}$ was asserted by the logical master. This is possible because normal synchronization delays are not imposed.

The critical factor in the synchronous mode of operation is that the logical bus master must provide bus timings with *exactly* the characteristics of the MC68020. This requirement includes all signals that are active during address translation as well as all those that are active during communications between the synchronous master and the MC68851 register set.

The above restriction requires that there be no intervening delay between the bus control signals of the synchronous logical bus master and the MC68851 inputs. In addition, no delay may be introduced between the address outputs of the synchronous master and the logical address inputs of the MC68851. Finally, the frequency and phase of the clock driving the MC68851 must be identical to that of the bus master. System designers must ensure that the address and control signals do not exceed worst case values specified by the MC68020 due to signal loading or routing constraints.

4.2.2.2 ASYNCHRONOUS OPERATION. In contrast to the synchronous requirements outlined above, operation of the MC68851 in the asynchronous mode imposes minimal restrictions on the bus timing of the logical master, but at the expense of increasing the logical-to-physical address strobe delay by the time required to internally synchronize the $\overline{\text{LAS}}$ input.

Operating in the asynchronous mode, the MC68851 makes no assumptions concerning signal relationships to clock edges or address/data setup times relative to the bus control strobes (except that they must be non-negative). When operating in the asynchronous mode, it is assumed, but not required, that the logical master and the MC68851 are operating at different clock frequencies.

4.2.3 Functional Descriptions

The following paragraphs provide a functional description of the bus operations of the MC68851 during address translation.

NOTE

In order to clarify the diagrams that are presented in this manual, different line widths are used to distinguish the actions of different devices. Signals that are driven by the MC68851 are drawn using a bold line; signals driven by the CPU are drawn using a normal width line, and signals driven by other external devices (for example, a memory controller, alternate bus masters, . . ., etc.) are drawn using a fine line.

4.2.3.1 NORMALLY TERMINATED ADDRESS TRANSLATION (NON-CPU SPACE). An address translation with normal termination refers to those cycles initiated by the logical master that have corresponding translation descriptors resident in the MC68851 address translation cache (ATC) and do not generate any conditions that are detected as exceptions by the MC68851 (for example, write violation, . . ., etc.). This type of bus cycle is terminated by an external device and the termination sequence may consist of any of the allowable M68000 bus conditions (normal, bus error, retry, etc.) without affecting the MC68851.

A normal translation is initiated when the master drives a valid address and function code onto the logical bus and sets the R/W output to indicate the direction of transfer. The MC68851 detects the transition in the address bus from its previous state and initiates a lookup in the ATC. After a period, determined by the worst case translation time, the MC68851 drives valid address onto the physical bus. When LAS is asserted by the logical bus master, the MC68851 checks the validity of the access using the status information stored in the ATC.

After the physical address has been driven, PAS and, if appropriate, CLI is/are asserted and the physical address bus cycle is validated. As long as LAS remains asserted, the MC68851 performs no further activity during the bus cycle.

When external hardware determines that the bus cycle should be terminated, some combination of the DSACKx signals is/are asserted (or BERR could be asserted with or without HALT) and the logical bus master negates its bus control strobes. Immediately after the negation of LAS, the MC68851 negates PAS in order to allow physical devices to prepare for the next cycle.

In the synchronous mode, as shown in Figure 4-3, the bus cycle is initiated at the rising edge of (entering into) clock state S0 when logical address, function code, and R/W are driven valid. At the falling edge of S0, the master asserts its address strobe, which is connected to the LAS input of the MC68851. On the falling edge of S2, one clock after the master drives the logical address strobe, the MC68851 asserts the physical address strobe (PAS). Some period after this, as determined by the access time of the referenced device, the device signals termination of the bus cycle.

With certain system configurations, it is possible that some bus operations can deviate slightly from the above, particularly in those systems having a high-speed data/instruction cache. In this case, the CPU can run bus cycles at its maximum bandwidth (three clock periods for the MC68020) for those cycles whose target operands reside in the cache. In order to execute such a bus cycle, the MC68020 requires that DSACKx be asserted, with the proper setup time, prior to the falling edge of clock state S2. Since PAS is generated from this same edge, it is clearly not possible to include PAS in the qualification equations for the generation of DSACKx for these cycles. Instead, the cache control circuitry is allowed to assert DSACKx for appropriate cycles without regard to the state of PAS. Figure 4-4 illustrates a three-cycle access to a local cache.

If the MC68851 determines that the bus cycle should not be allowed to complete, PAS is not asserted and a relinquish and retry or a bus error is signaled in time to abort or retry the bus cycle using the delayed bus error or retry capabilities of the M68000 bus, provided that additional decision timeout delay has not been enabled (refer to **4.1.2.3 DECISION TIMEOUT DELAY**). Refer to **APPENDIX B HARDWARE CONSIDERATIONS** for further discussion of cache considerations.

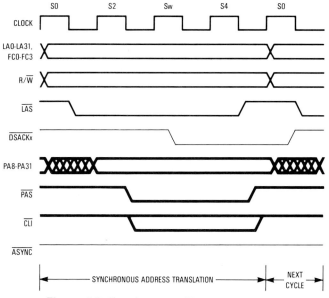

Figure 4-3. Synchronous Mode Translation

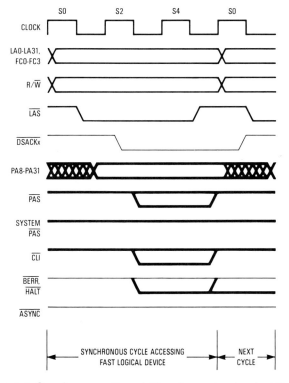

Figure 4-4. Synchronous Translation Accessing Logical Cache

In the asynchronous mode of operation, the MC68851 samples LAS on falling edges of the clock. If LAS meets the asynchronous input setup time specification (#47A) relative to the falling edge of the clock and the translation is successful, PAS is asserted on the next falling edge of the clock. If LAS does not meet this setup time, an additional one-clock delay in the assertion of PAS may be imposed. Additionally, if the negation period (high time) for LAS is less than one clock period, the assertion of PAS by the MC68851 will be delayed one clock period in addition to the delay described above. Figure 4-5 illustrates an asynchronous mode address translation.

4.2.3.2 ADDRESS TRANSLATION TERMINATED BY RELINQUISH AND RETRY SEQUENCE. Certain bus cycles initiated by a logical bus master require that the MC68851 acquire control of the bus and access the address translation tables in physical memory before that cycle can be successfully completed. Such cases include:
1) Translation descriptor for access not resident in ATC,
2) Modified bit not set in descriptor and pending cycle is a write,
3) Translation descriptor for a module descriptor not resident in ATC during execution of the CALLM instruction (refer to **SECTION 10 ACCESS LEVEL INTERFACE**), and
4) Restart of an aborted table search initiated by a PLOAD or PTEST instruction.

In any of the above cases the MC68851 forces the logical bus master into the relinquish and retry sequence by simultaneously asserting bus error (BERR), halt (HALT), and logical bus request out (LBRO).

Since the lower eight address lines and several bus control signals are shared between the logical and physical buses, the MC68851 must control both the logical and physical buses in order to

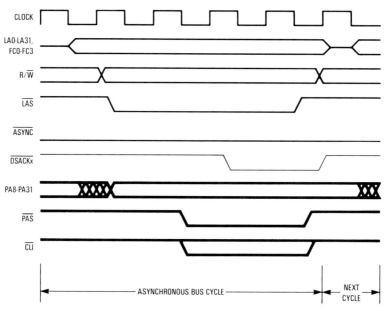

**Figure 4-5. Asynchronous Mode Translation
(LAS Meets Input Setup Time)**

perform physical bus activity. The MC68851 is the default physical bus master but it must arbitrate for the logical bus.

The relinquish and retry sequence signals to the logical master that it must abort the current bus cycle, release mastership of the logical bus to the requesting device, and retry the aborted cycle when it regains ownership of the bus. Before the master regains control of the bus, the MC68851 completes the arbitration sequence to take ownership of the logical bus (refer to **4.4 LOGICAL BUS ARBITRATION**), performs all table search operations that are required, and updates the ATC accordingly.

When the logical master acknowledges termination of the bus cycle by negating $\overline{LAS}$, the MC68851 immediately negates $\overline{BERR}$. $\overline{HALT}$ and $\overline{LBRO}$ remain asserted until the completion of the arbitration sequence (assertion of logical bus grant acknowledge ($\overline{LBGACK}$) by the MC68851). If there are no requests for bus mastership by alternate logical bus masters, $\overline{HALT}$ is negated one-half clock prior to the assertion of $\overline{LBGACK}$ and $\overline{LBRO}$ is negated one-half clock period after the assertion of $\overline{LBGACK}$. If, however, the MC68851 is prevented from assuming mastership of the logical bus by external assertion of $\overline{LBRI}$, both $\overline{HALT}$ and $\overline{LBRO}$ are negated one-half clock period prior to the assertion of $\overline{LBGO}$.

The MC68851 does not assert $\overline{PAS}$ for any cycles that are terminated with the relinquish and retry sequence or for any other fault.

The following paragraphs discuss the relinquish and retry sequence for the different translation modes. The arbitration phase and subsequent table search operations are discussed in **4.4 LOGICAL BUS ARBITRATION** and **4.3 TABLE SEARCH OPERATIONS**, respectively.

Similar to the normal assertion of $\overline{PAS}$ for a synchronous master, and provided that all relevant setup times are met, the MC68851 asserts $\overline{BERR}$, $\overline{HALT}$, and $\overline{LBRO}$ on the falling edge of the clock one clock period (plus any additional decision timeout delay specified during reset) after the logical master asserts $\overline{LAS}$ when operating in the synchronous translation mode.

The assertions of $\overline{BERR}$ and $\overline{HALT}$ occur early enough in the bus cycle to satisfy all timing requirements of the MC68020 for the late assertion of $\overline{BERR}$. Therefore, devices that operate on the logical bus (for example, a logical cache controller) need not monitor the state of $\overline{PAS}$ for cycles that do not access a physical address space device — that is, the validity of the bus cycle can be correctly implied by the absence of an abort or retry signal from the MC68851.

Figure 4-6 illustrates the synchronous relinquish and retry sequence.

In the asynchronous mode, $\overline{BERR}$, $\overline{HALT}$, and $\overline{LBRO}$ are asserted on the falling edge of the MC68851 clock one period (plus any additional decision timeout delay specified during reset) after $\overline{LAS}$ is detected as being asserted. If $\overline{LAS}$ meets the asynchronous input setup time specified (#47A) relative to the falling edge of the clock, and the cycle cannot be completed for reasons as discussed above, the signals are asserted on the next falling edge of the clock. If $\overline{LAS}$ does not meet this setup time, an additional one-clock delay in the assertion of the relinquish and retry sequence may be imposed.

Normally, when operating in the asynchronous translation mode, the $\overline{BERR}$, $\overline{HALT}$, and $\overline{LBRO}$ signals are not asserted early enough during a bus cycle to allow use of late bus error or retry features of the logical bus master when coupled with a fast logical data cache that operates with no wait states. However, this is dependent on the exact bus timing of the particular master.

Figure 4-7 illustrates the asynchronous relinquish and retry sequence.

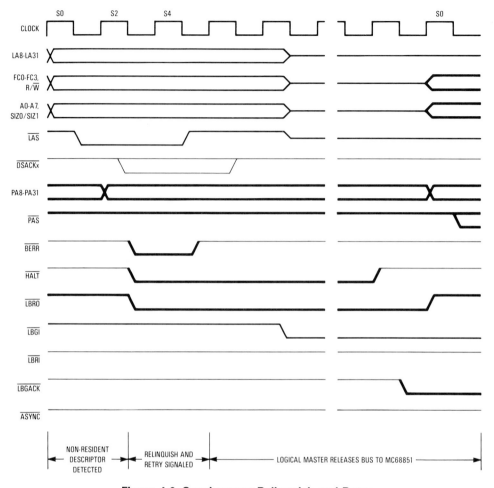

Figure 4-6. Synchronous Relinquish and Retry

4.2.3.3 ADDRESS TRANSLATION TERMINATED BY BUS ERROR. Certain bus cycles initiated by a logical bus master must not be allowed to be completed due to exceptional conditions generated by those accesses. Such cycles include:

1) Attempt to write to a write-protected page,
2) An access that exceeds the current access level,
3) An access that references an ATC descriptor that has its bus error bit set,
4) A breakpoint acknowledge cycle that references a breakpoint acknowledge control register that has a skip count equal to zero,
5) A breakpoint acknowledge cycle that references a breakpoint acknowledge control register that has its E bit (enable) clear, and
6) A read-modify-write operation is attempted to a page that does not have a corresponding descriptor resident in the address translation cache, has its modified bit clear, or is write-protected.

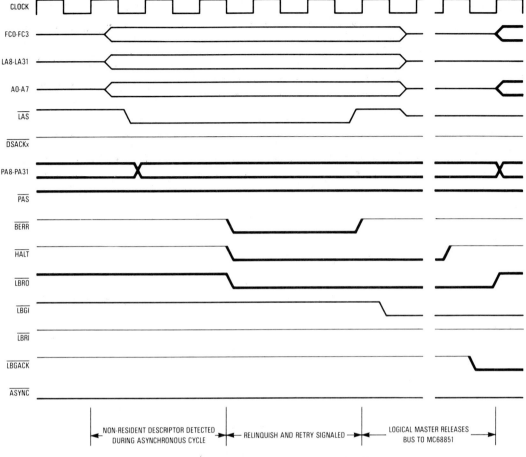

**Figure 4-7. Asynchronous Relinquish and Retry
($\overline{\text{LAS}}$ Misses Input Setup Time)**

The MC68851 aborts any of the above types of cycles by asserting bus error ($\overline{\text{BERR}}$) which signals the logical master that the cycle can neither be completed nor is it appropriate to retry the cycle without intervention from the operating system. Bus cycles may also be terminated by the assertion of $\overline{\text{BERR}}$ by an external device.

The MC68851 does not assert $\overline{\text{PAS}}$ for any bus cycle that it terminates with $\overline{\text{BERR}}$.

The timing of $\overline{\text{BERR}}$ in each of the translation modes corresponds exactly to the $\overline{\text{BERR}}$ assertion timing for the relinquish and retry sequence discussed above. Figures 4-8 and 4-9 illustrate the assertion of $\overline{\text{BERR}}$ during address translation.

4.2.3.4 CPU SPACE ACCESS WITH RELINQUISH REQUEST. The MC68851 PTEST and PLOAD instructions require that the MC68851 perform table search operations. As part of the normal dialog between the main processor and the MC68851 during execution of memory management

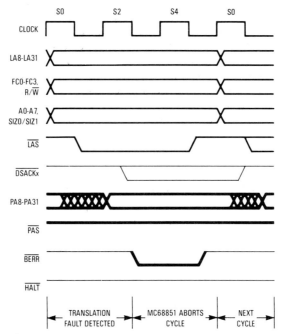

Figure 4-8. Synchronous Cycle Terminated by Bus Error

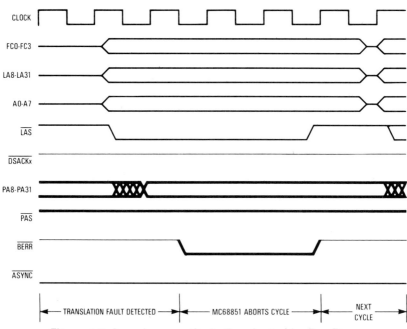

**Figure 4-9. Asynchronous Cycle Terminated by Bus Error
($\overline{\text{LAS}}$ Meets Input Setup Time)**

instructions, the CPU writes requests for action to the MC68851 coprocessor interface command register and then reads the MC68851 response to this request from the MC68851 coprocessor interface response register (refer to **SECTION 9 COPROCESSOR INTERFACE**).

When the request written by the main processor requires that the MC68851 perform a table search operation, the MC68851 initiates this activity by terminating the access of its registers with an appropriate combination of the $\overline{\text{DSACKx}}$ signals and also asserting the logical bus request output ($\overline{\text{LBRO}}$) and the halt signal ($\overline{\text{HALT}}$). This sequence causes the main processor to proceed with the next portion of the instruction dialog (reading the response register) but not without first granting bus mastership to the MC68851. The MC68851 can then perform the required service before resuming communication with the CPU.

Interprocessor communication between the MC68851 and the logical master does not result in the assertion of the physical bus control signals ($\overline{\text{PAS}}$ or $\overline{\text{CLI}}$).

Figure 4-10 illustrates the above termination. The asynchronous mode operations differ from those in the synchronous mode in two ways. First, additional synchronization delay may be introduced between the assertion of $\overline{\text{LAS}}$ and the MC68851 termination of the cycle. Second, during a read cycle from an MC68851 register, $\overline{\text{DSACKx}}$ is asserted two clock periods after data is driven onto the data bus instead of being driven on the same clock edge as data as would occur during synchronous operation.

When the MC68851 terminates an access to its register set with a relinquish request and is initialized for early processing startup (refer to **4.1.2.5 EARLY PROCESSING STARTUP**), the logical master *must* release control of the bus to the MC68851 (which may release it to an alternate master). Neither the CPU nor any other logical bus master may initiate a logical bus cycle prior to the assertion of $\overline{\text{LBGO}}$ and the negation of $\overline{\text{HALT}}$ by the MC68851 during this arbitration sequence. Note that the M68000 Family of processors fully satisfy this requirement. Use of the MC68851 with other processor families may necessitate the use of additional hardware to satisfy this requirement.

4.2.3.5 TRANSLATION OF CPU SPACE ACCESSES. A CPU space access is any access to the address space identified by the function code value of seven ($7). The CPU space accesses are used for special CPU functions, including coprocessor communications, access level control, breakpoint acknowledge, and interrupt acknowledge operations. The MC68851 treats these accesses differently than references generated in other address spaces. The MC68851 response to a CPU space cycle is dependent on whether the access is being made to the MC68851 or to another device.

CPU space accesses that reference the MC68851 include the breakpoint acknowledge functions, coprocessor operations with a Cp-ID of zero, and all access level operations (refer to Sections 8, 9, and 10). These accesses are decoded by the bus interface unit and are not passed through to the physical address bus. Cycles that access the coprocessor interface or the access level control registers are terminated by the MC68851 with the assertion of some combination of the bus termination signals after the appropriate action has been taken (for example, data latched during a write cycle or driven during a read cycle). In cases where the cycle in progress is requesting an MC68851 configuration change, $\overline{\text{DSACKx}}$ is not asserted until the reconfiguration is complete in order that the next bus cycle may be properly translated.

CPU space cycles that access the MC68851 breakpoint hardware may be terminated by the assertion of either $\overline{\text{DSACKx}}$ or $\overline{\text{BERR}}$, as appropriate (refer to **SECTION 8 BREAKPOINTS**). Figures 4-11 and 4-12 illustrate the functional timing of CPU space cycles that access the MC68851.

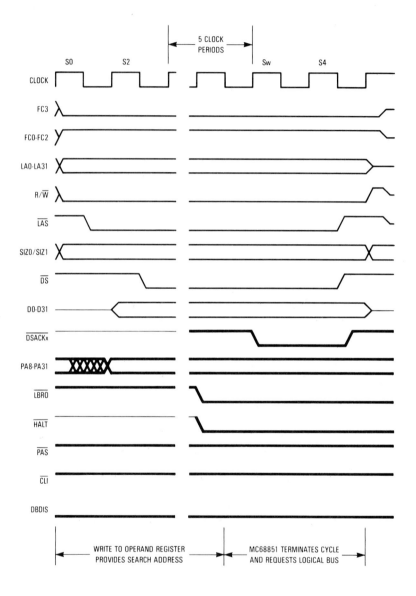

Figure 4-10. Synchronous CPU Space Cycle Accessing MC68851 Registers Terminated by Relinquish Request

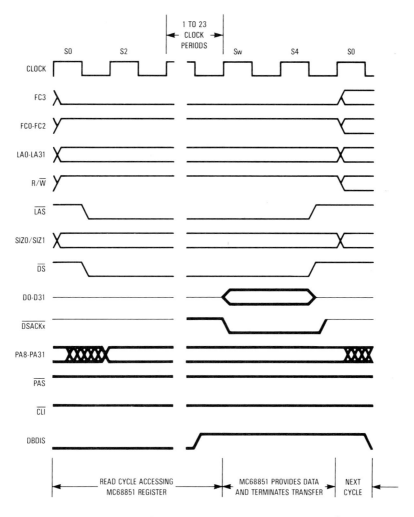

Figure 4-11. Synchronous CPU Space Read Cycle Accessing MC68851 Register

CPU space accesses that do not access the MC68851 are passed directly through to the physical bus with a unity mapping (i.e., unmapped). However, unlike normal address translations, mappings of CPU space accesses do not result in assertion of physical address strobe. Instead, $\overline{\text{CLI}}$ is asserted with timing similar to that of $\overline{\text{PAS}}$ and the combination of $\overline{\text{CLI}}$ with a CPU space indicator (FC3–FC0 = $7) can be used to generate a CPU space address strobe. The functional timing for CPU space cycles that do not access the MC68851 is shown in Figure 4-13.

$\overline{\text{PAS}}$ is not asserted for CPU space accesses in order that external controllers for physical memory devices not be required to monitor the function codes in addition to normal address decode in order to qualify the accesses. Figure 4-14 shows a typical representation of the logic required to generate a CPU space address strobe. Logical address strobe ($\overline{\text{LAS}}$) is included in order to negate the strobe immediately upon termination of the bus cycle.

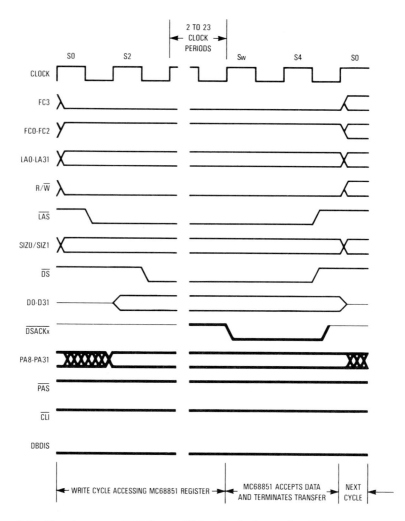

Figure 4-12. Synchronous CPU Space Write Cycle Accessing MC68851 Register

Also shown in Figure 4-14 are two alternative (though not mutually exclusive) methods for generating other required physical address space control strobes. The first method conditions the data strobe output of the logical bus master with $\overline{PAS}$ to generate a physical data strobe ($\overline{PDS}$). The second method conditions the R/$\overline{W}$ signal of the logical master with $\overline{PAS}$ to generate a physical R/$\overline{W}$ signal (PR/$\overline{W}$). One or both of these methods should be employed as dictated by the control requirements for a particular system.

4.2.3.6 CPU SPACE ACCESS WITH RELINQUISH AND RETRY. The MC68851 terminates accesses to its register set with a relinquish and retry request (assertion of $\overline{BERR}$, $\overline{HALT}$, and $\overline{LBRO}$) under two conditions. The first case occurs when a value is written to the descriptor address ALCR (refer to **SECTION 10 ACCESS LEVEL PROTECTION MECHANISM**) that does not have a corresponding entry resident in the MC68851 ATC. The relinquish and retry is issued in order that the MC68851

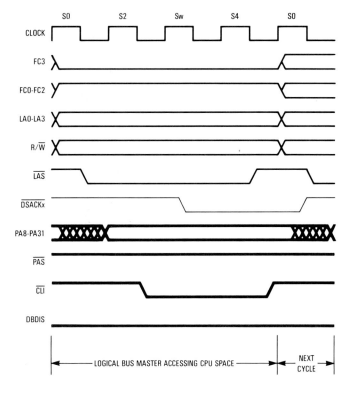

Figure 4-13. Synchronous CPU Space Cycle Accessing Physical Address Space

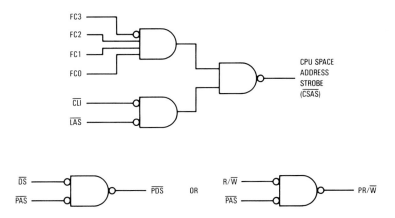

Figure 4-14. Typical Physical Address Space Strobe and R/W̄ Generation

can gain control of the logical bus in order to load the referenced entry into the ATC prior to being re-queried by the CPU. The second case occurs when a PLOAD or PTEST instruction is interrupted by the activity of an alternate logical bus master. Should this event occur, the table search is suspended by the MC68851 until the CPU reads the response register at which time the MC68851 issues a relinquish and retry and restarts the table search.

The functional timing for this operation is similar to that of a relinquish and retry issued during an address translation, as shown in Figure 4-6, with the exception that $\overline{BERR}$, $\overline{HALT}$, and $\overline{LBRO}$ are asserted one-half clock period later than shown in this figure.

4.3 TABLE SEARCH OPERATIONS

The following paragraphs describe the control signal and bus operation of the MC68851 during table search operations. For this discussion, it is assumed that the MC68851 possesses mastership of the logical bus. The operations required to gain this mastership are discussed in detail in **4.4 LOGICAL BUS ARBITRATION**.

During table search operations, the bidirectional signals $\overline{DSACK0}$, $\overline{DSACK1}$, $\overline{BERR}$, and $\overline{HALT}$ are always used as bus control inputs. The signals $\overline{RMC}$, $\overline{DS}$, SIZ0, SIZ1, R/$\overline{W}$, FC3–FC0, A7–A0, and $\overline{LBGACK}$ are used as three-state outputs. The MC68851 drives the data bus during all write cycles and inputs data from the bus during read cycles.

4.3.1 Operand Transfer Mechanism

When performing table search operations as the physical bus master, the MC68851 provides a very powerful operand transfer mechanism utilizing parallel, non-multiplexed buses.

The MC68851 architecture supports byte, word, and long word operands and allows 8-, 16-, and 32-bit ports through the use of the data transfer and size acknowledge signals ($\overline{DSACK0}$ and $\overline{DSACK1}$). The DSACKx signals are controlled by the slave devices currently being accessed and are discussed further in **4.3.1.1 DYNAMIC BUS SIZING**.

The current implementation of the MC68851 utilizes only long word and byte operands. Address and status information in the translation tables is normally accessed as long words; the descriptor status bytes containing the used, or used and modified bits (refer to **SECTION 5 ADDRESS TRANSLATION**) are accessed using byte write or byte read-modify-write cycles when the MC68851 must update these bits. The MC68851 performs write operations only to update descriptor status information and, as such, all write cycles are byte operations as are all read-modify-write cycles.

As opposed to the MC68020, which does not place any alignment restrictions on operands in memory, the MC68851 always operates on data that is aligned to long word boundaries. This requires that all entries in the translation table be aligned to long word boundaries. Although table pointers utilized by the MC68851 for address calculations (root, table, and page pointers) may contain values that are not long word aligned (i.e., A1/A0 ≠ 00), the MC68851 implicitly sets these bits to zero before performing physical address calculations.

4.3.1.1 DYNAMIC BUS SIZING. The MC68851 allows operand transfers to or from 8-, 16-, and 32-bit ports by dynamically determining the port size during each bus cycle. During an operand transfer cycle, the slave device signals its port size (byte, word, or long word) and transfer status (complete or not complete) to the MC68851 through the use of the $\overline{DSACKx}$ signals. The $\overline{DSACKx}$ signals perform the same transfer akcnowledge function as does the $\overline{DTACK}$ signal of other M68000 Family devices as well as informing the MC68851 of the current port width. Refer to Table 4-3 for $\overline{DSACKx}$ encodings and assertion results.

For example, if the MC68851 is executing a table search operation to read a page or table pointer (a long word operand) it attempts to read 32 bits during the first bus cycle. If the port responds that it is 32 bits wide, the MC68851 latches all 32 bits of data and continues with the next operation. If the port responds that it is 16 bits wide, the MC68851 latches the 16 bits of valid data and initiates another bus cycle to obtain the other 16 bits. An 8-bit port is handled similarly, but with four read cycles.

Table 4-3. DSACK Codes and Results

DSACK1	DSACK0	Result
H	H	Insert Wait States in Current Bus Cycle
H	L	Complete Cycle – Data Bus Port is 8 Bits
L	H	Complete Cycle – Data Bus Port is 16 Bits
L	L	Complete Cycle – Data Bus Port is 32 Bits

Each port is fixed in assignment to particular sections of the data bus. A 32-bit port is located on data bus bits 0 through 31, a 16-bit port is located on bits 16 through 31, and an 8-bit port is located on bits 24 through 31. The MC68851 makes these assumptions in order to locate valid data and to minimize the number of transfers required to access 8- and 16-bit ports. The MC68851 always attempts to transfer the maximum amount of data on all bus cycles; i.e., for a long word operation, it always assumes that the port is 32 bits wide when beginning the bus cycle.

Figure 4-15 shows the required organization of data ports on the MC68851 bus for 8-, 16-, and 32-bit devices, and also illustrates the internal organization of operands used by the MC68851, the internal multiplex and routing hardware, and the operand organization in memory required to provide this organization regardless of the port size.

The internal multiplexer shown in Figure 4-15 takes the four bytes of the 32-bit bus and routes them to their required positions. For example, OP3 can be routed to D0–D7, as would be the normal case, or it can be internally routed to D23–D16 or D31–D24 to support transfers to 16- or 8-bit ports, respectively.

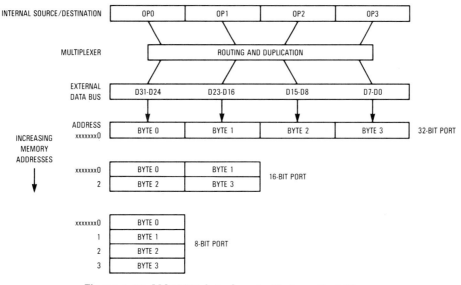

Figure 4-15. MC68851 Interface to Various Port Sizes

The positioning of the bytes on the internal data bus is determined by the size (SIZ1 and SIZ0) and address (A1 and A0) outputs. The size outputs indicate the number of bytes of the operand that remain to be transferred.

The number of bytes transferred during a bus cycle is always equal to or less than the operand size indicated by the SIZ1 and SIZ0 outputs, depending on the port width. For example, during the first bus cycle of a long word transfer from a word port, the size outputs indicate that four bytes are to be transferred although only two bytes are read on that cycle. The MC68851 executes another bus cycle to read the remainder of the operand with the size outputs indicating that a word remains to be read. Table 4-4 shows the encodings for SIZ1 and SIZ0.

It is important to recognize the distinction between port size and operand size. The port size is a function of the physical width of the device being accessed and is considered, but not required, to be static for any particular device. In contrast, the operand size, as indicated by the SIZ0 and SIZ1 signals, provides the size of the operand that remains to be transferred. The $\overline{DSACKx}$ signals **always indicate port size**.

The address lines A1 and A0 also affect the operation of the internal data bus multiplexer. During an operand transfer, A2–A31 indicate the long word base address of the operand to be accessed, while A1 and A0 give the byte offset from that base. For example, consider the transfer of a long word from a word port requiring two bus cycles to complete. For the first transfer, the MC68851 initiates an aligned long word read (A1/A0 = 00, SIZ1/SIZ0 = 00), accepting OP0 and OP1 on D24–D31 and D16–D23, respectively. To access the remainder of the operand, the MC68851 increments the access address by one word and initiates an aligned word read (A1/A0 = 10, SIZ1/SIZ0 = 10), accepting OP2 and OP3, again, on D24–D31 and D16–D23, respectively. Table 4-5 shows the encodings of A1 and A0 and the corresponding byte offsets from the long word base.

Table 4-4. Size Output Encodings

SIZ1	SIZ0	Size
0	1	Byte
1	0	Word
1	1	3 Byte
0	0	Long Word

Table 4-5. Address Offset Encodings

A1	A0	Offset
0	0	+ 0 Bytes
0	1	+ 1 Bytes
1	0	+ 2 Bytes
1	1	+ 3 Bytes

Table 4-6 describes the use of SIZ1, SIZ0, A1, and A0 in defining the transfer pattern between the internal multiplexer of the MC68851 and the external data bus. Transfer patterns that are not supported by the MC68851 due to operand alignment restrictions are not shown in this table. To summarize this description, the MC68851 initiates only aligned long word read, byte write, and byte read-modify-write cycles. All other permutations of alignment and size are in response to dynamic sizing request from slave devices that do not support single-cycle 32-bit transfers.

Table 4-6. MC68851 Internal to External Data Bus Multiplexer

Size	Transfer Size		Address		Source/Destination External Data Bus Connection			
	SIZ1	SIZ0	A1	A0	D31–D24	D23–D16	D15–D8	D7–D0
Byte	0	1	1	1	OP3	OP3	OP3	OP3
Word	1	0	1	0	OP2	OP3	OP2	OP3
3 Byte	1	1	0	1	OP1	OP1	OP2	OP3
Long Word	0	0	0	0	OP0	OP1	OP2	OP3

Figure 4-16 shows the basic control flow associated with an aligned long word transfer from a 16-bit port. Refer to Figure 4-17 for timing relationships. The high order word of the long word (OP0 and OP1) are transferred from the port located on D16–D31 during the first bus cycle. For the first transfer, the size outputs indicate that four bytes remain to be transferred and the A1/A0 indicate that the transfer is aligned (SIZ1/SIZ0/A1/A0 = 0000). The port responds to the MC68851 by asserting the $\overline{\text{DSACKx}}$ signals to indicate completion of a 16-bit transfer ($\overline{\text{DSACK1}}/\overline{\text{DSACK0}}$ = LH). The MC68851 latches the word of data, terminates this cycle and begins a second cycle to complete the transfer. For the second cycle, the size and address lines indicate that a word transfer is to take place on D16–D31 (SIZ1/SIZ0/A1/A0 = 1010). The base address has been incremented by two (bytes) in order to access the next highest word location in memory. The slave device places data on D16–D31 (OP2 and OP3) and again responds by asserting the $\overline{\text{DSACKx}}$ inputs ($\overline{\text{DSACK1}}/\overline{\text{DSACK0}}$ = LH).

The control flow for a long word transfer from an 8-bit port is shown in Figure 4-18. Four bus cycles are required to transfer this operand, moving one byte per cycle. Similar to the previous example, the size outputs indicate a long word transfer during the first cycle, three bytes during the second, a word during the third, and a byte during the final cycle. Refer to Table 4-6 for internal multiplexer operation during this transfer. Figure 4-19 shows timing relationships for these bus cycles.

4.3.1.2 EFFECTS OF DYNAMIC BUS SIZING. The dynamic sizing capabilities of the MC68851 allow placement of the address translation tables in 8-, 16-, and 32-bit memories or any desired mixture of these port widths. However, since the table search operations access primarily long word operands, residence of the translation tables in memory that is less than 32 bits wide has detrimental effects on system performance due to the increased number of bus cycles required to access this information. First, the overall average translation time increases, simply due to the increased number of bus cycles that are required to load translation descriptors from memory. Second, since the CPU cannot access the bus during MC68851 table search operations, any increase in the time required to perform a table search produces a corresponding increase in interrupt latency (refer to **SECTION 11 OPERATIONS TIMINGS**).

4.3.1.3 ADDRESS, SIZE, AND DATA BUS RELATIONSHIPS. The dynamic bus capabilities of the MC68851 create a very powerful and flexible bus structure. Correct external interpretation of bus control signals is critical to ensure valid data transfer operation.

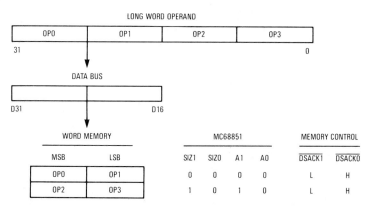

Figure 4-16. Example of Long Word Transfer from 16-Bit Port

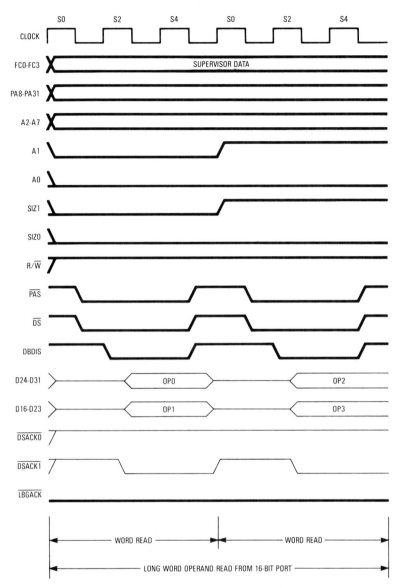

Figure 4-17. Long Word Operand Read Timing (16-Bit Data Port)

The MC68851 system designer should ensure that data ports are aligned as discussed in **4.3.1.1 DYNAMIC BUS SIZING** such that the MC68851 is able to route data to the correct locations. It is also required that the correct byte data strobes (four, for long word memory) be generated which enable only those sections of the data port(s) that are active during the current bus cycle. The MC68851 always drives all portions of the data bus during a write cycle, so this necessitates careful control of the enable signals for independent bytes of a data port. During write operations, those ports that are not active in that transfer must not be enabled.

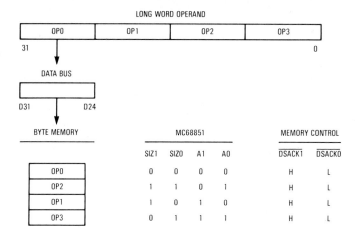

Figure 4-18. Example of Long Word Transfer from Byte Port

The required active bytes of the data bus for any given MC68851 bus transfer are a function of the size (SIZ1/SIZ0) and lower address (A1/A0) outputs and are shown in Table 4-7.

Table 4-7. Data Bus Activity for Byte, Word, and Long Word Ports

Transfer Size	Size		Address		Data Bus Active Sections Byte (B) – Word (W) – Long Word (L) Ports			
	SIZ1	SIZ0	A1	A0	D32–D24	D23–D16	D15–D8	D7–D0
Byte	0	1	1	1	B	W	—	L
Word	1	0	1	0	B W	W	L	L
3 Byte	1	1	0	1	B	W L	L	L
Long Word	0	0	0	0	B W L	W L	L	L

The MC68851 bus interface is a proper subset of the MC68020 bus structure and thus, coupled with the fact that all bus control strobe signals are wire-ORed with those of the CPU, the MC68851 can directly share all byte data strobe circuitry utilized by the processor. Refer to the *MC68020 32-Bit Microprocessor User's Manual* for additional information.

4.3.2 Physical Bus Operation

Transfer of translation information between the MC68851 and the translation tables located in physical memory involves the following signals:
1) Physical address PA8 through PA31,
2) Shared address A0 through A7,
3) Data bus D0 through D31,
4) Bus control signals, and
5) Transfer size SIZ0 and SIZ1.

The physical address and data buses are parallel, non-multiplexed buses used to transfer data using an asynchronous protocol. In all bus cycles the bus master is responsible for deskewing

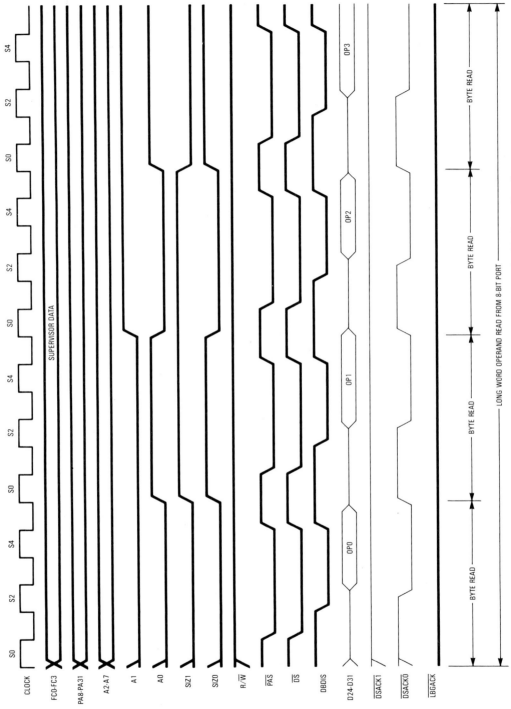

Figure 4-19. Long Word Operand Read Timing (8-Bit Data Port)

all signals issued at both the start and the end of the cycle. In addition, the bus master is responsible for deskewing the acknowledge and data signals from the slave devices.

The following paragraphs describe the MC68851 data transfer operations.

4.3.2.1 READ CYCLE. During a read cycle the MC68851 receives data from an external memory device. The MC68851 always reads a byte, or bytes, as determined by the operand and port sizes (refer to **4.3.1 Operand Transfer Mechanism**). If the $\overline{\text{DSACKx}}$ inputs or $\overline{\text{BERR}}$ are not asserted during the sample window of the falling edge of S2, wait states are inserted in the bus cycle until either $\overline{\text{DSACK1}}/\overline{\text{DSACK0}}$ or $\overline{\text{BERR}}$ is recognized as being asserted.

A flowchart of an MC68851 read cycle is shown in Figure 4-20. At the initiation of the bus cycle, the MC68851 outputs the operand size on the SIZ1/SIZ0 signals. If the transfer response from the accessed device indicates that the port size is smaller than the operand size, then the MC68851 immediately initiates another transfer to read the remainder of the operand. During successive cycles required to complete the operand transfer, the size outputs of the MC68851 indicate the size of the operand remaining to be transferred, that is, the operand size less the number of bytes previously acquired.

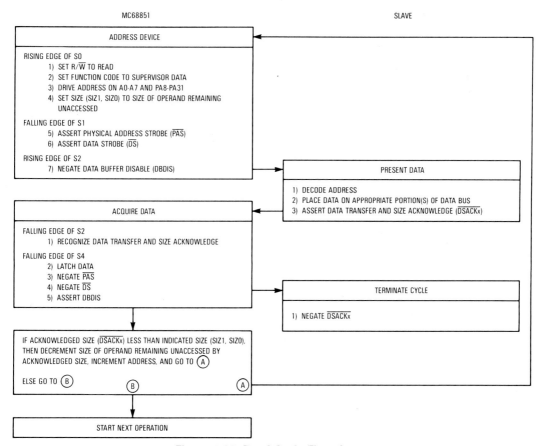

Figure 4-20. Read Cycle Flowchart

Recalling that the MC68851 performs read cycles only on aligned long word operands, all multiple cycle transfers are the result of long word accesses to ports that are not 32 bits wide. The various combinations of read cycles performed by the MC68851 are illustrated in Figures 4-17, 4-19, and 4-21. The parametric timing information for read cycles is shown in **SECTION 12 ELECTRICAL SPECIFICATIONS**.

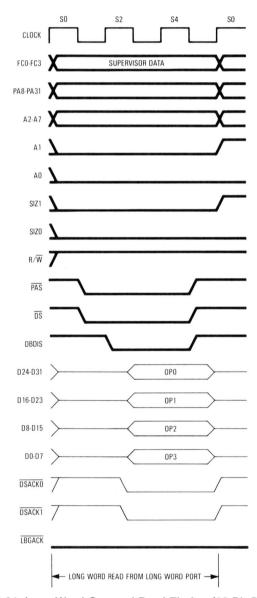

Figure 4-21. Long Word Operand Read Timing (32-Bit Data Port)

4.3.2.2 WRITE CYCLE. During a write cycle, the MC68851 sends data to a memory device. The function of the operand transfer mechanism during a write cycle is identical to that during a read cycle (refer to **4.3.1 Operand Transfer Mechanism**).

The only write cycles initiated by the MC68851 are byte operations to update the used bit, modified bit, or both in order to ensure that information contained in the translation tables is consistent with information stored in the address translation cache (refer to **5.1 ADDRESS TRANSLATION CACHE**).

A flowchart of the MC68851 write operation is shown in Figure 4-22. The functional timing for this operation is shown in Figure 4-23. The parametric timing information for write cycles is shown in **SECTION 12 ELECTRICAL SPECIFICATIONS**.

4.3.2.3 READ-MODIFY-WRITE CYCLE. The read-modify-write cycle performs a read, modifies the data in the EU, and writes the data back to the same address. During the entire read-modify-write sequence the MC68851 asserts the $\overline{RMC}$ signal to indicate that an indivisible operation is occurring. During this operation, the MC68851 will not issue a physical bus grant ($\overline{PBG}$) in response to a physical bus request ($\overline{PBR}$) nor will it release logical bus grant acknowledge ($\overline{LBGACK}$) in response to a logical bus request ($\overline{LBRI}$).

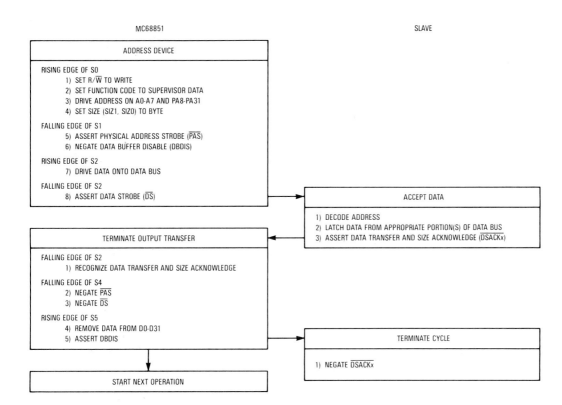

Figure 4-22. Write Cycle Flowchart

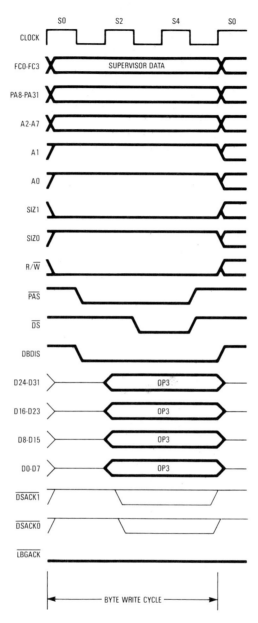

Figure 4-23. Byte Write Timing Diagram

The read-modify-write sequence is implemented to allow multiple MC68851s, in a multi-processing environment, to utilize the same address translation tables without corrupting critical status information contained in the tables. For example, consider the case where the MC68851 is setting the used bit in a page descriptor status byte that has not been modified (M = 0). The update is accomplished by reading the status byte (as part of the read of the descriptor), setting the appropriate bit (U = 1), and writing the entire status byte back to its original location. Effectively, the only bit that is changed is the used bit although all of the status byte has been overwritten. However, suppose that another MC68851, using the same page descriptor, initiates a cycle to set the modified bit (M = 1) and succeeds in setting it while the first MC68851 is still performing the data modification in its EU. The first MC68851 completes the modification and writes the byte back to memory. At this point the status byte has been corrupted since the image of the byte originally read by the first MC68851 had the modified bit clear and this is the value that will be written back, clearing the bit that had just been set by the second MC68851. The use of read-modify-write cycles during transfers that can cause corruption of the modified bit solves this problem by performing the entire operation in an indivisible sequence that does not allow alternate physical bus masters concurrent access to the information.

The MC68851 utilizes a read-modify-write sequence to update the descriptor status byte whenever it is required to set the used bit but not affect the state of the modified bit. Pointer table descriptors, which do not contain modified bits, are not referenced using read-modify-write sequences.

The use of read-modify-write cycles prevents multiple MC68851s, that are setting status bits in shared translation tables, from corrupting status information. However, it does not prevent alternate bus masters from rendering the table status information inconsistent if they are capable of accessing the translation tables and clearing the used or modified bits during an MC68851 table search operation. Devices capable of clearing the used and modified bits, or otherwise modifying a descriptor, should have their accesses to the translation tables synchronized with MC68851 table search operations (i.e., they should not be allowed access to the tables during table search operations).

A flowchart of the read-modify-write operation is shown in Figure 4-24. Figure 4-25 depicts the functional timing of the read-modify-write sequence. The parametric timing information for the read-modify-write cycle is shown in **SECTION 12 ELECTRICAL SPECIFICATIONS**.

4.3.2.4 BUS ERROR AND HALT OPERATION. In a bus architecture that requires a handshake from an external device to signal that a bus cycle is complete, the possibility exists that the handshake might not occur. Since different systems require different maximum response times, a bus error signal is provided; refer to **3.8.3 Bus Error (BERR)**. External circuitry must be used to determine the maximum allowable duration between the assertion of physical address strobe ($\overline{PAS}$) and data size and transfer acknowledge ($\overline{DSACKx}$) and it should issue a bus error signal when that time is exceeded. When a $\overline{BERR}$ signal is received the MC68851 immediately terminates its table search operation. When both $\overline{BERR}$ and $\overline{HALT}$ are received the MC68851 retries the cycle that was terminated.

4.3.2.4.1 Bus Error Operation. When the bus error signal is issued to terminate a bus cycle and $\overline{HALT}$ is not asserted, the MC68851 immediately aborts the table search operation that was in progress and creates a translation descriptor in the address translation cache reflecting the error (refer to **5.2 ADDRESS TRANSLATION CACHE**).

The bus error signal is recognized during a bus cycle in any of the following cases:
1) $\overline{DSACKx}$ and $\overline{HALT}$ are negated and $\overline{BERR}$ is asserted, or
2) $\overline{HALT}$ is negated and $\overline{DSACKx}$ is asserted, $\overline{BERR}$ is asserted within one clock cycle of $\overline{DSACKx}$ assertion.

When the bus error condition is recognized, the current bus cycle is terminated in the normal fashion. Figures 4-26 and 4-27 show the timing diagrams for both the normal and the delayed bus error signals.

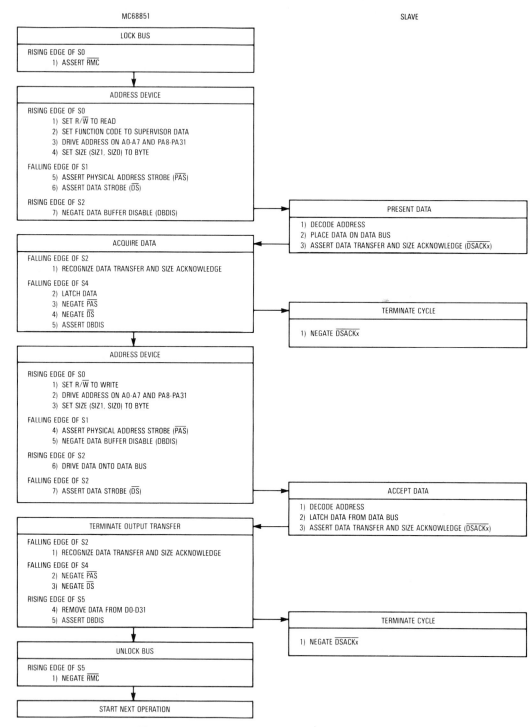

Figure 4-24. Read-Modify-Write Cycle Flowchart

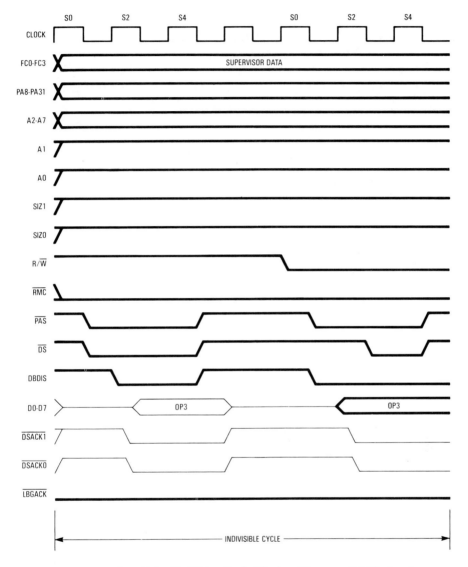

Figure 4-25. Read-Modify-Write Cycle Timing Diagram (32-Bit Port)

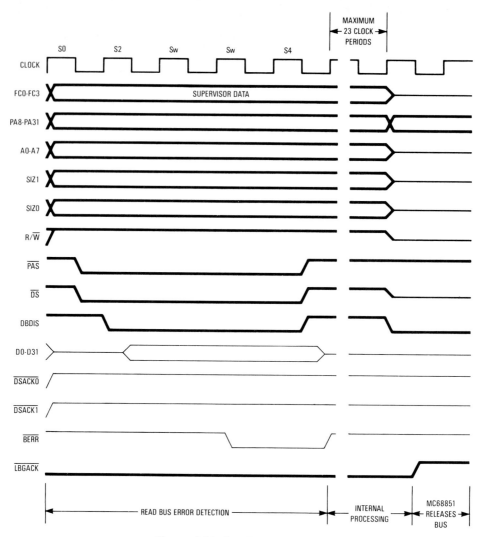

Figure 4-26. Bus Error Timing

4.3.2.4.2 Retry Operation. When, during a bus cycle, the $\overline{\text{BERR}}$ and $\overline{\text{HALT}}$ signals are both asserted by an external device, the MC68851 enters the retry sequence. A delayed retry may be used, similar to the delayed bus error described above. Figures 4-28 and 4-29 show the functional timing of both methods of retrying the bus cycle.

The MC68851 terminates the bus cycle, places the control signals in their inactive state and does not initiate further bus activity until both $\overline{\text{BERR}}$ and $\overline{\text{HALT}}$ are negated by external logic. The MC68851 then retries the previous cycle using the same access information (address, size, . . ., etc.). The $\overline{\text{BERR}}$ signal must be negated before or at the same time as the $\overline{\text{HALT}}$ signal.

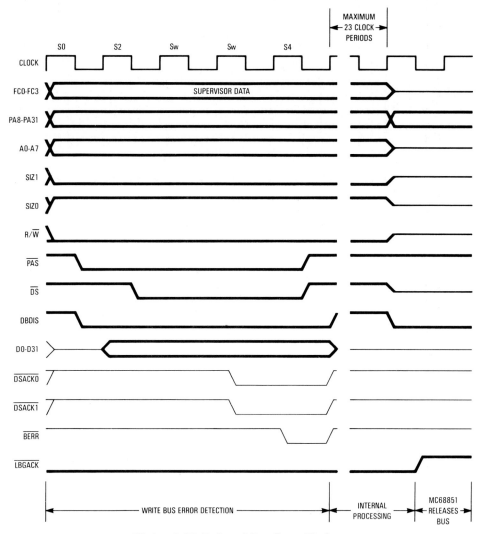

Figure 4-27. Delayed Bus Error Timing

The MC68851 imposes no restrictions on retrying any type of bus cycle. Specifically, any portion of a read-modify-write operation may be separately retried since the $\overline{\text{RMC}}$ signal remains asserted during the entire retry sequence.

4.3.2.4.3 Halt Operation. The $\overline{\text{HALT}}$ signal, when used as an input, performs a halt/run/single-step function. The halt and run modes are somewhat self-explanatory in that when, during a table search operation, the halt signal is constantly asserted the MC68851 'halts' (does nothing) and when the halt signal is constantly negated the MC68851 'runs' (does something).

The single-step mode is derived from correctly timed transitions on the $\overline{\text{HALT}}$ line. If $\overline{\text{HALT}}$ is asserted when the MC68851 begins a bus cycle (see below) and remains asserted, the bus cycle

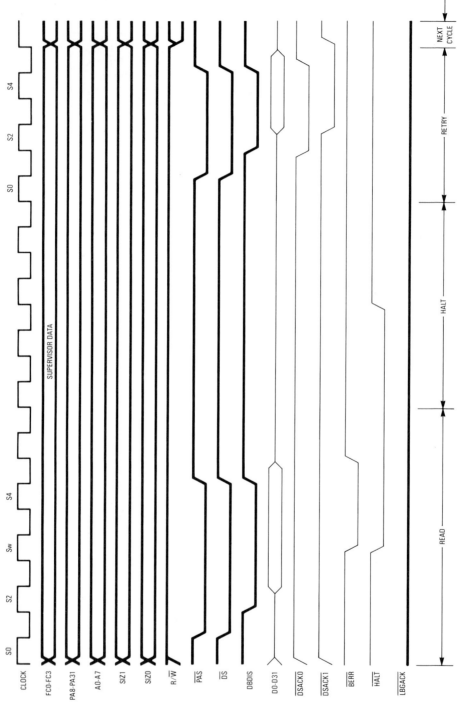

Figure 4-28. Bus Cycle Retry Timing

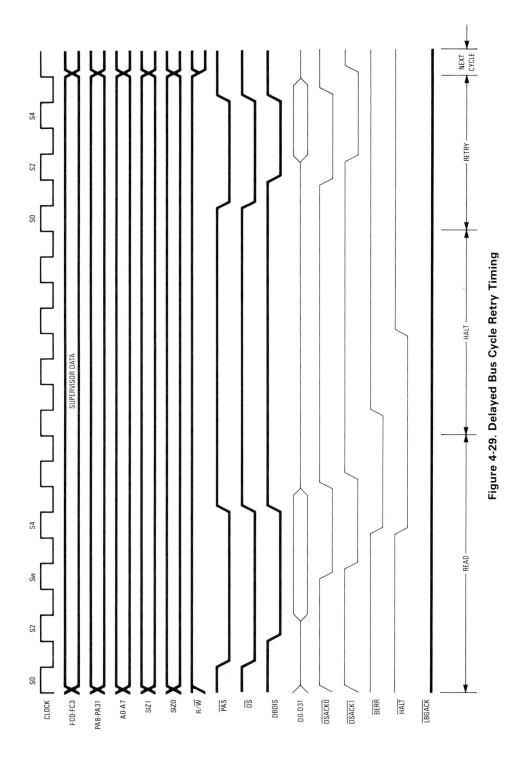

Figure 4-29. Delayed Bus Cycle Retry Timing

will complete, but another bus cycle is not allowed to start. When it is desired to continue, $\overline{\text{HALT}}$ is then negated and reasserted when the next bus cycle is started. Thus, the single-step mode allows the user to step through (and debug) MC68851 table search operations, one bus cycle at a time.

The timing required for correct single-step operation is detailed in Figure 4-30. Some care must be exercised to avoid harmful interactions between the $\overline{\text{BERR}}$ and $\overline{\text{HALT}}$ signals (refer to **4.3.2.4.2 Retry Operation**) when using the single-step mode as a debugging tool.

When the MC68851 completes a bus cycle after recognizing that the $\overline{\text{HALT}}$ line is active, all bus control signals are placed in their inactive states, buses remain driven with their previous values, and the logical and physical bus arbitration circuitry functions normally.

4.3.2.4.4 The Relationship of $\overline{\text{DSACKx}}$, $\overline{\text{BERR}}$, and $\overline{\text{HALT}}$. In order to properly control termination of a bus cycle for a retry or a bus error condition, $\overline{\text{DSACKx}}$, $\overline{\text{BERR}}$, and $\overline{\text{HALT}}$ should be asserted and negated on the rising edge of the MC68851 clock. This assures that when two signals are asserted simultaneously, the required setup time to the falling edge of the clock (#47A) and hold times (#47B) for both of them will be met during the same bus state. This, or some equivalent precaution, must be designed external to the MC68851.

The preferred bus cycle terminations may be summarized as follows (case numbers refer to Table 4-8).

Normal Termination: $\overline{\text{DSACKx}}$ is asserted, $\overline{\text{BERR}}$ and $\overline{\text{HALT}}$ remain negated (case 1).

Halt Termination: $\overline{\text{HALT}}$ is asserted at the same time as, or before $\overline{\text{DSACKx}}$ and $\overline{\text{BERR}}$ remains negated (case 2).

Bus Error Termination: $\overline{\text{BERR}}$ is asserted in lieu of, at the same time as, or before $\overline{\text{DSACKx}}$ (case 3) or within one clock cycle after $\overline{\text{DSACKx}}$ (case 4) and $\overline{\text{HALT}}$ remains negated; $\overline{\text{BERR}}$ is negated at the same time as or after $\overline{\text{DSACKx}}$.

Retry Termination: $\overline{\text{HALT}}$ and $\overline{\text{BERR}}$ are asserted in lieu of, at the same time as, or before $\overline{\text{DSACKx}}$ (case 5) or within one clock cycle after $\overline{\text{DSACKx}}$ (case 6); $\overline{\text{BERR}}$ is negated at the same time as or after $\overline{\text{DSACKx}}$. $\overline{\text{HALT}}$ may be negated at the same time as, or after $\overline{\text{BERR}}$.

Table 4-8 details the resulting bus cycle terminations under various conditions of control signal sequences. The correct timing for negation of $\overline{\text{BERR}}$ and $\overline{\text{HALT}}$ must also be used to ensure predictable operation. Note that for cases 4 and 6, $\overline{\text{BERR}}$ and/or $\overline{\text{HALT}}$ must meet the input setup time specified by #27a. For bus cycle retry operation $\overline{\text{BERR}}$ must be negated prior to, or at the same time as $\overline{\text{HALT}}$. $\overline{\text{DSACKx}}$, $\overline{\text{BERR}}$, and $\overline{\text{HALT}}$ may be negated when $\overline{\text{PAS}}$ is negated. If $\overline{\text{DSACKx}}$ or $\overline{\text{BERR}}$ remain asserted past the maximum hold time specified (#47B), the operation of the MC68851 bus is not predictable (i.e., $\overline{\text{DSACKx}}$ or $\overline{\text{BERR}}$ may or may not be recognized early in the next bus cycle).

4.3.2.5 ASYNCHRONOUS VERSUS SYNCHRONOUS PHYSICAL BUS OPERATION. The following paragraphs describe the asynchronous and synchronous physical bus operation.

4.3.2.5.1 Asynchronous Operation. To achieve clock frequency independence at a system level, the MC68851 can be used in an asynchronous manner. This requires using only the bus handshake lines ($\overline{\text{PAS}}$, $\overline{\text{DS}}$, $\overline{\text{DSACKx}}$, $\overline{\text{BERR}}$, and $\overline{\text{HALT}}$) to control the data transfer. Using this method, $\overline{\text{PAS}}$ signals the start of a bus cycle and $\overline{\text{DS}}$ is used as a condition for valid data on a write cycle. Decode of the size outputs and lower address lines A1 and A0 provide strobes that indicate which

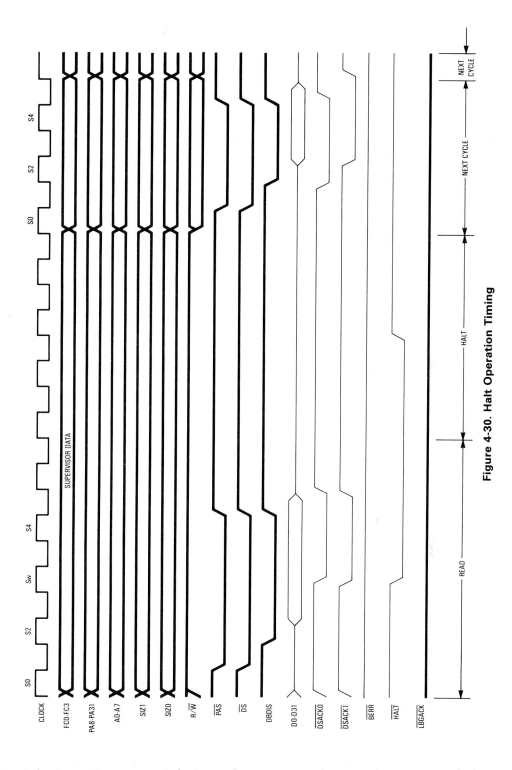

Figure 4-30. Halt Operation Timing

Table 4-8. $\overline{\text{DSACK}}$, $\overline{\text{BERR}}$, and $\overline{\text{HALT}}$ Assertion Results

Case No.	Control Signal	Asserted on Rising Edge of State		Result
		N	N + 2	
1	$\overline{\text{DSACKx}}$ $\overline{\text{BERR}}$ $\overline{\text{HALT}}$	A NA NA	S NA X	Normal Cycle Terminate and Continue
2	$\overline{\text{DSACKx}}$ $\overline{\text{BERR}}$ $\overline{\text{HALT}}$	A NA A/S	S NA S	Normal Cycle Terminate and Halt Continue when $\overline{\text{HALT}}$ Removed
3	$\overline{\text{DSACKx}}$ $\overline{\text{BERR}}$ $\overline{\text{HALT}}$	NA/A A NA	X S NA	Terminate and Abort Table Search
4	$\overline{\text{DSACKx}}$ $\overline{\text{BERR}}$ $\overline{\text{HALT}}$	A NA NA	X A NA	Terminate and Abort Table Search
5	$\overline{\text{DSACKx}}$ $\overline{\text{BERR}}$ $\overline{\text{HALT}}$	NA/A A A/S	X S S	Terminate and Retry when $\overline{\text{HALT}}$ Removed
6	$\overline{\text{DSACKx}}$ $\overline{\text{BERR}}$ $\overline{\text{HALT}}$	A NA NA	X A A	Terminate and Retry when $\overline{\text{HALT}}$ Removed

LEGEND:
- N — The number of the current even bus state (e.g., S2, S4, ..., etc.)
- A — Signal is asserted in this bus state.
- NA — Signal is not asserted in this state.
- X — Don't Care
- S — Signal was asserted in previous state and remains asserted in this state.

portion of the data bus is active. The slave device then responds by placing the requested data on the bus for a read cycle or latching the data on a write cycle and asserting data transfer and size acknowledge corresponding to the port size to terminate the cycle. If no slave responds, or the access is invalid, external control logic should assert the $\overline{\text{BERR}}$, or $\overline{\text{BERR}}$ and $\overline{\text{HALT}}$ signal(s) to abort or retry the cycle.

The $\overline{\text{DSACKx}}$ signals are allowed to be asserted before the data from a slave device is valid on a read cycle. The length of time that $\overline{\text{DSACKx}}$ may precede data is given by parameter #31, and it must be met in any asynchronous system to ensure that valid data is latched by the MC68851. Notice that there is no maximum time specified from the assertion of $\overline{\text{PAS}}$ to the assertion of $\overline{\text{DSACKx}}$. This is because the MC68851 inserts wait cycles in one clock period increments until $\overline{\text{DSACKx}}$ is recognized as asserted.

The $\overline{\text{BERR}}$ and $\overline{\text{HALT}}$ signals are allowed to be asserted after $\overline{\text{DSACKx}}$ is asserted. $\overline{\text{BERR}}$, or $\overline{\text{BERR}}$ and $\overline{\text{HALT}}$ must be asserted within the time given by parameter #48 after $\overline{\text{DSACKx}}$ is asserted in any asynchronous system to ensure proper operation. If this maximum delay is violated, the MC68851 may exhibit erratic behavior.

4.3.2.5.2 Synchronous Operation. To support those systems that use the system clock as a signal to generate $\overline{\text{DSACKx}}$ and other asynchronous inputs, the asynchronous input setup time is given by parameter #47A, and the asynchronous input hold time is given by parameter #47B. If these setup and hold times are met for the assertion or negation of an input, such as $\overline{\text{DSACKx}}$, the MC68851 is guaranteed to recognize that signal level on that specific falling edge of the system clock. However, the converse is not true — if the input signal does not meet the setup and/or hold time, that level is not guaranteed not to be recognized. In addition, if the assertion of $\overline{\text{DSACKx}}$ is recognized on a falling edge of the clock, valid data will be latched into MC68851 (on a read cycle) on the next falling edge provided that the data meets the setup time given by parameter #27. Given this situation, parameter #31 may be ignored. Note that if $\overline{\text{DSACKx}}$ is asserted for the required setup time before the falling edge of S2, no wait states will be incurred and the bus cycle will run at its maximum speed of three clock cycles.

In order to assure proper operation in a synchronous system when $\overline{\text{BERR}}$ or $\overline{\text{BERR}}$ and $\overline{\text{HALT}}$ is/are asserted after $\overline{\text{DSACKx}}$, $\overline{\text{BERR}}$ or $\overline{\text{BERR}}$ and $\overline{\text{HALT}}$ must meet the setup time (parameter #27A) prior to the falling edge of the clock one clock cycle after $\overline{\text{DSACKx}}$ is recognized as asserted. This setup time is critical for proper operation, and the MC68851 may exhibit erratic behavior if it is violated.

4.3.3 Bus Cycle Sequence

During a table search operation, the MC68851 performs sequences of operand transfers and address calculations to locate a page descriptor for the referenced logical-to-physical address mapping (refer to **SECTION 5 ADDRESS TRANSLATION** for more detail). The MC68851 uses the information acquired during one operand transfer (or transfers) to generate the address for the next level of the search. In general, two clock periods are required for this calculation and, therefore, successive operand transfers are separated by two clock periods.

However, when accessing multiple operands within a single level of the table structure (for example, when fetching long-format descriptors) additional address calculation is not required after the fetch of the first operand and, therefore, subsequent operands within that level may be accessed with consecutive bus cycles (i.e., no intervening idle clock periods). Successive bus cycles required to fetch a single operand (for example, in response to a dynamic sizing request from a port that is smaller than the operand width) are also executed consecutively. Finally, the MC68851 access after the fetch of a table descriptor that required the update of a status bit (U or M), occurs immediately since the address calculation for the next level of a search is performed in parallel with the status bit update.

Examples of MC68851 bus cycle sequences are provided in **4.7 BUS OPERATION EXAMPLES**.

4.4 LOGICAL BUS ARBITRATION

Bus arbitration is the technique used by the MC68851 and other bus master-type devices to request, be granted, and acknowledge bus mastership.

NOTE
The following paragraphs make reference to a 'logical bus arbiter'. This is the control logic that processes bus mastership requests and issues bus grants in response to these requests. Normally, the logical bus arbiter is contained in the bus arbitration circuitry of the CPU. However, there is no constraint that dictates that this control function cannot be implemented externally. The MC68851 and other alternate logical bus masters are 'requesting' devices that contain logic to generate requests for bus access and, in general, are slaves in the arbitration process (i.e., they cannot initiate grants).

When the MC68851 must initiate a table search in physical memory to complete a service requested by the logical bus master, it must first arbitrate for the logical bus. This is required in order to avoid contention between the control signals, data bus, and lower address bus of the MC68851

and other logical bus masters. The MC68851 arbitrates for mastership of the logical bus for the following circumstances:
1) The logical address output by the current logical bus master does not have a corresponding translation descriptor resident in the MC68851 address translation cache,
2) The logical bus master attempts to write (not part of a read-modify-write sequence) to a previously unmodified page,
3) The CPU executes a module call operation that references a non-resident descriptor, or
4) The CPU executes any coprocessor instruction that either explicitly requests, or implicitly requires, that the MC68851 perform table search operations.

In addition to requesting control of the logical bus for its own requirements, the MC68851 also contains circuitry to monitor arbitration for the logical bus by other alternate bus masters.

Finally, the MC68851 logical bus arbitration circuitry must resolve conflicts resulting from higher priority alternate logical bus masters requesting control of the bus coincident with the initiation of MC68851 requests for the bus to service a current, lower priority master.

In its simplest form, the logical bus arbitration process consists of the following:
1) The MC68851 outputs a bus request to the logical bus arbiter,
2) The logical bus arbiter asserts a bus grant to indicate that the bus will be available at the end of the current bus cycle, and
3) The MC68851 either acknowledges that it has assumed bus mastership by asserting logical bus grant acknowledge or it passes the bus grant to another device if a higher priority request also has been signaled.

Figure 4-31 is a flowchart detailing the logical bus arbitration process for the MC68851. Figure 4-32 illustrates the functional timing of the arbitration process when the MC68851 is requesting the bus as part of a relinquish and retry sequence.

4.4.1 Requesting the Logical Bus

The MC68851 contains arbitration logic required to request control of the logical bus and to monitor the requests of other alternate bus masters. Requests for bus mastership are monitored using the logical bus request input ($\overline{LBRI}$) and signaled using the logical bus request output ($\overline{LBRO}$).

The $\overline{LBRO}$ signal should be logically ORed externally with the $\overline{LBRI}$ signal to generate a single 'bus request' to the logical bus arbiter. Requests generated by the MC68851 on $\overline{LBRO}$ must not be reflected on $\overline{LBRI}$ or a dead-lock situation will arise when the MC68851 requests access to the bus.

Figure 4-33 illustrates the signal connections required for the logical bus arbitration circuitry.

4.4.1.1 ALTERNATE MASTER REQUESTING THE LOGICAL BUS.
The $\overline{LBRI}$ input is used to signal the MC68851 that a logical master with a higher priority that the current master is requesting access to the bus.

In systems that employ a single alternate logical bus master (for example, a single DMA controller) $\overline{LBRI}$ is a function of the bus request output of that device. It is necessary to externally condition the bus request output of the alternate master such that after receiving a relinquish and retry from the MC68851, the alternate master does not again assert $\overline{LBRI}$ until the MC68851 has completed the table search required to support the access requested by the master. An illustration of the circuitry required to provide the above conditioning is shown in Figure 4-34.

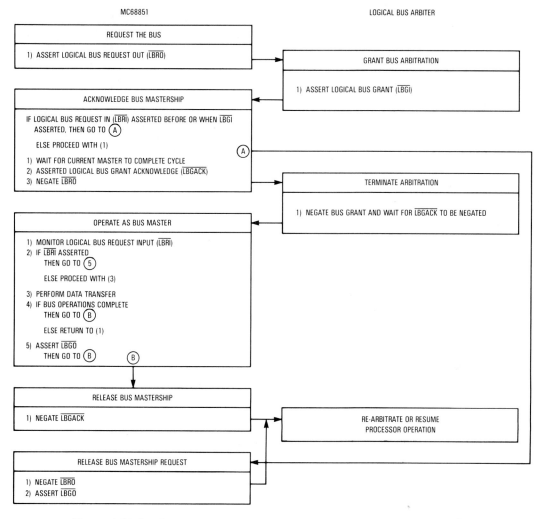

Figure 4-31. Logical Bus Arbitration Flowchart for MC68851 Bus Request

In systems that employ multiple alternate logical bus masters, $\overline{\text{LBRI}}$ should be the output of an external prioritization arbiter that signals that an alternate device with higher priority than the current master is requesting access to the bus. The external prioritization also ensures that table search operations for high priority masters are not interrupted by requests from lower priority devices.

In either of the above two system configurations $\overline{\text{LBRI}}$ is routed in parallel to the MC68851 and to the arbiter for the logical bus.

During a table search opertion, the MC68851 adopts the priority of the master that it is currently serving. Any time during the table operations that the MC68851 recognizes $\overline{\text{LBRI}}$ as being asserted, it aborts the table search in progress and relinquishes the bus, assuming that a master with higher priority than the one it is currently serving requires access to the bus. The table search is aborted

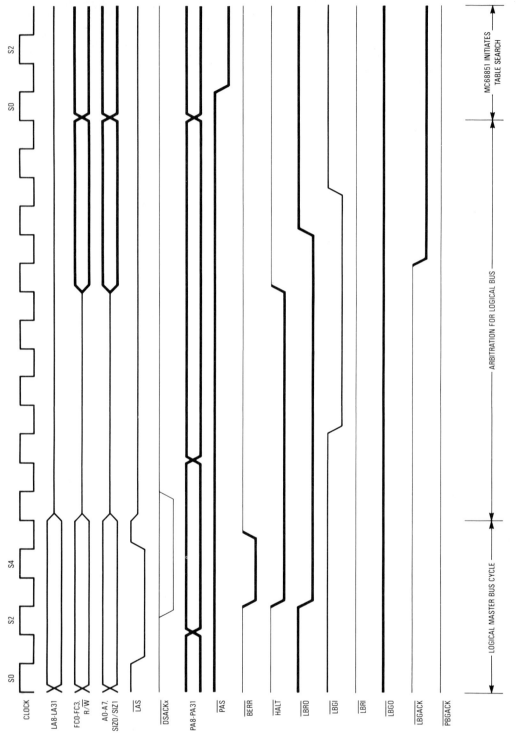

Figure 4-32. Logical Bus Arbitration During Relinquish and Retry Sequence

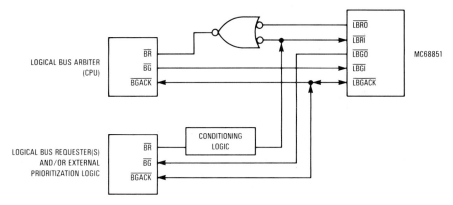

Figure 4-33. Logical Bus Arbitration Signal Inter-Connection

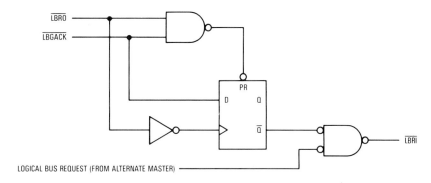

Figure 4-34. Single Alternate Logical Master Bus Request Conditioning Logic

immediately upon completion of the bus cycle (if any) in progress and the MC68851 then negates $\overline{\text{LBGACK}}$. Some time later, when the lower priority master regains control of the bus and retries the bus cycle for which the MC68851 was performing the table search, it will again encounter the exception from the MC68851 that originally caused it to initiate the table search. The MC68851 will then either continue or restart the search that was interrupted by the higher priority master depending on whether or not any other table search operations were performed between attempts to perform this search (refer to **4.4.1.2 MC68851 REQUESTING THE LOGICAL BUS**).

Figure 4-35 illustrates the case of an MC68851 table search operation being aborted by a higher priority bus request.

4.4.1.2 MC68851 REQUESTING THE LOGICAL BUS. The $\overline{\text{LBRO}}$ output signals to the logical bus arbiter that the MC68851 requires control of the bus to perform service for the current logical master. Since the MC68851 implicitly operates with the priority of the current bus master, the assertion of $\overline{\text{LBRO}}$ should not cause the external prioritization logic (if present) to update its current priority level (i.e., bus activity by the MC68851 should be viewed as an extension of that performed by the master it is currently serving).

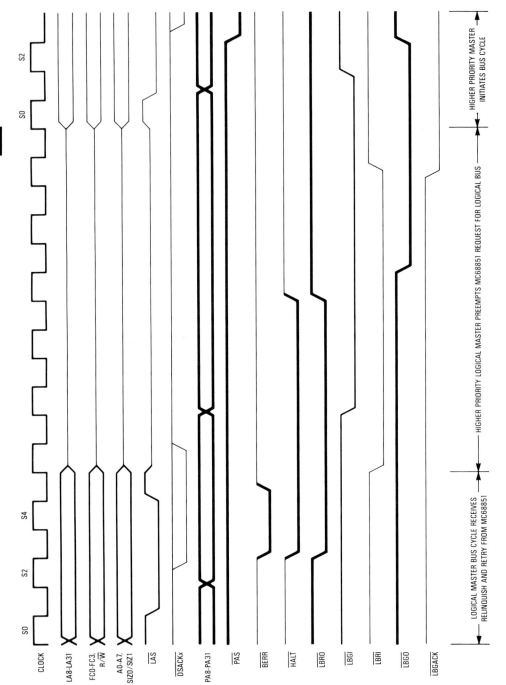

Figure 4-35. Relinquish and Retry Operation — MC68851 Arbitration for Logical Bus Preempted by Bus Request from Higher Priority Logical Master

If the MC68851 asserts $\overline{\text{LBRO}}$ and some time later, but before it receives a bus grant, $\overline{\text{LBRI}}$ is asserted (with an appropriate setup and synchronization time), the MC68851 will negate its bus request output and any other asserted logical bus control signals after ensuring that the current bus master has correctly recognized the termination sequence. For example, if during a relinquish and retry sequence, the MC68851 has not received a bus grant and detects that $\overline{\text{LBRI}}$ is asserted, it will wait until the current logical master has negated $\overline{\text{LAS}}$ and it will then negate $\overline{\text{BERR}}$ ($\overline{\text{LBRO}}$ and $\overline{\text{HALT}}$ are negated later). The negation of $\overline{\text{LAS}}$ ensures that the logical master recognized the relinquish and retry sequence and will retry its cycle and it regains control of the bus. This sequence is shown in Figure 4-35.

If a relinquish operation ($\overline{\text{DSACKx}}$, $\overline{\text{HALT}}$, and $\overline{\text{LBRO}}$) is interrupted before the MC68851 completes the required table search operations, upon regaining control of the logical bus, the CPU will query the MC68851 concerning the status of the request. If the MC68851 is required to perform table search operations before resumption of the interrupted service, the CPU will receive a relinquish and retry from the MC68851 in order that the aborted table search may be reinitiated. The relinquish and retry sequence is issued by the MC68851 in order to immediately gain mastership of the logical bus and to cause the CPU to automatically retry its query of the coprocessor interface response register upon regaining bus mastership. If the MC68851 was not required to perform any table search operations during the interruption of service, the CPU will receive a relinquish and retry on the read of the response register and the interrupted table search will be continued at the point that it was interrupted. Otherwise, the table search will be restarted from the point that the relinquish operation was signaled.

Normally, after a table search is aborted by a higher priority logical bus master, the MC68851 must completely restart the search since the internal state information concerning that search will have been lost while servicing the alternate master. However, in cases where the MC68851 is not required to perform any table search operations before control is returned to the master for which the MC68851 was performing the aborted search, the state information is not lost and the MC68851 will resume the table search at the point at which it was interrupted. This is common, for example, with spurious or transient bus requests or with logical DMA devices that have translation descriptors locked into the address translation cache and do not require table searches to load descriptors.

4.4.2 Receiving the Logical Bus Grant

The $\overline{\text{LBGI}}$ input should be connected to the bus grant output of the logical bus arbiter which indicates that an alterate master may take control of the logical bus as soon as the bus cycle in progress (if any) is complete and the bus is free.

This grant output of the logical bus arbiter is connected to the MC68851 and possibly to an external prioritization arbiter, but is not connected to any other requesting devices. The MC68851 controls the timing for when the grant may be passed to alternate requesting devices.

4.4.3 Passing the Logical Bus Grant

The $\overline{\text{LBGO}}$ output is generated from a synchronized version of the logical bus grant input and is asserted when the MC68851 passes a grant from the logical bus arbiter to an alternate requesting device.

If the MC68851 has requested the bus and $\overline{\text{LBRI}}$ is negated, the MC68851 will not assert $\overline{\text{LBGO}}$ and will, instead, take control of the bus to perform the required table searches. Should an alternate higher-priority master request the bus after the MC68851 has determined that it will initiate a table search but has not yet asserted $\overline{\text{LBGACK}}$, the requesting device will not receive a bus grant until the table search can be aborted and the MC68851 is ready to perform address translations for the higher priority device. If the MC68851 has asserted LBGACK when the external request is recognized, LBGO will be asserted as soon as possible but the MC68851 will not negate LBGACK until the table search has been aborted and the MC68851 is ready to perform address translations.

If LBGI is recognized as asserted and LBRI is also asserted, indicating that a higher priority master requires control of the bus, the MC68851 passes the grant by asserting LBGO immediately if the MC68851 has not also requested control of the logical bus or is not initialized for early processing startup (refer to **4.1.2.5 EARLY PROCESSING STARTUP**). Otherwise, the assertion of LBGO will be delayed until the MC68851 is again ready to perform address translation.

Finally, if LBGI is asserted and neither LBRI nor the LBRO output are asserted, a grant has occurred due to a spurious or transient request and the MC68851 does not pass the grant by asserting LBGO, but instead ignores the grant and continues monitoring LBRI.

Figure 4-36 illustrates the functional timing associated with the MC68851 passing a bus grant to an alternate bus master.

4.4.4 Acknowledgement of Logical Bus Mastership

Logical bus grant acknowledge (LBGACK) is asserted by an alternate logical bus master (including the MC68851) whenever it has taken control of the logical bus.

The bus grant acknowledge signals from all alternate logical masters should be directly connected to the LBGACK line which is also routed in parallel to the logical bus arbiter.

The MC68851 will not accept mastership of the bus until the following conditions are met:
1) The MC68851 has issued a request and the logical bus arbiter has issued a bus grant,
2) At the time the grant is issued, no other device has requested bus mastership,
3) LAS is negated indicating that the previous master has completed its bus activity,
4) DSACKx is negated indicating that the previous slave device has terminated its connection to the bus, and
5) LBGACK is not asserted, indicating that no other master is claiming ownership of the bus.

4.4.5 Read-Modify-Write Cycles

The RMC signal is driven by the logical bus master to indicate that an indivisible operation is in progress. The MC68020 will not issue a bus grant in response to a bus request during a read-modify-write operation that it initiated and, thus, will not release control of the bus to the MC68851, or any other device during this operation.

If the MC68851 observes an asserted level on RMC when it attempts to issue a relinquish and retry, it will instead assert bus error to force termination of the cycle (refer to **4.2.1.3 ADDRESS TRANSLATION TERMINATED BY BUS ERROR**).

If the MC68851 is performing a read-modify-write operation (RMC asserted by the MC68851) during a table search and observes an asserted level on LBRI, it will assert LBGO in response to an assertion of LBGI. However, the MC68851 will not negate LBGACK until it has completed the read-modify-write operation that was in progress and has idled its exception processing hardware.

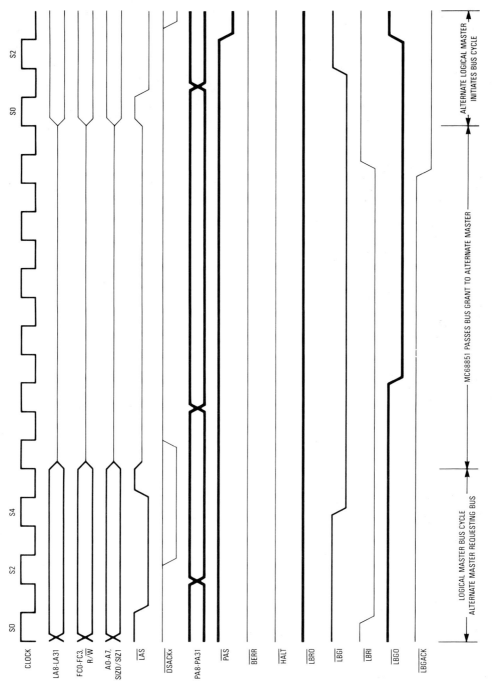

Figure 4-36. MC68851 Passes Logical Bus Grant to Alternate Master

4.5 PHYSICAL BUS ARBITRATION

Physical bus arbitration is the technique used by physical address space bus master-type devices to request, be granted, and acknowledge mastership of the physical bus. The MC68851 is the default master of the physical bus and any device that requires access to the bus must gain mastership through the arbitration process. In its simplest form, the physical bus arbitration process consists of the following:

1) An external device issues a physical bus request to the MC68851,
2) The MC68851 asserts physical bus grant to indicate that the bus will be available at the end of the current bus cycle, and
3) The external device acknowledges that it has assumed physical bus mastership by asserting physical bus grant acknowledge.

Figure 4-37 is a flowchart showing the details involved in physical bus arbitration for a single device. Figure 4-38 illustrates the functional timing of the arbitration circuitry when the MC68851 is performing address translation for the logical bus master. Figure 4-39 illustrates the same process when the MC68851 is performing table search operations.

The timing diagrams show that the bus request ($\overline{PBR}$) is negated at the time that bus grant acknowledge ($\overline{PBGACK}$) is asserted. This type of operation is true for a system consisting of the MC68851 and a single device capable of physical bus mastership. In systems having a number of devices capable of physical bus mastership, the requst line from each device is wire-ORed to the MC68851. In such a system, it is possible that there could be more than one bus request asserted simultaneously.

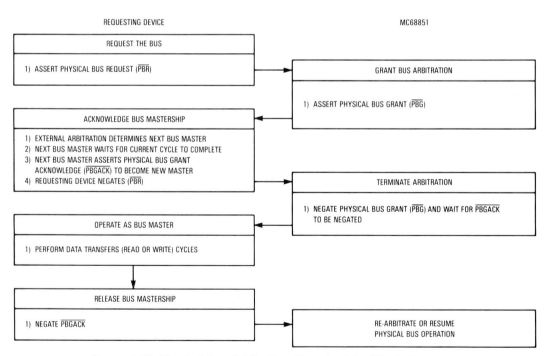

Figure 4-37. Physical Bus Arbitration Flowchart for Single Request

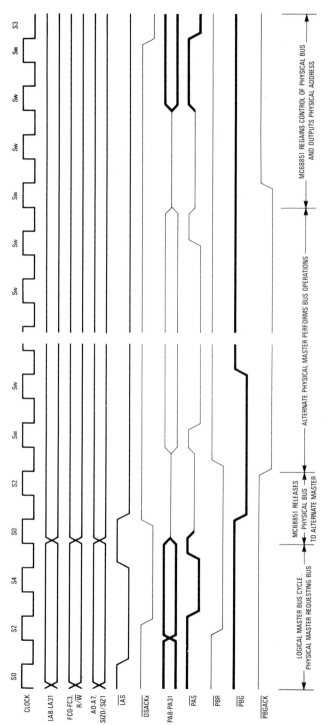

Figure 4-38. Physical Bus Arbitration During Address Translation

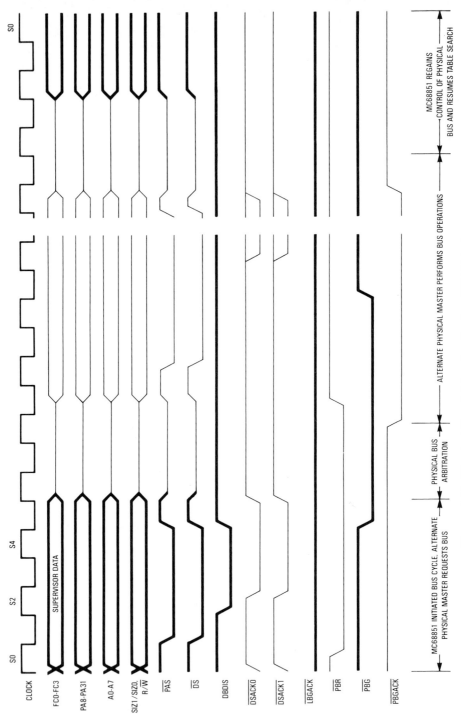

Figure 4-39. Physical Bus Arbitration During MC68851 Table Search

The timing diagram in Figure 4-38 shows that the bus grant ($\overline{\text{PBG}}$) signal is negated a few clocks after the transition of the bus grant acknowledge signal. However, if bus requests are still pending after the assertion of bus grant acknowledge, the MC68851 will assert another bus grant within a few clock cycles after the grant is negated. This additional assertion of bus grant allows external arbitration circuitry to select the next bus master before the current bus master has completed its use of the bus. The following three paragraphs provide additional information about the three steps in the arbitration process. The precise delays between signals are provided in **SECTION 12 ELECTRICAL SPECIFICATIONS**.

4.5.1 Requesting the Physical Bus

External devices that are capable of becoming physical bus masters request the bus by asserting the physical bus request ($\overline{\text{PBR}}$) signal. This can be a wire-ORed signal (although it need not be constructed from open-collector devices) that indicates to the MC68851 that some external device requires control of the physical bus. The MC68851 is effectively at a lower bus priority than all external physical devices and always relinquishes the bus after it has completed its current bus cycle or address translation, if one has started.

If no acknowledge is received before the bus request signal is negated, the MC68851 continues bus operations once it detects that the bus request is negated. This allows ordinary address translation and table search operations to continue if the arbitration circuitry inadvertently responded to noise or an external device determines that it no longer requires use of the bus before it has acknowledged mastership.

4.5.2 Receiving the Physical Bus Grant

The MC68851 asserts physical bus grant ($\overline{\text{PBG}}$) as soon as possible after the receipt of the physical bus request. Normally this is immediately following internal synchronization, but there are two exceptions to this rule. If the MC68851 has made an internal decision to execute a bus cycle or to output an address translation but has not progressed into the operation to assert the physical address strobe ($\overline{\text{PAS}}$) signal, then physical bus grant will be delayed until $\overline{\text{PAS}}$ is asserted to indicate to external devices that a bus cycle is in progress. The second exception occurs when a read-modify-write cycle is in progress regardless of whether that cycle was initiated by the MC68851 or the logical bus master. The MC68851 will not issue a physical bus grant if the $\overline{\text{RMC}}$ signal is driven either by the MC68851 or by a logical bus master.

The physical bus grant signal may be routed through a daisy-chained network or through a specific priority-encoded network. The MC68851 is not affected by an external method of arbitration as long as the protocol is obeyed.

4.5.3 Acknowledgement of Physical Bus Mastership

Upon receiving a physical bus grant, the requesting device waits until $\overline{\text{PAS}}$, $\overline{\text{DSACKx}}$, and $\overline{\text{PBGACK}}$ are negated before asserting its own $\overline{\text{PBGACK}}$. The negation of the $\overline{\text{PAS}}$ indicates that the previous master (including the MC68851) has completed its cycle. The negation of $\overline{\text{PBGACK}}$ indicates that the previous master (if any) has released the bus. The negation of $\overline{\text{DSACKx}}$ indicates that the previous slave has terminated its connection to the previous master. Note that in some applications, $\overline{\text{DSACKx}}$ might not enter into this function and devices are then connected such that they are only dependent on $\overline{\text{PAS}}$. When physical bus grant acknowledge is asserted, the device is bus master until it negates $\overline{\text{PBGACK}}$. Physical bus grant acknowledge should not be negated until after all bus cycles required by the alternate bus master are complete. Bus mastership is terminated at the negation of $\overline{\text{PBGACK}}$.

The bus request from the granted device should be negated after the physical bus grant acknowledge is asserted. If a bus request is still pending after the assertion of $\overline{\text{PBGACK}}$, another bus grant will be issued within a few clocks of the negation of the bus grant. Refer to **4.5.4 Physical Bus Arbitration Control**. Note that the MC68851 does not perform any external bus cycles before it reasserts the bus grant.

4.5.4 Physical Bus Arbitration Control

The physical bus arbitration control unit in the MC68851 is implemented using a finite state machine. As discussed previously, all asynchronous inputs to the MC68851 are internally synchronized in a maximum of two cycles of the system clock.

As shown in Figure 4-40, the inputs labeled R and A are internally synchronized versions of the physical bus request and physical bus grant acknowledge inputs, respectively. The physical bus grant output is labeled G and the internal three-state control signal T. If T is true, the physical address bus, $\overline{\text{PAS}}$, and other physical control signals are placed in the high-impedance state after $\overline{\text{PAS}}$ and $\overline{\text{RMC}}$ are negated (refer to **4.6 CONCURRENT DISSOCIATE LOGICAL AND PHYSICAL BUS ACTIVITY**). All signals are shown in positive logic (active high) regardless of their true active voltage level.

State changes (valid outputs) occur on the next rising edge of the clock after the internal signal is valid.

Timing diagrams of the physical bus arbitration sequence during address translation and table search operations are shown in Figures 4-38 and 4-39, respectively. The physical bus arbitration sequence while the physical bus is inactive is shown in Figure 4-41.

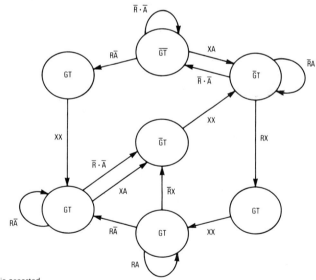

R – PHYSICAL BUS REQUEST
A – PHYSICAL BUS GRANT ACKNOWLEDGE
G – PHYSICAL BUS GRANT
T – THREE-STATE CONTROL TO PHYSICAL BUS CONTROL LOGIC
X – DON'T CARE

NOTE: The $\overline{\text{PBG}}$ output will not be asserted while $\overline{\text{RMC}}$ is asserted by the MC68851 or the Logical Bus Master

Figure 4-40. Physical Bus Arbitration State Diagram

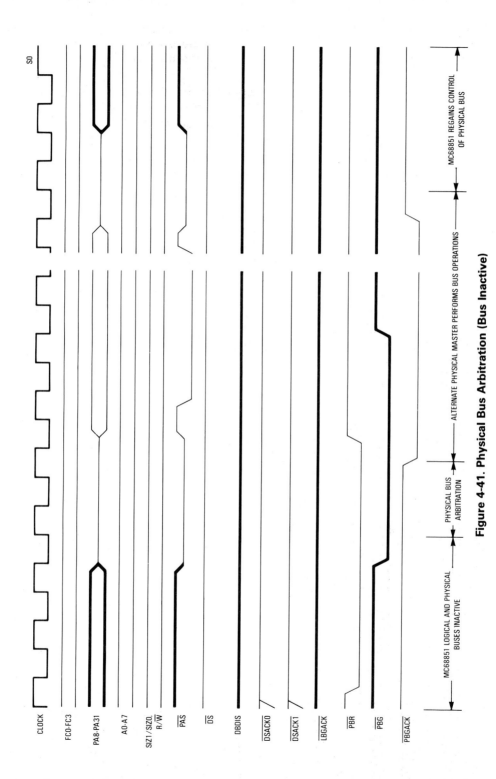

Figure 4-41. Physical Bus Arbitration (Bus Inactive)

4.6 CONCURRENT DISSOCIATE LOGICAL AND PHYSICAL BUS ACTIVITY

In systems that utilize alternate physical bus masters, the MC68851 allows independent operation of both the logical and physical buses while still performing access rights checking for logical bus activity. For example, it is possible for the logical master to access devices resident on the logical bus (a coprocessor, a logical cache, . . ., etc.) while the physical bus has been arbitrated away from the MC68851. This concurrence is obtained by the correct employment of the logical bus control signals and buffering of the control signals and buses that are shared between the logical and physical buses.

When the MC68851 does not possess ownership of the physical bus ($\overline{PBGACK}$ is asserted), the physical address bus and physical address strobe are in the high-impedance state. Also, the MC68851 does not drive the lower address A0-A7, size, function codes, data strobe, $\overline{RMC}$ or read/write, although these signals may be driven by the logical bus master. This requires that any of these that are used by external, physical address space devices must be buffered between the MC68851 and the alternate physical master.

If a bus cycle initiated by the logical master is held up pending the completion of alternate physical bus master activity, the MC68851 does not assert $\overline{PAS}$ for that cycle until it regains ownership of the physical bus. After the negation of $\overline{PBGACK}$ is detected by the MC68851 (subject to a synchronization delay), physical address will be driven and then $\overline{PAS}$ will be asserted on the next appropriate clock edge (as determined by the decision timeout delay).

In order to support logical bus activity, the MC68851 monitors logical addresses regardless of the state of $\overline{PBGACK}$ and uses the signals $\overline{LBRO}$, $\overline{HALT}$, $\overline{BERR}$, $\overline{CLI}$, $\overline{DSACKx}$, and D0-D31 to control and respond to accesses on the logical bus. Any of these signals that are employed by an alterate physical bus master must be buffered. Additionally, in order to prevent spurious assertions of $\overline{PAS}$, some provision must be made to block propagation of the $\overline{PAS}$ signal to physical address space devices when the target for a bus cycle resides on the logical bus. In order to prevent these transient assertions of $\overline{PAS}$ to physical address space devices, the logical bus control circuitry must block the propagation of $\overline{PAS}$ early enough in the bus cycle to account for the earliest possible assertion of $\overline{PAS}$ by the MC68851 and must maintain the blocking until the latest possible negation time. In general, the above requirement also applies to all systems that have memory devices resident on the logical bus.

In addition to proper buffering of signals, logical address space devices (henceforth referred to as logical devices) that are designed to operate independently of the physical bus must satisfy several criteria:

1) The address decode for the logical device must operate on only the logical address and function code,
2) The chip select, or similar function, for the logical device must be based on the state of the logical address strobe (i.e., independent of $\overline{PAS}$),
3) Likewise, the cycle termination response (for example, $\overline{DSACKx}$) must be generated from the logical address strobe, and
4) Any logical bus master capable of accessing the logical devices **must** be capable of aborting or retrying the bus cycle in response to a bus error or relinquish and retry signaled by the MC68851 (for example, refer to **4.2.2.1 SYNCHRONOUS OPERATION**).

In a suitably configured system, when a logical bus master is accessing a logical device, the MC68851 still provides access checking for the bus cycle and will assert the appropriate signals to terminate faulting cycles (bus error), to communicate across its coprocessor interface ($\overline{DSACKx}$ and the data bus), or to indicate the need to access the translation tables in physical memory (relinquish or relinquish and retry).

The above discussion of system configuration and buffering requirements applies only to those systems desiring to employ concurrent logical and physical bus activity for overall system performance enhancement, and should not be construed as a general requirement for all system configurations.

Figure 4-42 provides a simple block diagram of the buffering and control sections required to implement the above criteria.

Figure 4-43 illustrates several example sequences of concurrent logical and physical bus activity.

4.7 BUS OPERATION EXAMPLES

The following paragraphs contain several specific examples of MC68851 bus operations and is intended to provide better understanding of the MC68851 by demonstrating sequences of typical bus operations.

4.7.1 Table Search Operations

The bus operations required to initiate and complete a table search operation, including startup and terminate overhead, are shown in Figure 4-44. This figure demonstrates the timing for a translation descriptor fetch and address translation cache update assuming that the MC68851 is operating in the early processing startup and fast table search modes of operation (refer to **4.1.2 Bus Interface Initialization**) and that physical memory operates with no wait states. The table structure accessed consists of a function code index and two levels of long format descriptors.

The startup overhead associated with a table search operation is affected by the table structure used and operational mode of the MC68851. For example, if the first level of the table search is not an index by the function codes, the startup overhead is increased by the two clock periods required to perform a limit check of the root pointer used in the search. Also, if the early processing startup mode is disabled, an additional six clock periods of overhead is required to initiate a table search.

Figures 4-45 and 4-46 demonstrate the bus operations and timings associated with updating the used and modified descriptor status bits. The overall time required to perform a table search operation such as depicted in Figure 4-44 is affected by the number of status bits that must be updated during the search.

It should be noted that both the used and modified bits may be set in a single operation that does not require use of a read-modify-write operation. However, if only the used bit of a page descriptor is to be set and the status of the M bit is not to be changed, the MC68851 always uses a read-modify-write operation in order to maintain status consistency in systems that allow multiple MC68851s to share the same translation tables. It should also be noted that a simple write operation is always used to update the used bit at all levels of the translation table other than the page descriptor level.

4.7.2 Logical Bus Arbitration

Figure 4-47 illustrates an MC68851 table search operation that is interrupted by an alternate logical bus master requesting control of the logical bus. The MC68851 continues the table search until it detects an assertion of logical bus grant in ($\overline{\text{LBGI}}$) after which it asserts logical bus grant out ($\overline{\text{LBGO}}$) to indicate that it will relinquish control of the logical bus at the end of the current bus cycle. After placing all shared control lines in the high-impedance state, the MC68851 negates logical bus grant acknowledge ($\overline{\text{LBGACK}}$).

If the MC68851 was performing a table search to update the ATC as the result of a request for an address translation that did not have a descriptor resident in the address translation cache, the interrupted table search will not be resumed when the alternate logical bus master releases control of the bus; instead, the MC68851 will wait for the bus cycle that initiated the search to be retried by the logical master. When the master does retry that cycle, the MC68851 will resume the table search at the point it was terminated if, and only if, no operations have occurred between interruption of the table search and the retry of the cycle that require that the MC68851 perform any other internal operations. Otherwise, the table search will be completely re-executed.

If the MC68851 was performing a table search in response to a PTEST or PLOAD instruction, the table search will be automatically resumed or restarted (refer to **4.4.1.2 MC68851 REQUESTING THE LOGICAL BUS)**.

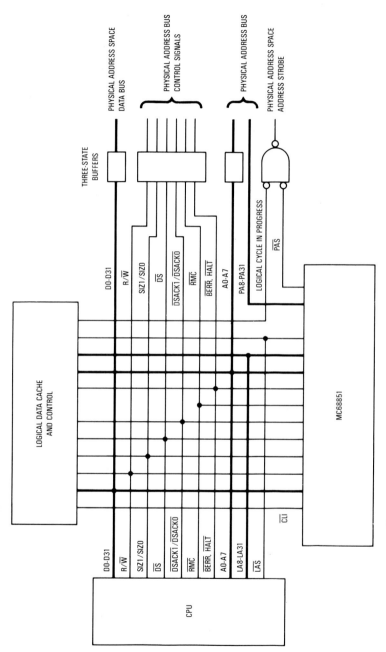

Figure 4-42. Example of Signal Buffering Requirements for Support of Concurrent Logical and Physical Bus Activity

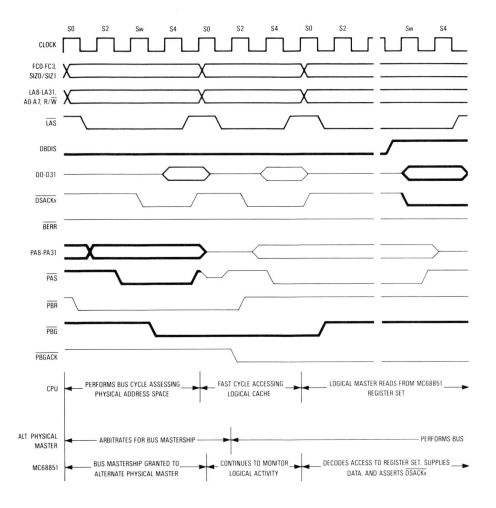

Figure 4-43. Example of Concurrent

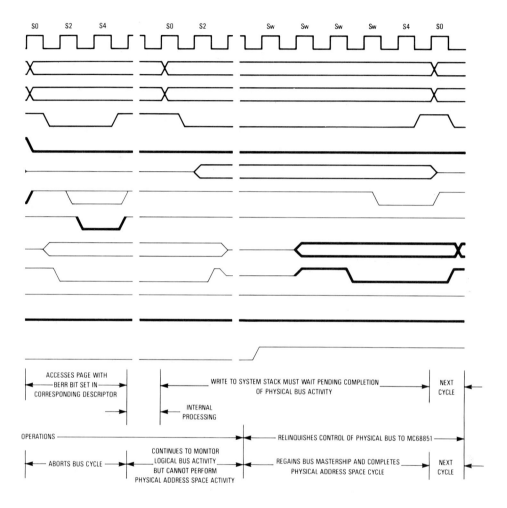

Logical and Physical Bus Activity

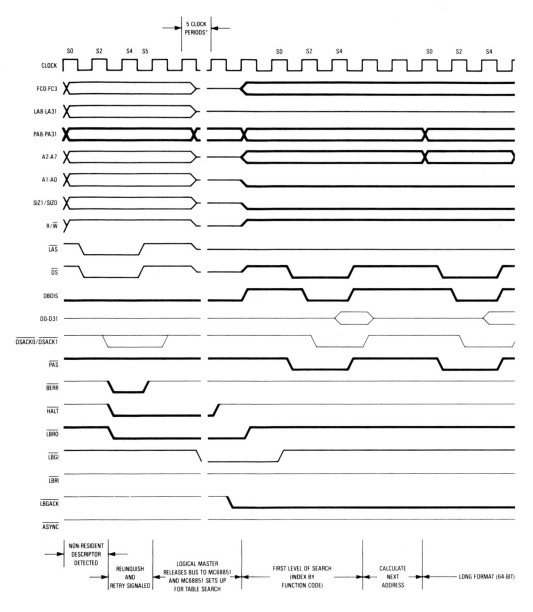

**Figure 4-44. MC68851
(Table Search with Function Code Lookup**

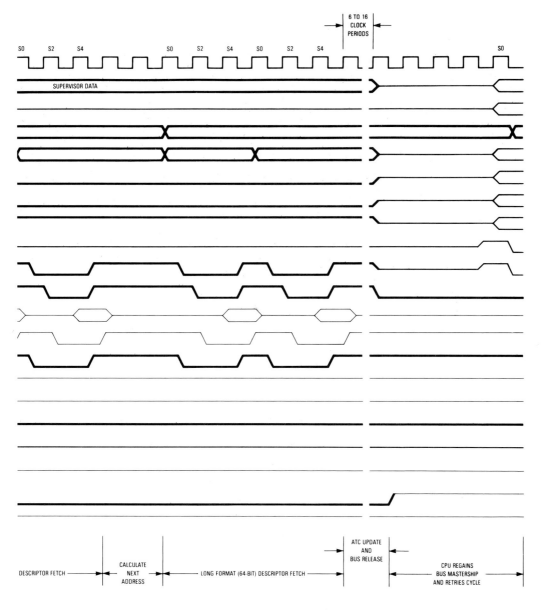

Table Search Example
and Two Levels of Long Format Descriptors)

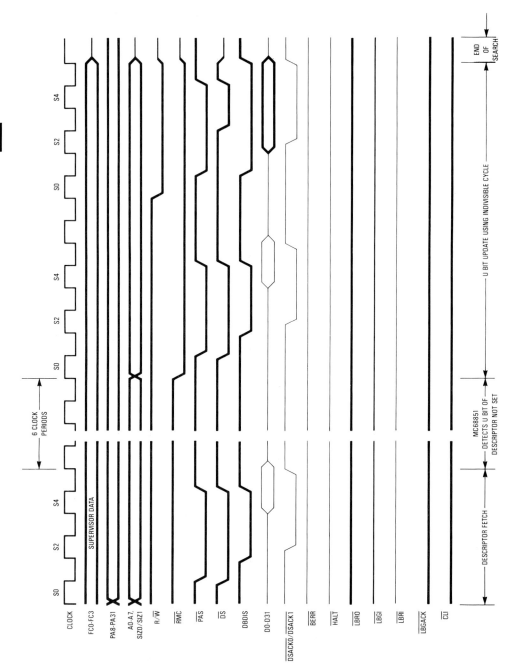

Figure 4-45. Page Descriptor U Bit Status Update

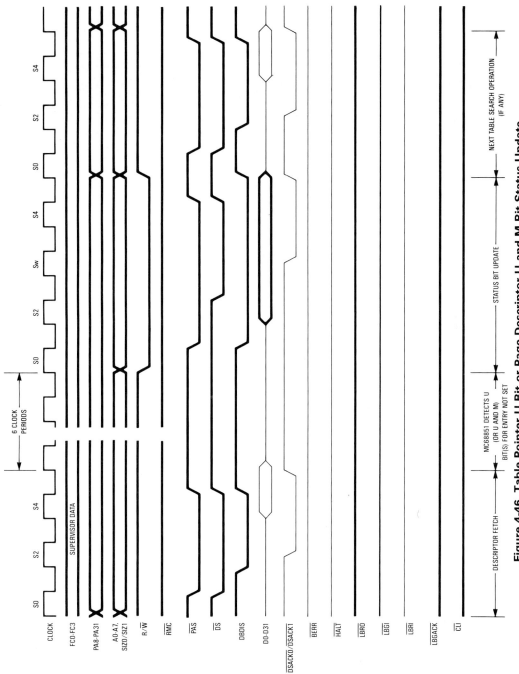

Figure 4-46. Table Pointer U Bit or Page Descriptor U and M Bit Status Update

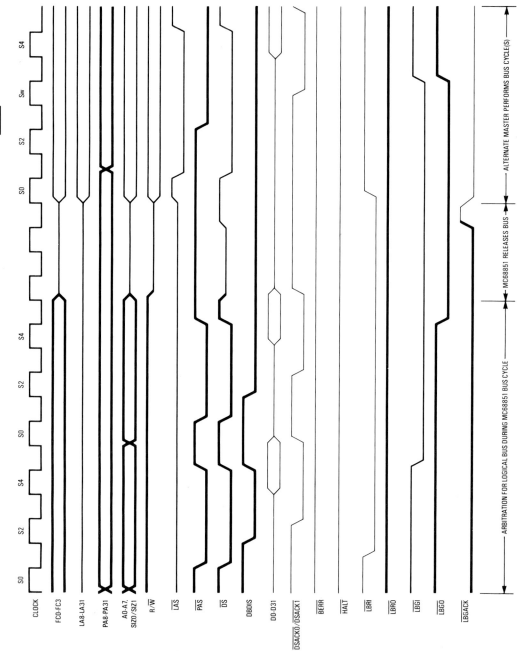

Figure 4-47. MC68851 Table Search Operation Interrupted by Alternate Logical Bus Master

SECTION 5
ADDRESS TRANSLATION

This section discusses the mapping of addresses from the logical address space to the physical address space by the MC68851. Included in this section is the description of the MC68851 translation table structure, formats and uses of translation descriptors, and operation of the MC68851 address translation cache (ATC).

5.1 ADDRESS TRANSLATION TABLES

In a paged virtual system, the logical address space is divided into a number of fixed-size pages and corresponding to each of these 'logical pages' there is (possibly) a unique mapping into the physical address space. The mapping may translate the logical address to the address of a page located in physical memory (a page frame), may indicate that the logical address is temporarily unuseable because the corresponding physical page is resident on a secondary storage device, or may indicate that the logical address does not (currently) have a corresponding physical mapping. The primary task for a memory management unit in such a system is to perform the translation from logical addresses to physical addresses for bus cycles executed by the logical bus master. Although the memory management unit performs address translation, it depends on the operating system to supply it with the information describing the logical-to-physical mapping.

In order to allow each 'logical page' to have a unique mapping into the physical address space, it is necessary to provide a translation descriptor corresponding to each page in the logical address space. In a system with a logical address space of size 2^n and a page size 2^m, there are 2^{n-m} logical pages. The highest order $n-m$ bits of the logical address specify the logical page address and the lowest order m bits specify an offset within the page to address an individual entry in that page. In order to locate a translation for a given logical address, a memory management unit uses the logical page address as an index into a table of translation descriptors to select the entry corresponding to that page address.

The descriptor table containing the logical-to-physical mappings for the system can be organized in one of two ways. A linear table is the simplest form and would consist of a single, contiguous table with one entry corresponding to each logical page. In order to locate a translation for a particular logical address, the memory management unit would use the logical page address as an index into this table selecting the entry at this location as the appropriate translation descriptor. Although the structure of this table is very simple and a translation descriptor could be fetched in a single bus operation, this type of table is not used since the entire table must always reside in the system's memory (i.e., there is no way to indicate that a portion of the address space is not (currently) mapped except by having an entry in the table indicating this). This disadvantage is significant in MC68020-based systems that are capable of supporting logical address spaces with several *million* pages.

Alternately, a tree structure could be used to contain the mapping information. Using this type of structure, a portion of the logical address space is mapped at each level of the translation tree. The higher levels of the tree subdivide the logical address space into relatively large blocks and the lower levels further subdivide these large blocks until, at the lowest level, the address space is broken down into individual pages. Compared to the linear table, a tree structure is somewhat more complex and may require that the memory management unit perform several bus operations to locate a translation descriptor. However, provided with an address translation cache of sufficiently high hit rate and a very efficient bus interface, these disadvantages are not significant. The significant advantage of using a tree structure is the ability to deallocate large portions of the logical address space with a single entry at the higher levels of the tree. Additionally, portions of the tree itself may reside on a secondary storage device or may not exist at all until they are required by the system. These advantages allow a tree structure to efficiently map a very large logical address space using only a fraction of the memory that would be required by a linear table.

The mapping of logical to physical addresses for a system is described to the MC68851 using trees of tables in physical memory. The physical addresses of the roots of these trees are contained in the MC68851 root pointer registers (refer to **6.1.1 Root Pointer Registers**). In addition to mapping information, the tables contain protection information and usage-history information for both translation tables and pages of physical memory. When the MC68851 needs to locate a logical-to-physical mapping, it uses the logical address to index into the translation tables and select the corresponding mapping. The MC68851 searches these tables to locate a logical-to-physical mapping when the ATC does not contain a translation for a bus cycle executed by a logical bus master, as part of a PTEST or PLOAD instruction, or when a module call operation references a module descriptor that does not have a corresponding entry in the ATC.

5.1.1 General Translation Table Structure

Address translation tables for the MC68851 are organized as trees of tables located in physical memory, each table being composed of pointers to other branches of the tree (table descriptors) or pointers to physical pages (page descriptors). The tables themselves may be termed to be either 'pointer tables' or 'page tables' depending on whether they contain table descriptors or page descriptors, respectively. The MC68851 can have as many as three of these trees active simultaneously, one pointed to by each of the root pointer registers: SRP, CRP, and DRP corresponding to translations for supervisor, user, or DMA accesses, respectively (refer to **6.1.1 Root Pointer Registers**).

Searching an address translation table tree for the physical address corresponding to a logical address consists of extracting a field from the logical address or function code, using the extracted field to select a descriptor in a table identified either by the root pointer or by a pointer table at a higher level of the translation tree, checking protection information, and using the selected descriptor to locate the next table. This process is repeated with successive fields in the logical address until a page descriptor is found, indicating the physical base address of the page frame, or until an error occurs, terminating the table search. A simplified flowchart of the address translation table search procedure is shown in Figure 5-1 (a complete flowchart is provided in Figure 5-23).

A translation tree may be composed of up to five levels of tables requiring the use of five separate index fields to locate a logical-to-physical mapping. Additionally, tables at different levels of the translation tree may all be of the same size or they may each have different sizes. The general structure of the translation tree is determined by the translation control (TC) register (refer to **6.1.3 Translation Control**). The IS field (initial shift) is used to set the size of the logical address space which is given by 2^{32-IS}. The PS field (page size) determines the page size to be used in the system (2^{PS}) and, together with the IS field, specifies the number of pages in the system ($2^{32-IS-PS}$). Additionally, if the logical address space is also mapped by the function code signals, there are eight separate logical address spaces of size 2^{32-IS}, one corresponding to each of the M68000 function code assignments, increasing the logical address space size to $2^{32-IS+3}$ and the number of pages in the system to $2^{32-IS-PS+3}$.

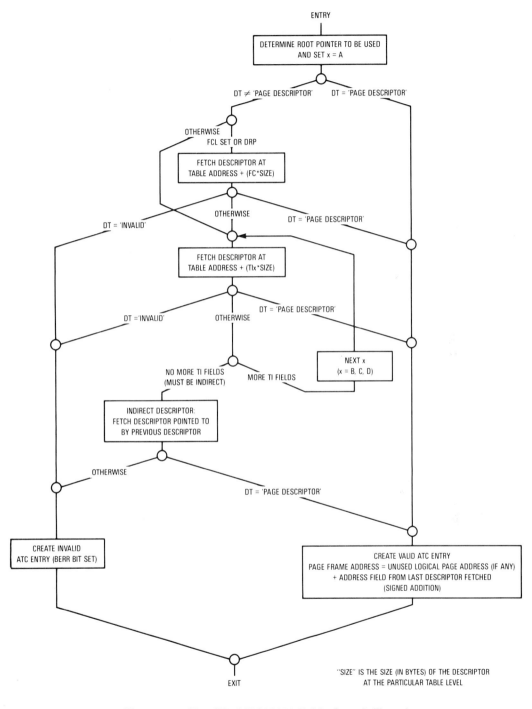

Figure 5-1. Simplified MC68851 Table Search Flowchart

In order to provide for a unique logical-to-physical mapping for each logical page, the logical page address (32-IS-PS + 3 bits) is used to index into the translation tables to select the appropriate mapping. The logical page address is divided into one or more fields, as determined by the FCL bit and the TIA, TIB, TIC, and TID fields of the TC register, to be used as indices into the tree structure at its various levels. This division of the logical address is illustrated in Figure 5-2.

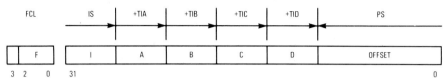

Figure 5-2. Derivation of Table Index Fields

The F field consists of function code bits FC2-FC0 (FC3 is used only to select use of the DMA root pointer (DRP)) and is used when the logical address space is mapped based on the function codes. Use of the F field is required for address translation trees pointed to by the DRP register. For address translation trees pointed to by the CRP and SRP registers, use of the F field is controlled by the FCL bit of the TC register (refer to **6.1.3.3 FUNCTION CODE LOOKUP**). An F level table is always eight entries long (one entry identifying a branch of the three corresponding to each of the M68000 function code assignments) and is always the first table accessed during a table search by the MC68851 (provided that function code lookup is enabled). If the F field is not used, the function codes are used only for protection purposes, the root pointer register points to the base of the A level table, and the first level of the address translation tree is indexed using the A field.

The table index fields (TIA, TIB, TIC, TID) specify the number of bits of the logical address to be used at each level of the translation tree thus specifying the division of the logical address space at each level. For example, if the TIA field is set to n then the table at the root level of the translation tree contains 2^n entries and the logical address space is subdivided into 2^n regions of equal size, one of these regions corresponding to each of the entries in this table. Further, if the TIA field is as above and the TIB field is set to m ($m + n \leq 32$-IS-PS) then each of the 2^n regions defined in the first level of the tree are further subdivided into 2^m regions of equal size. The table index fields are applied to tables in the sequence A, B, C, D. Use of the F, B, C, and D fields can be suppressed, so that the minimum number of levels in an address translation tree is one.

The A, B, C, and D fields of the logical address specified by the IS, TIA, TIB, TIC, and TID fields of the TC register are subject to restrictions as follows:

Field	Starting Bit Position	Width Restrictions
A	31-IS	1-15 (TIA Must be Non-Zero)
B	31-IS-TIA	0-15 if TIB = 0, then TIC = TID = 0 is Required
C	31-IS-TIB-TIB	0-15 if TIC = 0, then TID = 0 is Required
D	31-IS-TIB-TIB-TIC	0-15

In addition to the restrictions listed above, the fields of the TC register (when treated as unsigned integers) must satisfy the following relationship:

$$IS + PS + TIA + TIB + TIC + TID = 32$$

The logical-to-physical mappings for a system can be described to the MC68851 using two different formats of translation descriptors. The descriptors may be either of the long format (eight bytes) or the short format (four bytes) and these different formats may be freely intermixed in different tables of the translation tree. The determination of field widths described above does not determine the format (long or short) of descriptors in various tables of the tree. The format of the descriptors in a table is independent of all index field widths and the formats of all other tables of the tree. The MC68851 is informed of the format of descriptors in a table during the table search by the descriptor type fields in the pointers at the higher levels of the tree and the MC68851 uses this to scale the index into the table by four or eight bytes, as appropriate. Thus, tables at the same level in different branches of the tree may have different format descriptors, although mixing of descriptor formats within a single table is not allowed.

Figure 5-3 shows an example of a simple address translation table tree and a logical address translated using this tree. The 32-bit logical address is divided into three fields: A (12 bits), B (10 bits), and PS (10 bits). The function code lookup is suppressed such that the index by function code is not used. This division would be set at system initialization time by writing the value $80A0CA00 to the TC register (refer to **6.1.3 TRANSLATION CONTROL**). The bold lines indicate the sequence of descriptors used to translate the logical address ($00A01A00 for this example). The shaded descriptor on the right contains the physical page address that corresponds to the logical address. At the end of the table search, an entry will be made in the ATC pairing the logical address with this physical address. Subsequent references to this logical page, until the ATC is flushed of this entry, will not require the table search.

Figure 5-4 shows one possible arrangement of this translation tree in main memory. For convenience, all of the tables are shown as contiguous in physical memory; however, this is not required since all page frames are equivalent. Note that all addresses in the tables are physical addresses.

5.1.2 Variations in Translation Table Structure

Many aspects of the MC68851 translation tree structure are software configurable, allowing the system designer a great range of flexibility to optimize the performance of the MC68851 for a particular system. The following paragraphs discuss the variations of the tree structure from the general structure discussed above.

5.1.2.1 CONTIGUOUS MEMORY. The MC68851 provides the ability to translate a contiguous range of the logical address space (an integral number of logical pages) to an equivalent contiguous physical address range with a single descriptor. This is done by placing the code for 'page descriptor' ($1) in the descriptor type (DT) field of a descriptor at a level of the tree that would normally contain a table pointer, thereby deleting a sub-tree of the table.

When the MC68851 is performing a table search operation and encounters a descriptor with a DT field indicating 'page descriptor' it terminates the search and creates an entry in the ATC. In a normal table search, the MC68851 will have exhausted the page address field of the logical address (the most significant 32-IS-PS bits) indicating that the descriptor resides in a page table at the leaf level of the translation tree. In this case, the page frame address is simply the value contained in the 'page address' field of the descriptor. If the MC68851 has not exhausted the page address field (i.e., has not encountered a TIx field with a value of zero or has not used the most significant 32-IS-PS bits of the logical address) when it encounters the 'page descriptor' encoding, this indicates to the MC68851 that the range of the logical page address that was not used in the table search is to be defined as a contiguous range of memory. The MC68851 terminates the table search and creates an ATC entry. The physical address contained in this entry is the sum of the logical page address (bits already used in the table search are set to zero) and the page frame address (the most significant 32-PS bits in the page address field of the descriptor). If n bits of the logical page address are unused when a page descriptor encoding is encountered, the single

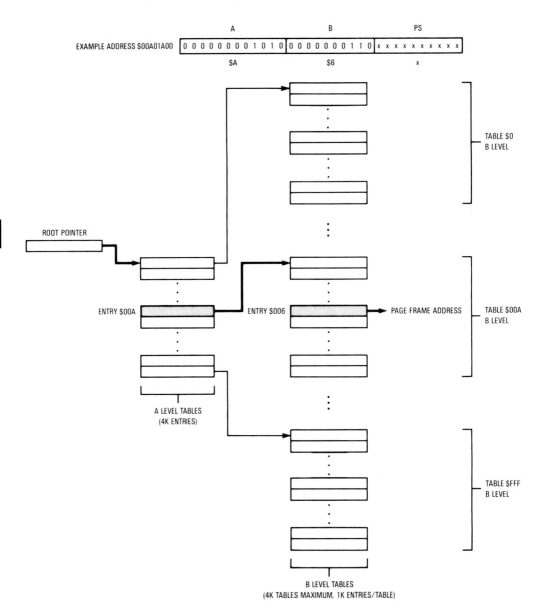

Figure 5-3. Example Translation Table Tree

descriptor creates a mapping of a contiguous region of the logical address space starting at the logical page address (with the *n* unused bits set to zero) to a contiguous region in the physical address space starting at the page frame base address with a size of $2^{PS} + n$ bytes.

This type of descriptor is referred to as a 'type-2 page descriptor' and is characterized by having a descriptor type of 'page descriptor' but not being located at the lowest level of the translation tree. If the type-2 page descriptor is of the long format, the limit field is applied to the next index

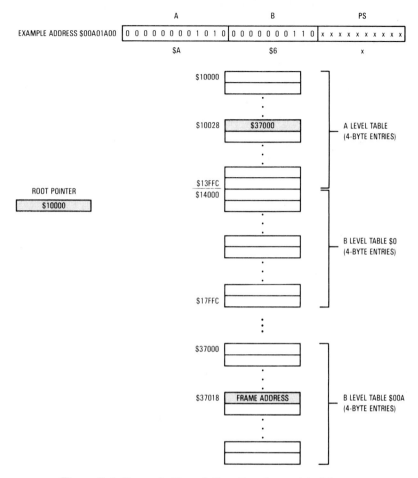

Figure 5-4. Example Translation Tree Layout in Memory

field. This allows the number of pages mapped contiguously to be restricted. Refer to **5.1.5 Descriptor Types** for additional information.

Although the type-2 page descriptor creates a contiguous logical-to-physical mapping without having to maintain individual descriptors in the translation tree for each page that is a member of the contiguous region, the ATC will contain one entry for each page mapped. These entries are created internally by the MC68851 each time a page boundary (as determined by the page size) is crossed in the contiguous region. Figure 5-5 shows an example translation table with a portion of the logical address space translated as a contiguous block.

Note that the DT field may be set to 'page descriptor' at any level of the translation tree including the root pointer level. Setting the DT field of a root pointer to 'page descriptor' creates a direct mapping from the logical to the physical address space with a constant offset as determined by the value in the table address field of the root pointer.

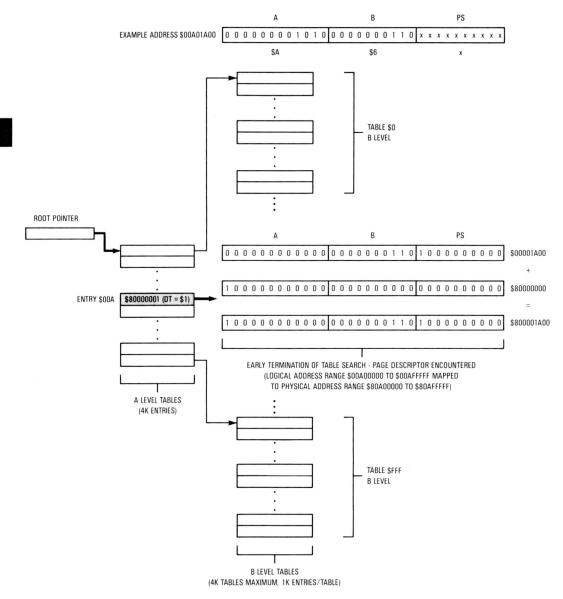

Figure 5-5. Example Translation Using Contiguous Memory

5.1.2.2 INDIRECTION. The MC68851 provides the ability to replace an entry in a page table with a pointer to an alternate entry. The indirection capability of the MC68851 allows multiple tasks to share a physical page while maintaining only a single set of history information for the page (i.e., the 'modified' indication is maintained only in the single descriptor). The indirection capability also allows the page frame to appear at arbitrarily different addresses in the logical address spaces of each task. Using the indirection capability, single entries or entire tables may be shared between multiple tasks. Figure 5-6 shows two tasks sharing a page using indirect descrtiptors.

When the MC68851 has completed a normal table search (has exhausted all index fields of the logical page address), it examines the descriptor type field of the last entry fetched from the translation tables. If the DT field contains a 'valid long' ($2) or 'valid short' ($3) encoding, this indicates to the MC68851 that the address contained in the highest order 30 bits of the table address field of the descriptor is a pointer to the page descriptor that is to be used to map the logical address. The MC68851 then fetches the type-1 page descriptor of the indicated format at this address and uses the page address field of this entry as the physical mapping for the logical address.

The page descriptor located at the address given by the address field of the indirect descriptor must not have a DT field with the long or short code (it must either be 'page descriptor' or 'invalid'). Otherwise, the descriptor will be treated as invalid and the MC68851 will create an ATC entry with an error condition signaled (BERR bit set).

5.1.2.3 TABLE SHARING BETWEEN TASKS. A page or pointer table may be shared between tasks by placing a pointer to the shared table in the address translation tables of more than one task. The upper (non-shared) tables may contain different settings of protection bits, allowing different tasks to use the area with different permissions. In Figure 5-7, two tasks share the memory translated by the table at the B level. Note that task 'A' cannot write to the shared area. Task 'B', however, has the WP bit clear in its pointer to the shared table, so it can read and write the shared area. Also note that the shared area appears at different addresses for each task.

5.1.2.4 PAGING OF TABLES. It is not required that the entire address translation tree for an active task be resident in main memory at once. In the same way that only the working set of pages need be kept in main memory, only the tables needed to describe the resident set of pages need be kept. This is done by placing the 'invalid' code ($0) in the DT field of the pointer descriptor that points to the absent table(s). When a task attempts to use an address that would be translated by an absent table, the MC68851 will be unable to locate a translation and asserts the bus error signal when the CPU retries the bus cycle that caused the table search to be initiated.

It is the responsibility of the system software to determine that the 'invalid' code in the descriptor indicates non-resident tables. This determination can be facilitated by using the descriptor to store status information concerning the 'invalid' encoding. When the MC68851 encounters an 'invalid' descriptor, it makes no interpretation (or modification) of any fields of this descriptor other than the DT field allowing the operating system to store system-defined information in this location. Typical information that might be stored includes the reason for the 'invalid' encoding (tables paged-out, region not allocated, . . ., etc.) and possibly the disk address for non-resident tables.

Figure 5-8 shows an address translation table in which only a single page table (table n) is resident and all other page tables are not resident.

5.1.2.5 DYNAMIC ALLOCATION OF TABLES. Similar to the case discussed above concerning table residence in memory, it is not required that a complete translation tree exist for an active

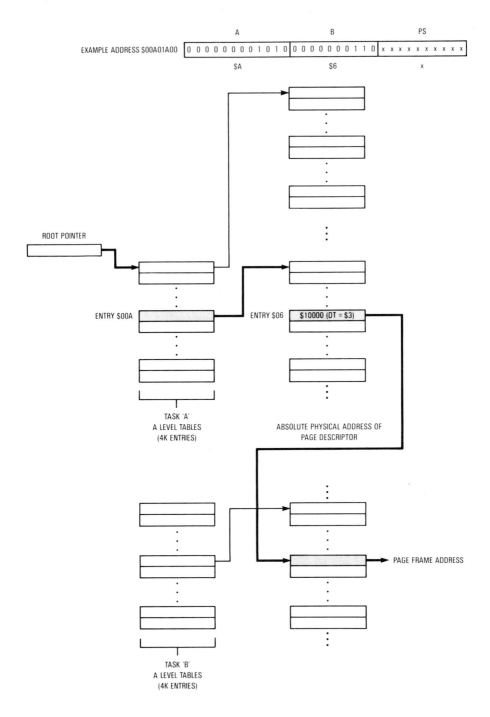

Figure 5-6. Example Translation Tree Using Indirect Descriptors

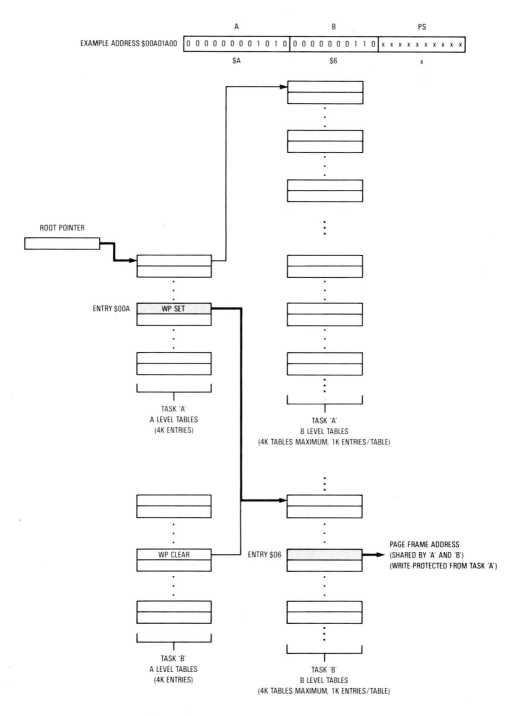

Figure 5-7. Example Translation Tree Using Shared Tables

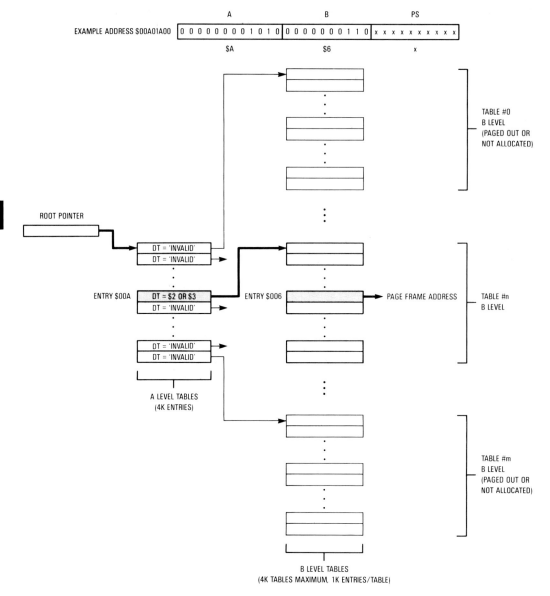

Figure 5-8. Example Translation Tree With Non-Resident Tables

task. The translation tree may be dynamically allocated by the operating system based on requests for access to particular areas.

As in the case of demand paging, it is difficult, if not impossible, to predict the areas of memory that will be used by a task over any extended period of time. Instead of attempting to predict the requirements of the task, the operating system performs no action for a task until a 'demand' is made requesting access to a previously unused area or an area that is no longer resident in memory. This same technique can be used to efficiently create a translation tree for a task.

For example, consider an operating system that is going to dispatch for execution a previously unexecuted task that has no translation tree. Rather than trying to guess what the memory usage requirements of the task will be, the operating system creates a translation tree for the task that maps one page corresponding to the initial value of the program counter for that task and possibly one page corresponding to the initial stack pointer of the task. All other branches of the translation tree for this task remain unallocated until the task requests access to the areas mapped by these branches. This technique allows the operating system to construct a minimal translation tree for each task conserving physical memory utilization and operating system overhead.

5.1.3 Functions Controlled by Address Translation Tables

The following paragraphs describe functions that are controlled by fields in the address translation tables. These topics are discussed further in **5.1.5 Translation Descriptors**.

5.1.3.1 PROTECTION. Protection information is indicated in the address translation tables. A page or segment is designated non-writable by setting the WP (write protect) bit in a descriptor, and a page or segment is restricted to access by only the supervisor by setting the S (supervisor) bit. Protections can be assigned based on access levels using the RAL (read access level) and WAL (write access level) fields. Finally, a page is permitted to contain module descriptors for the MC68020 CALLM instruction by setting the G (gate) bit. Refer to **SECTION 7 PROTECTION** for a complete discussion of the various aspects of the MC68851 protection mechanism.

5.1.3.2 ATC MANAGEMENT. Certain functions of the ATC are controlled using the address translation tables. Entries can be made exempt from removal by the ATC replacement algorithm by setting the L (lock) bit. Entries can be made exempt from removal by the RPT replacement algorithm by setting the SG (shared globally) bit. Setting the SG bit is also an indication to the ATC that the same ATC entry is to be used by all tasks (i.e., the task alias field is ignored for entries loaded with the SG bit set). ATC entries made with both bits set cannot be removed except by a PFLUSHS or PFLUSHA instruction (or by altering the TC register or the corresponding root pointer register).

5.1.3.3 DATA CACHE INHIBIT. The MC68851 provides the ability to indicate that pages should not be cached in external data caches. If the translation descriptor for a page has the CI (cache inhibit) bit set, the $\overline{\text{CLI}}$ (cache load inhibit) signal is asserted when that page is accessed. Local caches should use this signal to inhibit loading of entries when asserted.

The cache inhibit function allows system software to determine whether or not a particular area in the memory map should be cacheable. For example, interface registers for peripheral devices should be non-cacheable locations and so, when creating a mapping for these registers, the operating system should set the CI bit in the corresponding translation descriptor. In multi-processor systems, the CI function can be used to prevent caching of shared data areas and can resolve cache consistency problems (stale data) by marking all shared data areas as non-cacheable.

5.1.4 Root Pointers

The MC68851 locates the root of a translation tree by using one of its three root pointer registers: the CPU root pointer (CRP), the supervisor root pointer (SRP), or the DMA root pointer (DRP). These registers contain the physical address of the root of the corresponding translation tree as well as control information about the trees.

5.1.4.1 ROOT POINTER FORMAT. The format of the root pointer registers is discussed in detail in **6.1.1 Root Pointer Registers**. A brief summary is included below and the format of these registers is shown in Figure 5-9.

5.1.4.1.1 Lower/Upper (L/U). The L/U bit specifies whether the value contained in the limit field is to be used as the upper or lower limit of indices into the translation table. If L/U equals zero, the limit field contains the unsigned upper limit of indices. If L/U equals one, the limit field contains the unsigned lower limit of indices.

5.1.4.1.2 Limit. The limit field specifies a maximum or minimum value for the index to be used at the next level of the tables search operation (with the exception of the function code lookup) and is used to limit the size of the translation table at the root level. The limit field and L/U bit of the root pointer are ignored if the first level of the table search is a lookup by function code.

5.1.4.1.3 Shared Globally (SG). The SG bit indicates that the entire logical address space mapped by the root pointer is shared globally by all tasks within the system. Setting the SG bit to one informs the MC68851 that the logical-to-physical mappings identified by this root pointer are identical for all tasks and that only an single descriptor for the translation needs to be maintained in the ATC.

The shared globally attribute can significantly effect the performance of the MC68851 ATC and, thus, merits further discussion. The MC68851 task aliasing mechanism (refer to **5.3 ROOT POINTER TABLE**) assigns a task alias to *all* entries that are created in the ATC; this includes all supervisor and DMA entries. The value assigned to an entry is the current value of the internal task alias. In order for a logical address to match an entry in the ATC, the logical page address, function code, and task alias fields must match exactly. Without use of the shared globally attribute, this would mean that all supervisor and DMA entries in the ATC that are used during the execution of multiple user tasks would require individual ATC entries to be created, one corresponding to each user task during which the entry is used. The SG attribute allows the task alias compare to be suppressed during address translation and thus allows that only a single ATC entry be created regardless of the number of tasks in which the entry is used.

It is recommended that the SG bit be set in the DMA root pointer and, either in the supervisor root pointer, if enabled, or in one of the higher levels of the translation tree if supervisor accesses are translated using the CPU root pointer.

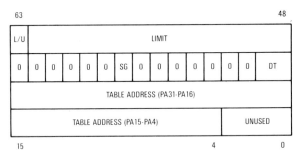

Figure 5-9. Root Pointer Register Format

5.1.4.1.4 Descriptor Type (DT). The DT field specifies the type of descriptor contained in either the root pointer or in the first level of the translation field identified by that root pointer. The values are defined as follows:

- $0 INVALID
 This value is not allowed for root pointers.
- $1 PAGE DESCRIPTOR
 Indicates that a translation table for this root pointer does not exist and that the MC68851 should internally create an ATC entry (page descriptor) for accesses using this root pointer. A limit check is performed regardless of the state of the FCL bit when the DT field of a root pointer is set to $1.
- $2 VALID 4 BYTE
 This value indicates that the translation table at the root of the translation tree contains short format descriptors.
- $3 VALID 8 BYTE
 This value indicates that the translation table at the root of the translation tree contains long format descriptors.

5.1.4.1.5 Table Address. The table address field specifies the physical base address of the root-level translation table for that particular root pointer or the constant offset if the DT = 1.

5.1.4.1.6 Unused. These bits of the root pointer are not used by the MC68851 and may be used by the operating system for other purposes.

5.1.4.2 SELECTION OF ROOT POINTER. The selection of which root pointer to use in translating an address is based on the function code of the logical address and the setting of the SRE bit in the TC register.

FC3	FC2	SRE	Root Pointer Used
0	0	0	CRP
0	0	1	CRP
0	1	0	CRP
0	1	1	SRP
1	x	x	DRP

The DRP is used for translating all accesses for which FC3 = 1. It is intended that peripheral devices using the MC68851 generate logical addresses with FC3 = 1 so that their address spaces may be separate from that of the main processor. Any DMA-type coprocessors should generate addresses with FC3 = 0 so that they may share the main processor's address space. With the SRE bit of the TC register clear, the CRP is used for translating all accesses that have FC3 = 0. With the SRE bit of the TC register set, the CRP translates logical addresses with FC3/FC2 = 00 (user mode), while the SRP translates logical addresses with FC3/FC2 = 01 (supervisor mode). It is intended that the main processor generate logical addresses with FC3 = 0.

5.1.5 Translation Descriptors

The MC68851 uses several types of descriptors as described in the paragraphs below. Each type of descriptor has a long and a short format. All descriptors share one characteristic: the lowest order two bits of the first long word of the descriptor contain a descriptor type (DT) field. The value of these bits affect the interpretation of other bits in the descriptor. In particular, if the value of the DT field is 'invalid' (refer to **5.1.4 FIELD DEFINITIONS**), then the descriptor is of one of the 'invalid' types and the other bits are undefined and are available for use by the system software.

The exact interpretation of the bits in a descriptor is determined by three factors: the value of the DT field of the descriptor, the state of the table search, and the value of the DT field of the previous descriptor used in the search. The value of the previous descriptor determines whether the current descriptor is of the long or short format. The type of a descriptor is determined according to the table in Figure 5-10. The table entries marked "illegal" are not valid configurations and are treated as the 'invalid' type by the MC68851.

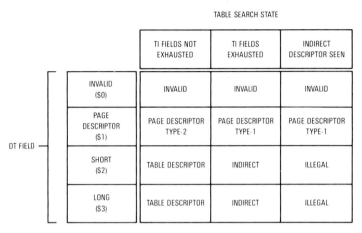

Figure 5-10. Descriptor Type Determination

5.1.5.1 DESCRIPTOR FORMATS. There are two formats of address translation descriptors: long (64 bits) and short (32 bits) and each descriptor type exists in both a long and a short format. Long format descriptors contain all fields that short format descriptors of the same type do, and (possibly) additional information. The MC68851 features that are controlled only by long format descriptors are limit checking on indices (L/U and limit fields), access level protection (RAL and WAL fields), supervisor-only protection (S bit) and sharing of ATC entries (SG bit).

All descriptors in an individual table must be of the same format. The format of the descriptors in different tables may be determined individually. There is no requirement that all tables at the same level of the address translation tree contain descriptors of the same format, or that all descriptors in a table contain DT fields with the same code. An example translation tree with different format descriptors is shown in Figure 5-11.

5.1.5.2 DESCRIPTOR TYPES. The following describes the format of the five basic descriptor types supported by the MC68851. Each of the descriptor types exist in a long and a short format.

5.1.5.2.1 Table Descriptors. This descriptor type is used to identify pointer or page tables at lower levels of the translation tree. The formats of this type of descriptor are shown in Figures 5-12 and 5-13.

5.1.5.2.2 Type-1 and Type-2 Page Descriptors. This descriptor type is found in the page tables and is used to define page frames when a table search terminates having used all fields of the logical page address (as specified by the TC register) as indices into the translation tree (i.e., the

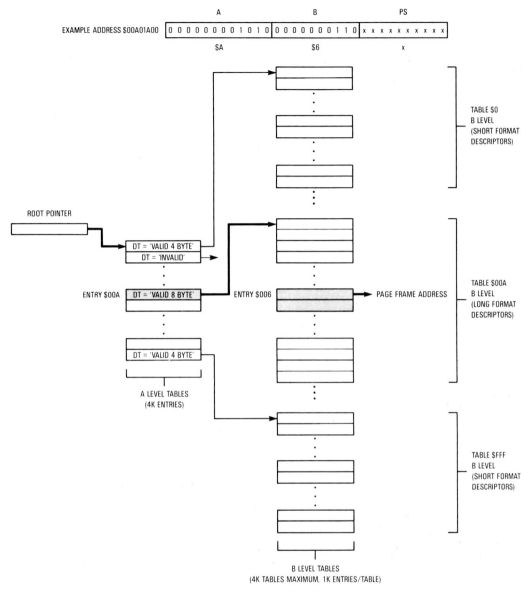

Figure 5-11. Example Translation Tree Using Different Format Descriptors

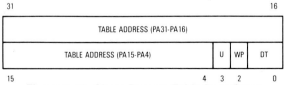

Figure 5-12. Short Format Table Descriptor

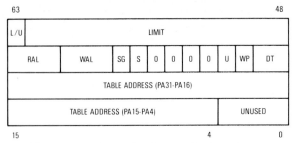

Figure 5-13. Long Format Table Descriptor

table search was not terminated early due to encountering a 'page descriptor' DT field in a pointer table). The formats of this type of descriptor are shown in Figures 5-14 and 5-15.

Note that the only difference in the long format of the type-1 and type-2 page descriptors is the presence of the LIMIT field and L/U bit in the long format of the type-2 descriptor. The type-1 and type-2 short format descriptors are identical.

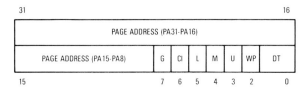

Figure 5-14. Type-1 and Type-2 Short Format Page Descriptors

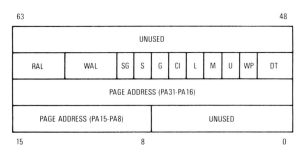

Figure 5-15. Type-1 Long Format Page Descriptor

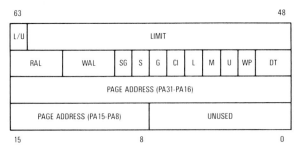

Figure 5-16. Type-2 Long Format Page Descriptor

5.1.5.2.3 Indirect Descriptors. This descriptor type is found in the page tables and is used to identify a page descriptor in another page table to be used to perform the logical-to-physical mapping. The formats of this type of descriptor are shown in Figures 5-17 and 5-18.

Figure 5-17. Short Format Indirect Descriptor

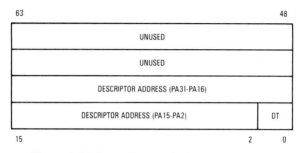

Figure 5-18. Long Format Indirect Descriptor

5.1.5.2.4 Invalid Descriptors. This descriptor type may be found at any level of the translation tree except at the root. The formats of this type of descriptor are shown in Figures 5-19 and 5-20.

Figure 5-19. Short Format Invalid Descriptor

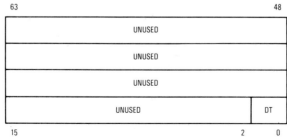

Figure 5-20. Long Format Invalid Descriptor

5.1.5.3 DESCRIPTOR FIELD DEFINITIONS. The following defines the fields that are found in the various types of table and page descriptors discussed in **5.1.5.2 DESCRIPTOR TYPES**. Not all of these fields are found in all descriptor formats and some fields are mutually exclusive of others.

5.1.5.3.1 Lower/Upper (L/U). The L/U bit (bit [63] of a long format table or type-2 page descriptor) specifies whether the value contained in the limit field (see below) is to be used as the upper or lower limit of indices into the translation table at the next level of the table search. If L/U equals zero, the limit field contains the unsigned upper limit of the index and all table indices for the next level must be less than or equal to the value contained in the limit field or a limit violation will occur. If L/U equals one, the limit field contains the unsigned lower limit of the index and all table indices for the next level must be greater than or equal to the value contained in the limit field; otherwise, a limit violation will occur.

5.1.5.3.2 Limit. The limit field (bits [62-48] of a long format table or type-2 page descriptor) specifies a maximum or minimum value for the table index to be used at the next level of the table search and is used to limit the size of the translation tables. The limit field may contain any value between 0 and 2^{15} (inclusive) in powers of two.

The limit function can be effectively suppressed by either setting L/U to zero and setting the limit field to all ones ($7FFF) or by setting L/U to one and clearing the limit field ($8000).

5.1.5.3.3 Read Access Level (RAL). The RAL field (bits [47-45] of a long format table or page descriptor) indicates the maximum value (minimum privilege) that the access level field of the logical address can contain to allow a translation for a read or write operation using this descriptor (refer to **7.2 ACCESS LEVEL PROTECTION**).

5.1.5.3.4 Write Access Level (WAL). The WAL field (bits [44-42] of a long format table or page descriptor) indicates the maximum value (minimum privilege) that the access level field of the logical address can contain to allow a translation for a write operation using this descriptor (refer to **7.2 ACCESS LEVEL PROTECTION**).

5.1.5.3.5 Shared Globally (SG). The SG bit (bit [41] of a long format table or page descriptor) indicates that the portion of the logical address space mapped by the descriptor is shared globally by all tasks within the system. Setting the SG bit informs the MC68851 that the logical-to-physical mappings identified by this descriptor are identical for all tasks and that only a single descriptor for the translation needs to be maintained in the ATC (as opposed to one descriptor for each task that uses that mapping).

Clearing the SG bit informs the MC68851 that the logical-to-physical mapping identified by the descriptor is unique for a particular task.

5.1.5.3.6 Supervisor (S). The S bit (bit [40] of long format table and page descriptors) is used to specify that a task must be operating in the supervisor mode in order to access the portion of the logical address space mapped by the descriptor. If this bit is set, accesses using this descriptor are restricted to supervisor-only. If this bit is clear, accesses using this descriptor are not restricted to supervisor-only unless the access is restricted at some other level of the translation tree.

5.1.5.3.7 Gate (G). The G bit (bit [39] of long format page descriptors, bit [7] of short format page descriptors) is used to indicate whether or not the corresponding page is allowed to contain module descriptors (gates) for the MC68020 CALLM instruction. If this bit is set, the page is allowed to contain gates. If this bit is clear, the page is not allowed to contain gates (refer to **7.2 ACCESS LEVEL PROTECTION**).

5.1.5.3.8 Cache Inhibit (C). The CI bit (bit [38] of long format page descriptors, bit [6] of short format page descriptors) is used to indicate whether or not the data contained in the corresponding page is cacheable by local caches. When CI is set, the MC68851 asserts the $\overline{\text{CLI}}$ output during accesses to this page signaling to local caches that the data of the current bus cycle should not be placed in the cache. If CI is clear, the MC68851 does not assert the $\overline{\text{CLI}}$ output during accesses that reference this descriptor.

5.1.5.3.9 Lock (L). The L bit (bit [37] of long format page descriptors, bit [5] of short format page descriptors) is used to inform the MC68851 that the corresponding page descriptor should be made exempt from the actions of the ATC replacement algorithm. When set, L indicates that ATC entries formed with this descriptor should be unavailable for replacement. When clear, L indicates that ATC entries formed with this descriptor are available for replacement.

Although the action of the L bit is to make the entries exempt from the actions of the ATC replacement algorithm, ATC entries with a set L bit may be removed as part of a task whose root pointer table entry is being replaced. To avoid this removal for supervisor and DMA ATC entries that are not task-specific, the SG bit should also be set (refer to **5.3 ROOT POINTER TABLE**). Additionally, the L bit will be ignored if the ATC already contains 63 locked entries (refer to **5.2.1.2 DATA SECTION**).

5.1.5.3.10 Modified (M). The M bit (bit [36] of long format page descriptors, bit [4] of short format page descriptors) is used to indicate whether or not the corresponding page has been written to by a logical bus master. This bit is set by the MC68851 to indicate that the page corresponding to the descriptor has been written to; the MC68851 never changes this bit from a one to a zero. Refer to **5.1.5.3.11 Used** for information regarding how the M bit is set by the MC68851.

5.1.5.3.11 Used (U). The U bit (bit [35] of long format page or table descriptors, bit [3] of short format page or table descriptors) is used to indicate whether or not the corresponding descriptor has been used. In a page descriptor table, this bit is set by the MC68851 to indicate that the page corresponding to the descriptor has been accessed. In a pointer table, this bit is set to indicate that the pointer has been fetched by the MC68851 as part of a table search. Note that a pointer may be fetched, and its U bit set, for an address to which access is denied at another level of the tree.

Updates of the U and M bits are performed before the MC68851 allows a page to be accessed or written. The MC68851 optimizes its activity by examining the U and M bits in descriptors as they are fetched, and only performing write cycles to modify these bits are required. For a pointer descriptor, a write cycle to set the U bit occurs only if the U bit was clear. For page descriptors, the update is done as described below:

Action by MC68851	Previous U	Previous M	R/$\overline{\text{W}}$	New U'	New M'
RMW Cycle to Set U (M Not Changed)	0	0	R	1	X
Write to Set U and M	0	0	$\overline{\text{W}}$	1	1
Write to Set U	0	1	R	1	1
Write to Set U	0	1	$\overline{\text{W}}$	1	1
No Write	1	0	R	1	0
Write to Set M (U Written Set)	1	0	$\overline{\text{W}}$	1	1
No Write	1	1	R	1	1
No Write	1	1	$\overline{\text{W}}$	1	1

A bus cycle executed by a logical bus master is considered to be a write for updating purposes if either R/$\overline{W}$ or $\overline{RMC}$ is low.

5.1.5.3.12 Write Protect (WP). The WP bit (bit [34] of long format page or table descriptors, bit [2] of short format page or table descriptors) is used to write-protect a range of the logical address space. When WP is set, the MC68851 does not allow the portion of the logical address space mapped by that descriptor to be written by any logical bus master operating at any privilege level (i.e., this protection is absolute). If the WP bit is clear, the MC68851 allows write accesses using this descriptor unless access is restricted at some other level of the translation tree.

Conditional write-protection can be designed by using the WAL (refer to **7.2 ACCESS LEVEL PROTECTION**).

5.1.5.3.13 Descriptor Type (DT). The DT field (bits [33-32] of all long format descriptors, bits [1-0] of all short format descriptors) specifies the type of descriptor contained in either the descriptor itself or in the next level of the translation tree, depending on the value in the field and the state of the table search. The values are defined as follows:

$0 INVALID
Regardless of the state of the table search, the current descriptor is invalid and all other bits are unused. When a descriptor of this type is encountered, the table search terminates and an ATC entry for the logical address is made with the BERR bit set.

$1 PAGE DESCRIPTOR
This value is used to terminate the table search with a valid translation. It indicates either a type 1 or type 2 page descriptor, depending on the state of the table search (refer to **5.1.5.2 DESCRIPTOR TYPES**).

$2 VALID 4 BYTE
This value indicates that the translation table at the next level of the translation tree contains short format descriptors. The current descriptor is of the table, indirect, or invalid type depending on the state of the table search.

$3 VALID 8 BYTE
This value indicates that the translation table at the next level of the translation tree contains long format descriptors. The current descriptor is of the table, indirect, or invalid type depending on the state of the table search.

5.1.5.3.14 Table Address. This field (bits [31-4] of all table descriptors) contains the most significant 28 bits of the physical base address of a table of descriptors.

5.1.5.3.15 Page Address. This field (bits [31-8] of all page descriptors) contains the most significant 24 bits of the physical address of a page of memory. If the page size is greater than 256 bytes, then the least significant bits of this field are unused by the hardware. Specifically, [LOG_2 (page size)]–8 bits are not used by the MC68851 and may be used by system software.

5.1.5.3.16 Indirect Address. This field (bits [31-2] of all indirect descriptors) contains the most significant 30 bits of the physical address of an individual page descriptor.

5.1.5.3.17 Unused. All fields marked 'unused' do not affect the operation of the MC68851 and are guaranteed not to be modified by the MC68851. They may be used by software for system-specific functions.

5.1.6 Protections

Some information may be stored in multiple levels of a translation tree. In general, the effective protection assigned to a page is the most strict of those indicated at any level. The supervisor-only, write-protect, and shared attributes may be specified at any level of the translation tree when using long format descriptors. An attribute will be conferred if the corresponding bit is set at any level. The effective RAL of a page will be the minimum (most privileged) of all RAL fields encountered. The effective WAL of a page will be the minimum (most privileged) of all WAL fields encountered, with the exception that if a WP bit is set for the page at any level, the page will not be writable for any access level. If there are no long format descriptors in the path through the translation tree that is used to translate an address, then the shared attribute is as indicated in the root pointer used, the page is not restricted to supervisor-only, and the effective RAL and WAL are both $7 (least privileged).

5.2 ADDRESS TRANSLATION CACHE

The address translation cache (ATC) of the MC68851 provides a mechanism for translating recently used logical addresses without the table search overhead. It consists of a fully-associative or content addressable memory (CAM) in which information about recently used logical addresses (tags) is stored, a RAM for storing the physical address (data) corresponding to the logical addresses in the CAM, and circuitry implementing the cache replacement algorithm. There are 64 entries in the CAM array and 64 corresponding entries in the RAM array.

5.2.1 Internal Organization

The information contained in the ATC is not directly accessible to the programmer. The following paragraphs provide an overview of the internal cache organization.

5.2.1.1 TAG SECTION. The tag, or CAM, section of the ATC contains logical addresses and control information for use inside the ATC. A diagram of an entry in the tag section of the cache is shown in Figure 5-21. The FC and logical address fields are compared with the values on the similarly named pins during bus cycles run by the logical bus master and the lower order bits of the logical address field are ignored during compare operations if the page size is larger than 256 bytes. The TA and SG fields are managed internally by the MC68851 to allow ATC entries for more than one task to be resident simultaneously. For a CAM entry to match a logical address presented by a logical bus master, both the logical address field (exclusive of low order bits representing the page offset) and the FC field must match exactly. In addition, the task alias (TA) field must match the current TA value of the MC68851 (refer to **5.3 ROOT POINTER TABLE**), or the entry's SG bit must be set in order for a match to occur.

Figure 5-21. ATC Tag Entry

5.2.1.2 DATA SECTION. The data, or RAM, section of the ATC contains the physical addresses and control information corresponding to the logical addresses stored in the tag section. A diagram of an entry in the data section is shown in Figure 5-22.

Figure 5-22. ATC Data Entry

The physical address field contains the physical page frame address corresponding to the logical address in the respective tag entry. The lower order bits of this field are unused if the page size is larger than 256 bytes. The data in this field of the logical address is not interpreted by the MC68851 but is presented on the physical address outputs during an address translation.

The G, L, and CI bits are copies of the similarly named bits extracted from the page descriptor in the translation table when the ATC entry is formed. The internal L bit exempts the entry from replacement using the ATC replacement algorithm. However, it will not be a copy of the page descriptor L bit if there are already 63 entries with set L bits in the ATC. In this case, the L bit for new entries will always be clear (indicating that the entry can be replaced). The inverse of the CI bit is presented on the $\overline{\text{CLI}}$ output during address translations. The WP bit is the effective write protection determined during the translation table search. The M bit is a copy of the M bit in the page descriptor in the translation table when the ATC entry is loaded. If it is clear and a write is attempted and permitted through the ATC entry, both the internal M bit and the M bit in the page descriptor will be set by the MC68851.

The B bit, when set, indicates that no translation should be performed using this ATC entry and that a bus error will be signaled to the logical bus master when a logical address matches the corresponding entry in the tag array. Primarily, this bit indicates that no translation is available for the logical address. This may be because an invalid descriptor or bus error was encountered during the table search. The B bit is also used to implement supervisor-only protection and access level protection with the RAL translation descriptor field. In these cases a task may generate the address of a restricted memory page, and instead of maintaining the RAL field and S bit in the ATC, the validity of the access is evaluated when the ATC entry is made. If access is to be denied, an ATC entry is made with the B bit set.

5.2.1.3 REPLACEMENT ALGORITHM. The MC68851 contains circuitry to automatically determined which tag/data pair to use for a new ATC entry. The algorithm is as follows: locate an invalid entry and use it. If no invalid entries are found, use a psuedo least-recently-used (LRU) algorithm to select an entry without its L bit set and replace that entry.

To implement this replacement algorithm, the ATC contains two additional bits for each entry. One is a valid bit to indicate that an entry contains a valid translation. The other is a history bit to indicate that the entry has been recently used.

During an ATC replacement operation when the ATC is full (all entries valid), the LRU algorithm attempts to locate the entry that was last used longest ago and, as such, allows the ATC to maintain a very close approximation to a proper working set of page descriptors. Although cache hit rates are very dependent on the nature of CPU activities, performance of the MC68851 ATC with psuedo-LRU replacement algorithm can be expected in the range of 95% to 99%.

5.2.2 ATC Operation

The following paragraphs describe the ATC operation.

5.2.2.1 ADDRESS TRANSLATION BY THE ATC. When the MC68851 is enabled and is not itself bus master, it performs an ongoing comparison between the address currently on the logical bus and in the ATC tag section. When $\overline{\text{LAS}}$ is asserted, the ATC allows time for the circuitry to settle and determines if any of its tag entries indicate a match. There are several actions that the ATC may take, depending on the number of entries in the tag section that match, the contents of a matching entry, and the state of the physical bus.

If the bus cycle addresses the MC68851 on-chip registers, the MC68851 peforms the action required by the bus cycle. If the bus cycle accesses an address in the CPU space (function code = $7) and is not an access to an MC68851 register, then the logical address is placed on the physical address outputs and the $\overline{CLI}$ signal is asserted with the same functional timing as $\overline{PAS}$ would have if an ATC hit had occurred.

If the cycle is not a CPU space access, there are no ATC entries that match, and the logical master does not have the $\overline{RMC}$ signal asserted, then $\overline{BERR}$, $\overline{HALT}$, and $\overline{LBRO}$ signals are asserted and the MC68851 initiates a translation table search to load an ATC entry. If the cycle does have $\overline{RMC}$ asserted, only $\overline{BERR}$ is asserted. The signals are asserted by the MC68851 after the time specified by the decision timeout (refer to **4.1.2.3 DECISION TIMEOUT DELAY**).

If one ATC entry matches, and the MC68851 owns the physical bus, the MC68851 gates the PA and CI fields of the data section to the appropriate pins, and the B, W, M, and G bits to access checking circuitry. Then the time specified by the decision timeout is allowed to elapse (refer to **4.1.2.3 DECISION TIMEOUT DELAY**). If the access is to be denied, $\overline{BERR}$ is asserted. If the access is to be granted, $\overline{PAS}$ is asserted. If the MC68851 does not own the physical bus, the MC68851 does not drive $\overline{PAS}$, but continues checking protections and will assert $\overline{CLI}$ or $\overline{BERR}$ as appropriate. This allows the use of a logical data cache with protection checking in parallel with other activity on the physical bus. The MC68851 will not assert the $\overline{PAS}$ signal until it regains control of the physical bus (provided that the logical bus master is still requesting the translation).

If more than one ATC entry matches, then all of the matching entries are flushed and the condition is treated as a cache miss. This condition may occur through improper use of the SG translation descriptor attribute (i.e., not having the SG bit set in all translation trees mapping a logical address that is marked as shared in another tree).

5.2.2.2 TRANSLATION MODES. The MC68851 can perform address translations in one of two modes: synchronous or asynchronous. The translation mode is selected on a bus cycle-by-bus cycle basis by the state of the $\overline{ASYNC}$ pin.

In the synchronous mode, the logical bus master must present bus cycles with the same timing as an MC68020 would if running with the same clock as the MC68851. The relationships between the clock, address timing, and $\overline{LAS}$ assertion are known for the MC68020. This allows elimination of synchronization delays in the address translation. The earliest that $\overline{PAS}$ can be asserted in synchronous mode is one clock period from the clock edge from which the logical bus master initiates the assertion of $\overline{LAS}$.

In asynchronous mode, no assumptions are made about the relationships of signals to the clock. All decisions are delayed until after the internally synchronized version of $\overline{LAS}$ is asserted. The earliest that $\overline{PAS}$ can be asserted in asynchronous mode is one and one-half clock periods after the clock edge on which $\overline{LAS}$ is asserted at the MC68851 input pin.

5.3 ROOT POINTER TABLE

In order to improve ATC utilization, the MC68851 internally maintains eight recently-used values of the CRP register in the root pointer table (RPT). These values are associated with eight recently active tasks. The MC68851 assigns each of these tasks a task alias for tagging ATC entries. The mapping of tasks to task alias values, and re-assignment of task alias values, is performed by the MC68851 hardware with no software intervention. When an entry is made in the ATC, the RPT index (a three bit value) corresponding to the current CRP value is stored in the TA field of the ATC entry. The TA field is then treated as part of the logical address to determine if a match has occurred in the ATC.

5.3.1 Loading the RPT

The RPT is checked whenever ther CRP register is loaded by a PMOVE or PRESTORE instruction. If the new CRP value is found in the RPT, the index of the matching entry becomes the current task alias. This value is then displayed in the TA field of the PCSR register, and the F bit of the PCSR register is cleared. The current task alias is then used as part of the logical address for succeeding bus cycles until the CRP is loaded with a new value.

If the new CRP value matches the address field and L/U bit of a value in the RPT, but does not match the limit and DT fields, the RTP entry is overwritten with the new value and the RPT index becomes the new current task alias. All ATC entries that match the new current task alias are invalidated, the current task alias is displayed in the TA field of the PCSR register, and the F bit of the PCSR register is set.

If no RPT entries matching the new CRP value are found, an entry from the RPT is selected from the RPT using the same replacement algorithm as the ATC (psuedo-LRU). If there is an invalid entry in the RPT, it is selected and its index becomes the current task alias. The new CRP value is loaded, the current task alias is displayed in the TA field of the PCSR register, and the F bit of the PCSR register is set. If a valid entry must be selected, the RPT entry is overwritten with the new value and the RPT index becomes the new current task alias. All ATC entries that match the new current task alias are invalidated, the current task alias is displayed in the TA field of the PCSR register, and the F bit of the PCSR register is set.

5.3.2 Flushing the RPT

Entries are normally flushed from the RPT by the replacement algorithm without explicit action by system software. When a task is destroyed, software should ensure that all ATC entries for it have been invalidated by executing the PFLUSHR instruction giving the CRP value of the destroyed task as the operand. This also invalidates the corresponding RPT entry thus improving utilization of the RPT.

5.4 DETAIL OF TABLE SEARCH OPERATIONS

Figures 5-23 through 5-27 provide a detailed description of the MC68851 table search operations in the form of several flowcharts. These flowcharts document the logical flow of control for table search operations and are not intended to convey any timing-related information. Refer to **SECTION 11 OPERATIONS TIMING** for timing information for table search operations.

The master flowchart for table searches is shown in Figure 5-23 and the detailed description of various sub-functions of the table search are provided in the subsequent diagrams. The initialization for a table search, creation of an ATC entry, limit check procedure, and descriptor fetch detail are shown in Figures 5-24, 5-25, 5-26, and 5-27 respectively.

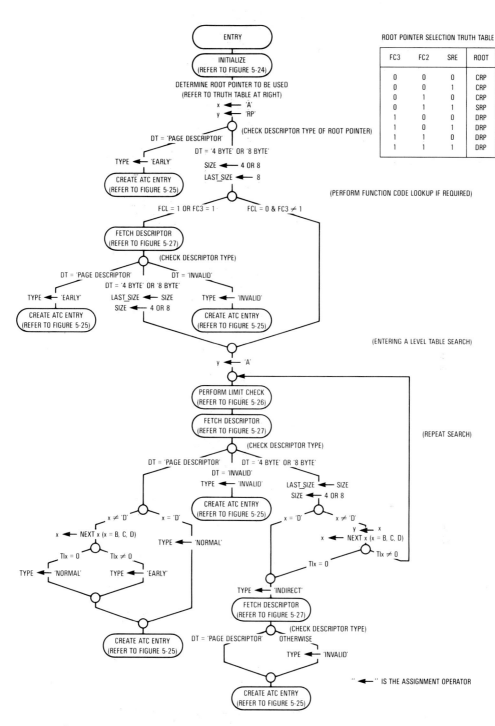

Figure 5-23. Detailed Flowchart of MC68851 Table Search Operation

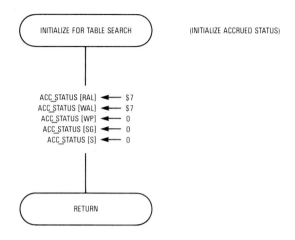

Figure 5-24. Table Search Initialization Detail

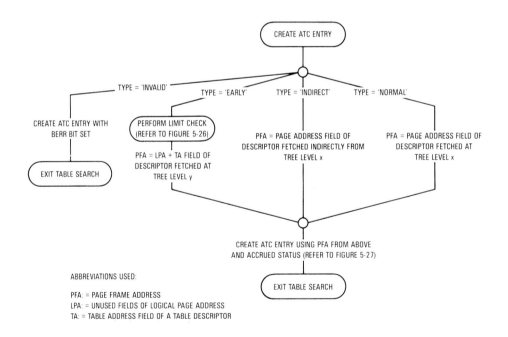

Figure 5-25. Detail of ATC Entry Creation During Table Search

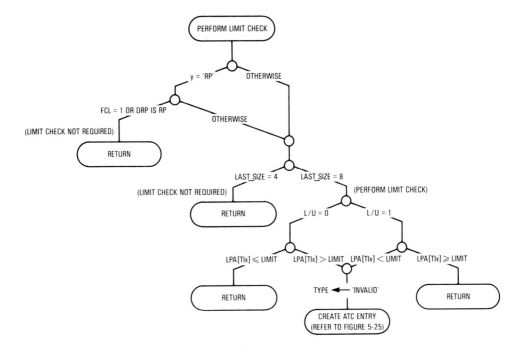

Figure 5-26. Detail of Limit Check Procedure

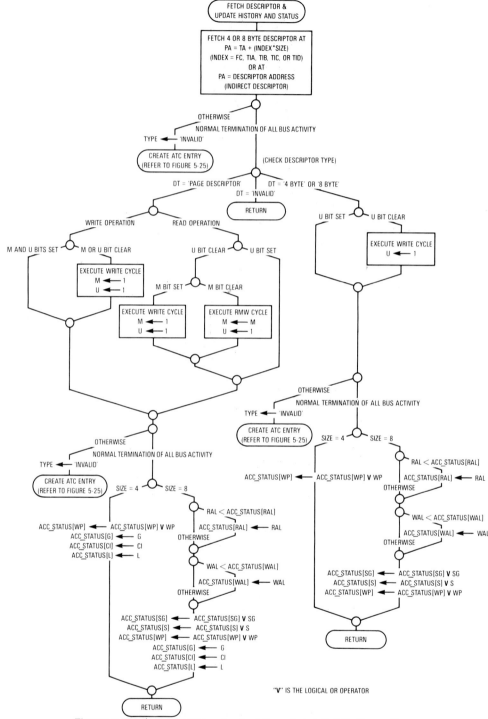

Figure 5-27. Detailed Flowchart of Descriptor Fetch Operation

SECTION 6
INSTRUCTION SET PROCESSOR

This section describes the instruction set processor for the MC68851.

6.1 REGISTERS

The MC68851 contains programmer-visible registers as shown in Figure 1-1. There are ten registers that control the translation and protection functions of the MC68851. They are: the CPU root pointer register (CRP), the supervisor root pointer register (SRP), the DMA root pointer register (DRP), the PMMU cache status register (PCSR), the translation control register (TC), the access control register (AC), the current access level register (CAL), the validate access level register (VAL), the stack change control register (SCC), and the PMMU status register (PSR). The other registers control the breakpoint functions. They are: the breakpoint acknowledge data registers (BAD0–BAD7) and the breakpoint acknowledge control registers (BAC0–BAC7).

All MC68851 registers are directly accessible only to programs operating in the supervisor state, although certain user mode instructions can access some registers in a limited fashion. The MC68020 instructions CALLM and RTM can read and alter CAL and VAL under control of the MC68851 access level protection mechanism. The PVALID instruction reads the contents of the VAL register to determine if a trap should be taken (refer to **SECTION 7 PROTECTION**).

6.1.1 Root Pointer Registers

The three MC68851 root pointer registers, CRP, SRP, and DRP contain the physical address of the root of the translation tree for user, supervisor, and DMA accesses, respectively. The format of these registers is shown in Figure 6-1.

The CPU root pointer (CRP) contains the pointer to the root of the translation tree for the current user mode task of the CPU. Before the operating system dispatches a new user task for execution,

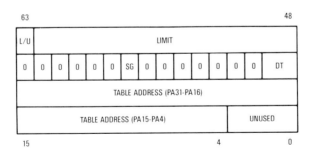

Figure 6-1. Root Pointer Register (CRP, SRP, DRP) Format

it reloads the CRP to point at the root of the translation tree for that task. The CRP register works in conjunction with the root pointer table (RPT) and writing to the CRP may cause ATC entries to be invalidated and the PCSR register to be updated (refer to **5.3 ROOT POINTER TABLE**).

If the SRE bit of the translation control register is set, the supervisor root pointer (SRP) register points to the root of the translation table to be used for translating supervisor accesses. Writing to this register causes all ATC entries marked as supervisor to be flushed (this includes globally shared entries). If the SRE bit of the translation control register is clear, this register is unused and the CRP is used to translate supervisor accesses.

The DMA root pointer (DRP) register points to the root of the translation table to be used when FC3 = 1. Entries in the ATC loaded when an alternate bus master begins translation will be tagged as such. Writing to this register causes all ATC entries marked as 'DMA' to be flushed (this includes globally shared entries).

6.1.1.1 LOWER/UPPER (L/U) The L/U (bit [63]) specifies whether the value contained in the limit field (see below) is to be used as the upper or lower limit of indices into the next level of the translation tree. If L/U equals zero, the limit field contains the unsigned upper limit of indices and all table indices must be less than or equal to the value contained in the limit field or a limit violation will occur (refer to **6.3.1.2 LIMIT FIELD EXCEEDED**). If L/U equals one, the limit field contains the unsigned lower limit of indices and all table indices must be greater than or equal to the value contained in the limit field; otherwise a limit violation will occur.

6.1.1.2 LIMIT. The limit field (bits [62-48]) specifies a maximum or minimum value for the index to be used at the next level of the table search with the exception of the function code lookup and is used to limit the size of the next level of the translation tree. The limit field may limit the size of the next level of the translation tree to any value between 0 and 2^{15} (inclusive) in powers of two.

The limit function can be effectively suppressed by either setting L/U to zero and setting the limit field to all ones ($7FFF) or by setting L/U to one and clearing the limit field ($8000).

If function code lookup is enabled (refer to **6.1.3 Translation Control**), the limit field and the L/U bit of a root pointer are ignored.

6.1.1.3 SHARED GLOBALLY (SG). The SG bit (bit [41]) indicates that the logical address space mapped by the root pointer is shared globally by all tasks within the system. Setting the SG bit to 'one' informs the MC68851 that the logical-to-physical mappings identified by this root pointer are identical for all tasks and that only a single descriptor for the translation needs to be maintained in the ATC (as opposed to one descriptor for each task that uses that mapping). Setting the SG bit to zero informs the MC68851 that the logical-to-physical mapping identified by the root pointer is unique for a particular task (user, supervisor, or DMA).

The shared globally attribute can significantly effect the performance of the MC68851 ATC. The MC68851 task aliasing mechanism (refer to **5.3 ROOT POINTER TABLE**) assigns a task alias to *all* entries that are created in the ATC; this includes all supervisor and DMA entries. The value assigned to an entry is the current value of the internal task alias maintained by the MC68851. In order for a logical address to match an entry in the ATC, the logical page address, function code, and task alias fields must match exactly. Without use of the shared globally attribute, this would mean that all supervisor and DMA entries in the ATC that are used during the execution of multiple user tasks would require individual ATC entries be created, one corresponding to each user task during which the entry is used. The SG attribute allows the task alias compare to be suppressed during address translation and thus allows that only a single ATC entry be created regardless of the number of tasks in which the entry is used.

It is recommended that the SG bit be set in the DMA root pointer and, either in the supervisor root pointer, if enabled, or in one of the highest levels of the translation tree if supervisor accesses are translated using the CPU root pointer.

6.1.1.4 DESCRIPTOR TYPE (DT). The DT field (bits [33–32]) specifies the type of descriptor contained in either the root pointer or in the first level of the translation table identified by that root pointer. The values are defined as follows:

$0   INVALID
       Indicates that the value contained in the table address field does not point to a valid translation table. The MC68851 does not allow the operating system to load a root pointer with an 'invalid' descriptor type with the PMOVE instruction. An 'invalid' descriptor may be loaded by the PRESTORE instruction; however, the operation of the MC68851 is undefined should this occur and care must be taken to avoid this.

$1   PAGE DESCRIPTOR
       Indicates that a translation table for this root pointer does not exist and that the MC68851 should internally create an ATC entry (page descriptor) for accesses using this root pointer. The page descriptor is formed by adding (unsigned) the value in the table address field to the incoming logical address. This operation yields a direct-mapping of the logical address space with a constant offset (the table address field) for all accesses that use this root pointer. If the DT field of a root pointer is set to $1, the MC68851 performs a limit check regardless of the state of the FCL bit.

$2   VALID 4-BYTE
       The value indicates that the translation table at the root of the translation tree contains short format descriptors and that the MC68851 must scale the table index for this level of the table search by four bytes.

$3   VALID 8-BYTE
       This value indicates that the translation table at the root of the translation tree contains long format descriptors and that the MC68851 must scale the table index for this level of the table search by eight bytes.

6.1.1.5 TABLE ADDRESS. The table address field (bits [31–4]) specifies the physical base address of the translation table for that particular root pointer. If the DT field is set to $1 (page descriptor), the value in the table address field provides a constant offset (may be zero) to the logical address when the MC68851 creates a page descriptor.

6.1.1.6 UNUSED. Bits [3–0] of the root pointer are not used by the MC68851 and may be used by the operating system for other purposes. All other unused bits of the root pointer registers must be zero.

6.1.2 PMMU Cache Status (PCSR)

The format of this 16-bit read-only register is shown in Figure 6-2. This register contains information about the MC68851 ATC to aid the operating system in maintaining a logical cache.

PCSR is updated whenever the CPU root pointer register is written by either the PMOVE or PRESTORE instructions. The contents of PCSR reflect the results of the root pointer table search (refer to **5.3 ROOT POINTER TABLE**) and it can be read with the PMOVE instruction. When written, all unused bits must be zero.

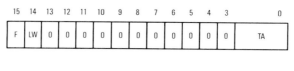

F — FLUSH
LW — LOCK WARNING
TA — TASK ALIAS

Figure 6-2. Cache Status Register (PCSR) Format

6.1.2.1 TASK ALIAS (TA). The TA field (bits [2–0]) contains the current internal task alias maintained by the MC68851 (refer to **5.3 ROOT POINTER TABLE**).

6.1.2.2 FLUSH (F). When the MC68851 flushes entries from the ATC as the result of a write to the CRP, bit [15] (F) of PCSR is set to indicate that entries with the task alias shown in the TA field have been flushed. Otherwise, this bit is cleared.

In a system incorporating a logical cache that maintains entries for multiple user tasks, the operating system should read PCSR after writing to the CRP and, if F is set, it should flush all entries in the logical cache corresponding to the TA encoding.

6.1.2.3 LOCK WARNING (LW). The lock warning flag (LW) is set when all entries in the ATC but one have been locked. When this bit is set, no additional entries will be locked into the ATC until others are removed, regardless of the state of L bits in translation descriptors. In systems that frequently lock descriptors into the ATC, it is recommended that this flag be checked periodically since severe performance degradation will result from having only a single entry in the ATC available for replacement.

6.1.3 Translation Control (TC)

This register contains control fields to configure the address translation mechanism of the MC68851. The format of this 32-bit register is shown in Figure 6-3. All unimplemented fields of this register are read as zeros and must always be written as zeros.

Manipulation of this register has side effects: writing a value with its enable bit clear to this register cause a flush of the entire ATC. When written with the E bit (bit 31) set (translation enabled), a consistency check is performed on the values of PS, IS, and TIx as follows. TheTIx

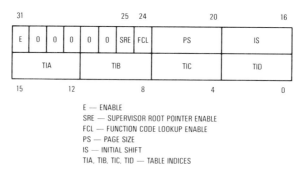

E — ENABLE
SRE — SUPERVISOR ROOT POINTER ENABLE
FCL — FUNCTION CODE LOOKUP ENABLE
PS — PAGE SIZE
IS — INITIAL SHIFT
TIA, TIB, TIC, TID — TABLE INDICES

Figure 6-3. Translation Control Register Format

fields are added together and this sum is added to PS and IS. The total must be 32, or an MMU configuration exception (refer to **6.3.2.3 CONFIGURATION ERROR**) is signaled to the processor through the coprocessor interface. If an exception is taken, the TC register is updated with the data except that the E bit is cleared.

6.1.3.1   ENABLE (E).   When set, the MC68851 translation mechanism is enabled and execution of the PLOAD, PTEST, and CALLM instructions is allowed. When clear, the MC68851 performs no translation operations, terminates all PTEST, PLOAD, and CALLM/RTM (type $1) instructions with an exception. Additionally, when the translation mechanism is disabled, logical addresses are routed directly from the logical address bus to the physical address bus, the physical address strobe ($\overline{\text{PAS}}$) is asserted for all non-CPU space cycles, and $\overline{\text{CLI}}$ is asserted for all CPU space cycles that do not access the MC68851.

This bit is cleared during reset and it may also be cleared by software. The E bit must be clear before it can be written set (i.e., the MC68851 must be disabled before the TC contents can be updated).

6.1.3.2   SUPERVISOR ROOT POINTER ENABLE (SRE).   When SRE is set, all supervisor accesses are translated using the translation tree identified by the supervisor root pointer. When SRE is clear, use of the supervisor root pointer is disabled, and the CPU root pointer is used for supervisor space translations.

6.1.3.3   FUNCTION CODE LOOKUP (FCL).   The function code lookup field determines whether or not the top level table in the translation tree should be indexed with the function code when using the CRP or SRP. When clear, function code lookup is disabled. If the function code lookup is suppressed, then the first lookup is made using the portion of the logical address specified by IS and TIA as the index. When set, function code lookup is enabled and the limit field of the root pointer used for translations is ignored.

A function code lookup is always performed when the MC68851 executes a table search using the DMA root pointer.

6.1.3.4   PAGE SIZE (PS).   The page size field indicates the current page size that the MC68851 is supporting. Its defined values are:

    $8 — 256 Bytes
    $9 — 512Bytes
    $A — 1K Bytes
    $B — 2K Bytes
    $C — 4K Bytes
    $D — 8K Bytes
    $E — 16K Bytes
    $F — 32K Bytes

Page size bit [3] must always be one. Writing values of zero to bit [3] of this field will cause an MMU configuration exception to be generated (refer to **6.3.2.3 CONFIGURATION ERROR**).

6.1.3.5   INITIAL SHIFT (IS).   This IS field determines how many upper logical address bits are ignored by the MC68851 during table search operations. The value of this field is an integer from 0 to 15 indicating the number of bits to discard from the logical address, starting with bit [31]. This allows the MC68851 to adapt to systems using logical addresses consisting of 17 to 32 bits.

Although the MC68851 ignores high-order logical address bits during table searches as determined by the IS encoding, all bits of the logical address are significant during address translation. Therefore, any unused bits should be tied to a constant voltage source (i.e., either V_{CC} or GND).

6.1.3.6 TABLE INDEX (TIA, TIB, TIC, AND TID). The table index fields specify the number of bits of the logical address to be used as an index into the translation tables at each level during a table search operation. Four fields are provided. The first lookup using logical address bits (which will be the second lookup if the function code lookup is enabled) uses TIA, the second TIB, . . ., etc.

The value of the field is an unsigned integer from 0 to 15 that represents the number of bits to be extracted from the logical address as an index. A zero value in a TIx field specifies that the lookup process is over when that field is encountered during a table search.

6.1.4 Current Access Level (CAL)

This register contains the encoded access level of the current user task. The register is eight bits wide, but only the upper three bits are implemented. Unimplemented bits always read as zeros and are ignored when written. This register is automatically loaded by the CALLM and RTM instructions of the MC68020 and can also be loaded with the PMOVE or PRESTORE instructions. The format of the CAL register is shown in Figure 6-4.

Figure 6-4. CAL and VAL Register Formats

When the access level protection mechanism is enabled, the value in CAL is compared against a field of the high-order logical address to ensure that a user task does not exceed the privilege assigned to it by the operating system. If a violation occurs, the MC68851 aborts the bus cycle in progress preventing the errant access. For a complete description of the use of this register refer to **SECTION 10 ACCESS LEVEL PROTECTION MECHANISM**.

6.1.5 Validate Access Level (VAL)

This register contains the access level of the caller of the current routine (called using the CALLM instruction). The register is eight bits wide, but only the upper three bits are implemented. Unimplemented bits always read as zeros and are ignored when written. This register is automatically loaded with the contents of the CAL register by the CALLM instruction of the MC68020 and can also be loaded with the PMOVE or PRESTORE instructions. The format of the VAL register is shown in Figure 6-4.

6.1.6 Stack Change Control (SCC)

SCC is an 8-bit register that determines if a stack change should occur during an MC68020 CALLM instruction. The format of the SCC register is shown in Figure 6-5. A one in a bit position indicates that a stack pointer change will occur on a module call operation to an equal or more privileged level.

This register is initialized by the operating system to dictate the requirements for stack changes during module call operations. The MC68851 examines this register during execution of the CALLM instruction to determine whether or not the CPU should be instructed to change stack pointers

Figure 6-5. Stack Change Control Register Format

before passing program execution control to the called module. If the current access level is n and the MC68020 requests a call to a module of privilege m where $m < n$ (greater privilege), the MC68851 will instruct the CPU to change stack pointers if any bit of SCC between n and m (inclusive) is set. For a complete description of the use of this register refer to **SECTION 10 ACCESS LEVEL PROTECTION MECHANISM**.

6.1.7 Access Control (AC)

This 16-bit register is used to configure the various access controls that the MC68851 supports. The register controls whether or not access levels are enabled, how many upper address bits contain access level information (up to a maximum of three), and also designates the size of a module descriptor and consequently the boundary on which a module descriptor is allowed to fall. The format of this register is shown in Figure 6-6.

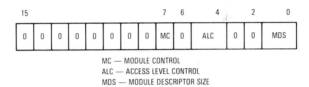

MC — MODULE CONTROL
ALC — ACCESS LEVEL CONTROL
MDS — MODULE DESCRIPTOR SIZE

Figure 6-6. Access Control Register Format

6.1.7.1 MODULE CONTROL (MC).
When MC is set, module operations are enabled and MC68020 module call/return instructions function as described in **7.2 ACCESS LEVEL PROTECTION**. If MC is clear, module operations are disabled, writes to the IAL and DAL access level control registers (ALCRs) do not change CAL, and all reads of the access status ALCR return the illegal code ($0) causing all MC68020 CALLM and RTM instructions to trap. In addition, the PVALID instruction will always cause an exception when MC is clear.

6.1.7.2 ACCESS LEVEL CONTROL (ALC).
This field determines the number of upper logical address bits used as access level information and whether access levels are enabled. The field is encoded as:
  $0 — No Address Bits Used: Access Level Checking is Disabled
  $1 — One Address Bit Used: Two Access Levels are Used
  $2 — Two Address Bits Used: Four Access Levels are Used
  $3 — Three Address Bits Used: Eight Access Levels are Used
This field is initialized to zero during reset.

6.1.7.3 MODULE DESCRIPTOR SIZE (MDS).
This field designates the boundaries on which a module descriptor is permitted to fall. The field is encoded as:
  $0 — All Module Descriptors are Invalid
  $1 — Valid Module Descriptors are Aligned to 16-Byte Boundaries
  $2 — Valid Module Descriptors are Aligned to 32-Byte Boundaries
  $3 — Valid Module Descriptors are Aligned to 64-Byte Boundaries

6.1.8 PMMU Status Register (PSR)

This 16-bit register contains status information for use by the operating system in determining the cause of system faults. The contents of PSR are affected only by the PTEST instruction. The format for this register is shown in Figure 6-7 and the fields are defined in the following paragraphs.

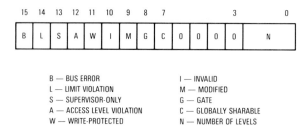

B — BUS ERROR
L — LIMIT VIOLATION
S — SUPERVISOR-ONLY
A — ACCESS LEVEL VIOLATION
W — WRITE-PROTECTED
I — INVALID
M — MODIFIED
G — GATE
C — GLOBALLY SHARABLE
N — NUMBER OF LEVELS

Figure 6-7. PMMU Status Register Format

6.1.8.1 BUS ERROR (B). For the PTEST instruction with a level specification of one through seven, this bit is set if a bus error is returned to the MC68851 from physical memory during the table search and is cleared otherwise. For the PTEST instruction with a level specification of zero, this bit is set if a matching descriptor is found in the ATC with its BERR bit set and is cleared otherwise.

6.1.8.2 LIMIT VIOLATION (L). For the PTEST instruction with a level specification of one through seven, this bit is set if a table index exceeded a limit field during a table search and is cleared otherwise. For the PTEST instruction with a level specification of zero, this bit is always clear.

6.1.8.3 SUPERVISOR VIOLATION (S). For the PTEST instruction with a level specification of one through seven, this bit is set if the tested address had a user function code and a set S bit of a long format descriptor was encountered and is cleared otherwise. For the PTEST instruction, with a level specification of zero, this bit is always clear.

6.1.8.4 ACCESS LEVEL VIOLATION (A). For the PTEST instruction with a level specification of one through seven, this bit is set if the address tested exceeded RAL for the PTESTR instruction, or exceeded WAL or RAL for the PTESTW instruction (refer to **SECTION 7 PROTECTION**) and is cleared otherwise. For the PTEST instruction with a level specification of zero, this bit is always clear.

6.1.8.5 WRITE PROTECTED (W). For any PTEST instruction, this bit is set if the address tested is not writeable. This may occur if any descriptor encountered in the search contained a set WP bit, or if the address tested exceeded the WAL field of any long descriptor encountered. It is cleared otherwise.

6.1.8.6 INVALID (I). For the PTEST instruction with a level specification of one through seven, this bit is set if the address has no translation in the table (i.e., an 'invalid' descriptor type, bus error, or limit violation was encounted during the table search). It is also set if the PTEST instruction requested a level zero search (search ATC only) and no corresponding entry was found in the ATC or an entry was found in the ATC but had its BERR bit set. The I bit is cleared for all other cases.

6.1.8.7 MODIFIED (M). For the PTEST instruction with a level specification of zero, this bit is set if the address is found in the ATC and it has the M bit set. For the PTEST instruction with a level specification of one through seven, this bit is set if a translation is located in the table and the M bit of the page descriptor is set. It is cleared otherwise.

6.1.8.8 GATE (G). For the PTEST instruction with a level specification of zero, this bit is set if an address is found in the ATC with its G bit set. For the PTEST instruction with a level specification of one through seven, this bit is set if a translation for the address is found in the table and the G bit of the page descriptor is set. It is cleared otherwise.

6.1.8.9 GLOBALLY SHARED (C). For any PTEST instruction, this bit is set if a translation for the address is found in the table and the SG bit in a long format descriptor is set. It is cleared otherwise.

6.1.8.10 LEVEL NUMBER (N). For the PTEST instruction with a level specification of one through seven, this bit is set to the number of tables used in the translation of an address. For the PTEST instruction with a level specification of zero, this field is always zero.

The bits of the PSR are ordered to allow use of the MC68020 'bit field find first one' (BFFO) instruction to determine the cause of a fault. An example sequence is:

```
PTESTR    ⟨fc⟩,⟨ea⟩,7           *TEST ADDRESS
PMOVE     PSR,D0                *GET PMMU STATUS RESULTS
BFFFO     D0{16:6},D1           *LOOK FOR SET BITS
BEQ       NOT__PMMU             *NO SET BITS = NOT PMMU (MAYBE)
JMP       ([TABLE,D1.W*4])      *JUMP TO APPROPRIATE CODE TABLE
DS.L      B_CODE
DS.L      L_CODE
DS.L      S_CODE
DS.L      A_CODE
DS.L      W_CODE
DS.L      I_CODE
```

The code fragment shows a move of the PSR register into a main processor register, followed by a 'bit field find first one' operation to determine the cause of the fault. If the bit field is entirely clear, then either the MC68851 did not cause the value, or the fault was caused by a descriptor miss for a TAS, CAS, or CAS2 instruction (refer to **6.3.1.7 RMC CYCLE**), or a user task attempted to exceed the current access level assigned to it. The 'BEQ' instruction branches to code to handle these cases. The JMP uses scaled, indexed memory indirect addressing implementing a case structure to go immediately to code to handle the fault. The different cases typically have these implications:

    B — Bad Pointer in Table or Main Memory Failure
    L — Addressing Error by Task or Request for Stack Extension
    S — Attempt by User to Access Supervisor-Only Information
    A — Attempt to Exceed Access Level
    W — Attempt to Write to Protected Memory
    I — Page Fault

6.1.9 Breakpoint Acknowledge Data (BAD0–BAD7)

There are eight BADx registers (BAD7–BAD0), each of which is 16 bits wide. These registers hold the opcodes that are provided to the CPU during a breakpoint acknowledge cycle. The format of this register is shown in Figure 6-8. For a complete description of the use of these registers refer to **SECTION 8 BREAKPOINTS**.

Figure 6-8. Breakpoint Acknowledge Data Register Format

6.1.10 Breakpoint Acknowledge Control (BAC0–BAC7)

There are eight BACx registers (BAC7–BAC0), each of which is 16 bits wide. They contain the enable and count functions for the instruction breakpoint acknowledge mechanism. The format of these registers is shown in Figure 6-9. For a complete description of the use of these registers refer to **SECTION 8 BREAKPOINTS**.

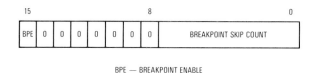

BPE — BREAKPOINT ENABLE

Figure 6-9. Breakpoint Acknowledge Control Register

6.1.10.1 BREAKPOINT ENABLE (BPE).
When set, this bit enables the breakpoint instruction corresponding to this register.

6.1.10.2 SKIP COUNT.
This field contains an unsigned integer that specifies how many times the data from the corresponding BADx register should be returned to the CPU before signaling a bus error. When this field is zero and a breakpoint instruction corresponding to this register is executed, the MC68851 terminates the breakpoint acknowledge cycle by asserting bus error.

6.2 INSTRUCTIONS

The MC68851 implements instruction extensions to M68000 Family processors using the M68000 Family coprocessor interface. These instructions provide control functions for loading and storing of MC68851 registers, testing access rights and conditionals based on the results of the tests, and setting the MC68851 control functions.

The functions provided by these instructions are described briefly below. For detailed descriptions, refer to **APPENDIX A INSTRUCTION SET DETAILS**. For a description of the M68000 Family coprocessor interface, refer to **SECTION 9 COPROCESSOR INTERFACE**.

All MC68851 instructions are privileged except PVALID. An attempt to execute any other MC68851 instruction while the CPU is in user state will cause a privilege exception.

The MC68851 participates in the execution of the CALLM and RTM instructions of the MC68020. These instructions use the CAL, access status, IAL, DAL, and descriptor address access level control registers. The MC68851 also provides a breakpoint acknowledge function in support of the MC68020 breakpoint instructions.

6.2.1 Data Movement (PMOVE)

The PMOVE instruction is provided to move data to or from MC68851 registers using the addressing modes available on the CPU. The operation can be byte, word, long word, or double long word, depending on the size of the MC68851 register involved. Data movement into the MC68851 may cause side effects, depending on the register moved.

6.2.2 Parameter Validation (PVALID)

The PVALID instruction examines the access level bits of its operand and executes an unsigned compare against the access level bits of the VAL register or to a surrogate level provided by the instruction. If the operand bits are arithmetically less than the VAL (or surrogate VAL) bits, this instruction causes a trap with the access level violation exception.

The purpose of this instruction is to prevent a routine from passing parameters to a module that the calling routine does not have access to but to which the called does (i.e., a module can be prevented from requesting that a higher-privilege module operate on data to which the lower-privileged module does not have access).

This instruction is intended for use in systems that use the access level protection mechanism. It allows a routine to verify that a pointer passed to it can be legally used by its caller. The addressing mode specification is the same as a data movement instruction would use. For example, if a routine is passed parameters on the stack, the following sequence may be used to verify that the calling routine has sufficient privilege to use these parameters itself:

```
PVALID   ([A7,offset])         *VALIDATE ADDRESS
MOVE     ([A7,offset]),D0      *USE ADDRESS
```

If the data will be frequently used, loading the data into a register may be more efficient:

```
LEA      ([A7,offset]),A0      *CALCULATE ADDRESS
PVALID   (A0)                  *VALIDATE ADDRESS
MOVE     (A0),D0               *USE ADDRESS
```

6.2.3 Address Attribute Testing (PTEST)

The PTEST instruction takes an address and function code and searches the ATC and/or translation tables for an entry that translates this address. The results of the search are available in the PSR. Optionally, the physical address of the last descriptor fetched may be returned.

This instruction is primarily used in bus error handling routines. For example, if a bus error has occurred, then the handler can execute an instruction such as:
```
PTESTW   #1, ([A7,offset]), #7, A0
```
This instruction requests that the MC68851 search the translation tables for an address in user data space (#1) and to examine protection information as if a write cycle were occurring. This particular address is stored at *offset* from the current stack pointer ([A7,offset]). The MC68851 is instructed to search to the bottom of the table (#7 — there cannot be more than six levels) and return the physical address of the last table entry used in register A0. After executing this instruction, the handler can examine PSR for the source of the fault, and use A0 to access the last descriptor.

6.2.4 Cache Pre-Loading (PLOAD)

The PLOAD instruction takes an address and function code, searches the translation table, and loads the ATC with an entry to translate the address. Any existing entry in the ATC that will translate the specified address is removed. The pre-load can be executed for either read or write attributes. If the write attribute is selected (PLOADW), the MC68851 performs the table search and updates all history information in the translation tables (used and modified bits) as if a write operation to that address had occurred. Similarly, if the read attribute is selected (PLOADR), the history information in the translation table (used bit) is updated as if a read operation had occurred.

6.2.5 Cache Flushing

The following paragraphs describe cache flushing.

6.2.5.1 PFLUSH/PFLUSHS. The PFLUSH instruction allows ATC entries to be invalidated in several ways: by effective address, by function code, or by both effective address and function code. Only entries that are associated with the current task alias and that are not globally shared may be flushed with the PFLUSH instruction. Entries that are globally shared can be flushed from the ATC with the PFLUSHS instruction.

6.2.5.2 PFLUSHR. The PFLUSHR instruction invalidates an entry in the root pointer table. The operand is compared against the values in the root pointer table. If a match is found, that entry in the RPT and all ATC entries associated with the matching RPT entry (i.e., that task alias) are invalidated. If no entry is found in the RPT that matches the operand for this instruction, neither the RPT nor the ATC are flushed.

6.2.5.3 PFLUSHA. The PFLUSHA instruction unconditionally invalidates all ATC entries.

6.2.6 Conditionals

The M68000 Family coprocessor interface provides several conditional instructions that are used to test for the following bits in the PSR: B, L, S, A, W, I, G, and C (refer to **6.1.8 PMMU STATUS REGISTER (PSR)**). The negation of these conditions may also be tested.

6.2.6.1 BRANCH CONDITIONALLY (PBcc). This instruction tests a condition based on one of the bits listed above and branches if the condition is true.

6.2.6.2 DECREMENT AND BRANCH (PDBcc). This instruction is a looping primitive identical to the DBcc instruction of the M68000 Family.

6.2.6.3 SET CONDITIONALLY (PScc). This instruction tests a condition and sets the byte specified by the effective address to all ones if the condition is true.

6.2.6.4 TRAP CONDITIONALLY (PTRAPcc). This instruction tests a condition and causes an exception if the condition is true.

6.2.7 State Save and Restore

The following paragraphs describe the state save and restore instructions.

6.2.7.1 PSAVE. This instruction saves the task-specific state of the MC68851. This consists of the CRP, SRP, CAL, VAL, SCC, breakpoint registers (if enabled) and internal state information. The saved data also contains additional internal state information if the MC68851 had an instruction execution in progress at the time of the save. The PSAVE instruction is intended for use in context switch operations. Refer to **APPENDIX C SOFTWARE CONSIDERATIONS** for further implications concerning the use of the PSAVE instruction.

6.2.7.2 PRESTORE. This instruction restores the internal state of the MC68851 that was saved with PSAVE. Refer to **SECTION 9 COPROCESSOR INTERFACE** for details on the restore operation. Refer to **6.3 EXCEPTIONS** for information on the format of the data to be restored.

6.2.7.3 STATE FORMATS. Data saved by the PSAVE instruction can have three formats as shown in Figures 6-10, 6-11, and 6-12. Note that these figures depict the memory organization for the state formats when using the predecrement addressing mode. When using other addressing modes, the first word of the state frame (identified by "SP" in Figures 6-10 through 6-12) is located at the specified effective address and successive words are located in higher memory.

The idle format is used when there is no coprocessor instruction in progress at the time of the PSAVE. The mid-coprocessor format is used when a coprocessor instruction is in progress. Both of these formats are used only when there are no breakpoints enabled. If there are any breakpoints enabled, the breakpoint enabled format is used regardless of the state of any coprocessor or module call/return instructions.

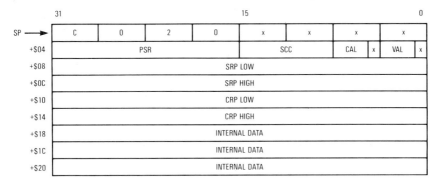

Figure 6-10. Idle Format Frame

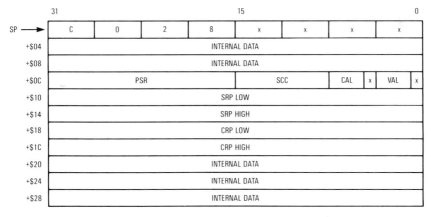

Figure 6-11. Mid-Coprocessor Format Frame

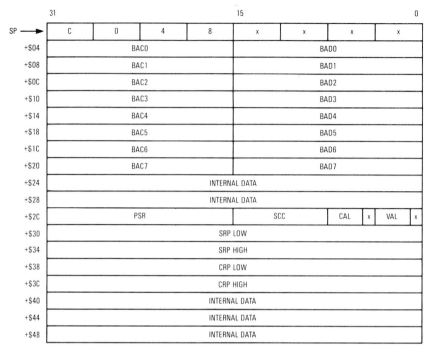

Figure 6-12. Breakpoint Enabled Format Frame

All data marked as 'internal' should not be modified by software. Modifying this data may result in erroneous behavior of the MC68851.

If the length field of the restored data is zero (i.e., the reset format frame), the MC68851 is reset (i.e., placed in the idle state with no operations in progress). Configuration data from the data bus is not read as it is during a hardware reset and no MC68851 register contents are altered. This state frame format is shown in Figure 6-13.

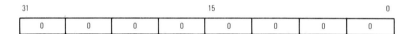

Figure 6-13. Reset Format Frame

6.3 EXCEPTIONS

The following paragraphs describe the exceptions.

6.3.1 Bus Error

The bus error exception (vector #8 in M68000 systems) is signaled to the main processor by assertion of the $\overline{\text{BERR}}$ signal. Due to the limited number of signals available for error reporting, the $\overline{\text{BERR}}$ signal may be asserted for several different reasons. The handler for the bus error exception of the main processor must be prepared to handle all of these cases. Normal bus error handler action should be to execute a PTEST instruction (after ensuring that no other MC68851 coprocessor instructions are in progress) giving the fault address stored by the CPU or returned by the logical bus master (if the CPU was not the logical bus master). If the MC68851 has denied access to the location due to restrictions in the translation table, the reason will be indicated by the bits of the PSR register. The following conditions must be detected by software: main memory failure (transient or otherwise), access exceeded value of CAL at the time the bus cycle was run, an ATC miss during a TAS, CAS, or CAS2 instruction, or an alteration in the translation tables between the time the bus cycle was aborted by the MC68851 and time of the PTEST instruction.

6.3.1.1 BUS ERROR SIGNALED FROM MAIN MEMORY. Main memory may assert the $\overline{\text{BERR}}$ signal to the MC68851 during a table search operation. If the table search was initiated by a bus cycle run by a logical bus master or by a PLOAD instruction, an ATC entry will be made with its internal bus error (B) bit set. When a logical bus master attempts an access using this ATC entry, the MC68851 will assert the $\overline{\text{BERR}}$ signal. If the table search was initiaited by a PTESTR or PTESTW instruction, the B bit of the PSR register will be set.

This error indicates that a bad pointer was loaded into a translation table, or that there is a main memory failure. If there is a main memory failure, the error may be transient and the PTEST instruction may not indicate any fault.

6.3.1.2 LIMIT FIELD EXCEEDED. If a table index extracted from a logical address exceeds the limit field of a corresponding long format descriptor, an ATC entry will be made with its internal bus error (B) bit set. When a logical bus master attempts an access using this ATC entry, the MC68851 will assert the $\overline{\text{BERR}}$ signal. The PTEST instruction signals that a limit violation has occurred by setting the 'L' bit in the PSR.

6.3.1.3 ATTEMPTED USER ACCESS OF SUPERVISOR ADDRESS. If bit FC[2] of a logical address is zero, and a set S bit is encountered during the table search in a long format descriptor for that address, an ATC entry will be made with its internal bus error (B) bit set. When a logical bus master attempts an access using this ATC entry, the MC68851 will assert the $\overline{\text{BERR}}$ signal. The PTEST instruction signals that this condition has arisen by setting the 'S' bit in the PSR.

6.3.1.4 ACCESS LEVEL VIOLATION. If access levels are enabled, and the access level bits of a logical address indicates a higher privilege (numerically less) than the value of the CAL register, the MC68851 will assert the $\overline{\text{BERR}}$ signal. Note that the PTEST instruction will not detect this condition and the fault handler of the main processor should compare the access level field of the fault address with the value contained in the MC68851 CAL register at the time of the fault to determine whether or not this condition caused the fault.

Additionally, if access levels are enabled and the access level bits of a logical address indicate less privilege (numerically greater) than that indicated by the RAL field of a long descriptor in the table search path for a read, or less privilege than the RAL or WAL fields for a write, an ATC entry will be made with its internal bus error (B) bit set. When a logical bus master attempts an access using this ATC entry, the MC68851 will assert the $\overline{\text{BERR}}$ signal. The PTEST instruction signals that this condition has arisen by setting the 'A' bit in the PSR.

6.3.1.5 WRITE PROTECTION VIOLATION. If a write cycle is attempted with a logical address for which the WP bit is set in any descriptor in the table search path, or access levels are enabled and the access level bits of the logical address are less privileged (numerically greater) than the value of a WAL field in a long descriptor, an ATC entry will be made with its internal bus error

(B) bit set. When a logical bus master attempts an access using this ATC entry, the MC68851 will assert the $\overline{\text{BERR}}$ signal. The PTEST instruction signals that this condition has arisen by setting the 'W' bit of the PSR.

6.3.1.6 INVALID ADDRESS. If the DT field of any descriptor in the table search path for a logical address contains the valid 'invalid', an ATC entry will be made with its internal bus error (B) bit set. When a logical bus master attempts an access using this ATC entry, the MC68851 will assert the $\overline{\text{BERR}}$ signal.

This error indicates that a valid translation is not available to the MC68851. Typical system implications would be that the page requested is allocated but paged out, or the page requested is currently unallocated. The PTEST signals that this error has occurred by setting the 'I' bit in the PSR.

6.3.1.7 READ-MODIFY-WRITE (RMW) CYCLE. The MC68851 asserts the $\overline{\text{BERR}}$ signal if the logical bus master attempts to execute a bus cycle with the $\overline{\text{RMC}}$ signal asserted to an address that does not have a descriptor in the ATC, or to an address whose ATC entry does not have the modified (M) bit set. The action on the part of the bus error exception handler should be to execute a PTESTR or PTESTW instruction giving the faulted address, determine that the access should be valid (by examining the 'I' bit of the PSR), execute PLOADW instruction giving the faulted address, and return to the faulted instruction with the rerun bit of the SSW set (refer to the *MC68020 32-Bit Microprocessor User's Manual*). The MC68020 will return to the beginning of the set of interlocked bus cycles and rerun the set. To reduce the average response time for this situation, the following heuristic is suggested: maintain the address of the most recent RMW fault in a local static data area. If the current fault is an RMW (as indicated by the SSW), and it does not match the stored address or there is no stored address, update the stored address with the current address, execute a PLOAD and return. Otherwise, search for other causes of the fault.

This action, by the MC68851, is necessary to allow the uninterrupted sequence of bus cycles required by the TAS, CAS, and CAS2 instructions of the MC68020, without increasing bus arbitration latency to an unacceptable level. Note that software intervention is not required on every instruction execution that asserts $\overline{\text{RMC}}$, but only on those that require a table search. The operating system can reduce the frequency of table searches by maintaining the page descriptors of semaphore areas with their L (lock), M (modified), and U (used) bits always set. Preceding sequences of TAS, CAS, and/or CAS2, instructions by non-RMW writes to a location in the shared pages also reduces the frequency of table searches during RMW cycles.

Note that it is possible, by locking ATC entries, to create a situation in which there are too few unlocked ATC entries to allow an RMW instruction to complete. The minimum number of unlocked entries required depends on the system software configuration. It can be computed as follows: four entries for the longest RMW instruction itself (CAS2 where both operands cross page boundaries), two entries for the supervisor stack, one entry for the exception vector table, one entry for each page of the bus error handler routine, and enough entries for any interrupt routines that may execute during the bus error handler. The MC68851 lock warning facility does not detect the locking of this number of entries. Therefore, the bus error handler must infer the existence of this condition from the fact that the same fault address has been processed more than once in succession with no other discernible cause.

6.3.2 Coprocessor Interface Exceptions

The MC68851 may return the 'take exception' coprocessor primitive through the coprocessor interface. The following paragraphs describe the exceptions that may be returned and their causes.

6.3.2.1 F-LINE EMULATION.
The MC68851 returns this exception (exception vector #11 ($0B)) when presented with an unrecognized command or condition. It is returned as a pre-instruction exception.

6.3.2.2 PROTOCOL VIOLATION.
The MC68851 returns this exception (exception vector #13 ($0D)) when it detects a coprocessor protocol violation. It is returned as a pre-instruction exception. When an RTE is performed by the main processor, the MC68851 will attempt to execute the instruction again. This behavior is based on the assumption that the most likely cause of this error is faulty system software that attempted an MC68851 instruction, other than PSAVE, during a fault in another MC68851 instruction. The pre-instruction exception causes the faulted MC68851 instruction to be discarded and the more recent instruction to be executed after the RTE.

6.3.2.3 CONFIGURATION ERROR.
The MC68851 returns this exception (exception vector #56 ($38)) when the data to be loaded into the TC, CRP, SRP, or DRP registers is not valid. It is returned as a post-instruction exception. The scanPC (on an MC68020) is moved to the next instruction.

6.3.2.4 ILLEGAL OPERATION ERROR.
The MC68851 returns this exception (exception vector #57 ($39)) when a PTEST or PLOAD instruction is executed and the E (enable) bit of the TC register is clear. It is returned as a post-instruction exception. The scanPC (on an MC68020) is moved to the next instruction.

6.3.2.5 ACCESS VIOLATION.
The MC68851 returns this exception vector #58 ($3A) when a PVALID instruction check fails. It is returned as a post-instruction exception. The scanPC (on an MC68020) is moved to the next instruction.

SECTION 7
PROTECTION

This section discusses the facilities provided by the MC68851 to protect address spaces and portions of address spaces. These facilities include protection of the supervisor from user tasks, of user tasks from each other, and of user tasks from themselves. In addition, the access level protection mechanism and its use with the MC68020 CALLM and RTM instructions is discussed.

The MC68851 provides two protection mechanisms that can be used either independently or together, as dictated by the protection requirements for a particular system, to provide a comprehensive protection scheme. The primary protection mechanism utilizes the function code outputs of the logical bus master to define address space based on the current operating mode of the master and the type of operand that is being accessed. The more comprehensive access level protection mechanism subdivides the logical address spaces of user mode tasks into discrete regions of distinct privilege with a hierarchical structure.

7.1 PROTECTION USING ADDRESS SPACE ENCODINGS

M68000 Family processors and other bus master-type devices (DMA controllers, . . ., etc.) provide an indication of the context in which they are operating on a cycle-by-cycle basis through the function code outputs. The function codes indicate the current privilege mode of the bus master (supervisor or user) and the type of operand that is being accessed (program or data). Other distinctions provided by the function code signals (for example, CPU space accesses) are used for special purposes and are not of concern in discussion of the protection mechanism.

All mapping and protection information used by the MC68851 is contained in the translation tables in physical memory and the basis for the protection mechanism based on address space encodings is the structure of these translation tables and how they are accessed by the MC68851. Tasks or routines are prevented from gaining access to valid translation descriptors mapping those areas. In essence, the translation tables are structured such that the MC68851 cannot locate a valid translation ('valid' indicating that the mapping exists in the translation tables and that the access status information contained in it results in the assertion of the physical address strobe by the MC68851 for that access) for any access to an area that should be protected from that access.

The function code signals provide the basis for the MC68851 protection mechanism by forcing different translation tables or branches of a single table to be used to locate logical-to-physical mappings for accesses to different address spaces.

7.1.1 Supervisor/User and User/Supervisor Protection

Supervisor mode programs and data can be protected from access by user mode programs in one of two ways. The first method uses the function code of the logical address to index into the first level of the address translation table. Using this method, a branch of the active translation table (pointed to by the CPU root point register) is dedicated to contain mapping information for each of the address spaces (supervisor program and data, user program and data). This has the effect of breaking the logical address space of the system into four separate address spaces, as shown in Figure 7-1.

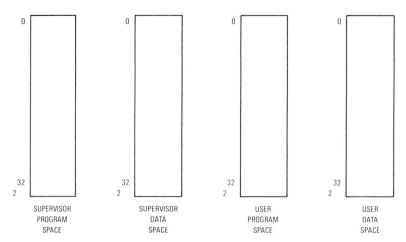

Figure 7-1. Logical Address Map Using Function Code Lookup

Since a user mode program cannot generate addresses with either the supervisor program or supervisor data function codes, supervisor code and data can be protected from any user mode accesses by not placing any valid logical-to-physical mappings in the user branch of the translation table that references supervisor-only information. Additionally, since the supervisor cannot generate user program or data address space references with normal effective address calculations (although these spaces are accessible using the MOVES (move to alternate address space) instruction of the MC68020), user information is protected against all but deliberate supervisor accesses. Figure 7-2 illustrates an example of the upper portion of the address translation table for a task using this method.

If it is desired to separate the supervisor and user address spaces, but to make no distinction between program and data, the supervisor root pointer register can be used and the function code lookup can be suppressed. Use of the supervisor root pointer is enabled by setting the SRE bit of the translation control (TC) register and the function code lookup is suppressed by clearing the FCL bit of the TC register (refer to **6.1.5 TRANSLATION CONTROL**). When SRE is set, all supervisor mode references are translated using the address translation table pointed to by the SRP register and user mode references are translated using the address translation table pointed to by the CRP register.

If the system requires that the user task and the supervisor share the same address space, an alternate method of providing protection for supervisor code and data is provided. The CRP is used to map both supervisor and user mode accesses, and individual pages or entire sections of memory may be restricted to supervisor-only access by setting the S bit in the long format page or table descriptors. Additionally, if the function code lookup is enabled (in order to provide distinction between program and data references) the corresponding user and supervisor entries in the function code table (for example, the user data and supervisor data) should contain the same values such that they point to the same sub-branch of the translation table. Finally, each user task may have a different supervisor mapping if desired. Figure 7-3 shows an example address space using this structure, and Figure 7-4 shows a two level translation table that implements this space.

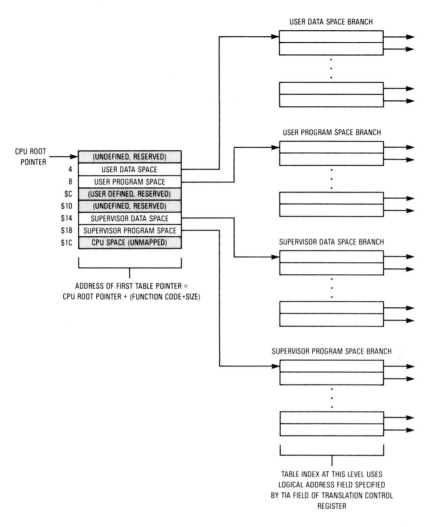

Figure 7-2. Example Translation Tree Using Function Code Lookup

7.1.2 User/User Protection

Similar to the requirements for providing protection of the supervisor, the essential requirement for providing protection between multiple user tasks is to prevent a task from accessing areas to which it does not have access rights by preventing the MC68851 from locating a valid descriptor to translate errant accesses. In order to enforce protection, each user mode task must have its own translation table. The recommended method to perform this function is to provide each task with a complete address translation table, including a function code table, duplicating the supervisor program and supervisor data pointers in each function code table. Changing the address mapping during a context switch is done by loading the CPU root pointer register with the pointer to the address translation table of the new task. This method takes advantage of the automatic

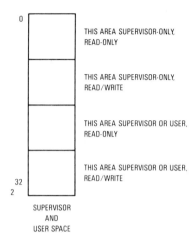

Figure 7-3. Example Logical Address Map With Shared Supervisor and User Spaces

flushing, task aliasing, and other address translation cache management facilities of the MC68851. Figure 7-5 depicts an example of the upper portion of the address translation table for tasks using this method. When using this table structure, it is recommended that the SG bit be set in all long format descriptors in the supervisor branches of the tables (refer to **SECTION 5 ADDRESS TRANS-LATION**). This allows sharing of supervisor entries among tasks and makes more efficient use of the address translation cache.

It is possible to maintain one function code table for the entire system and alter the address mapping on a context switch by replacing the user program and user data entries in the function code table. However, this method requires that the address translation tables in memory be modified and the MC68851 address translation cache be explicitly flushed at each context switch and is therefore not recommended.

7.1.3 Write Protection

Another means to protect certain pages or entire areas of memory is to designate them write-protected (read-only). There are two ways to accomplish this. The first is to set the WP bit in the page or table descriptor for the memory that is to be protected. This write-protection is absolute in that neither user nor supervisor mode programs can write to the protected area. In translation table structures with more than one level of tables there may be more than one WP bit encountered during the table search for any individual page. A page is protected if the WP bit is set in *any* of the descriptors used in the translation.

If access levels are being used, individual pages or areas of memory may be write-protected based on access level. This protection is indicated using the WAL field of the long page and table descriptors and is discussed further in **7.2 ACCESS LEVEL PROTECTION MECHANISM**, and in **SECTION 5 ADDRESS TRANSLATION**. Use of the WAL field and WP bits may be combined to provide both conditional and absolute write protection.

In addition, if the logical address space is separated into program and data spaces through the use of function code lookup, the program space is effectively write-protected since M68000 Family microprocessors cannot generate writes to program space under normal circumstances. The privileged MOVES instruction can be used only by a supervisor mode program to perform writes to program space.

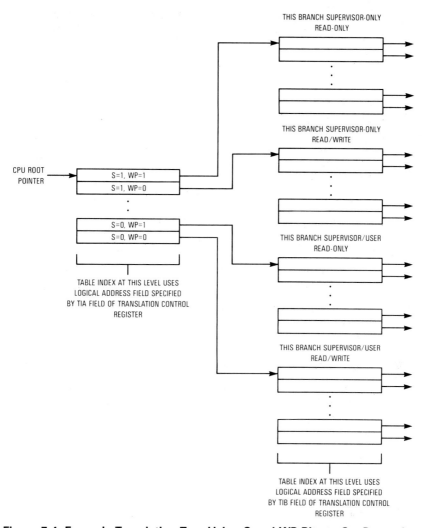

Figure 7-4. Example Translation Tree Using S and WP Bits to Set Protection

7.1.4 Access (Read and Write) Protection

A fourth type of access protection for individual pages or areas of memory can be enforced by setting the DT (descriptor type) field of a page or table descriptor to 'invalid' (refer to **5.1.3 Translation Descriptors**). When the MC68851 is performing a table search and reads a page or table descriptor that has an 'invalid' descriptor type, the table search is terminated and an entry for the logical address that caused the table search to be initiated is created in the ATC with its BERR bit set. When the logical master retries the bus cycle that caused the MC68851 to initiate the table search, the MC68851 aborts the bus cycle by asserting the bus error signal.

When a descriptor is created in the translation tables with an 'invalid' descriptor type, the other bits of the descriptor may be used by the operating system to store other information. The

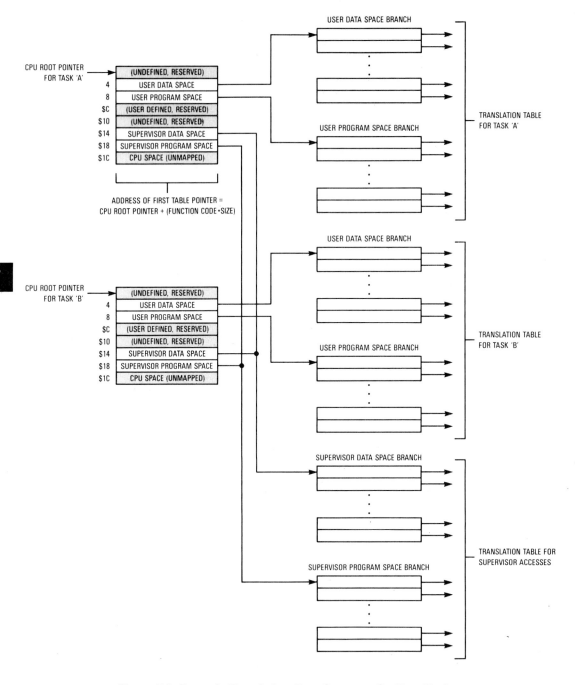

Figure 7-5. Example Translation Tree Structure for Two Tasks Sharing a Common Supervisor Table

MC68851 makes no interpretation of the information stored in a descriptor marked 'invalid'. Typically, information stored in the invalid descriptor might include the reason for the invalid setting and any other information that may be required by the operating system. Access to a page may be denied because the page is not currently resident in memory or because DMA activity that affects that page is in progress. Additionally, the invalid descriptor type can be used to deny access to the portion of the logical address space that is mapped by the branch (or page) of the translation table for the task whose logical-to-physical mappings are contained in that translation table.

7.1.5 Protection Examples

Using the facilities described, some of the protection classes that can be created are listed below.

No Access
> Set the descriptor type for all areas of the logical address to which access is to be denied to invalid. This protection can be set for individual pages or ranges of the logical address by setting the descriptor type fields in the page descriptors or table pointers, respectively.

Supervisor-Only (Read/Write)
> If a single logical address space is shared by the supervisor and the user, set the S bit in the status field of all long format descriptors that map areas to be protected. If both the supervisor and user have separate logical address spaces (using either function code lookup or the supervisor root pointer), all supervisor information is protected if the translation tables for user accesses do not contain logical-to-physical mappings that reference areas of physical memory owned by the supervisor.

Supervisor-Only (Read-Only)
> Similar to the previous example except that the WP bit is set in addition to the S bit. The WP bit must also be set in descriptors in the supervisor's translation table for all protected areas.

Supervisor/User (Read/Write)
> No protection is required for these areas. This type of protection (and those discussed below) is applicable to those systems in which the supervisor and user share a common logical address space.

Supervisor/User (Read-Only)
> Set the WP bit in the status field of all long format descriptors that map read-only areas.

Supervisor/User Data-Only (Read/Write)
> Function code lookup is enabled. All data-only areas are contained in the branch of the translation table pointed to by the user data or supervisor data entries in the function code table.

Supervisor/User Program-Only (Read-Only)
> Function code lookup is enabled. All program-only areas are contained in the branch of the translation table pointed to by the user program or supervisor program entries in the function code table. Note that this does not provide execute-only protection if the PC-relative effective addressing mode is used for data accesses.

7.2 PROTECTION USING THE ACCESS LEVEL PROTECTION MECHANISM

In addition to the user/supervisor distinction provided by M68000 Family microprocessors, a system containing an MC68020 and MC68851 can use the access level protection mechanism to construct up to eight additional levels of protection. These levels subdivide the user mode logical address space, providing the ability to restrict read and write accesses based on the privilege level assigned to the current task. The MC68020 module call and return instructions (CALLM and RTM) interface with the MC68851 to allow a task to alter its access level in a manner that is controlled by the operating system (refer to **SECTION 10 ACCESS LEVEL CONTROL INTERFACE** for further information on the mechanics of these instructions).

7.2.1 Overview of Operation

The access level protection mechanism provides a hierarchy of two, four, or eight distinct privilege levels within the user logical address space. The mechanism is hierarchical in the sense that a task operating at a given level of privilege n has access to all areas of the logical address space that require a privilege level of n or less but cannot access areas corresponding to higher levels of privilege. Figure 7-6 illustrates this concept. In the figure, four access levels are in use with lower numbers representing higher levels of privilege. The shaded areas in the Figure 7-6 represent areas to which accesses by a task operating at level n are allowed while the unshaded areas are not accessible to the task except through use of the CALLM instruction.

The MC68020 CALLM (call module) instruction allows a task operating at one level of privilege to request temporary transfer of program execution control to a module operating at a higher (or same) privilege level and to pass parameters to the called module. The calling routine cannot access or otherwise disrupt the higher privilege module since the only control the calling routine has over the called module is the value and number of parameters that are passed. The MC68020 RTM (return from module) instruction reverses the operation of the CALLM instruction and provides a secure means of returning program execution control to a routine from a module of higher privilege.

Note that when the CALLM instruction is used to pass program control to a module operating at a higher level of privilege than the calling routine, the called module is effectively rendered 'execute-only' since the calling routine cannot access the module through any means other than passing program execution control to that module.

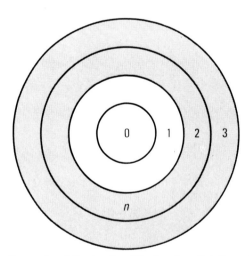

Figure 7-6. Example of Protection Mechanism Privilege Hierarchy

Access levels are useful in any system where more than two levels of privilege are required. For example, a system may contain a data base manager that requires access to sensitive tables. It may be undesirable to require a task switch in order to invoke a data base manager function, or to allow the manager to run in supervisor mode. Using the access level mechanism, both the application and data base manager code can reside in the same address space. Data base functions can be invoked as module calls from the application code to predefined entry points in the data base manager. Data base manager code and data can be protected from being read or written by the application code. This allows the data base manager to be made execute-only from the application. By structuring the system tables properly, the data base manager can be invoked from several tasks simultaneously, and each instance can have some shared and some private data areas.

Another use for the access level mechanism is to create an operating system with an interface that appears as an external subroutine call to application programs. In such a system, most of the operating system executes in user mode at the most privileged access level. The access level mechanism is used to protect system tables and peripheral device interface registers. Application code can request operating system services through the CALLM instruction in the MC68020. Supervisor mode is then considered to be an extension of the processor microcode for functions that are either too complex or too system specific to be implemented in the microprocessor itself. Code that must run in supervisor mode includes the front end of exception handlers and code that must use privileged instructions for context switching and processor control.

An address map demonstrating an example of the access level mechanism is shown in Figure 7-7. In this figure, four access levels (or more if the application code area is further subdivided by several different access levels) are implemented. The most privileged level contains the bulk of the operating system code and is directly accessible only to itself; the application code or the data base manager can request operating system services by using the CALLM instruction. The next most privileged level contains the data base management code and is directly accessible by both the data base manager and the operating system and is callable by the application code. The application code occupies the next access level and, similar to above, is accessible to itself, the data base manager, and the operating system. The lowest level of privilege is allocated to a data area that is shared by the data base manager and the application code. However, the protection attributes of the shared area are set such that the application code has rights only to read from the shared area and cannot write to it (refer to **7.2.3.1 Write Protection**). Figure 7-8 illustrates one method of configuring a translation table to provide this type of function.

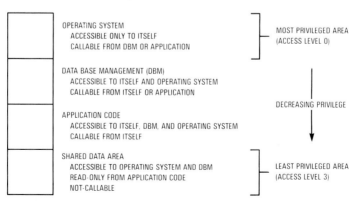

Figure 7-7. Example Logical Address Map for System Using Access Level Mechanism

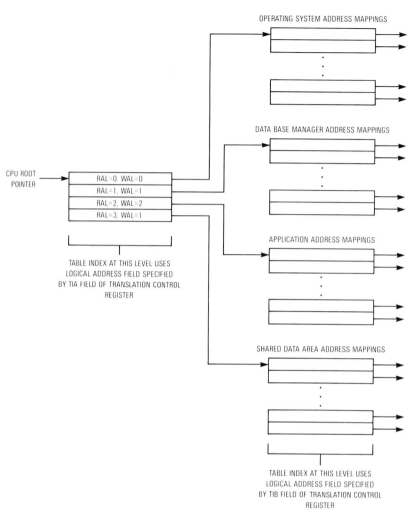

Figure 7-8. Translation Table for Example System

7.2.2 Access Level Protection Mechanism Operation

Throughout the system, access levels are one, two, or three bit quantities describing the level of privilege possessed or required. The number of bits used for access levels, and hence the number of levels, is set by the ALC field of the AC register in the MC68851 (refer to **6.1.9 ACCESS CONTROL (AC)**). An access level of zero represents the most privileged or protected level. Larger numbers indicate lower privilege. The access level mechanism is hierarchical; if access to an address is permitted from a given level, it is permitted from all levels with greater privilege (smaller values of access level). If access to an address is denied from a given level, it is denied from all levels with less privilege (larger values of access level).

Access levels are associated with logical addresses, pages in the logical address space, and tasks. The access level of a logical address is contained in the most significant one, two, or three bits of the logical address (determined by the ALC field of the AC register). It is interpreted as the level of privilege requested by an access using the address. It is not directly related to the access level of the page to which it refers, as described below.

A page in the logical address space (corresponding to a page in physical memory as determined by the current logical-to-physical mapping) has two access levels associated with it: one for read accesses and one for write accesses. These are interpreted as protection information. An access to the page must indicate a privilege of at least the read access level to read or write the page, and a privilege of at least the write access level in order to write to it. The access levels of a page are determined from information contained in the address translation tables. Long format page and table descriptors have read access level (RAL) and write access level (WAL) fields. When the address translation tables are searched for a translation for a logical address, the access level bits of the logical address are compared against the RAL and WAL fields of all long descriptors encountered in the search. The effective read access level of the page is the most privileged (numerically least) of all RAL fields encountered. The effective write access level is the most privileged (numerically least) of all WAL and RAL fields encountered.

The access level of the current task is contained in the current access level (CAL) register of the MC68851. It is interepreted as the level of privilege possessed by the task. A task may use only those logical addresses with equal or less privilege than it possesses. That is, the access level encoded in the highest-order logical address bits must be greater than (less privileged) or equal to the value in CAL; otherwise, the MC68851 aborts the access.

Before the operating system dispatches a task for execution, the physical address of the root for the translation table for that task is loaded into the MC68851 CRP and the access level for the task is written to the CAL register.

The MC68851 uses the access level information in the following way. Since a task is capable of formulating a logical address with any access level, the MC68851 compares the access level of each logical address that the task tries to use with the access level of the task stored in the CAL register. If the task attempts to use an access level more privileged than it is permitted, the MC68851 aborts the access by asserting the bus error signal. If the access is permitted, the MC68851 translates it, using the address translation tables if necessary. If the access is a read and the logical address indicates an access level less privileged (numerically greater) than the effective read access level of the page, the MC68851 aborts the access by asserting the bus error signal. Similarly, the MC68851 aborts the cycle if the access is a write with an access level less privileged than either the effective write access level or read access level of the page.

The MC68851 performs the above protection functions as follows. When the access level protection mechanism is enabled (refer to **6.1.9 Access Control (AC)**), the access level bits of the logical address for each bus cycle with FC3/FC2 = 00 (indicating an access to one of the user address spaces) are compared (unsigned) with the access level bits of the CAL register. If the access level value in the logical address is numerically less than that in CAL, the address requests more privilege than the task possesses, and the MC68851 terminates the bus cycle by asserting bus error. Otherwise the access is allowed and the address is translated. When the address translation cache is searched, all bits of the logical address, including the access level bits and function code bits are significant. If an exact match is found, and the BERR bit is set in the entry or the WP bit is set and the access is a write cycle, the MC68851 terminates the bus cycle by asserting the bus error signal. Otherwise, the MC68851 outputs the physical address. If no match is found in the ATC, a search of the translation tables is required.

When a search of the translation tables occurs, the access level bits of the logical address are compared (unsigned) against all RAL and WAL fields encountered. If any RAL field contains a value less than the access level bits of the logical address, the resulting entry in the ATC will have its BERR bit set. If any WAL field contains a value less (greater privilege) than the access level bits of the logical address, or if any set WP bits are encountered, the resulting ATC entry will have its WP bit set.

When access levels are enabled and a bus cycle has FC2 equal to one (a supervisor space reference) the check against the CAL register is *not* performed. When access levels are enabled and a bus cycle has FC3 equal to a one (a DMA access) the check against the CAL register is *not* performed but the RAL and WAL fields *are* checked during table search operations initiated due to misses in the ATC caused by these accesses. It is the responsibility of the operating system to ensure that sensitive areas of the user address space are not misused by the supervisor resources.

7.2.3 Constructing Address Spaces Using Access Levels

The access level mechanism supports three basic types of address spaces, depending on how the MC68851 is instructed to interpret access level bits. In the first of these, the access level bits are treated as address information as well as protection information and are used to index into the address translation tables during table search operations. This type of structure separates objects by both access level and logical address and results in an address map as shown in Figure 7-9. Lower levels of privilege are associated with the higher ranges of the logical address space and, conversely, higher levels of privilege are associated with the lower ranges. When using this type of address space, use of the RAL and WAL fields in the address translation tables is not required since any access to an area more privileged than the access level of executing task fails the check against the CAL register and will be aborted by the MC68851.

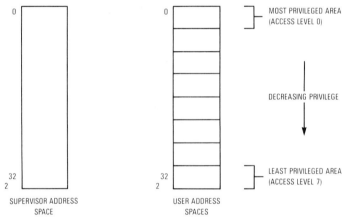

Figure 7-9. Logical Address Map Using Access Level Information as Address Information

The second type of address space uses the access level bits of the logical address as protection information only and they are not used to index into translation tables during a table search. This is done by setting the IS field of the TC register to discard them (refer to **6.1.5.5 INITIAL SHIFT**). When using this type of protection, the logical address space is now smaller, since fewer bits are used as addressing information and the resulting logical address map is as shown in Figure 7-10. Although the access level bits are not used as table indices, they are compared against RAL and WAL fields during table search operations and against the CAL register during all bus cycles by the CPU as described above. Using this type of address map has several benefits. Code and

Figure 7-10. Logical Address Map Using Access Level Information as Control Information Only

data need not be arranged in the address space according to the access level required to use them. This type of organization is of particular benefit in systems that allow dynamic loading of memory since the protection attributes are no longer location dependent. It also allows areas of memory to be accessible to different parts of a program with different access rights; areas may be read/write to code executing at one access level, read-only to code executing at a less privileged level, and inaccessible to code executing at a still less privileged level.

The third type of address space uses the access level bits of the logical address selectively to provide access level and address information for certain accesses while providing only access level information for other accesses. To implement such an address space, the translation tables are used to provide the necessary distinction. For example, consider a system that uses the highest order three bits of the logical address (as determined by the TIA field of the translation control register) to index into the first level of the translation tree. By manipulating the values in this eight entry table, the operating system can separate or merge access level and address information at will. If all entries in this first-level table have the same value, then the access level information is effectively not used as address information. Similarly, if the entries in the table point to different sub-branches of the translation table tree, then the high-order address information is used for both access level and addressing information. By using the CRP, SRP, and DRP, the translation tables for each type of access (user, supervisor, and DMA) can be configured to either use or to ignore the high-order logical address bits for addressing purposes.

An additional variable in the design of the address space for a system is the treatment of supervisor space accesses. Figures 7-9 and 7-10 show supervisor space to be a separate and disjoint space. This is not required as supervisor and user spaces may overlap. Supervisor space references are treated specially as described in **7.2.2 Access Level Protection Mechanism Operation**.

7.2.3.1 WRITE PROTECTION. The access level protection mechanism allows areas of the logical address space to be conditionally write-protected based on the privilege level associated with the address used to reference the area.

When using the access level encodings presented by the CPU as protection information only, the WAL fields of long format page and table descriptors are used to specify the minimum access level that must be used to write to the page or range of the logical address, respectively. Additionally, since denying a task read access to an area implies that the task also does not have sufficient privilege to write to that area, the MC68851 prohibits write accesses to all areas to which a task does not have read access. This is true regardless of the write access level associated with that area.

In order to write to an area, a task must have an access level reflecting a privilege of at least the most privileged of all RAL and WAL fields encountered in the table search performed by the MC68851 when loading the translation descriptor for that access. This requires that the access level used by the task to access the protected area be less than (more privileged than) or equal to the lowest value (most privileged) of all WAL or RAL fields in the branch of the translation table containing the logical-to-physical mapping for that access.

For example, consider a page that has RAL and WAL settings both equal to five (eight access levels in use). In order to read or write that area, a task must use an address with a privilege level of at least five. An access with a privilege of six or seven would be aborted by the MC68851. Now consider a page with a RAL encoding of five and a WAL encoding of four; a task may read from this page using a privilege level of five but must use an access level of four or lower (more privileged) to write to the page. Finally, consider a page with a RAL encoding of five and a WAL encoding of six; a task must use an access level of five or lower to read from or write to this page. An attempt to write to this page using an access level of six would be aborted by the MC68851 since it is less privileged than the read access level of the page.

If the access level encoding is used both as address and protection information, areas are either accessible or not accessible to a task, as described below; there is no distinction between read-only and read/write protection except as provided by settings of the WP bit in page or pointer descriptors.

7.2.3.2 ACCESS (READ AND WRITE) PROTECTION. Similar to the case described above for write protection in a system that uses access level information as protection information only, an area can be protected from all accesses (read and write) by tasks operating at or below a particular level of privilege by setting the RAL fields of the page and/or table descriptors to the access level of the lowest privilege level from which the area should be accessible.

For example, setting the RAL field of a page descriptor to four prevents access to that page from access levels five, six, and seven while allowing access from levels zero through four.

When using the access level encodings presented by the CPU as both address and protection information, access protection of an area or areas of the logical address space is achieved through the use of the CAL register. Since areas of different privilege are separated by logical address range, the MC68851 prevents a task from gaining access to an area to which it does not have sufficient access rights by aborting all accesses to that area by that task. All that is required for this protection is that the logical addresses generated by the task be compared against the privilege level of that task contained in the CAL register. Any time that the access level encoding of a logical address is greater than (less privileged than) the value in the CAL register the MC68851 aborts the access by asserting bus error.

7.2.4 Transfers Between Access Levels

Transfers between access levels are done in hardware using the MC68020 module call instruction (CALLM) and module return instruction (RTM). These instructions provide an indivisible transfer of program execution control and change in access level, under the control of module descriptors provided by the operating system. A module descriptor contains information including the entry point address of the called routine, and the access level at which it should execute. For a detailed description of the descriptor formats used by the CALLM and RTM instructions refer to the *MC68020 32-Bit Microprocessor User's Manual*.

The CALLM and RTM instructions communicate with the MC68851 through a special set of bus interface registers. During the CALLM or RTM instruction, the MC68851 is responsible for verifying that the requested change in access level is legal, for verifying that the address given for the module descriptor is legal, for updating its access level registers, and for determining whether the stack pointer of the microprocessor should be changed. The programmer-visible registers involved in a module call or return are the current access level (CAL) register, and the stack change control (SCC) register.

Routines are only allowed to call modules operating at a privilege level that is greater than or equal to the privilege level of the calling routine. Similarly, module return operations are allowed only when the return passes program execution control to a routine that is operating at a lower or equal level of privilege than the module from which the return is being made. This requirement is made because the M68000 Family stores return information about subroutine calls on the stack where it is accessible to the called routine. In the case of module calls, this return information includes the access level of the caller which is restored to the CAL register during execution of the RTM instruction. These restrictions prevent a routine from obtaining higher privilege through misuse of the RTM instruction (i.e., falsifying the stored value of the CAL register in the module stack frame).

The protection mechanism used by the MC68851 to ensure validity of all changes in access level is described in detail in **SECTION 10 ACCESS LEVEL CONTROL INTERFACE** and an example usage of the CALLM and RTM instructions is provided in **APPENDIX C SOFTWARE CONSIDERATIONS**.

7.2.5 Passing Parameters Between Routines at Different Access Levels

The MC68020/MC68851 combination provides several facilities to ease the passing of parameters between routines at different access levels. By selecting the appropriate value in the OPT field when creating a module descriptor, the MC68020 can be made to copy stacked parameters from the old stack to the new stack in the event a stack pointer change is required. In this way, the code for accessing stack arguments can be identical, regardless of whether a stack pointer change occurred or whether the caller was running at a different access level.

Address parameters are given special attention. A routine called with the CALLM instruction finds the access level of its caller in the VAL register. Although the VAL register is not directly readable by user programs, the MC68851 instruction PVALID allows a routine to compare the access level of a pointer with the access level in the VAL register. An exception is taken if the access level of the address is more privileged than that in the VAL register (refer to **6.3.2.5 ACCESS VIOLATION**). This allows a routine to quickly determine if its caller would have had permission to use an address. In effect, the PVALID instruction performs the check against the CAL register that would have taken place if the calling routine had used the address and thus verifies whether or not the calling routine has sufficient privilege to use the data areas identified by the pointers. Once this check has been done, the called routine is guaranteed that it can use the address with no greater access privileges than the calling routine would have had. Note that this instruction can be used with any address, so that each link in a chain of pointers can be validated.

7.2.6 Security

The security of the access level system is comprised of two separate parts. The first is the ability to guarantee that a low privileged routine cannot gain access to areas requiring higher privilege. The MC68851 check of addresses against the CAL register ensures that low privileged routines will not be able to use entries in the address translation cache that may have been left there by more privileged routines.

The second issue is the ability to forbid low privileged programs from creating, modifying, or misusing module descriptors. This is important because one of the features of the CALLM instruction is allowing a general effective address specification to locate the module descriptor, and so the module descriptor exists in the address space of the caller. The ability to call a routine is in fact granted by allowing its module descriptor to be readable by the caller. Unauthroized creation of module descriptors is prevented by the checks on the module descriptor address peformed by the MC68851. All module descriptors must reside in pages that have the G bit set in their page descriptor in the address translation tables. The security of the address translation tables must be guaranteed by the system software and, minimally, requires that all pages that have the G bit set in the corresponding page descriptors also be write-protected from user accesses. The requirement enforced by the MC68851 that module descriptors must fall on specified boundaries prevents a program from using data in the middle of a valid module descriptor as a module descriptor, and possibly causing an illegal increase in access level. Additionally, the alignment restriction prevents a module descriptor from crossing a page boundary which simplifies protection checking.

7.2.7 Relationship Between Access Levels and Supervisor Mode

The access level mechanism operates in addition to the user/supervisor mode distinction of the processor. Supervisor space accesses are treated specially in that they are not subject to the check against the CAL register or RAL and WAL during a table search, meaning that addresses generated by the supervisor can use any access level. This is similar to a program running with a value of zero in the CAL register. Supervisor and access level zero are, however, not equivalent. Supervisor mode is entered only via an exception or interrupt, and the MC68851 hardware does not update the value of the CAL register on these translations. When using access levels, it is recommended that systems run with most of the operating system in user mode, using the access level mechanism to protect code, data, and peripheral registers. Supervisor mode should only be used for code that must use privileged instructions.

7.2.8 Considerations for Non-32-Bit Systems

Since the access level protection information is carried in the highest-order logical address bits, there are special considerations that should be taken for those systems that do not utilize a 32-bit logical address bus. The access level bits of the logical address must be routed to the most significant one, two, or three logical address inputs (depending on the number of access levels in use) of the MC68851 in order to utilize the access level protection mechanism. Additionally, in order to use the PVALID instruction, the access level bits of the PVALID operand must be shifted (in software) to occupy the most-significant bits of the operand.

SECTION 8
BREAKPOINTS

The MC68851 provides a breakpoint acknowledgement facility to support software analysis and debugging for the MC68020 when used in conjunction with the M68000 breakpoint instructions.

The M68000 instruction set implements eight breakpoint opcodes ($4848 through $484F). When one of these opcodes is executed by the MC68020, the processor responds by performing a breakpoint acknowledge cycle to inform external hardware that a breakpoint instruction has been encountered. The breakpoint acknowledge cycle is executed by reading from the specific address in the system CPU space (function code = $7) corresponding to the particular breakpoint instruction. The required format for the address generated during a breakpoint acknowledge cycle is shown in Figure 8-1. The bits marked as 'x' are ignored by the MC68851 and are zero filled by the MC68020.

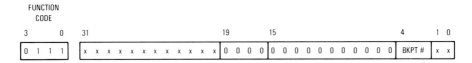

Figure 8-1. Breakpoint Acknowledge Cycle Address Encoding

Upon termination of the breakpoint acknowledge cycle, the MC68020 can proceed with one of two sequences. First, if the cycle is terminated by the assertion of bus error, the MC68020 immediately begins exception processing for an illegal instruction (M68000 exception vector #4). Alternately, a replacement opcode may be supplied on the processor data bus and the $\overline{DSACK}$ signals asserted. In response to this termination, the MC68020 replaces the breakpoint opcode in its instruction pipeline with the opcode supplied during the acknowledge cycle and continues with normal program execution.

The MC68851 contains special hardware to fully control the MC68020 breakpoint instruction features and supply additional capabilities for program debug and analysis.

8.1 INSTRUCTION BREAKPOINT MECHANISM

The MC68851 contains eight pairs of breakpoint registers, one pair corresponding to each of the breakpoint opcodes, which control the breakpoint operations. The breakpoint register set is shown in Figure 8-2.

The register pair BAD0/BAC0 corresponds to the breakpoint opcode $4848, BAD1/BAC1 to $4849, . . ., etc.

8.1.1 Breakpoint Acknowledge Data Registers

Each of the breakpoint acknowledge data registers, BAD0 through BAD7, can be loaded with an opcode to be transferred to the MC68020 during the breakpoint acknowledge cycle. These registers

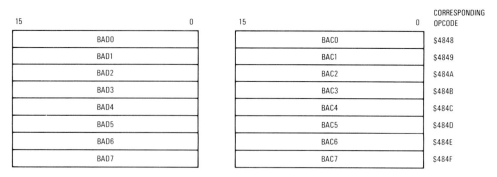

Figure 8-2. MC68851 Breakpoint Registers

may be loaded with any 16-bit value, but in order to provide useful operation, the value should be a recognizable, legal MC68020 opcode. For example, it is possible to load BAD0 with $4848 (breakpoint zero opcode) causing the breakpoint acknowledge cycle to be repeated until the skip count, as described below, is exhausted. However, the value of this operation is questionable. These registers may be read or written using the PMOVE instruction.

The format of these registers are shown in Figure 8-3.

Figure 8-3. Breakpoint Acknowledge Data Register Format

8.1.2 Breakpoint Acknowledge Control Registers

The operation of each of the breakpoint acknowledge data registers is controlled by the corresponding breakpoint acknowledge control register, BAC0 through BAC7. The format of the BACx registers is shown in Figure 8-4.

Figure 8-4. Breakpoint Acknowledge Control Register Format

Bit [15] of the BACx register is the breakpoint enable control. If this bit is clear, breakpoint acknowledgement for the corresponding breakpoint instruction is disabled and any breakpoint acknowledge cycle generated by execution of that opcode is terminated by the MC68851 with the assertion of bus error. The BPE bit is cleared at reset; the skip count field is not.

The breakpoint skip count contained in bits [0–7] specifies the number of times that the replacement opcode contained in the corresponding BADx register is returned with $\overline{\text{DSACKx}}$ in response to a breakpoint acknowledge cycle before the MC68851 signals the MC68020 to initiate exception processing for the breakpoint by asserting bus error.

If, at the beginning of a breakpoint acknowledge cycle, the breakpoint skip count is non-zero, the MC68851 will return the corresponding replacement opcode and assert $\overline{DSACKx}$. During the breakpoint cycle, the skip count is decremented by one. If, at the beginning of a breakpoint acknowledge cycle, the breakpoint skip count is zero, the MC68851 terminates the cycle by asserting bus error, causing the MC68020 to initiate illegal instruction exception processing for the breakpoint.

The breakpoint acknowledge control registers may be read or written using the PMOVE instruction. All unimplemented bits (bits [8–14]) are always read as zeros and must be written as zeros.

A flowchart for the breakpoint operation is shown in Figure 8-5. Figure 8-6 illustrates the functional timing for the breakpoint acknowledge cycle when the MC68851 supplies the replacement opcode and asserts $\overline{DSACKx}$. Figure 8-7 illustrates the functional timing of the cycle, when the MC68851 asserts bus error due to either the corresponding enable bit being clear or the skip count having been decremented to zero.

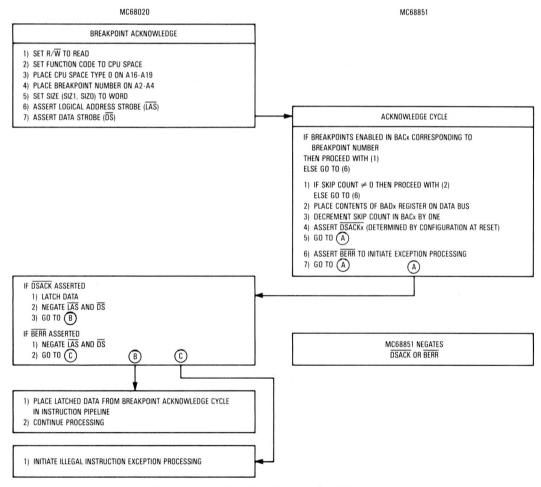

Figure 8-5. Instruction Breakpoint Flowchart

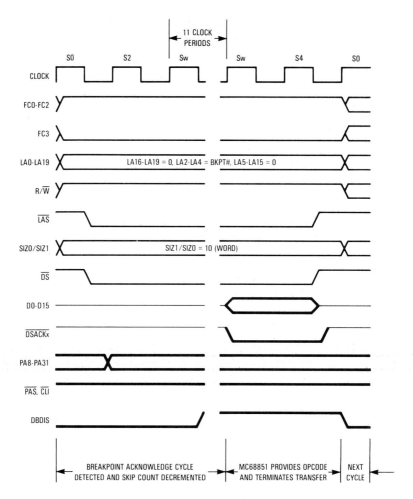

Figure 8-6. Breakpoint Acknowledge Cycle — MC68851 Supplies Replacement Opcode

8.2 BREAKPOINT USAGE

The instruction breakpoint facilities of the MC68020 and MC68851 provided simplified program monitoring and debug capabilities without the need for additional hardware.

The most typical use of the instruction breakpoints is in the monitoring of program execution flow. For example, when it is desired to observe the entry of program execution into a particular segment of code, the first instruction in the target segment can be replaced with one of the eight breakpoint opcodes and the original opcode stored in the breakpoint acknowledge data register corresponding to the breakpoint opcode used. If the corresponding breakpoint acknowledge control register is disabled or the skip count is zero, the MC68851 will assert bus error on the first pass through the program segment. At this point control is passed to the illegal instruction exception handler that can perform any activities required to report or log the breakpoint and, if

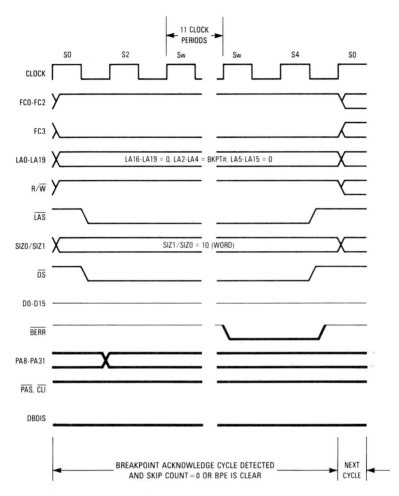

Figure 8-7. Breakpoint Acknowledge Cycle — Bus Error Asserted

desired, replace the original opcode in memory and allow the program to continue with normal execution.

In order to resume execution of a program that has been interrupted by a breakpoint exception, the breakpoint opcode can be left in memory and the breakpoint skip count set to one in the breakpoint acknowledge control register for that opcode. When the MC68020 executes a return from exception (RTE) instruction from the illegal instruction handler, it attempts to re-execute the instruction that caused the fault (the stacked program counter points to the instruction that caused the exception). Setting the skip count to one causes the MC68851 to provide the replacement opcode the first time the breakpoint is executed (immediately upon completion of the RTE) and to force exception processing on subsequent accesses.

In an alternate use, if the MC68851 breakpoint control register is enabled and the skip count is non-zero, program execution continues unaffected by the fact that one of the opcodes for the program was supplied by the MC68851 during the breakpoint acknowledge cycle. In this manner it is possible to take the breakpoint exception only after n ($1 \leq n \leq 255$) repetitions of a program segment. When the skip count is exhausted and control is passed to the illegal instruction exception handler, the occurrence of n passes through the program segment can be reported to the user, or the skip count register can be reinitialized, the n passes added to a static counter maintained by the exception handling routine and program execution resumed for another n passes.

By using the breakpoint instructions with non-zero skip counts, it is also possible to keep a log of the relative frequency of execution of up to eight different sections of code without significantly affecting program execution time. To perform this function, an instruction from each of the relevant code sections is replaced with a different breakpoint opcode, the replaced opcode is placed in the correct breakpoint acknowledge data register and the skip counts set to n. When an illegal instruction exception occurs due to an exhausted skip count, a master counter for the particular breakpoint is incremented by n and the skip count is reset to n. At the termination of the program, the residual skip counts (n – remainder in count register) for each of the breakpoints are added to the corresponding master counts providing a history of the relative frequency of execution of each of the code sections.

Note that the execution of the instruction breakpoints is unaffected by whether the breakpoints reside in external memory or in the MC68020 on-chip cache.

SECTION 9
COPROCESSOR INTERFACE

This section describes the coprocessor interface with respect to the communication protocol utilized by the MC68851 and MC68020. This communication protocol includes electrical and command level mechanisms that allow a coprocessor to act as an extension to the main processor.

9.1 COPROCESSOR INTERFACE SIGNAL CONNECTION

The connection between the MC68020 and the MC68851 is a simple extension of the M68000 bus interface with the MC68851 directly connected to the MC68020. The selection of the MC68851 is based upon an internally generated chip select signal that is decoded from the logical address and function code inputs.

The MC68851 contains a set of coprocessor interface registers (CIRs) by which the main processor and coprocessor communicate. These registers are not related to the programming model implemented by the MC68851. Rather, they are used as communication ports that have specific functions associated with each register. When the MC68851 is used as a coprocessor to the MC68020, the programmer is never required to explicitly access these interface registers, since the coprocessor interface is implemented in the hardware and microcode of the MC68020. When the MC68020 is not used as the main processor, the MC68851 CIRs can be explicitly accessed by a software routine that emulates the behavior of the MC68020 with respect to the coprocessor interface.

For more information on the electrical interconnection between the main processor and the MC68851, refer to **APPENDIX B HARDWARE CONSIDERATIONS**.

9.1.1 Selecting the MC68851

The MC68851 does not require any special bus signals, beyond the normal M68000 Family bus control signals, for connection to the MC68020. The former MC68000 interrupt acknowledge address space (function code $7) is extended in the MC68020 to be the CPU address space. A portion of this space, identified by the MC68020 address bus, is dedicated to coprocessor devices. Figure 9-1 illustrates the required address bus encoding for coprocessor accesses in the CPU address space. The bit positions marked with an 'x' are zero-filled by the MC68020 but are ignored by the MC68851.

During CPU space cycles, address bits A16–A19 indicate the CPU space function that the main processor is performing. The MC68020 utilizes four of the possible 16 encodings of A16–A19 as listed in Table 9-1.

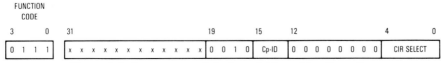

Figure 9-1. Coprocessor Interface Address Bus Encoding

The coprocessor identification (Cp-ID), A13–A15, is taken from the coprocessor instruction operation word (refer to **9.2 COPROCESSOR INSTRUCTIONS** and to the *MC68020 32-Bit Microprocessor User's Manual*). The MC68851 always operates as coprocessor zero and, therefore, selects itself for coprocessor communications (CPU space type = $2) when the Cp-ID is set to zero. The coprocessor interface register (CIR select) field, A0–A12, is decoded by the MC68851 to select the appropriate CIR.

Table 9-1. MC68020 CPU Space Type Field Encodings

CPU Space Type Field (A19–A16)	CPU Space Transaction
0 0 0 0	Breakpoint Acknowledge
0 0 0 1	Access Level Control
0 0 1 0	Coprocessor Communications
1 1 1 1	Interrupt Acknowledge

Although the MC68851 decodes the full address range specified on A0–A12, the MC68851 register set occupies only the lower 32 bytes of this range. Any access above this range (A0–A12 ⩾ $20) is ignored for a write cycle and returns the null response (all ones) for a read (the MC68851 terminates these cycles by asserting $\overline{\text{DSACKx}}$). For a map of the coprocessor interface registers implemented on the MC68851, refer to Figure 9-2. Since address bits A20–A31 are not present on all implementations of M68000 processors, these bits are not essential for decoding CPU space accesses.

The internal M68851 chip select decode is therefore based upon the function code signals (FC0–FC3), the CPU space type field (A16–A19), and the Cp-ID field (A13–A15). The MC68851 decodes the address bits A0–A4 (A5–A12 must be zero) to determine the CIR involved in any coprocessor access.

9.1.2 Coprocessor Interface Registers

Table 9-2 identifies the MC68851 coprocessor interface register locations in the CPU space that are used for communications between the MC68020 and the MC68851. Figure 9-2 illustrates the memory map of the CIRs on a 32-bit bus. When a coprocessor communication cycle is executed with a Cp-ID of zero, the MC68851 decodes the CIR select field of the address bus, A0–A4 (A5–A12 = 0), to select the appropriate coprocessor interface register.

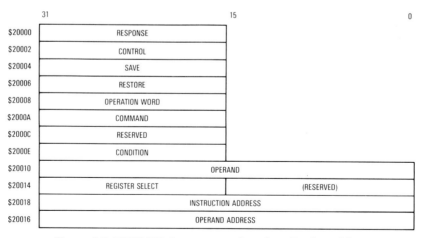

Figure 9-2. MC68851 Coprocessor Interface Register Map

Table 9-2. Coprocessor Interface Register Characteristics

Register	A4–A0	Offset	Width	Type
Response	0 0 0 0 x	$00	16	Read
Control	0 0 0 1 x	$02	16	Write
Save	0 0 1 0 x	$04	16	Read
Restore	0 0 1 1 x	$06	16	Read/Write
Operation Word*	0 1 0 0 x	$08	16	Write
Command	0 1 0 1 x	$0A	16	Write
(Reserved)	0 1 1 0 x	$0C	16	—
Condition	0 1 1 1 x	$0E	16	Write
Operand	1 0 0 x x	$10	32	Read/Write
Register Select	1 0 1 0 x	$14	16	Read
(Reserved)	1 0 1 1 x	$16	16	—
Instruction Address*	1 1 0 x x	$18	32	Read/Write
Operand Address	1 1 1 x x	$1C	32	Write

*Unimplemented

The following paragraphs describe the characteristics of each of the coprocessor interface registers as implemented by the MC68851. In these descriptions, the read/write attributes of each register are given. If a register is read-only, write accesses to that location are ignored; read accesses of a write-only register always return all ones. In all cases, the MC68851 asserts $\overline{\text{DSACKx}}$ in response to all CPU space cycles accessing coprocessor zero (FC0–FC3 = $7, CPU space type = $2, and Cp-ID = 0) to terminate the bus cycle.

9.1.2.1 RESPONSE CIR ($00). This 16-bit read-only register is used to communicate service requests from the MC68851 to the main processor. A read of the response CIR is always legal, regardless of the state of an instruction dialog. The format of the response primitives that are returned through this register are detailed in **9.2.2 Response Primitives**.

In general, the primitive encoding returned in the response register is not changed until the action requested by the primitive is performed by the processor. For example, if an evaluate and transfer effective address primitive is encoded in the response CIR and the main processor reads that primitive, the response register will not be updated until the processor completes a long-word (32-bit) transfer to the operand address CIR (refer to **9.1.2.11 OPERAND ADDRESS CIR ($1C)**).

Primitive responses that do not request explicit service from the processor are discarded by the MC68851 when the response register is read. The supervisor check primitive is one example of such a primitive in that it requires only that the processor perform a check of its internal status and either re-read the status register or take an exception (refer to **9.2.2.4 SUPERVISOR CHECK PRIMITIVE**).

Although a read of the response register is legal at any time, the read may not be the access that is expected by the MC68851. In such cases, the MC68851 returns the null done primitive (refer to **9.2.2.1 NULL PRIMITIVE**) unless the expected access was to the register select CIR in which case an unimplemented response ($0 or $1) is returned (refer to **9.2.2.6 TRANSFER MAIN PROCESSOR CONTROL REGISTER PRIMITIVE**).

Unexpected accesses are not a normal occurrence but may occur due to either improper synchronization of multiple devices accessing the MC68851 or a memory fault generated during the execution of an MC68851 instruction. Since the instruction dialog is interrupted and program control is passed to the bus error handler, it is possible to initiate another coprocessor instruction that will cause an unexpected access or protocol violation due to the incomplete state of the previous instruction. A protocol violation will be signaled if the dialog for a new MC68851 instruction is initiated (by writing to the command register). Unexpected accesses receive either a 'null done' or 'unimplemented' primitive in order to prevent potential lockups by signaling the errant device that communication should be terminated.

9.1.2.2 CONTROL CIR ($02). This 16-bit write-only register is utilized by a main processor to issue an exception acknowledge or instruction abort to the MC68851. Figure 9-3 illustrates the format of this register. Only two of the 16 bits are defined: the exception acknowledge (XA) and abort (AB) bits.

Figure 9-3. Control CIR Register

The MC68851 does not utilize these two bits; instead, it simply interprets a write to this CIR address as an abort command, regardless of the data pattern written. Thus, an exception acknowledge (in response to a take exception primitive) or abort (in response to an illegal format word, an invalid request primitive, or a supervisor check violation) issued during any MC68851 instruction protocol, or an explicit write (for example, with the MOVES instruction) to the control CIR always has the same effect on the MC68851. Also, write cycles to this register are never illegal, since the MC68851 always responds in the same manner.

The response of the MC68851 to a write of the control CIR is to:
1) Immediately terminate processing of any instruction that may be in progress. If an operation involving an MC68851 user-visible register is aborted and the abort was not requested by the MC68851, the contents of the register is undefined,
2) Clear any pending exceptions, and
3) Reset the coprocessor interface state to the idle condition. Thus, the MC68851 is ready to begin a new instruction protocol following the write cycle.

9.1.2.3 SAVE CIR ($04). This 16-bit read-only register is used by the main processor to issue a context save command to the MC68851, and to return the format word of the MC68851 state frame to the main processor. A read of this register causes the operation currently being executed by the MC68851 (except a state save or restore) to be suspended, and a state save operation is initiated.

After the read of the save register, the next expected access is to the operand CIR (to transfer the state frame).

The only time that a read of this register is illegal is when the MC68851 is executing a PSAVE or PRESTORE instruction; a read of the save CIR is legal at any other time. If the main processor reads the save CIR at an illegal time, the invalid format word is returned. In response to the invalid format word, the main processor must issue an abort to the MC68851 to return it to the idle state (the MC68020 does this automatically).

In systems that support multiple devices accessing the MC68851, an external synchronization protocol (for example software semaphores) must be employed to ensure that the coprocessor instruction execution by one device is never interrupted by attempts to access MC68851 registers by any other device.

9.1.2.4 RESTORE CIR ($06). This 16-bit read/write register is used by the main processor to issue a context restore command to the MC68851 and to validate the format word of a state frame. A write of this register causes the MC68851 to immediately stop any operation that may be executing and prepare to load a new internal state context from the memory resident state frame.

After the main processor writes a format word to the restore CIR, it must read the restore CIR to receive the results of the format word verification. If the previously written format word is valid, that format word will be read back from the restore CIR to indicate the successful verification. If the format word is invalid, the 'invalid format take exception' value is placed in the restore CIR to indicate the verification failure. After a successful verification is signaled, the next expected access is to the operand CIR (to transfer the state frame). After a verification failure is signaled, the main processor should write an abort to the control CIR in order to return the MC68851 to the idle state (the MC68020 does this automatically).

9.1.2.5 OPERATION WORD CIR ($08). This 16-bit write-only register is not used by the MC68851. The only time that this CIR location is used by the M68000 Family coprocessor interface is when a coprocessor issues the transfer operation word primitive, in which case the main processor writes the F line word of the instruction to the operation word CIR. Since the MC68851 never issues the transfer operation word primitive, the operation word CIR location should never be written by the main processor. If a write to this location occurs, it will be ignored and will not cause a protocol violation.

9.1.2.6 COMMAND CIR ($0A). This 16-bit write-only register is used by the main processor to initiate the dialog for a general type coprocessor instruction. When the MC68851 detects a write to this CIR location, the data value is latched from the data bus. If the MC68851 is executing a previous instruction when the command CIR is written, a protocol violation pre-instruction exception is signaled to the processor indicating a fault in the coprocessor dialog.

Due to the implications that many MC68851 instructions have on system configuration, the MC68851 does not allow concurrent instruction processing (that is, upon initiation of an MC68851 instruction, the main processor cannot proceed with the next instruction until completion of all MC68851 activities). Normally, synchronization is forced since the MC68851 does not issue a release primitive until completion of the instruction in progress. However, since the MC68851 may request evaluation of effective addresses during the coprocessor instruction dialog, it is possible to generate an exception (for example, a page fault) during the communication that would leave the previous instruction incomplete. If, after such an error occurs, the processor attempts to initiate another MC68851 instruction, the MC68851 signals the protocol violation and then aborts the uncompleted instruction that caused the fault. This causes a protocol violation exception handler to return and rerun the instruction that received the protocol violation. The exception handler must be capable of correcting the problem that caused the fault and, additionally, since the entire instruction that was aborted must be rerun, the exception handler must be able to correct problems associated with the predecrement addressing mode, if employed.

A write to this CIR location is legal only when the MC68851 is in the idle state (i.e., not currently executing an instruction). If a write to the command CIR occurs when it is not expected, a protocol violation occurs, the command word that is written is not saved by the MC68851 and the previous command word is discarded.

9.1.2.7 CONDITION CIR ($0E). This 16-bit write-only register is used by the main processor to initiate the dialog for a conditional type coprocessor instruction. When the MC68851 detects a write to this CIR location, the data value is latched from the data bus. If the MC68851 is executing a previous instruction when the condition CIR is written, a protocol violation is signaled. If the MC68851 is in the idle or reset state when a write to the condition CIR occurs, it first returns the supervisor check primitive. After a read of the response register, the MC68851 then evaluates the selected condition and returns the null (CA = 0, TF = 0/1) primitive (where the TF bit indicates whether the conditional evaluation is true or false).

A write to this CIR location is legal only when the MC68851 is in the idle or reset state. If a write to the condition CIR occurs when it is not expected, a protocol violation occurs, the conditional predicate that is written is not saved by the MC68851, and the operation in progress is aborted.

9.1.2.8 OPERAND CIR ($10). This 32-bit read/write register is used by the main processor to transfer data to and from the MC68851. The MC68851 transfers data through this CIR location in the following cases:
1) Following an evaluate effective address and transfer data primitive,
2) Following a transfer single main processor register primimtive,
3) Following a read of an idle or busy format word from the save CIR,
4) Following a read of an idle or busy format word to the restore CIR, and
5) Following the read of the register select CIR in response to a transfer main processor control register primitive.

These five cases are the only times when an access to the operand CIR is legal. At any other time, an access to this CIR location causes a protocol violation.

The MC68851 expects all operands that are to be transferred through this CIR location to be aligned with the most-significant byte of the register. Any operand larger than four bytes is transferred through this register using a sequence of long-word transfers. Figure 9-4 illustrates the operand CIR data alignment expected by the MC68851 when transferring data through the operand CIR.

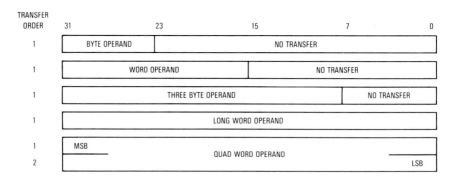

Figure 9-4. Operand CIR Data Alignment

9.1.2.9 REGISTER SELECT CIR ($14). This 16-bit read-only register is read by the main processor to transfer the register select code from the MC68851 in response to a transfer main processor control register primitive. The MC68851 instructions PFLUSH, PLOAD, and PTEST may require access to operands residing in the MC68020 source and destination function code registers (SFC and DFC). Values returned by the MC68851 in this register are $0 and $1 to request transfer of the SFC and DFC, respectively.

This register may be accessed by the processor only in response to a transfer main processor control register primitive. Accesses at any other time will cause the MC68851 to return a protocol violation on the next read from the response register.

9.1.2.10 INSTRUCTION ADDRESS CIR ($18). This 32-bit read/write register is used by the main processor to transfer the address of a coprocessor instruction being executed when the PC bit of any primitive is set. This CIR is used to support concurrent processor/coprocessor instruction execution and is not implemented by the MC68851. Primitives returned by the MC68851 do not have the PC bit set.

All writes to this CIR are ignored and reads return all ones. Accessing this register will not cause a protocol violation.

9.1.2.11 OPERAND ADDRESS CIR ($1C). This 32-bit read/write register is used by the main processor to transfer an operand address in response to the evaluate and transfer effective address primitive issued by the MC68851 during the PFLUSH, PLOAD, PTEST, and PVALID instructions.

Writes to this CIR are legal only in response to the evaluate and transfer effective address primitive. Any other write will cause a protocol violation, the faulting cycle will be ignored, and the instruction currently being executed (if any) will be aborted.

Reads from this register are ignored and always return all ones.

9.1.3 Interprocessor Transfers

All interprocessor transfers are initiated by the MC68020. During the processing of an MC68851 instruction, the MC68020 transfers instruction information and data to the MC68851 via standard write bus cycles; it receives data, requests for service, and status information from the MC68851 via standard read bus cycles. A detailed description of the electrical characteristics of the MC68851 bus interface is contained in **SECTION 4 BUS OPERATION** and **SECTION 12 ELECTRICAL SPECIFICATIONS**.

9.2 COPROCESSOR INSTRUCTIONS

MC68851 instructions are from one to eight words in length. The first word of the instruction is called the operation word, and the second word of the instruction, for the general instruction type, is called the coprocessor command word. Additional words specify the operands, and are either extensions to the effective addressing mode specified in the operation word, or immediate operands which are part of the instruction. The general format of an MC68851 instruction is illustrated in Figure 9-5.

All coprocessor operations are based on the F-line operation codes (i.e., operand words with bits [15:12] = $F) which instruct the MC68020 to call upon a coprocessor for execution of the instruction. Figure 9-6 illustrates the format of this word.

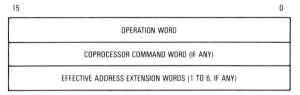

Figure 9-5. Coprocessor Instruction General Format

Figure 9-6. MC68851 Instruction Operation Word

The Cp-ID field indicates which coprocessor is to be selected. Cp-IDs of 0—$5 are reserved by Motorola, and Cp-IDs $6 and $7 are reserved for user definition. The MC68851 always corresponds to Cp-ID zero. The type field indicates to the MC68020 which type of coprocessor operation is selected: general, branch, conditional, save, or restore. The type and type-dependent fields and the coprocessor command word for all MC68851 instructions are described in **6.2 INSTRUCTION DETAILS**.

9.2.1 Instruction Protocol

All MC68851 instructions have a typical protocol which the MC68020/MC68851 pair follows. This communication protocol is as follows:

1) When the MC68020 detects an F-line operation word, communication is initiated by writing information (a command, condition selector, or restore format word) to the appropriate MC68851 coprocessor interface register location (the MC68851 save instruction is initiated by a read operation).
2) The MC68020 then reads the coprocessor response to the previous write operation. The response may indicate any of the following:
    a) An exception condition exists, and the MC68851 instructs the MC68020 to take an exception, using a specific exception vector. The MC68020 acknowledges the exception and initiates exception processing.
    b) There is an MC68851 service request; for example, to evaluate the effective address and transfer data to/from the effective address from/to the MC68851. The MC68851 may also request that the MC68020 query the coprocessor after the service is performed.
    c) No service is requested but the processor is instructed to read from the response register again.
    d) A supervisor check is requested.

Each MC68851 instruction type has specific requirements based upon this simplified protocol. The main processor service requests required for each MC68851 instruction are described in **6.2 INSTRUCTION DETAILS**. All MC68851 main processor service requests (response primitives) are described in the following paragraphs. In addition, the dialog used by the MC68020 and the MC68851 during the execution of each instruction is detailed in **9.3 INSTRUCTION DIALOGS**.

9.2.2 Response Primitives

Data read form the MC68851 coprocessor interface response register is referred to as a primitive. Although the M68000 Family coprocessor interface defines 18 response primitives, the MC68851 only uses eight of those primitives. For additional information on the complete set of response primitives and how they are serviced, refer to the *MC68020 32-Bit Microprocessor User's Manual*. The following paragraphs summarize all MC68851 response primitives and how they are used.

The M68000 coprocessor response primitives are encoded in a 16-bit word that is transferred to the main processor through the response CIR. Figure 9-7 illustrates the general format of a response primitive.

Figure 9-7. M68000 Coprocessor Response Primitive General Format

The encoding of bits [0–12] of a coprocessor response primitive is dependent on the individual primitive being implemented. Bits [13–15], however, are used to specify particular attributes of the response primitive which can be utilized in most of the primitives defined for the M68000 coprocessor interface.

Bit [15] of the primitive format, denoted by CA, is used to specify the come-again operation of the main processor. Whenever the main processor receives a response primitive from the MC68851 with the CA bit set to one, it should perform the service indicated by the primitive and then return to read the response CIR again.

Bit [14] of the primitive format, denoted by PC, is used to specify the pass program counter operation. The MC68851 never issues a primitive with the PC bit set.

Bit [13] of the primitive format, denoted by DR, is the direction bit; and is used in conjunction with operand transfers between the main processor and the MC68851. If DR is zero, the direction of the transfer is from the main processor to the MC68851 (a main processor write). If DR is one, the direction of the transfer is from the MC68851 to the main processor (a main processor read). If the operation indicated by a given response primitive does not involve an explicit operand transfer, the value of this bit is dependent on the particular primitive encoding.

The following paragraphs detail the response primitive encodings used by the MC68851 and the expected main processor response to each one.

9.2.2.1 NULL PRIMITIVE. This primitive is used by the MC68851 to indicate completion of a coprocessor instruction. The format of the null primitive is shown in Figure 9-8. In addition to the bits CA and PC that are discussed above, the null primitive uses three other bits to identify the required action to be taken by the main processor. When set to one, bit [8], denoted by IA, is used to specify that the main processor may process pending interrupts if necessary. The IA bit is never set in any MC68851 primitive. Bit [1], denoted by PF, is used to indicate the status of the MC68851 during instruction execution; if PF equals zero, then the MC68851 is executing an instruction; otherwise it is idle. Bit [0], denoted by TF, is used to communicate the result of a conditional evaluation. If TF equals one, then the condition is true; otherwise it is false.

15	14	13	12	11	10	9	8	7	6	5	4	3	2	1	0
CA	PC	0	0	1	0	0	IA	0	0	0	0	0	0	PF	TF

Figure 9-8. Null Primitive Format

As indicated by the format of this primitive, there are 32 possible null primitive encodings of which the MC68851 uses only three. Table 9-3 lists the MC68851 null primitive encodings, and the circumstances in which they are used.

Table 9-3. Null Primitive Encodings

CA	PC	IA	PF	TF	Usage
0	0	0	1	0	Returned when the MC68851 is in the idle state or as the final primitive of an instruction dialog. The PF bit indicates that no instruction is being executed; thus, there is no expected response to this primitive.
1	0	0	0	0	Returned when the MC68851 is executing an instruction and requires further service from the main processor before the next instruction can be executed. The expected response is for the main processor to re-read the response CIR.
0	0	0	1	0/1	Returned by the MC68851 in response to the write of a conditional predicate to the condition CIR. The TF bit indicates the result of the conditional evaluation; TF = 1 if the condition is true, TF = 0 if the condition is false.

The meaning of the CA, PC, and IA bits are as described above. The PF bit is an indicator that reflects the processing state of the MC68851 during instruction execution. In normal operation, the PF bit is of no concern to the main processor. However, if the main processor is in the trace mode, it should wait until the MC68851 has completed execution of an instruction before taking the trace exception. This is always enforced since the MC68851 does not allow the processor to proceed with the next instruction until the coprocessor operation is complete.

The TF bit is utilized only for the conditional instructions. When the main processor writes a conditional predicate to the condition CIR, the MC68851 uses the null primitive to return the true or false result of the conditional evaluation. If TF equals one, then the condition is true; otherwise it is false. For all reads of the response CIR for other instruction types, the TF bit is a don't care.

9.2.2.2 EVALUATE EFFECTIVE ADDRESS AND TRANSFER DATA PRIMITIVE. This primitive is used by the MC68851 during the execution of the PMOVE instruction to request the transfer of a data item between the MC68851 internal registers and an external location (either memory or a main processor register). The format of this primitive is shown in Figure 9-9. The main processor services this request by evaluating the effective address indicated by the F line word of the instruction and transferring the number of bytes indicated by the length field of the primitive to or from the operand CIR.

15	14	13	12	11	10	9	8	7	6	5	4	3	2	1	0
CA	0	DR	1	0	VALID <ea>			LENGTH							

Figure 9-9. Evaluate Address and Transfer Data Primitive Format

This primitive encoding remains in the response register until the requested data transfer is complete.

The meaning of the CA bit is as described above. The PC bit is always zero. The DR bit indicates the direction of data transfer between the effective address location and the operand CIR of the coprocessor. If DR equals zero, the operand is transferred from the effective address location to the coprocessor. If DR equals one, the operand is transferred from the coprocessor to the effective address location.

The effective address that is to be evaluated is specified in the F-line operation word, and any required extension words are fetched by the main processor, as needed. If the predecrement or postincrement addressing mode is used, the address register is decremented or incremented before or after the transfer by the size of the operand, as indicated in the length field.

The 'valid EA' field specifies various classes of addressing modes with the encodings shown in Table 9-4. If the effective address in the operand word is not of the specified class, then the main processor should write an abort to the control CIR and take an F-line emulator trap. The addressing categories below are as defined for all M68000 Family processors.

Table 9-4. Coprocessor Valid Effective Address Codes

$0	Control Alterable
$1	Data Alterable
$2	Memory Alterable
$3	Alterable
$4	Control
$5	Data
$6	Memory
$7	Any Effective Address

The number of bytes transferred to or from an effective address location is indicated in the length field. If the effective address is a main processor register (register direct), only lengths of one, two, or four bytes are used. If the effective addressing mode is immediate, the length is always one or even, and the transfer is effective address to coprocessor. If the effective address is a memory location, any length is legal (including odd). The PMOVE instruction uses lengths of one, two, four, or eight bytes depending on the MC68851 register involved in the transfer. If the effective address mode is predecrement or postincrement, with A7 as the specified register and a length of one, the transfer causes the stack pointer to be decremented or incremented by two, in order to keep the stack aligned to a word boundary.

Table 9-5 lists the encodings of the evaluate effective address and transfer data primitive that are used by the MC68851 and the cases for which they are used.

Table 9-5. Evaluate Effective Address and Transfer Data Primitive Encoding

Usage	CA	PC	DR	Valid ⟨ea⟩	Length
PMOVE PMMUreg,⟨ea⟩ Issued during the PMOVE instruction dialog to request the transfer of an operand from the MC68851 to memory or to a main processor data register. The length field indicates the size of the operand; byte, word, long, or quad word.	0 0 0 0	0 0 0 0	1 1 1 1	$3 $3 $3 $2	1 2 4 8
PMOVE ⟨ea⟩,PMMUreg Issued during the PMOVE instruction dialog to request the transfer of an operand from memory or a main processor data register to the MC68851. The length field indicates the size of the operand; byte, word, long, or quad word.	0 1 0 1 0 1 0 1	0 0 0 0 0 0 0 0	0 0 0 0 0 0 0 0	$7 $7 $7 $7 $7 $7 $6 $6	1 1 2 2 4 4 8 8

9.2.2.3 TRANSFER SINGLE MAIN PROCESSOR REGISTER PRIMITIVE. This primitive is used by the MC68851 to request the transfer of one main processor register. The format of this primitive is shown in Figure 9-10. The D/A bit is used to specify whether the register is a data or an address register. A value of one for the D/A bit specifies an address register; a value of zero specifies a

15	14	13	12	11	10	9	8	7	6	5	4	3	2	1	0
CA	0	DR	0	1	1	0	0	0	0	0	0	D/A	REGISTER		

Figure 9-10. Transfer Single Main Processor Register Primitive

data register. When the DR bit in this primitive is set, the direction of transfer is from the MC68851 to the main processor. The main processor services this request by reading a long word from the operand CIR and transferring it to the appropriate main processor register. When the DR bit is clear the transfer is from the main processor to the MC68851. The main processor services this request by taking the appropriate register and writing it to the MC68851 operand CIR.

This primitive remains in the response CIR until the register transfer is complete.

9.2.2.4 SUPERVISOR CHECK PRIMITIVE. The supervisor check primitive allows the MC68851 to verify that the main processor is operating in the supervisor state during MC68851 instruction execution. When this primitive is read, the main processor checks the S bit in its status register. If the bit is set, indicating that the processor is operating in the supervisor state, the instruction dialog may be continued by again reading the response register. Otherwise, the instruction must be aborted and a privilege violation exception taken. The MC68020 does this automatically. The format of the supervisor check primitive returned by the MC68851 is illustrated in Figure 9-11.

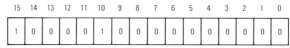

Figure 9-11. Supervisor Check Primitive Format

As with all other primitives returned by the MC68851, the PC bit (bit [15]) is always returned clear.

The supervisor check primitive is always returned during the dialog for a privileged instruction before any user-visible state is altered. A read of the response register following a read of the supervisor check primitive is an indication to the MC68851 that the check passed. This primitive is returned only once during an MC68851 instruction.

9.2.2.5 EVALUATE AND TRANSFER EFFECTIVE ADDRESS PRIMITIVE. This primitive is used by the PFLUSH, PLOAD, PTEST, and PVALID instructions to instruct the main processor to evaluate the effective address specified by the coprocessor instruction operation word and transfer the address to the MC68851 operand address register. The format of this primitive is shown in Figure 9-12.

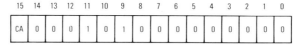

Figure 9-12. Evaluate and Transfer Effective Address Primitive Format

This primitive is retained in the response register until the requested effective address has been completely transferred to the MC68851.

9.2.2.6 TRANSFER MAIN PROCESSOR CONTROL REGISTER PRIMITIVE. This primitive is used by the MC68851 to request the transfer of the MC68020 source or destination function code registers (SFC or DFC) to the MC68851. The format of this primitive is shown in Figure 9-13.

Figure 9-13. Transfer Main Processor Control Register Primitive Format

In response to this primitive, the main processor reads the register select field from the register select CIR and transfers either the SFC or DFC to the MC68851 operand CIR. This primitive is issued only once during the MC68851 instruction dialog.

After this primitive is read from the response CIR, the next expected access is to the register select CIR. If the response register is read when the next expected access is to the register select CIR, the MC68851 will return an illegal primitive ($0 or $1) (refer to **9.1.2.1 RESPONSE CIR**).

9.2.2.7 TAKE EXCEPTION PRIMITIVES. These primitives are used by the MC68851 to instruct the main processor to abort the current operation and initiate exception processing. The main processor services these requests by writing an exception acknowledge to the control CIR (which clears the pending exception in the MC68851), creates the appropriate stack frame on the currently active supervisor stack, and begins execution of an exception handler. The exception handler is located by using the vector number that is supplied as part of the take exception primitive. Table 9-6 lists the vector numbers used by the MC68851.

Table 9-6. MC68851 Vector Numbers

Vector Number (Decimal)	Vector Offset (Hexidecimal)	Assignment	Type
11	$02C	F-Line Emulator	Pre-Instruction
13	$034	Coprocessor Protocol Violation	Pre-Instruction
56	$0E0	Configuration Error	Post-Instruction
57	$0E4	Illegal Operation	Post-Instruction
58	$0E8	Access Violation	Post-Instruction

The take exception primitive remains in the response CIR until an abort is signaled through the control CIR or a further exception (for example, protocol violation) occurs.

The MC68851 returns one of these primitives until the control CIR is written. When an exception acknowledge is written to the control CIR, the take exception primitive is discarded by the MC68851, and the response encoding is changed to the null primitive. By doing this, the MC68851 assures that the take exception request is received by the main processor.

While the M68000 coprocessor interface defines three take-exception primitives, the MC68851 utilizes only two of them. The following paragraphs describe the two take exception primitives that are used by the MC68851.

9.2.2.7.1 Take Pre-Instruction Exception Primitive. This primitive is used by the MC68851 if an illegal command word is written to the command CIR or if a protocol violation occurs. The format of this primitive is shown in Figure 9-14.

15	14	13	12	11	10	9	8	7	6	5	4	3	2	1	0
0	0	0	1	1	1	0	0	VECTOR NUMBER							

Figure 9-14. Take Pre-Instruction Exception Primitive Format

The CA bit is always zero for this primitive since there is an implied protocol preemption in this service request. The vector number identifies the type of the exception and is used by the main processor to locate the appropriate exception handling routine.

In response to this primitive, the MC68020 creates a four word stack frame on top of the currently active supervisor stack. The format of this stack frame is shown in Figure 9-15. The value of the program counter in the stack frame is the address of the F-line operation word of the MC68851 instruction that was preempted by the exception. Thus, if no modifications are made to the stack frame within the exception handler, an RTE instruction causes the MC68020 to return and reinitiate the instruction that was being attempted when the primitive was received. Refer to the *MC68020 32-Bit Microprocessor User's Manual* for further details on exception handling by the MC68020.

	15 … 0
SP →	STATUS REGISTER
+$02	PROGRAM COUNTER
+$06	0 0 0 0 / VECTOR OFFSET

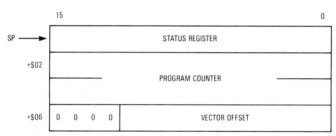

Figure 9-15. Pre-Instruction Exception Stack Frame

9.2.2.7.2 Take Post-Instruction Exception Primitive. This primitive is used by the MC68851 when an exception occurs during the execution of a PMOVE ⟨ea⟩,reg instruction, an invalid operation is requested by the PTEST or PLOAD instructions, or to signal failure of a PVALID instruction. The format of this primitive is shown in Figure 9-16.

15	14	13	12	11	10	9	8	7	6	5	4	3	2	1	0
0	0	0	1	1	1	1	0	VECTOR NUMBER							

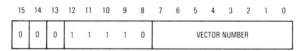

Figure 9-16. Take Post-Instruction Exception Primitive Format

The CA bit is always zero for this primitive, since there is an implied protocol preemption in this service request. The vector number identifies the type of the exception, and is used by the main processor to locate the exception handler routine.

In response to this primitive, the MC68020 creates a six word stack frame on top of the currently active supervisor stack. The format of this stack frame is shown in Figure 9-17. The value of the

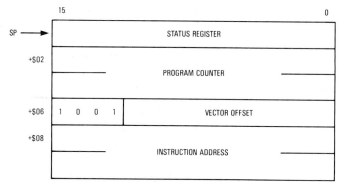

Figure 9-17. Post-Instruction Stack Frame

scanPC at the time the take exception primitive was encountered is stored in the program counter field of the frame and points to the next instruction after the coprocessor instruction that generated the exception. The address of the F-line operation word of the MC68851 instruction that caused the exception is stored in the instruction address field of the stack frame.

When the MC68020 receives the take post-instruction exception primitive it assumes that the coprocessor either completed or aborted the instruction in progress with an exception. The MC68851 always adjusts the MC68020 scanPC to point to the next instruction before returning a take post-instruction exception primitive. If no modifications are made to the stack frame within the exception handler, an RTE instruction causes the MC68020 to return to program execution at the location specified by the program counter field of the stack frame, which is the address of the next instruction to be executed.

9.2.2.8 RESPONSE PRIMITIVE SUMMARY. Table 9-7 lists a summary of all primitive responses utilized by the MC68851 in numeric order. The utilization of these primitives is implementation-dependent and is subject to future change without notice.

9.3 INSTRUCTION DIALOGS

The following paragraphs detail the coprocessor communication dialogs that are executed by the MC68851 and MC68020 during each memory management instruction. In this discussion, a dialog refers to the sequence of command and data transfers to/from the MC68851, and the service request primitives that are returned to control that sequence. Although the following discussion assumes that the main processor is an MC68020, information is also presented that may be used by designers of systems that utilize a different main processor.

The diagrams presented in the following paragraphs represent the activity of the MC68020 and the MC68851 during the execution of an MC68851 instruction. In these diagrams, boxes are used to depict periods of time during which a device is actively participating in the execution of an instruction; the absence of a box during a period indicates that a device is waiting on the other one to complete an operation.

Each box in the following diagrams is labeled to indicate the activity depicted by that box. The labels above or to the right of the boxes identify the actions taken by the main processor, while the labels below or to the left of the boxes identify the encoding of the response CIR at any time during a dialog. Usually, when a response CIR encoding is indicated, the encoding will be received by the main processor any time that the response CIR is read until the next primitive encoding

Table 9-7. MC68851 Primitive Responses

Primitive Value	Primitive Type	Comments
$0802	Null	CA = 0, PC = 0, IA = 0, PF = 1, TF = 0
$0803		CA = 0, PC = 0, IA = 0, PF = 1, TF = 1
$0A00	Evaluate and Transfer Effective Address	CA = 0, PC = 0
$0C00	Transfer Single Main Processor Register CA = 0, PC = 0, DR = 0 (Main Processor to MC68851)	D0
$0C01		D1
$0C02		D2
$0C03		D3
$0C04		D4
$0C05		D5
$0C06		D6
$0C07		D7
$0D00	Transfer Main Processor Control Register	CA = 0, PC = 0, DR = 0
$1608	Evaluate (ea) and Transfer Data CA = 0, PC = 0, DR = 0 (External to MC68851)	Quad Word (Memory Only)
$1701		Byte
$1702		Word
$1704		Long Word
$1C0B	Take Pre-Instruction Exception PC = 0	F-Line Emulation
$1C0D		Protocol Violation
$1E38	Take Post-Instruction Exception PC = 0	Configuration Error
$1E39		Illegal Operation
$1E3A		Access Violation
$2C08	Transfer Single Main Processor Register CA = 0, PC = 0, DR = 1 (MC68851 to Main Processor)	A0
$2C09		A1
$2C0A		A2
$2C0B		A3
$2C0C		A4
$2C0D		A5
$2C0E		A6
$2C0F		A7
$3208	Evaluate (ea) and Transfer Data CA = 0, PC = 0, DR = 1 (MC68851 to External)	Quad Word (Memory Only)
$3301		Byte
$3302		Word
$3304		Long Word
$8400	Supervisor Check	
$8800	Null	CA = 1, PC = 0, IA = 0, PF = 0, TF = 0
$8A00	Evaluate and Transfer Effective Address	CA = 1, PC = 0
$8C00	Transfer Single Main Processor Register CA = 1, PC = 0, DR = 0 (Main Processor to MC68851)	D0
$8C01		D1
$8C02		D2
$8C03		D3
$8C04		D4
$8C05		D5
$8C06		D6
$8C07		D7
$8C08		A0
$8C09		A1
$8C0A		A2
$8C0B		A3
$8C0C		A4
$8C0D		A5
$8C0E		A6
$8C0F		A7
$8D00	Transfer Main Processor Control Register	CA = 1, PC = 0, DR = 0
$9608	Evaluate (ea) and Transfer Data CA = 1, PC = 0, DR = 0 (External to MC68851)	Quad Word (Memory Only)
$9701		Byte
$9702		Word
$9704		Long Word

is indicated. Additionally, if the MC68020 fails a supervisor check performed as the result of the MC68851 supervisor check primitive, the resulting trap is the privilege violation exception.

In all of the following paragraphs, the following assumptions are made:
1) Before the start of an instruction dialog, except for the PSAVE and PRESTORE instructions, the MC68851 is in the idle state,
2) The MC68020 and the MC68851 communicate via a 32-bit data bus, and
3) The memory width is 32 bits, and all memory operands are long-word aligned.

9.3.1 General Instructions

This group of instructions includes the MC68851 instructions: PFLUSH, PFLUSHA, PFLUSHR, PFLUSHS, PLOADR, PLOADW, PMOVE, PTESTR, PTESTW, and PVALID. The common factor between these instructions is the format of the F-line operation word, which uses the CpGEN format of the M68000 Family coprocessor instruction set (refer to the *MC68020 32-Bit Microprocessor User's Manual*. Thus, the initial phase of the communication dialog for these instructions is identical, with the MC68020 writing the command word to the MC68851 and then relying on the MC68851 to control the remainder of the dialog through the use of the coprocessor interface response primitive set.

In general, the dialog for an MC68851 instruction does not advance to the next state until all activity has been completed in the current state. The MC68851 enforces this by controlling the assertion of the data transfer and size acknowledge ($\overline{\text{DSACKx}}$) signals and through the use of the come-again attribute of the response primitives.

The following paragraphs discuss the different protocols that are used by the MC68851 for this group of instructions.

9.3.1.1 PFLUSH INSTRUCTIONS. The dialogs for these instructions are initiated by a write to the command register and a read of the response register.

The PFLUSH instruction may require that one of the main processor function code registers (SFC of DFC) be transferred if a function code is required for the flush operation and the value is not encoded in the coprocessor operation word. If the transfer of SFC or DFC is required, the MC68851 issues a transfer main processor control register primitive and indicates the required register in the register select CIR. Alternately, the function code may reside in one of the main processor data registers. If so, the MC68851 will issue the transfer single main processor register primitive to have the appropriate register transferred. After the function code transfer is complete (if required), the evaluate and transfer effective address primitive is issued requesting the calculation and transfer of an effective address from the main processor to the MC68851 for use in the flush operation. The MC68851 performs the flush operation and releases the processor upon completion. Until the flush is complete, the MC68851 does not terminate the write cycle accessing the operand address CIR (i.e., the $\overline{\text{DSACKx}}$ signals are not asserted). This ensures that the next cycle is translated correctly.

The supervisor check for these instructions may be returned either before or after the function code transfer (if any) but always occurs before any entries are flushed from the ATC.

The dialogs for the PFLUSH instructions are shown in Figures 9-18 and 9-19. The key for all instruction dialogs presented in this section are shown in Figure 9-19.

9.3.1.2 PLOAD INSTRUCTIONS. The dialog for these instructions is similar to that used during the PFLUSH instructions. The major difference in the communication required for these instruc-

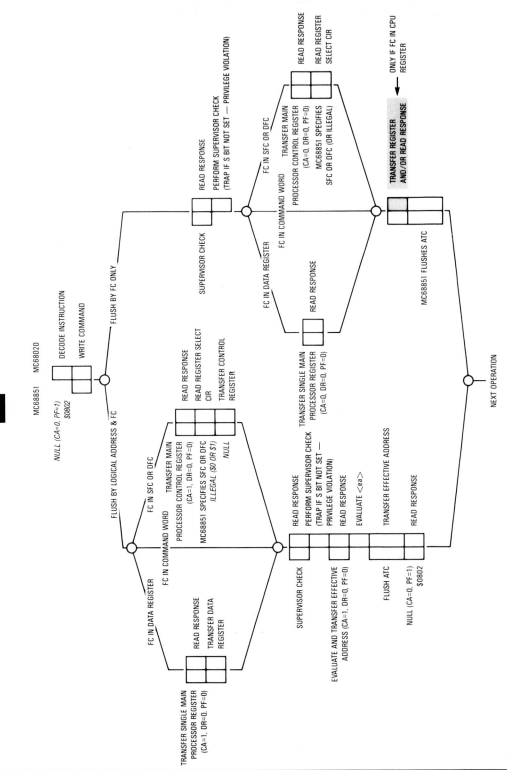

Figure 9-18. PFLUSH and PFLUSHS Instruction Dialog

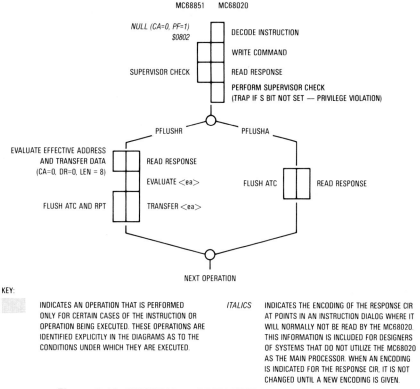

Figure 9-19. PFLUSHA and PFLUSHR Instruction Dialog

tions is that the MC68851 must take control of the logical bus in order to perform a search of the address translation tables (refer to **4.2.3.4 NORMALLY TERMINATED ADDRESS TRANSLATION WITH RELINQUISH REQUEST**). The MC68851 requests bus mastership simultaneously with the termination of the effective address transfer accessing the operand address CIR.

During the table search operation it is possible for an alternate higher priority bus master to request and receive control of the logical bus, preempting completion of the MC68851 operation. The state of the coprocessor instruction is always maintained although the table search may have to be restarted. However, unless a PSAVE is executed prior to access and a PRESTORE is executed prior to returning control to the main processor, alternate bus masters must not be allowed to access the MC68851 coprocessor interface register set during instruction execution as this may cause the context of the instruction in progress to be permanently lost. Systems employing multiple devices capable of accessing the MC68851 registers must provide for synchronization of instruction execution (refer to **APPENDIX C SOFTWARE CONSIDERATIONS**).

The only difference between the PLOADR and PLOADW instructions is that the translation tables are updated for a read or a write cycle, respectively, during the table search. The dialog for the PLOAD instructions is shown in Figure 9-20.

9.3.1.3 PMOVE INSTRUCTION. The dialogs for this instruction are used for all move operations to and from the MC68851 register set.

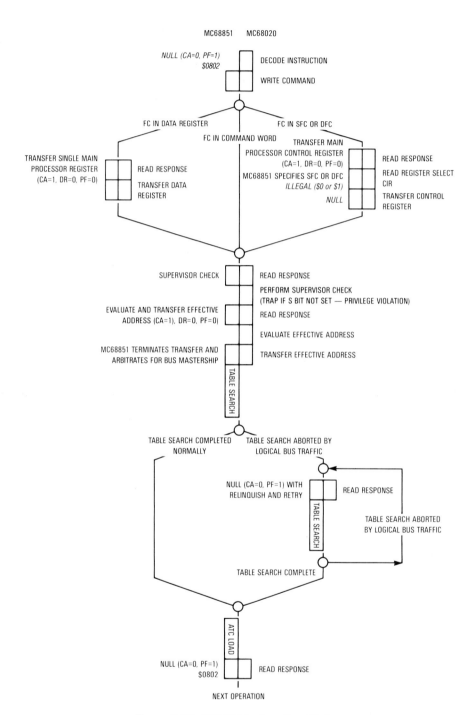

Figure 9-20. PLOAD Instruction Dialog

The dialog is initiated with the command CIR write and the supervisor check primitive response. After performing the supervisor check, the main processor is requested to evaluate the effective address encoded in the F-line coprocessor instruction word and transfer data to or from the MC68851.

After the data transfer is complete, the main processor is released from the MC68851-to-external instruction dialog as shown in Figure 9-21. For external transfers to the MC68851, the protocol is somewhat more complex. Data written to any of the root pointer registers must be checked for validity and the ATC must be updated before the processor can be allowed to continue with the next instruction. Data written to the translation control register undergoes several consistency checks to ensure that the logical address is completely mapped and the requested memory page size is greater than 256 bytes. Before the processor is allowed to continue, the ATC is flushed. The dialog for a write to the translation control register or the root pointer registers is shown in Figure 9-22.

The instruction dialog for write operations to other MC68851 registers is shown in Figure 9-23. The only operation that is not entirely straight-forward is the write to the breakpoint acknowledge control register. When the write operation enables the breakpoint corresponding to the register accessed, the MC68851 sets a save-breakpoint-state flag (if it is not already set) that indicates that the long format state frame including all the BADx and BACx registers, must be saved in response to a PSAVE instruction. When the write operation disables the corresponding breakpoint, the MC68851 checks the enable bits of all of the breakpoint acknowledge control registers to determine if there are any breakpoints still enabled. If no breakpoints remain enabled, the MC68851 clears the save-breakpoint-state flag indicating that the long format state no longer needs to be saved in response to a PSAVE instruction. Otherwise, the flag remains set.

The PMOVE external-to-MC68851 dialog for accesses to the CAL, VAL, SCC, AC, BADx, status, and BACx registers is shown in Figure 9-23.

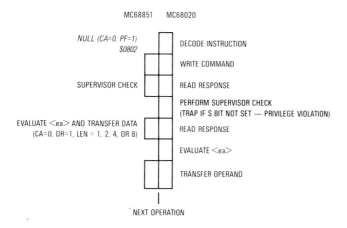

Figure 9-21. PMOVE PMMUreg,⟨ea⟩ Instruction Dialog

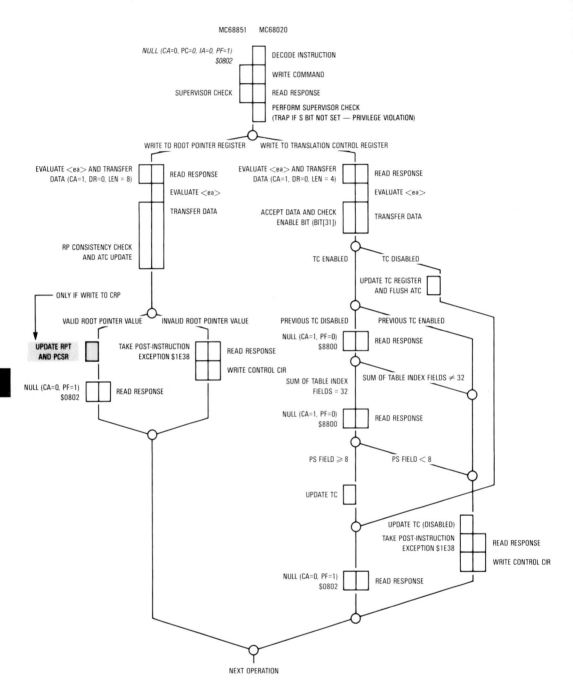

Figure 9-22. PMOVE ⟨ea⟩,PMMUreg (Root Pointer or TC Registers)

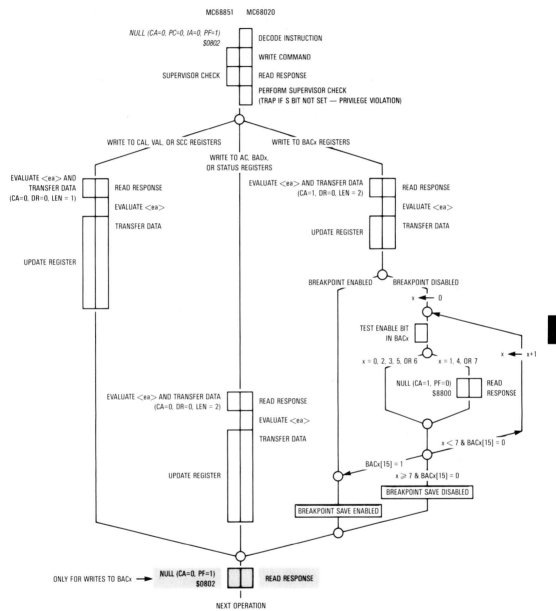

Figure 9-23. PMOVE ⟨ea⟩,PMMUreg (CAL, VAL, SCC, AC, PSR, PSCR, BADx, and BACx Registers)

9.3.1.4 PTEST INSTRUCTIONS. The beginning of the dialog for the PTEST instructions is similar to that of the PLOAD instructions described above. However, the MC68851 does not perform a table search operation if a level zero test is requested. At the termination of a PTEST instruction with a non-zero level specification, the MC68851 may optionally return the physical address used to perform the last level of the search. If this is requested, the MC658851 issues the transfer main processor register primitive that causes the main processor to transfer a long word address from the MC68851 operand register into one of the address registers of the processor.

The only difference between the PTESTR and PTESTW variations of this instruction is in the examination of access rights for the detection of an access level violation (refer to **6.1.10.4 ACCESS LEVEL VIOLATION**). The dialog of this instruction is shown in Figure 9-24.

9.3.1.5 PVALID INSTRUCTION. The PVALID instruction differs from other MC68851 general instructions in that the supervisor check primitive is not issued during the dialog for this instruction. Since this instruction terminates with an exception (access violation) if the task executing this instruction does not have sufficient access rights, no further protection is required. Furthermore, if the access level protection mechanism is disabled, the dialog for this instruction is always terminated with an access violation exception. The dialog for this instruction is shown in Figure 9-25.

9.3.2 Conditional Instructions

This group of instructions includes the PBcc, PDBcc, PScc, and PTRAPcc instructions. The common factor between these instructions is that the execution of each one is defined by the M68000 Family coprocessor instruction set, and the dialog used for all of them is the same. The dialog consists of only one write cycle and two read cycles; the main processor writes the conditional predicate to the MC68851 and then reads the response CIR, first to receive a supervisor check, and again to receive the result of the evaluation. After the supervisor check, the MC68851 always responds immediately with a true or false result, and the main processor then proceeds with the appropriate conditional action. This dialog is shown in Figure 9-26.

9.3.3 Context Switch Instructions

This group of instructions includes the PSAVE and PRESTORE instructions. The common factor between these instructions is that the execution of each one is defined by the M68000 Family coprocessor instruction set, and the coprocessor does not control the dialog in the flexible manner available with the general and conditional instruction types. The dialog consists of the save and restore command, followed by the transfer of the appropriate state information. These dialogs are discussed in the following paragraphs.

9.3.3.1 PSAVE. This dialog is utilized for the context save instruction. The dialog for this instruction is shown in Figure 9-27. No response primitives are issued during the dialog for the PSAVE instruction. The MC68851 controls the frame transfer to a limited extent through the use of the format word encoding.

The main processor initiates this dialog by reading from the save CIR. During this read cycle, the MC68851 returns a format word that indicates the current state of the machine. For most cases of this dialog, the first read of the save CIR returns the idle format word, and the main processor then proceeds to transfer nine long words from the operand CIR to memory. If the MC68851 is busy processing a coprocessor instruction when the PSAVE is encountered, a busy format word is returned and an 11 long word, mid-coprocessor instruction frame will be saved if all breakpoints were disabled. A 19 long word frame will be saved if any breakpoints were enabled. The invalid

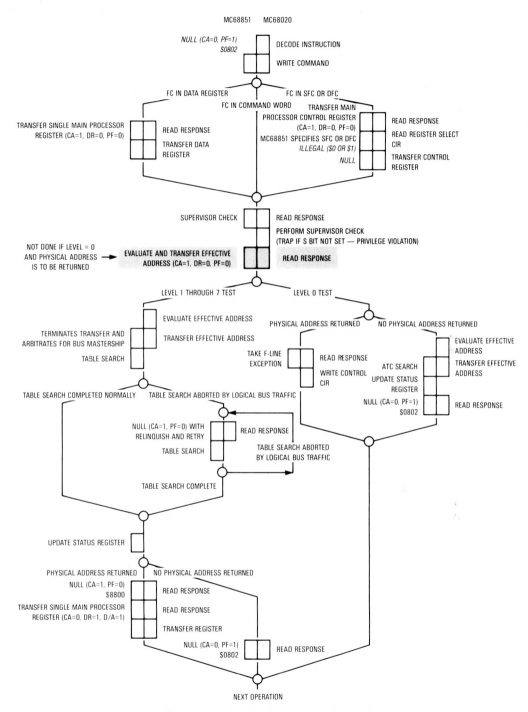

Figure 9-24. PTEST Instruction Dialog

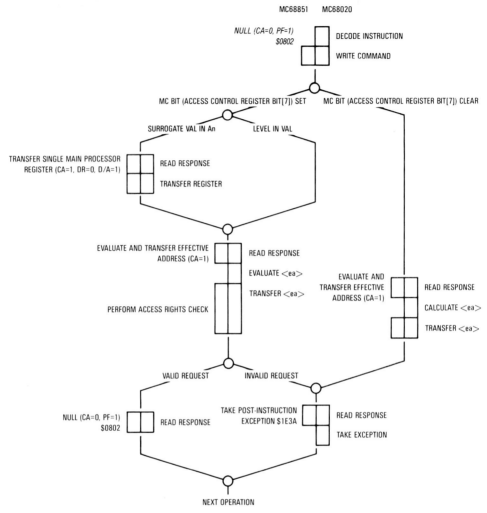

Figure 9-25. PVALID Instruction Dialog

format word may also be returned, as discussed in **9.3.4.6 FORMAT EXCEPTION, PSAVE INSTRUCTION**.

After the MC68020 receives a valid format word, it then evaluates the effective address and writes the format word to that address. The appropriate state frame is then transferred to the effective address, and the main processor is free to proceed with the execution of the next instruction.

Since the MC68851 does not return any primitives during execution of the PSAVE instruction, it is the responsibility of the processor to ensure that a PSAVE instruction is executed only in the supervisor mode of operation (the MC68020 does this automatically).

Note that after the state save operation is complete, the MC68851 is in the idle state with no pending exceptions.

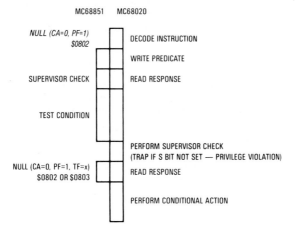

Figure 9-26. Conditional Instruction Dialog

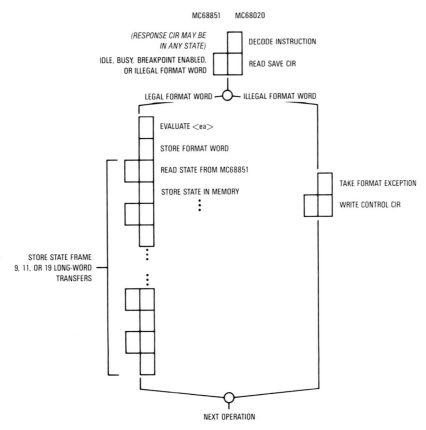

Figure 9-27. PSAVE Instruction Dialog

9.3.3.2 PRESTORE. This dialog is utilized for the context restore instruction. The dialog for this instruction is shown in Figure 9-28. As with the PSAVE instruction, no primitives are issued during the dialog for this instruction. The MC68851 controls the frame transfer to a limited extent through the use of the format word encoding.

The main processor initiates the restore dialog by evaluating the effective address, fetching a format word from that address, and writing the format word to the restore CIR. The main processor then reads the restore CIR to verify that the format word is valid. During this read cycle, the MC68851 returns a format word that indicates if the format word that was written is valid for the current revision of the device. If the format word is valid, the same value that was written is read back from the restore CIR, and the main processor proceeds to transfer the state frame appropriate for the format word. The state frame size is 0, 9, 11, or 19 long words for the current implementation of the MC68851. The invalid format word may also be returned as discussed in **9.3.4.7 FORMAT EXCEPTION, PRESTORE INSTRUCTION**. Note that after the state restore operation is complete, the MC68851 is in the state of the instruction (if any) that was previously suspended with a PSAVE instruction.

Since the MC68851 does not return any primitives during execution of the PRESTORE instruction, it is the responsibility of the processor to ensure that a PRESTORE instruction is executed only in the supervisor mode of operation (the MC68020 does this automatically).

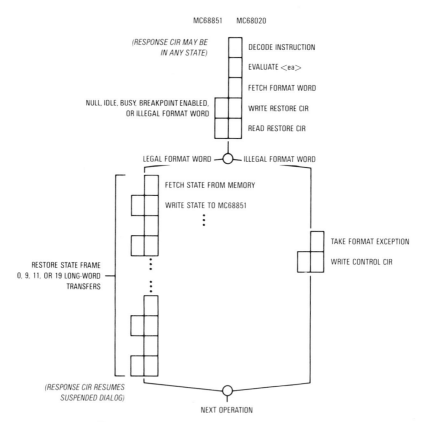

Figure 9-28. PRESTORE Instruction Dialog

9.3.4 Exception Processing

This group of dialogs is actually a set of special cases of the dialogs described previously; they are grouped here for quick reference, and to simplify the preceding discussions. For each of the exception processing dialogs, only the differences from the normal instruction dialogs shown above are discussed here. Also, it should be noted that these dialogs do not include all exception processing sequences that involve the MC68851; they only include those exceptions that are directly related to the coprocessor interface operation. For example, main-processor-detected F-line exceptions are not included, since no coprocessor interface dialog occurs as part of the exception processing for this type of an exception. Also not included in the diagrams below is the dialog for the coprocessor protocol violation exception. This is due to the fact that these exceptions are not expected to occur during the normal operation of a fully debugged system, and that the dialog is not readily predictable (either before or after the protocol violation occurs). For main-processor-detected protocol violations, the cause of the exception is, by definition, a hardware failure (since the MC68851 can not return an illegal response primitive).

For MC68851-detected protocol violations, the cause is most likely a software failure that causes a new instruction to be initiated before the previous instruction dialog is completed. In this case, both the previous and the new instruction dialogs are aborted immediately.

9.3.4.1 TAKE PRE-INSTRUCTION EXCEPTION.

This dialog is utilized by the MC68851 when the main processor writes an undefined, reserved command word to the command or condition CIR. The take pre-instruction exception dialog consists of two write cycles and one read cycle, as shown in Figure 9-29. First, the main processor attempts to initiate a new instruction by writing to the command CIR; it then reads the response CIR to determine the next required action. The MC68851 returns the take pre-instruction exception in this case, indicating the appropriate vector number. The main processor services this primitive by writing an exception acknowledge to the control CIR and initiates exception processing. An exception to this dialog is the F-line exception returned by the PTEST instruction as shown in Figure 9-24.

Note that the write of the exception acknowledge causes the response CIR encoding to be changed to the null primitive, thus assuring that the take exception primitive is received by the main processor while avoiding spurious request primitives in non-MC68020 based systems.

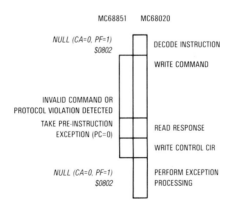

Figure 9-29. Take Pre-Instruction Exception Dialog

9.3.4.2 TAKE POST-INSTRUCTION EXCEPTION. This dialog is utilized by the MC68851 if an exception occurs as the result of execution of any MC68851 instruction that requests an illegal configuration, an invalid operation, or an access violation. In this case, the protocol for the normal execution of the instruction is followed and then the take post-instruction exception is reported as the last primitive (in lieu of the null primitive normally used to terminate the dialog). The MC68851 always adjusts the scanPC of the MC68020 to point to the next instruction before returning a take post-instruction exception primitives. The main processor services this primitive by initiating exception processing. The dialog for this operation is shown in Figure 9-30.

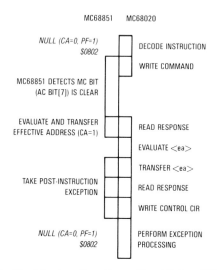

Figure 9-30. Take Post-Instruction Exception Dialog (PVALID Example)

Note that a read of the response register causes the response CIR encoding to be changed to the null primitive, thus assuring that the take exception primitive is received by the main processor while avoiding spurious request primitives in non-MC68020 based systems.

9.3.4.3 F-LINE EMULATOR EXCEPTION. This dialog is utilized by the MC68851 when a general instructon is initiated and the value written to the command CIR is not a legal MC68851 command word encoding or an unrecognized condition selector is written to the condition CIR. In this case, this dialog consists of two write cycles and one read cycle, as shown in Figure 9-31. First the main processor attempts to initiate a new instruction by writing to the command CIR; it then reads the response CIR to determine the appropriate action to be taken. In this case, the first read of the response CIR returns a take exception primitive with the F-line emulator vector number. The main processor services this primitive by writing an exception acknowledge to the control CIR and initiating exception processing.

Note that the write of the exception acknowledge causes the response CIR encoding to be changed to the null primitive, while avoiding spurious request primitives in non-MC68020 based systems.

9.3.4.4 FORMAT EXCEPTION, PSAVE INSTRUCTION. This dialog is utilized by the MC68851 when a PSAVE or PRESTORE instruction dialog is interrupted by an attempt to initiate a new PSAVE instruction (by reading from the save CIR). In this case, the MC68851 returns the invalid

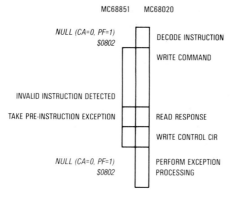

Figure 9-31. Take F-Line Emulation Exception Dialog

format word to signal the illegal nesting of the PSAVE instruction. The main processor services this format word by writing an abort to the control CIR and initiating exception processing. The dialog for this operation is shown in Figure 9-32.

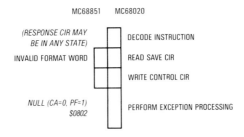

Figure 9-32. PSAVE Format Exception Dialog

Since the MC68020 writes an abort to the MC68851 in response to the illegal format word, the PSAVE or PRESTORE that was interrupted by the nested PSAVE is destructively aborted, with no indication to the suspended instruction that this has occurred. Thus, a suspended save operation continues to read the frame from the operand CIR if it is resumed, even though the data in the operand CIR is not valid. Likewise, a suspended restore operation writes the remainder of the frame to the operand CIR if it is resumed, even though the data written is ignored and the restore operation is not performed. Due to the destructive behavior of a nested PSAVE instruction, programmers must be certain that the MC68851 is not executing a PSAVE or PRESTORE instruction prior to an attempt to execute a new PSAVE instruction. The most likely cause of a nested PSAVE operation is the main processor receiving a bus error during a PSAVE or PRESTORE operation. This should not be allowed to occur and can be avoided by accessing the top of the system stack and the address 19 long words beyond it immediately before executing the PSAVE. This ensures that the stack area is properly allocated.

9.3.4.5 FORMAT EXCEPTION, PRESTORE INSTRUCTION. This dialog is utilized by the MC68851 when a PRESTORE instruction is initiated by writing an invalid format word value to the restore CIR (in this context, the term invalid format value refers to any value that is not a null, idle, or busy (mid-instruction, breakpoints enabled or disabled) format word value recognized by the MC68851). In this case, the MC68851 returns the explicit invalid format word ($02xx) to signal the unrecognized format word value. The main processor services this format word by writing an abort to the control CIR and initiating exception processing. The dialog for this operation is shown in Figure 9-33. Note that this is a destructive exception, since any instruction that was executing is aborted when the PRESTORE instruction is initiated.

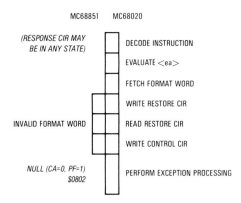

Figure 9-33. PRESTORE Format Exception Dialog

SECTION 10
ACCESS LEVEL CONTROL INTERFACE

This section describes the access level control interface with respect to the communication protocol utilized by the MC68020 and the MC68851 during the type $01 module operations, CALLM and RTM. This communications protocol includes electrical and command level mechanisms that allow the MC68851 to extend the protection mechanism of the main processor (refer to the *MC68020 32-Bit Microprocessor User's Manual*.

10.1 ACCESS LEVEL CONTROL INTERFACE SIGNAL CONNECTION

Identical to case of the coprocessor interface register set, the selection of the MC68851 access level interface register set is based upon an internally generated chip select signal that is decoded from the logical address and function code inputs when the processor initiates an access to this register set.

The MC68851 contains a set of access level control registers (ALCRs) by which the main processor and MC68851 communicate during module operations. These registers are not part of the programming model implemented by the MC68851. Rather, they are used as communication ports that have specific functions associated with each register. The programmer is never required to explicitly access these interface registers, since the access level control interface is implemented in the hardware and microcode of the MC68020 and the MC68851. When the MC68020 is not used as the main processor, the MC68851 ALCRs can be explicitly accessed by a software routine that emulates the behavior of the MC68020 with respect to the access level control interface.

For more information on the electrical interconnection between the main processor and the MC68851, refer to **APPENDIX B HARDWARE CONSIDERATIONS**.

10.1.1 Selecting the MC68851

A portion of the CPU space, identified by the MC68020 address bus is dedicated to access control functions. Figure 10-1 illustrates the required address bus encoding for access level control accesses in the CPU address space. The bit positions marked with an 'x' are zero-filled by the MC68020 but are ignored by the MC68851.

Figure 10-1. Access Level Control Interface Logical Address Bus Encoding

During CPU space cycles, address bits A16–A19 indicate the CPU space function that the main processor is performing. The MC68020 utilizes four of the possible 16 encodings of A16–A19 as listed in Table 9-1.

The MMU register (ALCR select) field, A0–A15, is decoded by the MC68851 to select the appropriate ALCR. Although the MC68851 decodes the full address range specified on A0–A15, the MC68851 ALCRs occupy only the lower 128 bytes of this range. Any access above this range (A7–A15 = 0) is ignored for a write cycle and returns the null value (all ones) for a read (the MC68851 terminates these accessses by asserting $\overline{\text{DSACKx}}$). For a map of the implemented MC68851 access control interface registers in the CPU address space, refer to Figure 10-2. Since address bits A20–A31 are not present on all implementations of M68000 processors, these bits are not essential for decoding CPU space transactions and are ignored for the purposes of decoding CPU space accesses.

	31	23	0
$10000	CL	(UNUSED, RESERVED)	
$10004	ACCESS STATUS	(UNUSED, RESERVED)	
$10008	IAL	(UNUSED, RESERVED)	
$1000C	DAL	(UNUSED, RESERVED)	
$10040	FUNCTION CODE 0 DESCRIPTOR ADDRESS		
$10044	FUNCTION CODE 1 DESCRIPTOR ADDRESS (USER DATA)		
$10048	FUNCTION CODE 2 DESCRIPTOR ADDRESS (USER PROGRAM)		
$1004C	FUNCTION CODE 3 DESCRIPTOR ADDRESS (USER, RESERVED)		
$10050	FUNCTION CODE 4 DESCRIPTOR ADDRESS (SUPERVISOR DATA)		
$10054	FUNCTION CODE 5 DESCRIPTOR ADDRESS (SUPERVISOR PROGRAM)		
$10058	FUNCTION CODE 6 DESCRIPTOR ADDRESS		
$1005C	FUNCTION CODE 7 DESCRIPTOR ADDRESS (CPU SPACE)		

Figure 10-2. MC68851 Access Level Control Interface Register Map

The internal MC68851 chip select decode for the access level control interface is therefore based upon the function code signals (FC0–FC3) and the CPU space type field (A16–A19). The MC68851 decodes the address bits A0–A6 (A7–A12 must be zero) to determine the function of any access level control access.

10.1.2 Access Level Control Interface Registers

Table 10-1 identifies the MC68851 access level control interface register locations in the CPU space that are used for communications between the MC68020 and the MC68851. Figure 10-2 illustrates the memory map of the ALCRs on a 32-bit bus. When an access level control cycle is executed, the MC68851 decodes the ALCR select field of the address bus, A0–A6 (A7–A15 = 0), to select the appropriate access level control interface register.

The access level control interface registers of the MC68851 appear at the logical addresses shown in Figure 10-2 and Table 10-1.

The following paragraphs describe the characteristics of each of the access level control interface registers as implemented by the MC68851. In these descriptions, the read/write attributes of each register are given. If a register is read-only, write accesses to that location are ignored; read accesses of a write-only register always return all ones. In all cases, the MC68851 asserts $\overline{\text{DSACKx}}$ in response to all CPU space cycles accessing the access level control interface (FC0–FC3 = $7, CPU space type = $1) to terminate the bus cycle.

Table 10-1. Access Level Control Interface Register Characteristics

Register	A6–A0	Offset	Width	Type
CL	0000000	$00	8	Read
Access Status	0000100	$04	8	Read
IAL	0001000	$08	8	Write
DAL	0001100	$0C	8	Write
FC0 Descriptor Address	10000xx	$40	32	Write
FC1 Descriptor Address	10001xx	$44	32	Write
FC2 Descriptor Address	10010xx	$48	32	Write
FC3 Descriptor Address	10011xx	$4C	32	Write
FC4 Descriptor Address	10100xx	$50	32	Write
FC5 Descriptor Address	10101xx	$54	32	Write
FC6 Descriptor Address	10110xx	$58	32	Write
FC7 Descriptor Address	10111xx	$5C	32	Write

10.1.2.1 CURRENT LEVEL (CL) ALCR ($00). When read by the CPU, this 8-bit read-only register supplies the highest-order three bits of the CAL register in the most significant three bits (bits [5–7]) and the highest-order three bits of the VAL register in bits [1–3]. This register is read by the MC68020 during the execution of a CALLM instruction in order to save the access information (CAL and VAL) of the calling module in the saved access level field of the module call stack frame.

10.1.2.2 ACCESS STATUS (AS) ALCR ($04). This 8-bit read-only register contains the status of an access level change that has been requested by the MC68020. During the execution of a CALLM instruction, the MC68851 uses the information contained in the current access level register (CAL), increase access level ALCR (IAL) and the stack change control register (SCC) to determine whether or not the requested module call is valid and whether or not a stack change should occur before program control is passed to the called module. This information is available in AS and is read by the processor to determine the validity of the module operation.

During the execution of an RTM instruction, the MC68851 uses the information contained in the CAL register and the decrease access level ALCR (DAL) to determine whether or not the requested module return operation is valid.

The encodings for the AS ALCR are shown in Table 10-2. The algorithm used to calculate the access status encoding for the CALLM instruction is shown in Figure 10-3.

10.1.2.3 INCREASE ACCESS LEVEL (IAL) ALCR ($08). This 8-bit write-only register is the register through which the MC68020 requests increased access rights during a module call operation. When this register is written, the MC68851 compares the access level contained in the highest-order bits of IAL (1, 2, or 3 bits as determined by the number of access levels in use) against the corresponding bits in the CAL register. If the IAL field is less than or equal to the CAL field (the call is to a module with equal or greater privilege), the requested change is valid, the MC68851 transfers the contents of the CAL register to VAL and transfers the new access level in IAL to CAL. If IAL is greater than CAL (the call is to a module with less privilege), the module operation is invalid, no transfer between registers is made, and the contents of the access status ALCR are updated to indicate that a formt exception should be taken by the CPU.

Table 10-2. Access Status Register Code

Value	Validity	Processor Action
00	Invalid	Format Error
01	Valid	No Change in Access Rights
02–03	Valid	Change Access Rights with No Change of Stack Pointer
04–07	Valid	Change Access Rights and Change Stack Pointer
Other	Undefined	Undefined (Take Format Error)

10.1.2.4 DECREASE ACCESS LEVEL (DAL) ALCR ($0C). This 8-bit write-only register is the register through which the MC68020 requests decreased access rights during a module return operation.

When written by the CPU, the MC68851 compares the access level contained in the highest order bits of DAL (1, 2, or 3 bits as determined by the number of access levels in use) against the corresponding bits in the CAL register. If the DAL field is greater than or equal to the CAL field (the return is to a module with equal or less privilege), the requested change is valid, the highest-order three bits of DAL (bits [5–7]) are placed in bits [5–7] of CAL and bits [1–3] of DAL are placed in bits [5–7] of VAL. If DAL is less than CAL, the return operation is invalid, no transfer between registers is made, and the access status ALCR is updated to indicate that a format exception should be taken by the CPU.

During the execution of an RTM instruction, the MC68020 writes the saved access level field from the module call stack frame to the DAL register to reverse the operation performed by reading the CL ALCR during the CALLM instruction.

10.1.2.5 DESCRIPTOR ADDRESS ALCRS ($40 THROUGH $5C). These eight 32-bit registers are used by the MC68020 to pass the module descriptor address to the MC68851 during a type $01 module call (requsting a change in access level). There is one descriptor address ALCR corresponding to each of the eight MC68020 address spaces (as defined by the function code outputs of the CPU).

During execution of the CALLM instruction, the MC68020 writes the logical address of the module call descriptor to the descriptor address ALCR corresponding to the address space in which the descriptor resides. If module operations are enabled (AC [7] = 1), and the module descriptor size is set to a valid size (AC[0–1] = 0), the MC68851 checks the validity of the descriptor. If any of the above conditions are not met, the access status ALCR is updated to indicate that a format exception should be taken by the CPU.

In order to verify that the module descriptor address is valid, the logical address formed by the contents of the descriptor address ALCR and the function code implicitly associated with that register are used by the MC68851 to perform a table search to locate the translation descriptor corresponding to that address. As part of the execution of the CALLM instruction, the MC68020 reads the first word of the module descriptor prior to writing its address to the descriptor address ALCR, so the ATC will usually contain the required entry. However, it may be necessary to perform an external search for the translation descriptor.

When the MC68851 locates the translation descriptor for the page containing the module descriptor (either in the ATC or from a search of the external tables), it first checks to ensure that the G bit of the page descriptor is set indicating that the page is allowed to contain module descriptors. If

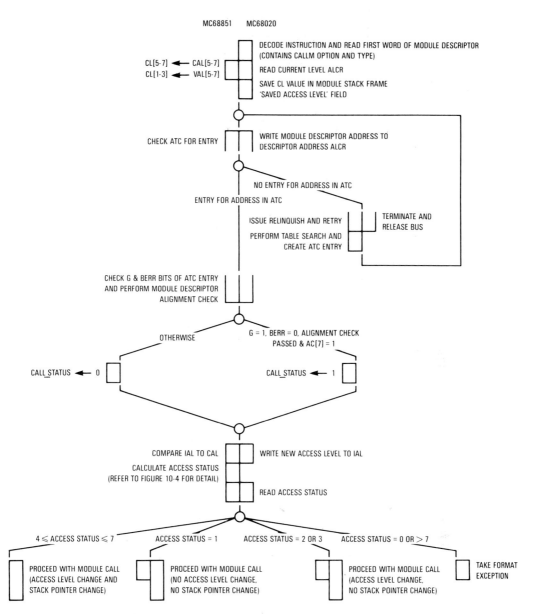

Figure 10-3. CALLM Instruction Dialog Flowchart

this check passes, the MC68851 examines the low-order bits of the module descriptor address to ensure that the descriptor begins on an appropriate byte boundary as determined by the MDS field of the access control (AC) register (bits [0–1]). For module descriptor sizes of 16, 32, and 64 bytes, the lowest order four, five, or six bits, respectively, of a module descriptor address must be zero in order for that address to be valid. If either of the above two conditions are not met, the access status ALCR is updated to indicate that a format exception should be taken by the CPU.

If the MC68851 cannot locate a translation for the module descriptor (table search terminated due to encountering an invalid descriptor or a bus error during the table search) the access status ALCR is updated to indicate that a format exception should be taken by the CPU.

10.2 CALLM AND RTM INSTRUCTIONS

The following paragraphs detail the communication dialog between the MC68020 and the MC68851 during execution of the module call and return instructions with the type $01 attribute (requesting a change in access level). This discussion assumes that the reader is familiar with the format of the module descriptors and stack frames. For further details concerning the CALLM and RTM instructions refer to Appendix D Advanced Topics of the *MC68020 32-Bit Microprocessor User's Manual*.

10.2.1 CALLM Instruction

The MC68020/MC68851 dialog for the CALLM type $01 instruction begins when the MC68020 reads the current access level information (CAL and VAL) from the MC68851 CL ALCR. The value supplied by the MC68851 is placed in the saved access level field of the module call stack frame.

The next operation performed is a verification of the validity of the module descriptor address. The MC68020 writes the address of the module descriptor to the descriptor address ALCR corresponding to the address space in which the descriptor is located. If a valid translation for the descriptor address can be located and module operations are allowed, the MC68851 checks to ensure that the page is allowed to contain module descriptors (G bit set), and that the module descriptor address resides on a proper byte boundary as determined by the value of the access control register.

The MC68020 then requests that the current access level be updated by writing the new access level, taken from the access level field of the module call descriptor, to the increase access level ALCR. If the new access level is less than or equal to the current access level contained in CAL (the called module has a privilege level that is the same as or higher than the calling module), the change is allowed and VAL is updated to contain the privilege level of the calling module (the old value of CAL) and CAL is updated with the contents of IAL to contain the privilege level of the currently active module.

After completion of the access level change verification, the MC68851 uses the information contained in the stack change control (SCC) register to determine whether or not the CPU should change stack pointers before entering the called module. During configuration of the MC68851, the operating system informs the MC68851 as to when stack pointer changes must occur during module operations by the values set in the SCC register.

There is one bit in SCC corresponding to each of the eight possible distinct access levels. If bit n of SCC is set, all module calls from a less privileged access level m ($m > n$) to an access level g of privilege n or higher ($g \leq n$) require a change of stack pointers before the module call can be completed. Module calls that do not change access levels ($m = g$) do not require stack pointer changes. Thus, the operating system can specify that stack pointer changes are required for all module calls that require a change in access level by setting SCC to all ones. Alternately, the operating system can specify that stack changes are never required by clearing all of SCC or could chose any combination of change requirements between these two extremes. For example, setting bit 3 of SCC causes the MC68851 to signal the processor that it must perform a stack change before entering a module at levels three, two, one, or zero when the calling module has a privilege level of four or greater (lower privilege). Similarly, setting bit zero of SCC and leaving all others clear dictates that a stack change must occur when a module operating at any lower privilege level (zero indicating highest priority) calls a level zero module. No other module operations require a stack change.

The final action required to complete the module call dialog between the MC68851 and the MC68020 is for the MC68020 to read the access status (AS) register to determine if the call is valid and to determine whether or not a stack change should occur. The AS encodings used by the MC68851 are shown in Table 10-2.

If any of the validity checks discussed above failed, the CAL and VAL registers are not updated and the access status register returns a format exception encoding. otherwise, one of the valid encodings is returned.

A flowchart of the MC68851/MC68020 dialog for the CALLM type $01 instruction is shown in Figure 10-4.

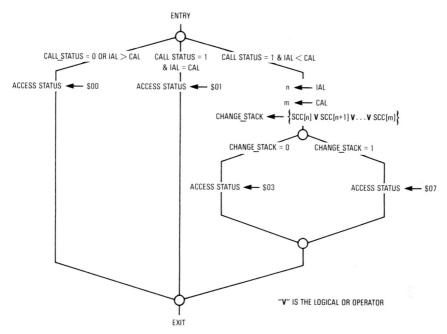

Figure 10-4. Access Status Computation Flowchart

10.2.2 RTM Instruction

Providing that the MC68851 access level mechanism is enabled and module operations are allowed, the MC68020/MC68851 dialog for the RTM instruction begins when the MC68020 writes the saved access level information (CAL and VAL) to the MC68851 DAL ALCR. The value written to the MC68851 was placed in the saved access level field of the module call stack frame by the CALLM instruction.

Following the write operation to DAL, the MC68851 compares the access level contained in the highest order bits of DAL (one, two, or three bits as determined by the number of access levels in use) against the corresponding bits in the CAL register. If the DAL field is greater than or equal to the CAL field (the return is to a module with equal or less privilege), the requested change is valid, the highest-order three bits of DAL (bits [5–7]) are placed in bits [5–7] of CAL and bits [1–3] of DAL are placed in bits [5–7] of VAL. If DAL is less than CAL, the return operation is invalid, no transfer between registers is made, and the access status ALCR is updated to indicate that a format exception should be taken by the CPU. Otherwise, AS is set to $01 to indicate that the return operation is valid.

A flowchart of the MC68851/MC68020 dialog for the RTM instruction is shown in Figure 10-5.

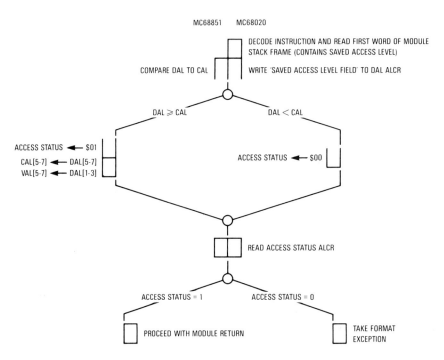

Figure 10-5. RTM Instruction Dialog Flowchart

SECTION 11
OPERATION TIMINGS

This section gives the instruction execution and operations (table searches, . . ., etc.) times for the MC68851 in terms of external clock cycles. This section provides the user with some reasonably accurate execution and operations timing guidelines, not exact timings for every possible circumstance. This approach is used since the exact execution time for an instruction or operation is highly dependent on such things as processor/coprocessor timing relationships, memory speeds, and external table structures. The timing numbers presented in the following tables allow the assembly language programmer or compiler writer to predict worse case timings needed to evaluate the performance of the MC68851. Additionally, the timings for exception processing, context switching, and interrupt processing are included so that designers of multitasking or real-time systems can predict such things as task switch overhead and maximum interrupt latency due to the presence of the MC68851.

11.1 FACTORS AFFECTING EXECUTION TIMES

When investigating instruction execution timing for the MC68851, it is assumed that a system designer requires the following information in order to make informed engineering decisions:
- Best case instruction execution and operating timing for the MC68851, for determining whether or not the MC68851-based system can meet certain performance criteria.
- The effects that an MC68851 might have on system related timings such as context switch overhead time in multi-tasking systems, or interrupt latency in real-time systems.

In this manual, instruction execution times are given in clock cycles to remove clock frequency dependencies from the times given, and the following assumptions are used to define the context of the times given.
- The main processor is an MC68020, acting as the host to the MC68851, and the two devices use the same clock input.
- All operands in memory, as well as the system stack, are long word aligned.
- A 32-bit data bus is used for communications between the MC68020 and both the MC68851 and system memory.
- All memory accesses occur with no wait states.
- No exceptions occur (except as specified).

11.2 ADDRESS TRANSLATION TABLE SEARCH TIMING

The time taken for an address translation table search by the MC68851 depends on the configuration of the translation tables, the states of U and M bits in the translation descriptors, the length of time that a bus cycle takes, and other factors. Since there are a large number of variables involved, a program is provided that calculates the time required for the MC68851 to perform a table search. To allow the time to be determined for any configuration, the following interactive program may be used. The program is a shell script suitable for use with **sh(1)** on either UNIX™ System V or BSD 4.2. To use this program, run the script and answer questions regarding the system configuration and current state as prompted by the program. When the routine prompts the user, the value in square brackets at the end of a question line is the default value that will be used if a carriage return is entered.

The shell script assumes that the data bus between the MC68851 and memory is 32 bits wide. To calculate the table search time for buses narrower than 32 bits, supply the time required for two bus cycles (16-bit data bus) or four bus cycles (8-bit data bus) when prompted for the basic bus cycle time.

The times provided by this procedure include all phases of the table search (bus arbitration, . . . , etc.).

Timings on various mask versions of the MC68851 may differ slightly from the values calculated by the shell script.

```
####################################################################
# This script is suitable for use with sh(1) on either System V or
# BSD 4.2. When run, it will prompt for several parameters, print a
# configuration message, and then print the number of clocks and bus
# cycles required for the table search. Questions may be answered with
# a return, and the default in square brackets will be selected.
#
# The following things should be noted by the user:
#
# 1. This script gives an approximation of the time taken for a table
#    search and associated overhead for a miss in the ATC. The exact
#    time may vary across different mask versions of the MC68851.
#
# 2. It does not give the time for table searches required by the PLOAD
#    and PTEST instructions. These will typically be longer.
#
# 3. It does not account for Delay Timeouts (DTOs) other than the default,
#    asyncronous operation with a master, write bus cycles of different
#    length than read bus cycles, or exception conditions that can
#    arise during a table search.
#
# 4. It does little error checking. It is possible to describe inconsistent
#    and impossible configurations to the script.
#
#    Note: On System V, the "-n" flag should be removed from the echo
#    commands

echo    "Enter bus arbitration time (clocks from S0 to first T1). "
echo -n "Minimum is 7 [7]: "
read busarb
if test ! "$busarb"; then
     busarb=7
fi

echo -n "Enter bus cycle time (in clocks) [3]: "
read bus
if test ! "$bus"; then
     bus=3
fi

echo    "Enter 1 if bus arb proceeds in parallel"
echo -n "with startup, 0 otherwise [1]: "
read early
if test ! "$early"; then
     early=1
fi
```

```
echo -n "Enter 1 if there is a function code lookup, 0 otherwise [0]: "
read fcl
if test ! "$fcl"; then
    fcl=0
fi


echo    "Enter number of long descriptors (page and pointer), "
echo -n "including FCL ones [0]: "
read long
if test ! "$long"; then
    long=0
fi

echo    "Enter number of short descriptors (page or pointer), "
echo -n "including FCL ones [0]: "
read short
if test ! "$short"; then
    short=0
fi

echo -n "Enter number of short to long transitions [0]: "
read s_to_l
if test ! "$s_to_l"; then
    s_to_l=0
fi

echo -n "Enter 1 if there is a long indirect descriptor, 0 otherwise [0]: "
read l_ind
if test ! "$l_ind"; then
    l_ind=0
fi

echo -n "Enter 1 if there is a short indirect descriptor, 0 otherwise [0]: "
read s_ind
if test ! "$s_ind"; then
    s_ind=0
fi

echo -n "Enter number of cleared ubits encountered in long pointers [0]: "
read l_pointer_ubits
if test ! "$l_pointer_ubits"; then
    l_pointer_ubits=0
fi

echo -n "Enter number of cleared ubits encountered in short pointers [0]: "
read s_pointer_ubits
if test ! "$s_pointer_ubits"; then
    s_pointer_ubits=0
fi

echo -n "Enter 1 if the page descriptor ubit is set, 0 otherwise [1]: "
read page_ubit
if test ! "$page_ubit"; then
    page_ubit=1
fi

echo -n "Enter 1 if the page descriptor mbit is set, 0 otherwise [1]: "
read page_mbit
if test ! "$page_mbit"; then
    page_mbit=1
fi
```

```
echo    "Enter 1 if the page descriptor is encountered unexpectedly,"
echo -n "0 otherwise [0]: "
read et
if test ! "$et"; then
     et=0
fi

echo    "Enter 1 if the walk occurred due to a"
echo -n "write to an unmodified page [1]: "
read unmod
if test ! "$unmod"; then
     unmod=1
fi

echo -n "Enter 1 if the page descriptor is long, and not root pointer [0]: "
read long_page
if test ! "$long_page"; then
     long_page=0
fi


####################################################################
#
# Variables:
#
#   overhead      - startup and termination overhead (boxes).
#   busarb        - the time from LBROUT asserted to first box.
#   bus_accesses  - number of bus accesses required.
#   s_to_l_penalty- dead time between a short to long transition.
#
#
####################################################################

####################################################################
#
# Print Configuration message.
#
####################################################################

levels=`expr $short + $long + $l_ind + $s_ind`

if test $fcl -eq 1; then
     tmp1=" one for FCL"
else
     tmp1=""
fi

out1="Configuration: $levels levels $tmp1  - "


if test $long -ne 0 ; then
out1="$out1 $long long descriptors "
fi

if test $short -ne 0 ; then
out1="$out1 $short short descriptors"
fi
```

```
if test $l_ind -eq 1 ; then
    out1="$out1 long indirection"
elif test $s_ind -eq 1 ; then
    out1="$out1 short indirection"
fi

out2="+"

if test $early -eq 0 ; then
    out2="$out2 no early startup, "
fi

if test $s_to_l -ne 0 ; then
    out2="$out2 $s_to_l short to long transitions, "
fi

if test $l_pointer_ubits -ne 0 ;  then
    out2="$out2 $l_pointer_ubits long pointer ubits clear, "
fi

if test $s_pointer_ubits -ne 0 ; then
    out2="$out2 $s_pointer_ubits short pointer ubits clear, "
fi

if test $page_ubit -eq 0 ; then
    out2="$out2 page ubit clear, "
fi

if test $page_mbit -eq 0 ;  then
    out2="$out2 page mbit clear, "
fi

if test $et -eq 1 ; then
    out2="$out2 early termination, "
fi

if test $unmod -eq 1 ; then
    out2="$out2 write to unmodified page, "
fi

if test $long_page -eq 1 ; then
    out2="$out2 page is long;"
else
    out2="$out2 page is short;"
fi


out3="$bus clock bus cycle time; $busarb clock busarb."

echo
echo $out1
echo "         " $out2
echo "         " $out3
```

```
####################################################################
#
# Calculate result.
#
####################################################################


# time from BEGINNING of bus cycle which misses to first box, early mode.
cough=4

# 3 boxes of startup, when no FCL.
startup=6

# 3 boxes of termination.
termination=6

# clocks between last box's T4 and S0 of the 020's retry (typical?).
post_busarb=4

# Bus accesses begin sooner if FCL - no limit check.
if test $fcl -eq 1 ; then
        startup=`expr $startup - 2`
fi

overhead=`expr $cough + $startup + $termination`

if test $early -eq 0 ; then
        overhead=`expr \( $overhead + $busarb \) - $cough`
elif test $busarb -gt `expr $startup + $cough` ; then
        overhead=`expr $busarb + $termination`
fi

overhead=`expr $overhead + $post_busarb`

bus_accesses=`expr \( $long \* 2 \) + $short + \( $l_ind \* 2 \) + $s_ind`

if test $bus_accesses -eq 0 ; then
      if test $et -ne 1 ; then
           echo Error: 0 bus accesses implies unexpected page encountered.
      fi
#     If the page is et, the startup + termination equals 14.
      clocks=`expr $overhead - \( $startup + $termination \) + 14`
else

# In transitions, DESCHL access is 4 clocks after DESCH access.
      if test $bus -lt 4 ; then
           s_to_l_penalty=`expr 4 - $bus`
      else
           s_to_l_penalty=0
      fi


      l_pointer_ubit_delay=2
      if test $bus -lt 4 ; then
           l_pointer_ubit_delay=`expr \( 4 - $bus \) \* 2`
      fi
# The next level's read dead time is hidden in the
# current level's write time.
      l_pointer_ubit_delay=`expr $l_pointer_ubit_delay - 2`
```

```
# ET vector parallels last descl fetch if page is long.
    if test $long_page -eq 1 ; then
        if test $bus -lt 8 ; then
            et_delay=`expr 8 - $bus`
        else
            et_delay=0
        fi
# ET vector occurs after all fetches if page is short.
    else
        et_delay=8
    fi

# This code decides if a write or RMC needs to be done to set
# the history bits in the page descriptor

    if test \( $page_ubit -eq 0 -a ! \
        \( $page_mbit -eq 0 -a $unmod -eq 0 \) \) \
        -o \
        \( $page_ubit -eq 1 -a $page_mbit -eq 0 -a $unmod -eq 1 \) ; \
    then
        write_page=1
    else
        write_page=0
    fi

    if test $page_ubit -eq 0 -a $page_mbit -eq 0 -a $unmod -eq 0 ; then
        rmc_page=1
    else
        rmc_page=0
    fi


####################################################################
#
# Perform the calculation.
#
####################################################################
#
    clocks=`expr $overhead                              \
        + \( $long \* \( 2 + 2 \* $bus \) \)            \
        + \( $short \* \( 2 + $bus \) \)                \
        + \( $s_to_l \* $s_to_l_penalty \)              \
                                                        \
        + \( $l_ind \* \( 5 + \( 2 \* $bus \) + $unmod \* 2 \) \)        \
        + \( $s_ind \* \( 5 +    $bus + $unmod \* 2 \) \)                \
        + \( $l_pointer_ubits \* \( $l_pointer_ubit_delay + $bus \) \)   \
        + \( $s_pointer_ubits \* \( 4 + $bus \) \)                       \
                                                                         \
        + \( $rmc_page   \* \( 3 + \( 2 \* $bus \) + $unmod \* 2 \) \)   \
        + \( $write_page \* \( 4 +    $bus + $unmod \* 2 \) \)           \
                                                                         \
        + \( $et \* \( $et_delay + $unmod \* 2 \) \)                     \
                                                                         \
        + \( $unmod \* 8 \)`

fi
```

```
out="   Clocks required from beginning of missed bus cycle: $clocks"
echo
echo $out

write_accesses=`expr $l_pointer_ubits + $s_pointer_ubits + $write_page`

out="Bus Reads: $bus_accesses"
echo $out

print_total=0
if test $write_accesses -ne 0 ; then
    out="Bus Writes: $write_accesses"
    echo $out
    print_total=1
fi

if test $rmc_page -eq 1; then
    out="   Bus RMCs:  1"
    echo $out
    print_total=1
fi

bus_accesses=`expr $bus_accesses + $write_accesses + \( $rmc_page \* 2 \)`

if test $print_total -eq 1 ; then
    out="Total Bus Cycles: $bus_accesses"
    echo $out
fi
########################################################################
########
```

The following table gives some sample times obtained using the shell script. Each row of the table indicates a translation table configuration. The identifier on each row consists of five positions. Each position may have either an "x" meaning that there is no table at the level, an "S" meaning that the table at the level is composed of short format descriptors, or an "L" meaning that the table at the level is composed of long format descriptors. The format of the entries is:

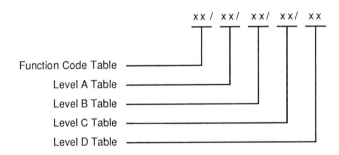

Each entry in the table consists of three numbers that give the number of clock cycles, the number of bus reads, and the number of bus writes required for a table search. An RMC cycle to set the U bit is counted as one read and one write. The format of the entries is:

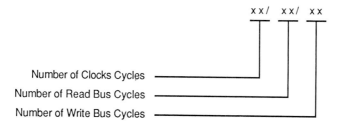

The table is calculated based on the following assumptions:
- Bus Arbitration Time is Seven Clock Cycles
- Bus Cycle Time is Three Clock Cycles
- Bus Arbitration Proceeds in Parallel with MC68851 Startup
- There are No Indirect Descriptors
- There are No Page Descriptors Encountered Unexpectedly (i.e., at the pointer table level)
- The Data Bus Between the MC68851 and Memory is 32-Bits Wide

Table Format	History Bit Maintenance Required by the Table Search			
	All U and M Bits Must be Set	Page U and M Bits Only Must be Set	Page U Bit Set with RMC	No U or M Bits Must be Set
L/L/x/x/x*	44/4/2	41/4/1	44/5/1	34/4/0
L/L/L/x/x*	55/6/3	49/6/1	52/7/1	42/6/0
L/L/L/L/x*	66/8/4	57/8/1	60/9/1	50/8/0
L/L/L/L/L	77/10/5	65/10/1	68/11/1	58/10/0
S/S/x/x/x*	42/2/2	35/2/1	38/3/1	28/2/0
S/S/S/x/x*	54/3/3	40/3/1	43/4/1	33/3/0
S/S/S/S/x*	66/4/4	45/4/1	48/5/1	38/4/0
S/S/S/S/	78/5/5	50/5/1	53/6/1	43/5/0
x/S/S/x/x	44/2/2	37/2/1	40/3/1	30/2/0
x/S/L/x/x	48/3/2	41/3/1	44/4/1	34/3/0
x/L/S/x/x	43/3/2	40/3/1	43/4/1	33/3/0
x/L/L/x/x	46/4/2	43/4/1	46/5/1	36/4/0
x/S/S/S/x	56/3/3	42/3/1	45/4/1	35/3/0
x/S/S/L/x	60/4/3	46/4/1	49/5/1	39/4/0
x/S/L/S/x	56/4/3	46/4/1	49/5/1	39/4/0
x/S/L/L/x	59/5/3	49/5/1	52/6/1	42/5/0
x/L/S/S/x	55/4/3	45/4/1	48/5/1	38/4/0
x/L/S/L/x	59/5/3	49/5/1	52/6/1	42/5/0
x/L/L/S/x	54/5/3	48/5/1	51/6/1	41/5/0
x/L/L/L/x	57/6/3	51/6/1	54/7/1	44/6/0

*For configurations without function code lookup and with one additional level (e.g., x/L/L/x/x instead of L/L/x/x/x), add two clocks.

11.3 INSTRUCTION TIMING

In the following paragraphs, timing tables are presented that allow the calculation of worst case execution times for any MC68851 instruction. The tables are based on the assumptions stated above, and include the total execution time for each instruction, from the time when an MC68020 begins execution of the coprocessor instruction (when the instruction has been prefetched and loaded into the instruction decode register) to the time when the MC68851 and/or MC68020 completes execution of the instruction (when a read of the response CIR indicates a null response, when conditional processing has been completed, or when the last transfer to or from the MC68851 is completed).

Bus cycle activity is also indicated by the tables, and includes all bus cycles generated by a particular operation. Note that instruction prefetch and operand write cycles requested by the execution of a given instruction may not actually be executed during the execution of the instruction, but are queued by the MC68020 bus interface unit for completion as soon as the bus is available (refer to *MC68020 32-Bit Microprocessor User's Manual* for more information on bus cycle overlap). When an MC68851 instruction is completed, a prefetch request will have been generated by the MC68020 to replace each word of instruction stream used by the instruction, or to refill the instruction pipe in the case of a conditional branch taken, a trap taken, or an exception.

The execution time entries in the following tables contain six numbers. The leftmost number is the total execution time for the instruction in clock cycles. In parenthesis is the bus cycle activity, which indicates the number of instruction prefetch, operand read, operand write, coprocessor read, and coprocessor write bus cycles that will be generated by the execution of the instruction. The format of the entries is:

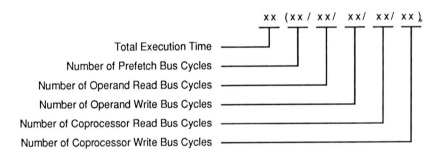

The set of tables provided in this section allow a quick determination of the typical execution time for any MC68851 instruction when the MC68020 is used as the main processor. The first table presented is for effective address calculations performed by the MC68020. Entries from this table are added to the entries in the other tables in this subsection, if necessary, to obtain the overall execution time for an operation. The assumptions for the following tables are:
- The main processor is an MC68020 and operates on the same clock as the MC68851. Instruction prefetches do not hit in the MC68020 cache (or it is disabled) and the instruction is aligned such that a prefetch occurs before the command CIR is written by the MC68020.
- A 32-bit memory interface is used, and memory accesses occur with zero wait states. All memory operands, as well as the stack pointers, are long-word aligned.
- No instruction overlap is allowed, so the coprocessor interface overhead is 11 clocks.
- No exceptions occur.

11.3.1 Effective Address Calculation

For any instruction that requires an operand external to the MC68851, an evaluate effective address and transfer data response primitive is issued by the MC68851 during the dialog for that instruction. The amount of time that is required by the MC68020 to calculate the effective address while processing this primitive for each addressing mode, excluding the transfer of the data to the MC68851, is shown below. The times given in this table include all bus cycles required to perform the calculation (prefetches and memory indirect fetches).

The PMOVE, PFLUSHR, PScc, PLOAD, PTEST, PVALID, PFLUSH, PFLUSHS, PRESTORE, and PSAVE instructions require an effective address to be calculated although not all require that data be transferred from that effective address. The following table is used for these instructions to adjust the basic instruction time to reflect the addressing mode that is used.

Note that the following table applies only to the MC68020 effective address calculation time for coprocessor instructions. The execution times included in this table are not the same as the calculate effective address times given in the *MC68020 32-Bit Microprocessor User's Manual* for non-coprocessor instruction execution.

Addressing Mode	Best Case	Cache Case	Worst Case
Dn or An	0 (0/0/0/0/0)	0 (0/0/0/0/0)	0 (0/0/0/0/0)
(An)	0 (0/0/0/0/0)	2 (0/0/0/0/0)	2 (0/0/0/0/0)
(An)+	3 (0/0/0/0/0)	6 (0/0/0/0/0)	6 (0/0/0/0/0)
–(An)	3 (0/0/0/0/0)	6 (0/0/0/0/0)	6 (0/0/0/0/0)
(d_{16},An) or (d_{16},PC)	0 (0/0/0/0/0)	2 (0/0/0/0/0)	3 (1/0/0/0/0)
(xxx).W	0 (0/0/0/0/0)	2 (0/0/0/0/0)	3 (1/0/0/0/0)
(xxx).L	1 (0/0/0/0/0)	4 (0/0/0/0/0)	5 (1/0/0/0/0)
#⟨data⟩	0 (0/0/0/0/0)	0 (0/0/0/0/0)	0 (0/0/0/0/0)
(d_8,An,Xn) or (d_8,PC,Xn)	1 (0/0/0/0/0)	4 (0/0/0/0/0)	5 (1/0/0/0/0)
(d_{16},An,Xn) or (d_{16},PC,Xn)	3 (0/0/0/0/0)	6 (0/0/0/0/0)	7 (1/0/0/0/0)
(B)	3 (0/0/0/0/0)	6 (0/0/0/0/0)	7 (1/0/0/0/0)
(d_{16},B)	5 (0/0/0/0/0)	8 (0/0/0/0/0)	9 (1/0/0/0/0)
(d_{32},B)	11 (0/0/0/0/0)	14 (0/0/0/0/0)	16 (2/0/0/0/0)
([B],I)	8 (0/1/0/0/0)	11 (0/1/0/0/0)	12 (1/1/0/0/0)
$([B],I,d_{16})$	8 (0/1/0/0/0)	11 (0/1/0/0/0)	12 (1/1/0/0/0)
$([B],I,d_{32})$	10 (0/1/0/0/0)	13 (0/1/0/0/0)	15 (2/1/0/0/0)
$([d_{16},B],I)$	10 (0/1/0/0/0)	13 (0/1/0/0/0)	14 (1/1/0/0/0)
$([d_{16},B],I,d_{16})$	10 (0/1/0/0/0)	13 (0/1/0/0/0)	15 (2/1/0/0/0)
$([d_{16},B],I,d_{32})$	12 (0/1/0/0/0)	15 (0/1/0/0/0)	17 (2/1/0/0/0)
$([d_{32},B],I)$	16 (0/1/0/0/0)	19 (0/1/0/0/0)	21 (2/1/0/0/0)
$([d_{32},B],I,d_{16})$	16 (0/1/0/0/0)	19 (0/1/0/0/0)	21 (2/1/0/0/0)
$(d[d_{32},B],I,d_{32})$	18 (0/1/0/0/0)	21 (0/1/0/0/0)	24 (3/1/0/0/0)

11.3.2 General Instructions

The following tables give the worst-case instruction execution time for each MC68851 general instruction. This group of instructions includes all MC68851 instructions except the conditionals and the save/restore operations. For memory operands, the timing for the appropriate effective addressing mode must be added to the numbers in this table to determine the overall instruction execution times.

Instruction	Worst Case
PMOVE (to CRP, DRP, SRP)*	108 (2/2/0/3/3)
PMOVE (to TC)*	155 (2/1/0/5/3)
PMOVE (to CAL, VAL, SCC, AC)*	54 (2/0/0/2/2)
PMOVE (to BADx, PSR, PCSR)*	54 (2/0/0/2/2)
PMOVE (to BACx)*	156 (2/1/0/6/2)
PMOVE (from CRP, DRP, SRP)*	84 (2/0/2/4/1)
PMOVE (from TC, CAL, VAL, SCC, AC)*	70 (2/0/1/3/1)
PMOVE (from BACx, BADx, PSR, PCSR)*	70 (2/0/1/3/1)
PFLUSHA	40 (2/0/0/2/1)
PFLUSH ⟨fc⟩,#⟨mask⟩	76 (2/0/0/4/2)
PFLUSH ⟨fc⟩,#⟨mask⟩,⟨ea⟩*	108 (2/0/0/5/3)
PFLUSHR*	86 (2/2/0/2/3)
PLOAD**	100 (2/0/0/5/3)
PTEST ⟨fc⟩,⟨ea⟩,#level**	110 (2/0/0/6/3)
PTEST ⟨fc⟩,⟨ea⟩,#level,An**	136 (2/0/0/8/2)
PVALID VAL,⟨ea⟩*	68 (2/0/0/2/2)
PVALID An,⟨ea⟩*	78 (2/0/0/3/3)

*Add the appropriate effective address calculation time.
**Add the appropriate effective address calculation time and the table search time.

The following table gives the execution times for the MC68851 conditional instructions. Each entry in this table, except those for the PScc instruction, is complete and does not require the addition of values from any other table. For the PScc instruction, the only additional factor that must be included is the calculate effective address time for the operand to be modified.

Since the conditional instructions are intrinsic to the M68000 Family coprocessor interface (i.e., they are not defined by the MC68851 through the use of response primitives), the MC68020 performs most of the processing associated with these instructions. The only part of the instruction that is performed by the MC68851 is the evaluation of the conditional predicate written to the condition CIR. Thus, the execution times given in the table below are heavily dependent on the environment in which the main processor executes.

Operation	Comments	Worst Case
PBcc.W	Branch Taken	28 (2/0/0/2/1)
	Branch Not Taken	24 (1/0/0/2/1)
PBcc.L	Branch Taken	28 (2/0/0/2/1)
	Branch Not Taken	26 (2/0/0/2/1)
PDBcc	True, Not Taken	29 (2/0/0/2/1)
	False, Not Taken	37 (4/0/0/2/1)
	False, Taken	31 (3/0/0/2/1)
PScc	Dn	26 (2/0/0/2/1)
	(An)+ or –(An)*	31 (2/0/1/2/1)
	Memory**	28 (2/0/1/2/1)
PTRAPcc	Trap Taken	52 (3/1/4/2/1)
	Trap Not Taken	27 (2/0/0/2/1)
PTRAPcc.W	Trap Taken	50 (3/1/4/2/1)
	Trap Not Taken	28 (2/0/0/2/1)
PTRAPcc.L	Trap Taken	57 (4/1/4/2/1)
	Trap Not Taken	32 (3/0/0/2/1)

*For condition true; subtract one clock for condition false.
**Add the appropriate effective address calculation time.

11.3.4 PSAVE and PRESTORE Instructions

The time required for a context save or restore operation is given in the table below. The appropriate calculate effective address times must be added to the values in this table to obtain the total execution time for these operations.

Operation	State Frame	Worst Case
PRESTORE	Null	22(1/1/0/1/1)
	Idle	76(1/10/0/1/10)
	Mid-Coprocessor	88(1/12/0/1/12)
	Breakpoint Enabled	136(1/20/0/1/20)
PSAVE	Null	18(1/0/1/1/0)
	Idle	72(1/0/10/10/0)
	Mid-Coprocessor	84(1/0/12/12/0)
	Breakpoint Enabled	132(1/0/20/20/0)

11.4 INTERRUPT LATENCY

In real-time systems, a very important factor pertaining to overall system performance is the response time required for a processor to handle an interrupt. In the M68000 Family of processors, interrupts are allowed to be asserted to the processor asynchronously, and they are handled on the next instruction boundary. While the average interrupt latency for the MC68020 is quite short, the maximum latency is often of critical importance, since real-time interrupts cannot require servicing in less than the maximum interrupt latency. The maximum interrupt latency for the MC68020 alone is approximately 250 clock cycles (for the MOVEM.L ([d32,An],Xn,d32), D0–D7/A0–A7 instruction where the last data fetch is aborted with a bus error; refer to the *MC68020 32-Bit Microprocessor User's Manual* for more detailed information), but the use of a memory management unit such as the MC68851 may cause some operations to take several times longer to execute.

Interrupt latency in systems using the MC68851 will be affected by the length of main processor instructions, the address translation table configuration, the number of address translation table searches required by the instructions, the access time of main memory, and the width of the data bus connecting the MC68851 with main memory. It is important to note that the address translation table configuration is under software control and can strongly affect the system interrupt latency. The maximum interrupt latency for a given system configuration can be computed by adding the length of the longest main processor instruction to the time required for the maximum number of address translation table searches that the instruction could require. For the MC68020 microprocessor, two instructions are of interest. The first is a memory-to-memory move with memory indirect addressing for both the source and destination, with all of the code and data items crossing page boundaries. The assembler syntax for this instruction is:

MOVE.L (od,[bd,An,Rm]),(od,[bd,An,Rm])

This instruction can cause ten address translation table searches (two for the instruction stream, two for the source indirect address, two for the destination indirect address, two for the source operand fetch, and two for the destination write). System software can reduce the maximum number of table searches by placing additional restrictions on generated code. For example, if the language translators in the system only generate long words aligned on long word boundaries, then the indirect address and operands can cause only one table search each. This will reduce the number of table searches for the instruction to a maximum of six.

In systems that use the MC68020 CALLM instruction:

CALLM #256,(od[bd,An,Rm])

with a stack copy indicated by the MC68851 SCC register can cause nine address translation table searches (two for the instruction stream, one for the module descriptor, two for the indirect address, and two each for the source and destination stack), and 64 bus cycles of stack copying (on a 32-bit data bus).

11.5 BUS ARBITRATION LATENCY

The bus arbitration latency in a system containing an MC68851 is affected by several factors. The MC68851 will not arbitrate away either the logical or physical buses while the main processor is performing an RMW (read-modify-write) operation (the TAS, CAS, or CAS2 instructions). The longest period of time that the bus can be locked in this fashion is for a CAS2 instruction, which may perform eight bus cycles on a 32-bit bus, 12 bus cycles on a 16-bit bus, or 16 bus cycles on an 8-bit bus. Note that address translation table search time is not added to these times because the MC68851 forces a bus error on an ATC miss for these instructions in order to avoid causing a large delay in bus arbitration.

Bus arbitration may also be delayed by the MC68851 not asserting the $\overline{DSACKx}$ signals during coprocessor instructions while it updates its internal state. The maximum delay from this source is 23 clock cycles.

SECTION 12
ELECTRICAL SPECIFICATIONS

This section contains the electrical specifications and associated timing information for the MC68851.

12.1 MAXIMUM RATINGS

Rating	Symbol	Value	Unit
Supply Voltage	V_{CC}	−0.3 to +7.0	V
Input Voltage	V_{in}	−0.5 to +7.0	V
Operating Temperature	T_A	0 to 70	°C
Storage Temperature	T_{stg}	−55 to +150	°C

This device contains protective circuitry against damage due to high static voltages or electrical fields; however, it is advised that normal precautions be taken to avoid application of any voltages higher than maximum-rated voltages to this high-impedance circuit. Reliability of operation is enhanced if unused inputs are tied to an appropriate logic voltage level (e.g., either GND or V_{CC}).

12.2 THERMAL CHARACTERISTICS — PGA PACKAGE

Characteristic	Symbol	Value	Rating
Thermal Resistance — Ceramic Junction to Ambient Junction to Case	θ_{JA} θ_{JC}	30* 15*	°C/W °C/W

*Estimated

12.3 POWER CONSIDERATIONS

The average chip-junction temperature, T_J, in °C can be obtained from:

$$T_J = T_A + (P_D \cdot \theta_{JA}) \quad (1)$$

where:

T_A = Ambient Temperature, °C
θ_{JA} = Package Thermal Resistance, Junction-to-Ambient, °C/W
P_D = $P_{INT} + P_{I/O}$
P_{INT} = $I_{CC} \times V_{CC}$, Watts — Chip Internal Power
$P_{I/O}$ = Power Dissipation on Input and Output Pins, Watts — User Determined

For most applications $P_{I/O} < P_{INT}$ and can be neglected.

An approximate relationship between P_D and T_J (if $P_{I/O}$ is neglected) is:

$$P_D = K \div (T_J + 273°C) \quad (2)$$

Solving equations (1) and (2) for K gives:

$$K = P_D \cdot (T_A + 273°C) + \theta_{JA} \cdot P_D^2 \quad (3)$$

where K is a constant pertaining to the particular part. K can be determined from equation (3) by measuring P_D (at equilibrium) for a known T_A. Using this value of K, the values of P_D and T_J can be obtained by solving equations (1) and (2) iteratively for any value of T_A.

The total thermal resistance of a package (θ_{JA}) can be separated into two components, θ_{JC} and θ_{CA}, representing the barrier to heat flow from the semiconductor junction to the package (case) surface (θ_{JC}) and from the case to the outside ambient (θ_{CA}). These terms are related by the equation:

$$\theta_{JA} = \theta_{JC} + \theta_{CA} \tag{4}$$

θ_{JC} is device related and cannot be influenced by the user. However, θ_{CA} is user dependent and can be minimized by such thermal management techniques as heat sinks, ambient air cooling and thermal convection. Thus, good thermal management on the part of the user can significantly reduce θ_{CA} so that θ_{JA} approximately equals θ_{JC}. Substitution of θ_{JC} for θ_{JA} in equation (1) will result in a lower semiconductor junction temperature.

Values for thermal resistance presented in this document, unless estimated, were derived using the procedure described in Motorola Reliability Report 7843, "Thermal Resistance Measurement Method for MC68XX Microcomponent Devices," and are provided for design purposes only. Thermal measurements are complex and dependent on procedure and setup. User derived values for thermal resistance may differ.

12.4 DC ELECTRICAL CHARACTERISTICS (V_{CC} = 5.0 Vdc ± 5%; GND = 0 Vdc; T_A = 0 to 70°C; see Figure 12-1)

Characteristic		Symbol	Min	Max	Unit
Input High Voltage		V_{IH}	2.0	V_{CC}	V
Input Low Voltage		V_{IL}	GND −0.5	0.8	V
Input Leakage Current @ 5.25 V	CLK, RESET, LA8–LA31, LAS, LBRI, LBGI, PBR, PBGACK, ASYNC	I_{in}	—	10	µA
Hi-Z (Off-State) Input Current @ 2.4 V/0.4 V	DSACK0, DSACK1, D0–D31, FC0–FC3, SIZ0–SIZ1, PAS, DS, R/W, RMC, BERR, HALT, LBGACK	I_{TSI}	—	20	µA
Output High Voltage (I_{OH} = −400 µA)	A0–A7, DSACK0, DSACK1, D0–D31, FC0–FC3, SIZ0–SIZ1, PAS, DS, R/W, RMC, BERR, HALT, LBGACK, PA8–PA31, DBDIS, LBRO, LBGO, PBG, CLI	V_{OH}	2.4	—	V
Output Low Voltage (I_{OL} = 5.3 mA)	DSACK0, DSACK1, HALT, PAS, DS, R/W, RMC, BERR, LBGACK, DBDIS, LBRO, LBGO, PGB, CLI	V_{OL}	—	0.5	V
Output Low Voltage (I_{OL} = 3.2 mA)	D0–D31, A0–A7, FC0–FC3, SIZ0–SIZ1, PA8–PA31	V_{OL}	—	0.5	V
Power Dissipation		P_D	—	1.50	W
Capacitance* (V_{in} = 0, T_A = 25°C, f = 1 MHz)		C_{in}	—	20	pF

*Capacitance is periodically sampled rather than 100% tested.

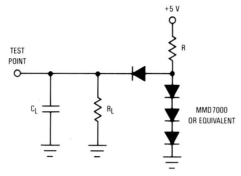

C_L = 130 pF (includes all parasitics)
R_L = 6.0 kΩ
R = 740 Ω for $\overline{DSACK0}$, $\overline{DSACK1}$, D0-D31, $\overline{PAS}$, $\overline{DS}$, R/$\overline{W}$, $\overline{RMC}$, $\overline{BERR}$, $\overline{HALT}$, $\overline{LBGACK}$, DBDIS, $\overline{LBRO}$, $\overline{LBGO}$, $\overline{PBG}$, $\overline{CLI}$
R = 1.22 kΩ for A0-A7, FC0-FC3, SIZ0/SIZ1, PA8-PA31

Figure 12-1. Test Loads

12.5 AC ELECTRICAL SPECIFICATIONS — CLOCK INPUT (V_{CC} = 5.0 Vdc ± 5%; GND = 0 Vdc; T_A = 0 to 70 °C; see Figure 12-2)

No.	Characteristic	Symbol	MC68851RC12 Min	MC68851RC12 Max	MC68851RC16 Min	MC68851RC16 Max	Unit
	Frequency of Operation	f	8.0	12.5	8.0	16.67	MHz
1	Cycle Time	t_{cyc}	80	125	60	125	ns
2, 3	Clock Pulse Width	t_{CL}, t_{CH}	32	125	24	95	ns
4, 5	Clock Rise and Fall Time	t_{Cr}, t_{Cf}	—	5	—	5	ns

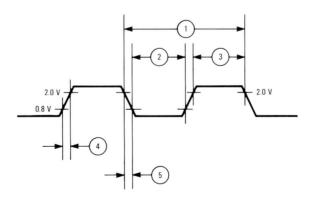

Figure 12-2. Clock Input Timing Diagram

NOTE

Notes referenced to in the following table have been placed after the final entry (see pages 12-8 and 12-9).

The timing diagrams (Figures 12-3 through 12-11) are intended to provide parametric timing information for the MC68851. For easy reference, these diagrams have been placed on foldout pages at the end of this document. Effort has been made to ensure that the diagrams provide correct functional signal relationships. However, not all relationships depicted are valid operations for the MC68851 (e.g., during a CPU space access as shown in Figure 12-8, accesses to the MC68851 will not cause assertion of $\overline{CLI}$).

12.6 AC ELECTRICAL SPECIFICATIONS — ALL BUS OPERATIONS (V_{CC} = 5.0 Vdc ± 5%; GND = 0 Vdc; T_A = 0 to 70°C; see Figures 12-3 through 12-11)

No.	Characteristic	Mode	MC68851RC12 Min	MC68851RC12 Max	MC68851RC16 Min	MC68851RC16 Max	Unit	Figure Reference
6	Clock High to FC, Size, $\overline{RMC}$, Physical Address, Shared Address Valid (see Note a)	T[b]	0	40	0	30	ns	3, 4
7	Clock High to FC, Size, $\overline{RMC}$, Data-Out, Physical Address, Shared Address High Impedance	T	0	40	0	30	ns	8
8	Clock High to FC, Size, $\overline{RMC}$, Physical Address, Shared Address Invalid	T	0	—	0	—	ns	3, 4
9	Clock Transition to $\overline{PAS}$ Asserted	T	0	35	0	25	ns	3, 4
9A[k]	$\overline{PAS}$ to $\overline{DS}$ Assertion (Read) (Skew)	T	−20	20	−15	15	ns	3
9B	Clock Transition to $\overline{DS}$ Asserted	T	0	40	0	30	ns	4
11[p]	FC, Size, $\overline{RMC}$, Physical Address, Shared Address Valid to $\overline{PAS}$, $\overline{DS}$ Asserted	T	20	—	15	—	ns	3, 4
12	Clock Low to $\overline{PAS}$ Negated	T	0	35	0	25	ns	3, 4
12A	Clock Low to $\overline{DS}$ Negated	T	0	40	0	30	ns	3, 4
13	$\overline{PAS}$, $\overline{DS}$ Negated to FC, Size, $\overline{RMC}$, Physical Address, Shared Address Invalid (see Note u)	T	20	—	15	—	ns	3, 4
14	$\overline{PAS}$, $\overline{DS}$ (Read) Width Asserted	T	120	—	100	—	ns	3, 4
14A	$\overline{DS}$ Width Asserted (Write)	T	50	—	40	—	ns	4
15	$\overline{PAS}$, $\overline{DS}$ Width Negated	T	50	—	40	—	ns	4
16	Clock High to $\overline{PAS}$, $\overline{DS}$, R/$\overline{W}$, DBDIS High Impedance	T	0	40	0	30	ns	3
17	$\overline{PAS}$, $\overline{DS}$ Negated to R/$\overline{W}$ Invalid (Read or Write)	T	20	—	15	—	ns	3, 4
18	Clock High to R/$\overline{W}$ High (Read)	T	0	40	0	30	ns	3
20	Clock High to R/$\overline{W}$ Low (Write)	T	0	40	0	30	ns	4
21	R/$\overline{W}$ High to $\overline{PAS}$ Asserted	T	20	—	15	—	ns	3
22	R/$\overline{W}$ Low to $\overline{DS}$ Asserted (Write)	T	90	—	70	—	ns	4
23	Clock High to Data-Out Valid	T/O	0	40	0	30	ns	4, 9
25	$\overline{DS}$ Negated to Data-Out Invalid	T/O	20	—	15	—	ns	4, 9
26	Data-Out Valid to $\overline{DS}$ Asserted	T	20	—	15	—	ns	4

12.6 AC ELECTRICAL SPECIFICATIONS — ALL BUS OPERATIONS (Continued)

No.	Characteristic	Mode	MC68851RC12 Min	MC68851RC12 Max	MC68851RC16 Min	MC68851RC16 Max	Unit	Figure Reference
27	Data-In Valid to Clock Low (Data Setup)	T	10	—	5	—	ns	3
27A	$\overline{BERR}$-i/$\overline{HALT}$-i Asserted to Clock Low (Late $\overline{BERR}$/$\overline{HALT}$ Setup Time) (see Note c)	T	25	60^d	20	45^d	ns	3
29	$\overline{DS}$ Negated to Data-In Invalid (Data-In Hold Time)	T	0	—	0	—	ns	3
29A	$\overline{DS}$ Negated to Data-In High Impedance	T	0	80	0	60	ns	3
31^l	$\overline{DSACKx}$ Asserted to Data-In Valid	T	—	60	—	50	ns	3
31A^m	$\overline{DSACKx}$ Asserted to $\overline{DSACKx}$ Valid (Assertion Skew)	T	—	20	—	15	ns	3, 4
32	$\overline{RESET}$ Input Transition Time	X	—	200	—	200	ns	11
33	Clock Low to $\overline{PBG}$ Asserted	X	0	40	0	30	ns	8
34	Clock Low to $\overline{PBG}$ Negated	X	0	40	0	30	ns	8
35A	$\overline{PBR}$ Asserted to $\overline{PBG}$ Asserted ($\overline{RMC}$ Not Asserted)	T	2.0	3.5	2.0	3.5	Clk Per	8
35B	$\overline{PBR}$ Asserted to $\overline{PBG}$ Asserted ($\overline{RMC}$ Not Asserted)	M	2.0	5.5	2.0	5.5	Clk Per	8
36	$\overline{PBR}$ Negated to $\overline{PBG}$ Negated (Transient or Spurious Request)	X	2.0	3.5	2.0	3.5	Clk Per	8
37	$\overline{PBGACK}$ Asserted to $\overline{PBG}$ Negated	X	2.0	3.5	2.0	3.5	Clk Per	8
39	$\overline{PBG}$ Width Negated	X	1.5	—	1.5	—	Clk Per	8
39A	$\overline{PBG}$ Width Asserted	X	1.5	—	1.5	—	Clk Per	8
40A	Clock High to DBDIS Negated (Read)	T	0	40	0	30	ns	3
40B	Clock Low to DBDIS Negated (Write (T)) (Read (O))	T/O	0	40	0	30	ns	4, 9
41A	Clock Low to DBDIS Asserted (Read (T)) (Write (O))	T/O	0	40	0	30	ns	3, 9
41B	Clock High to DBDIS Asserted (Write)	T	0	40	0	30	ns	4, 9
43	$\overline{PBGACK}$ Negated to $\overline{PAS}$, Physical Address Impedance Change (see Note j)	X	0.5	2.5	0.5	2.5	Clk Per	8
44	R/$\overline{W}$ Asserted to DBDIS Negated (Read or Write)	T	20	—	15	—	ns	3, 4
45A	DBDIS Width Negated (Read)	T	80	—	60	—	ns	3
45B^o	DBDIS Width Negated (Write)	T	160	—	120	—	ns	4
46	R/$\overline{W}$ Width Asserted (Read or Write)	T	180	—	150	—	ns	3, 4
47A	Asynchronous Input Setup Time to Sampling Clock Edge	T	10	60^d	5	45^d	ns	3, 4, 8
47B	$\overline{PAS}$, $\overline{DS}$ Negated to Asynchronous Input Negated	T	0	100	0	80	ns	3, 4
48^n	$\overline{DSACKx}$-i Asserted to $\overline{BERR}$-i/$\overline{HALT}$-i Asserted (Late Bus Error or Retry)	T	—	40	—	30	ns	3, 4
53	Data-Out Hold from Clock High	T	0	—	0	—	ns	4
53A	Data-Out Hold from $\overline{LAS}$ Negated	O	0	—	0	—	ns	9
55	R/$\overline{W}$ Low to Data Bus Impedance Change	T	40	—	30	—	ns	4
56	DBDIS Asserted to Data Bus Impedance Change	O	15	—	15	—	ns	9

12.6 AC ELECTRICAL SPECIFICATIONS — ALL BUS OPERATIONS (Continued)

No.	Characteristic	Mode	MC68851RC12 Min	MC68851RC12 Max	MC68851RC16 Min	MC68851RC16 Max	Unit	Figure Reference
56A	Data Bus Impedance Change to DBDIS Negated	O	0	—	0	—	ns	9
59	DBDIS High to R/$\overline{W}$ Low	T	20	—	15	—	ns	3
60	$\overline{BERR}$-i Negated to $\overline{HALT}$-i Invalid (Hold Time for Retry)	T	0	—	0	—	ns	3
63	$\overline{DS}$ Negated to DBDIS Asserted (Write)	T	20	—	15	—	ns	4
64	DBDIS Negated to Data Bus Impedance Change (Write)	T	20	—	15	—	ns	4
65	Clock Low to $\overline{LBGACK}$-o, $\overline{LBGO}$ Asserted	X	0	40	0	30	ns	6, 7
66	Clock Low to $\overline{LBGACK}$-o, $\overline{LBGO}$ Negated	X	0	40	0	30	ns	6, 7
67	$\overline{LBGACK}$-o Asserted to $\overline{LBRO}$ Negated	T	20	60	15	45	ns	6
68	$\overline{LBGACK}$-o Asserted to $\overline{CLI}$ Asserted	T	0	80	0	60	ns	6
69	$\overline{CLI}$ Negated to $\overline{LBGACK}$-o Negated	T	0	40	0	30	ns	6
70	$\overline{LBGACK}$-o Asserted to DBDIS Asserted	T	−20	20	−15	15	ns	6
71	$\overline{LBGI}$ Asserted to $\overline{LBGO}$ Asserted (Not Read-Modify-Write Cycle by MC68851)	X	2.0	12.5^h	2.0	12.5^h	Clk Per	7
72	$\overline{LBRI}$ Negated to $\overline{LBGO}$ Negated	X	2.0	3.5	2.0	3.5	Clk Per	7
73	$\overline{LBGO}$ Width Asserted	X	40	—	30	—	ns	7
74	$\overline{LBGO}$ Width Negated	X	40	—	30	—	ns	7
75	$\overline{LBGI}$ Negated to $\overline{LBGO}$ Negated	X	2.0	3.5	2.0	3.5	Clk Per	7
77	$\overline{LBGI}$ Asserted to $\overline{LBGACK}$-o Asserted	T	2.0	3.5	2.0	3.5	Clk Per	6
79	$\overline{RESET}$ Width Asserted (V_{CC} Active and Stable)	X	512	—	512	—	Clk Per	11
79A	$\overline{RESET}$ Width Asserted (V_{CC} Stable > 512 Clocks)	X	10	—	10	—	Clk Per	11
80	$\overline{RESET}$ Asserted to Bus Control Signals Negated (V_{CC} Active and Stable)	X	0	4	0	4	Clk Per	11
81	$\overline{RESET}$ Negated to $\overline{LAS}$ Asserted	X	4	—	4	—	Clk Per	11
82	$\overline{RESET}$ Negated to Mode Select Data Valid (Hold)	X	0	—	0	—	ns	11
83	Mode Select Data Valid to $\overline{RESET}$ Negated (Setup)	X	2	—	2	—	Clk Per	11
84	Clock Transition to $\overline{HALT}$/$\overline{BERR}$/$\overline{LBRO}$ Asserted (Logical Master Relinquish and Retry)	M	0	40	0	30	ns	5
86A	$\overline{LAS}$ Asserted to $\overline{HALT}$/$\overline{BERR}$/$\overline{LBRO}$ Asserted (Logical Master Relinquish and Retry)	MS	0.5	1.5^g	0.5	1.5^g	Clk Per	6
86B	$\overline{LAS}$ Asserted to $\overline{HALT}$/$\overline{BERR}$/$\overline{LBRO}$ Asserted (Logical Master Relinquish and Retry)	MA	1.0	3.0^f	1.0	3.0^f	Clk Per	6
89	$\overline{HALT}$ Negated to $\overline{LBGACK}$-o Asserted	M	20	60	15	45	ns	6
90	$\overline{LAS}$ Negated to $\overline{BERR}$-o Negated (Termination of Relinquish and Retry)	M	0	40	0	30	ns	6
91	Logical Address, FC, $\overline{RMC}$, R/$\overline{W}$ Valid to Clock High (Setup)	MS/OS	40	—	30	—	ns	5
92A	Logical Address, FC, $\overline{RMC}$, R/$\overline{W}$, Valid to $\overline{LAS}$ Asserted	MS/OS	20	—	15	—	ns	5, 9, 10

12.6 AC ELECTRICAL SPECIFICATIONS — ALL BUS OPERATIONS (Continued)

No.	Characteristic	Mode	MC68851RC12 Min	MC68851RC12 Max	MC68851RC16 Min	MC68851RC16 Max	Unit	Figure Reference
92B	Logical Address, FC, $\overline{RMC}$, R/$\overline{W}$ Valid to $\overline{LAS}$ Asserted	MA/OA	0	—	0	—	ns	7, 9, 10
93A	$\overline{LAS}$ Negated to Logical Address, FC, $\overline{RMC}$, R/$\overline{W}$ Invalid	MS/OS	20	—	15	—	ns	5, 9, 10
93B	$\overline{LAS}$ Negated to Logical Address, FC, $\overline{RMC}$, R/$\overline{W}$ Invalid	MA/OA	0	—	0	—	ns	7, 9, 10
95	Logical Address Valid to Physical Address Valid (Translation Cache Hit or CPU Space Cycle)	M	0	60[s]	0	45[s]	ns	5, 7, 9, 10
96	Size, Shared Address Valid to $\overline{LAS}$ Asserted (Access to MC68851 Register)	OS	20	—	15	—	ns	9, 10
97	$\overline{LAS}$ Negated to Size, Shared Address Invalid (Access to MC68851 Register)	OS	20	—	15	—	ns	9, 10
100	$\overline{LAS}$ Asserted to Clock Low (Setup Time)	MS	40	—	30	—	ns	5
103	$\overline{LAS}$ Width Asserted	M	1.5	—	1.5	—	Clk Per	5, 7
104	$\overline{LAS}$, $\overline{DS}$ Width Negated	MS	0.5	—	0.5	—	Clk Per	5
104A	$\overline{LAS}$, $\overline{DS}$ Width Negated	MA	30	—	20	—	ns	7
105	$\overline{ASYNC}$ Asserted to $\overline{LAS}$ Asserted	M	1.5	—	1.5	—	Clk Per	7
106	$\overline{LAS}$ Negated to $\overline{ASYNC}$ Negated	M	0	—	0	—	ns	5, 7
107	$\overline{ASYNC}$ Negated to $\overline{LAS}$ Asserted (For Synchronous Next Cycle)	M	1.5	—	1.5	—	Clk Per	5
108	Data Valid to $\overline{DS}$ Asserted (Write Setup Time to MC68851)	O	0	—	0	—	ns	10
109A	$\overline{DS}$ Negated to Data Invalid (Write Hold Time to MC68851)	O	0	—	0	—	ns	10
109B	$\overline{DS}$ Negated to Data High Impedance	O	0	80	0	60	ns	10
110	$\overline{DSACKx}$-o Asserted to $\overline{DSACKy}$-o Valid	O	0	20[r]	0	15[r]	ns	9, 10
111	Clock High to $\overline{DSACKx}$-o Asserted	O	0	40	0	30	ns	9, 10
112A	$\overline{LAS}$ Asserted to $\overline{DSACKx}$-o Asserted	OS	2.0	23	2.0	23	Clk Per	9, 10
112B	$\overline{LAS}$ Asserted to $\overline{DSACKx}$-o Asserted	OA	2.5	26	2.5	26	Clk Per	9, 10
113	$\overline{LAS}$ Negated to $\overline{DSACKx}$-o, $\overline{BERR}$-o Negated	O	0	40	0	30	ns	9, 10
114	$\overline{LAS}$ Negated to $\overline{DSACKx}$-o, $\overline{BERR}$-o High Impedance	O	0	60	0	40	ns	9
115	Clock Low to $\overline{PAS}$ Asserted	MS	0[e]	35[e]	0[e]	25[e]	ns	5
116	Clock Transition (Rising or Falling Edge) to $\overline{PAS}$ Asserted	M	0[e]	35[e]	0[e]	25[e]	ns	5, 7
116A	Clock Low to $\overline{CLI}$ Asserted	M	0[e]	40[e]	0[e]	30[e]	ns	5, 9
117	$\overline{LAS}$ Asserted to $\overline{PAS}$ Asserted (Synchronous Translation with ATC Hit)	MS	0.5[g]	1.5[g]	0.5[g]	1.5[g]	Clk Per	5
118	$\overline{LAS}$ Negated to $\overline{PAS}$ Negated	M	0	20	0	15	ns	5, 7
119	Physical Address Valid to $\overline{PAS}$ Asserted	M	20	—	15	—	ns	5
120A	$\overline{PAS}$ Negated to Physical Address Invalid	MS	15	—	10	—	ns	7

12.6 AC ELECTRICAL SPECIFICATIONS — ALL BUS OPERATIONS (Concluded)

No.	Characteristic	Mode	MC68851RC12 Min	MC68851RC12 Max	MC68851RC16 Min	MC68851RC16 Max	Unit	Figure Reference
120B	PAS Negated to Physical Address Invalid	MA	0	—	0	—	ns	7
121	LAS Asserted to PAS Asserted (Asynchronous Operation Only)	M	1.0^f	3.0^i	1.0^f	3.0^i	Clk Per	7
122	LAS Negated to PAS High Impedance (PBR Asserted by Alternate Physical Master)	M	—	80	—	60	ns	5, 8
123	Physical Address Valid to CLI Asserted (CPU Space Cycle Not Accessing MC68851)	M	20	—	15	—	ns	9, 10
124A	LAS Asserted to CLI Asserted (CPU Space Cycle Not Accessing MC68851)	MA	1.0^f	3.0^i	1.0^f	3.0^i	Clk Per	9, 10
124B	LAS Asserted to CLI Asserted (CPU Space Cycle Not Accessing MC68851)	MS	0.59	1.59	0.59	1.59	Clk Per	9, 10
126	LAS Negated to CLI Negated (CPU Space Cycle Not Accessing MC68851)	M	0	40	0	30	ns	9, 10
127	CLI Negated to Physical Address Invalid (CPU Space Cycle Not Accessing MC68851)	MS	10	—	5	—	ns	9, 10
128	PAS Asserted to CLI Asserted (Not CPU Space Access)	M	—	20	—	15	ns	5
129	PAS Negated CLI Negated (Not CPU Space Access)	M	5	40	5	30	ns	5

NOTES:

a) In this specification the terms 'high', 'low', 'asserted', 'negated', 'valid', and 'invalid' are used frequently to describe a signal state. For inputs to the MC68851, 'high' indicates that the signal conforms to the V_{IH} voltage specification while 'low' indicates that the V_{IL} specification is satisfied. Similarly, a MC68851 output is 'high' if it conforms to the V_{OH} specification and 'low' if it conforms to the V_{OL} parameter. An active low input (output) is asserted if it satisfies the respective V_{IH} (V_{OH}) requirements and negated if it satisfies the V_{IL} (V_{OL}) specification. A signal is 'valid' if it conforms to either the voltage high or the voltage low specifications and is an appropriate value for the current operation (for example, R/W should output a valid low during an MC68851 initiated write cycle). A signal is 'invalid' if it either does not conform to the V_H or V_L specifications or is an inappropriate value for the current operation as above.

b) In order to better understand the parameters given, a 'mode' identification is included with each specification: **X** indicates that this specification is valid in any operating mode whatever; **T** indicates that the MC68851 is the current bus master and is performing a table walk operation; **M** indicates that the MC68851 is mapping translations for the current bus master with the designation **MS** indicating that the master is operating synchronously with the MC68851, **MA** indicating an asynchronous master, and **MX** indicating that the parameter is valid for any type of logical master; **O** indicates that the parameter is valid for operations which access the internal registers of the MC68851.

c) Due to the numerous MC68851 signals that are used as inputs in one operating mode and as outputs in another, some attempt has been made to clarify whether a particular signal is acting as an input or as an output in cases where ambiguity is possible. The suffix ''-o'' indicates that the signal is an output of the MC68851 while the suffix ''-i'' indicates that this signal is acting as an input to the MC68851.

d) The maximum value for parameter #47A is specified in order that the system designer may deterministically identify the clock edge on which an asynchronous input to the MC68851 will be recognized. Any signal that meets the minimum specified setup time to an appropriate clock edge (rising/falling) for that signal to be recognized on, and does not exceed the maximum time, is guaranteed to be recognized as asserted on that edge. Signals that do not meet the minimum setup time may or may not be recognized; signals that exceed the maximum specified setup time may be recognized on the previous rising/falling clock edge.

e) The actual assertion delay from the low-going clock edge that causes the strobe(s) to assert includes the time specified in the parameter plus any additional delay specified on D3/D4 during MC68851 configuration at RESET.

f) The actual assertion delay from the assertion of LAS when mapping in the asynchronous mode is the time specified in the parameter plus any additional delay specified on D3/D4 during MC68851 configuration at RESET.

g) The actual assertion delay from the assertion of LAS is the time specified in the parameter plus any additional delay specified on D3/D4 during MC68851 configuration at RESET. This specification has a range of one clock period in order to allow for cases in which the CPU exhibits a best-case (minimum) assertion delay for the LAS signal relative to the clock while the MC68851 PAS or CLI outputs exhibit worst-case (maximum) assertion delays. When operating in the synchronous translation mode, the MC68851 asserts PAS (CLI) on the falling edge of the clock (plus additional specified delay) one clock period after the CPU drives LAS.

h) The worst case assertion delay for this specification can be reduced to 5.5 clock periods if the early processing startup mode of operation is disabled (refer to **4.1.2.5 EARLY PROCESSING STARTUP (D6)**).

i) This maximum can be reduced to 1.5 clock periods if the logical address strobe ($\overline{\text{LAS}}$) high time (negated period) is one clock period or greater.

j) This specification also applies to the signals A0–A7, FC0–FC3, SIZ0–SIZ1, and $\overline{\text{RMC}}$ if the MC68851 is awaiting the negation of $\overline{\text{PBGACK}}$ to initiate or complete a table search operation.

k) This number can be reduced to ±5 nanoseconds if the strobes have equal load.

l) If the asynchronous setup time (#47) requirements are satisfied, the $\overline{\text{DSACKx}}$ low to data setup (#31) and $\overline{\text{DSACKx}}$ low to $\overline{\text{BERR}}$ low setup time (#48) can be ignored. The data must only satisfy the data-in to clock low setup time (#27) for the following clock cycle. $\overline{\text{BERR}}$ must only satisfy the late $\overline{\text{BERR}}$ low to clock low setup time (#27A) for the following clock cycle.

m) This parameter specifies the maximum allowable skew between $\overline{\text{DSACK0}}$ to $\overline{\text{DSACK1}}$ asserted or $\overline{\text{DSACK1}}$ to $\overline{\text{DSACK0}}$ asserted. Specification #47 must be met by either $\overline{\text{DSACK0}}$ or $\overline{\text{DSACK1}}$.

n) In the absence of $\overline{\text{DSACKx}}$, $\overline{\text{BERR}}$ is an asynchronous input using the asynchronous input setup time (#47).

o) DBDIS may stay asserted on consecutive write cycles (e.g., a retry of an MC68851 write operation).

p) Actual value depends on the clock input waveform.

q) This number can be reduced to 5 nanoseconds if $\overline{\text{CLI}}$ and $\overline{\text{PAS}}$ have equal loading.

r) This specification is valid only if the loading of the $\overline{\text{DSACKx}}$ outputs are equal (±50 pF).

s) This specification can be reduced to 35 ns or 50 ns at 16.67 and 12.5 MHz, respectively for those bits of the logical address that are not translated by the MC68851. This includes all bits of the logical address if the MC68851 translation mechanism is disabled, and all bits, LAn, of the logical address (page size 2^m) such that $n \leq m$.

u) This specification also applies to the signals A0–A7, FC0–FC3, and SIZ0–SIZ1 if the MC68851 is granting physical bus mastership to an alternate device during a table search operation.

Table 12-1. AC Electrical Specifications Reference Summary

Signal Function	Signal Name	Relevant AC Electrical Specifications
Logical Address Bus	LA8–LA31	91, 92A, 92B, 93A, 93B, 95
Physical Address Bus	PA8–PA31	6, 7, 8, 11, 13, 43, 95, 119, 120A, 120B, 123, 127
Shared Address Bus	A0–A7	6, 7, 8, 11, 13, 43, 96, 97
Function Codes	FC0–FC3	6, 7, 8, 11, 13, 43, 91, 92A, 92B, 93A, 93B
Data Bus	D0–D31	7, 23, 25, 26, 27, 29, 29A, 31, 53, 56A, 64, 82, 83, 108, 109A, 109B
Size	SIZ0–SIZ1	6, 7, 8, 11, 13, 43, 96, 97
Cache Load Inhibit	$\overline{CLI}$	68, 69, 116, 123, 124A, 124B, 126, 127, 128, 129
Asynchronous Control	$\overline{ASYNC}$	105, 106, 107
Read-Modify-Write Cycle	$\overline{RMC}$	6, 7, 8, 11, 13, 43, 91, 92A, 92B, 93A, 93B
Logical Address Strobe	$\overline{LAS}$	81, 86A, 86B, 90, 92A, 92B, 93A, 93B, 96, 97, 100, 103, 104 104A, 105, 106, 107, 112A, 112B, 113, 117, 118, 121, 122, 124A, 124B, 126
Physical Address Strobe	$\overline{PAS}$	9, 9A, 9B, 11, 12, 12A, 13, 14, 15, 16, 17, 21, 43, 47B, 115, 116, 117, 118, 119, 120A, 120B, 121, 122, 128, 129
Data Strobe	$\overline{DS}$	9A, 13, 14, 14A, 15, 16, 17, 22, 25, 26, 29, 29A, 47B, 63, 104, 104A, 108, 109A, 109B
Read/Write	R/$\overline{W}$	16, 19, 20, 22, 44, 46, 55, 59, 91, 92A, 92B, 93A, 93B
Data Transfer and Size Acknowledge	$\overline{DSACK0}$–$\overline{DSACK1}$	31, 31A, 47A, 48, 110, 111, 112A, 112B, 113, 114
Data Bus Disable	$\overline{DBDIS}$	16, 40A, 40B, 41A, 41B, 44, 45A, 45B, 56, 56A, 59, 63, 64
Bus Error	$\overline{BERR}$	27A, 47A, 48, 60, 84, 86A, 86B, 90, 113, 114
Halt	$\overline{HALT}$	27A, 47A, 48, 60, 84, 86A, 86B, 89
Reset	$\overline{RESET}$	32, 47A, 79, 79A, 80, 81, 82, 83
Physical Bus Request	$\overline{PBR}$	35A, 35B, 36, 47A
Physical Bus Grant	$\overline{PBG}$	33, 34, 35A, 35B, 36, 37, 39, 39A
Physical Bus Grant Acknowledge	$\overline{PBGACK}$	37, 43, 47A
Logical Bus Request In	$\overline{LBRI}$	72, 47A
Logical Bus Request Out	$\overline{LBRO}$	67, 84, 86A, 86B
Logical Bus Grant In	$\overline{LBGI}$	47A, 71, 75, 77
Logical Bus Grant Out	$\overline{LBGO}$	65, 66, 71, 72, 73, 74, 75
Logical Bus Grant Acknowledge	$\overline{LBGACK}$	47A, 65, 66, 67, 68, 69, 70, 77, 89
Clock	CLK	1, 2, 3, 4, 5
Power Supply	V_{CC}	DC Only
Ground	GND	DC Only

12.7 AC ELECTRICAL SPECIFICATION DEFINITIONS

The AC specifications presented in the previous sub-section consist of output delays, input setup and hold times, and signal skew times. All signals are specified relative to an appropriate edge of the MC68851 clock input and, possibly, relative to one or more other signals.

The measurement of the AC specifications is defined by the waveforms in Figure 12-12. In order to test the parameters guaranteed by Motorola, inputs must be driven to the voltage levels specified in Figure 12-12. Outputs of the MC68851 are specified with minimum and/or maximum limits, as appropriate, and are measured as shown. Inputs to the MC68851 are specified with minimum and, as appropriate maximum setup and hold times, and are measured as shown. Finally, the measurements for signal-to-signal specifications are also shown.

Note that the testing levels used to verify conformance of the MC68851 to the AC specifications does not affect the guaranteed DC operation of the device as specified in **12.4 DC ELECTRICAL CHARACTERISTICS**.

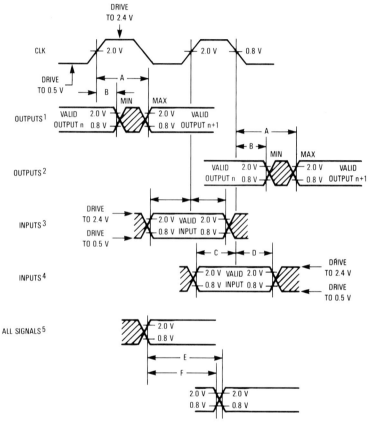

Notes:
1 - This output timing is applicable to all parameters specified relative to the rising edge of the clock
2 - This output timing is applicable to all parameters specified relative to the falling edge of the clock
3 - This input timing is applicable to all parameters specified relative to the rising edge of the clock
4 - This input timing is applicable to all parameters specified relative to the falling edge of the clock
5 - This timing is applicable to all parameters specified relative to the assertion/negation of another signal

Legend:
A - Maximum output delay specification
B - Minimum output delay specification
C - Minimum input setup time specification
D - Minimum input hold specification
E - Signal valid to signal valid specification (maximum or minimum)
F - Signal valid to signal invalid specification (maximum or minimum)

Figure 12-12. Drive Levels and Test Points for AC Specifications

SECTION 13
ORDERING INFORMATION AND MECHANICAL DATA

This section contains the pin assignments and package dimensions of the MC68851. In addition, detailed information is provided to be used when ordering.

13.1 STANDARD MC68851 ORDERING INFORMATION

Package Type	Frequency (MHz)	Temperature	Order Number
Pin Grid Array	12.5	0° to 70°C	MC68851RC12
RC Suffix	16.7	0° to 70°C	MC68851RC16

13.2 PIN ASSIGNMENTS

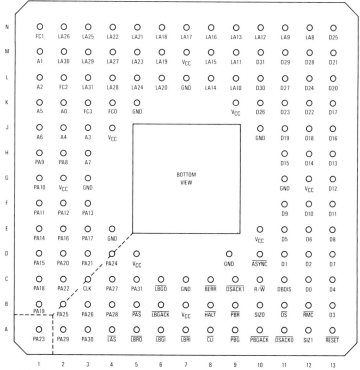

Pin Group	V_{CC}	GND
Physical Address	D5, G2, J4	E4, G3, K5
Logical Address, Internal Logic	M7	L7
D0–D31	E10, 0G12, K9	D9, G11, J10
Internal Logic, Clocks	B7	C7

13.3 MECHANICAL DATA

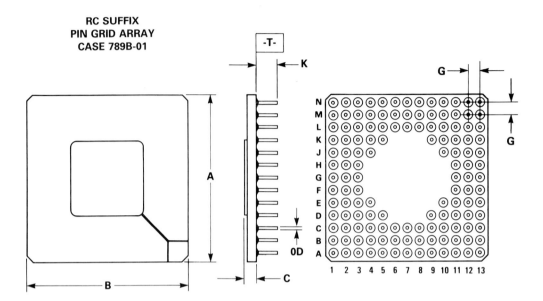

RC SUFFIX
PIN GRID ARRAY
CASE 789B-01

NOTES:
1. A AND B ARE DATUMS AND T IS A DATUM SURFACE.
2. POSITIONAL TOLERANCE FOR LEADS (132 PL).
   ⌖ ⌀ 0.13 (0.005) Ⓜ T AⓈ BⓈ
3. DIMENSIONING AND TOLERANCING PER Y14.5M, 1982.
4. CONTROLLING DIMENSION: INCH.

DIM	MILLIMETERS		INCHES	
	MIN	MAX	MIN	MAX
A	34.04	35.05	1.340	1.380
B	34.04	35.05	1.340	1.380
C	2.54	3.81	0.100	0.150
D	0.43	0.55	0.017	0.022
G	2.54 BSC		0.100 BSC	
K	4.32	4.95	0.170	0.195

APPENDIX A
INSTRUCTION SET

This appendix details the MC68851 instruction set using the Motorola assembly language syntax and notation. The instructions are arranged in alphabetical order with the mnemonic heading set in large bold type for easy reference. Also, included at the end of this appendix, is a listing of the binary patterns of all the instructions.

A.1 MC68020/MC68851 ADDRESSING MODES

Due to the nature of the MC68020/MC68851 coprocessor interface, the MC68851 supports all MC68020 addressing modes. The MC68020 effective address modes are categorized by the manner in which the modes are used. The following classifications are used in the instruction details.

Data If an effective address is used to refer to data operands, it is considered a data addressing mode.

Memory If an effective address is used to refer to memory operands, it is considered a memory addressing mode.

Alterable If an effective address is used to refer to alterable (writeable) operands, it is considered an alterable addressing mode.

Control If an effective address is used to refer to memory operands that do not have an associated size, it is considered a control addressing mode.

Table A-1 shows the various addressing categories of each addressing mode. These categories may be combined so that additional, more restrictive, classifications may be defined. For example, the instruction descriptions use such classifications as memory alterable or data alterable. The former refers to those addressing modes that are both memory and alterable addresses (i.e., the intersection of the two sets of modes), and the latter refers to addressing modes that are both data and alterable.

Table A-1. Effective Addressing Mode Categories

Address Modes	Mode	Register	Data	Memory	Control	Alterable	Assembler Syntax
Data Register Direct	000	reg. no.	X	—	—	X	Dn
Address Register Direct	001	reg. no.	—	—	—	X	An
Address Register Indirect	010	reg. no.	X	X	X	X	(An)
Address Register Indirect with Postincrement	011	reg. no.	X	X	—	X	(An)+
Address Register Indirect with Predecrement	100	reg. no.	X	X	—	X	–(An)
Address Register Indirect with Displacement	101	reg. no.	X	X	X	X	(d_{16},An)
Address Register Indirect with Index (8-Bit Displacement)	110	reg. no.	X	X	X	X	(d_8,An,Xn)
Address Register Indirect with Index (8-Bit Displacement)	110	reg. no.	X	X	X	X	(d_8,An,Xn)
Address Register Indirect with Index (Base Displacement)	110	reg. no.	X	X	X	X	(bd,An,Xn)
Memory Indirect Post-Indexed	110	reg. no.	X	X	X	X	([bd,An],Xn,od)
Memory Indirect Pre-Indexed	110	reg. no.	X	X	X	X	([bd,An,Xn],od)
Absolute Short	111	000	X	X	X	X	(xxx).W
Absolute Long	111	001	X	X	X	X	(xxx).L
Program Counter Indirect with Displacement	111	010	X	X	X	—	(d_{16},PC)
Program Counter Indirect with Index (8-Bit Displacement)	111	010	X	X	X	—	(d_8,PC,Xn)
Program Counter Indirect with Index (Base Displacement)	111	011	X	X	X	—	(bd,PC,Xn)
PC Memory Indirect Post-Indexed	111	011	X	X	X	—	([bd,PC],Xn,od)
PC Memory Indirect Pre-Indexed	111	011	X	X	X	—	([bd,PC,Xn],od)
Immediate	111	100	X	X	—	—	#⟨data⟩

A.2 OPERATION DESCRIPTION DEFINITIONS

The following definitions are used for the operation description details of the instruction set.

An	— Any Main Processor Address Register
Dn	— Any Main Processor Data Register
PC	— The Main Processor Program Counter
PSR	— The MC68851 Status Register
d	— Displacement
cc	— MC68851 Defined Condition Code
FC	— Function Code
⟨ea⟩	— The Operand Identified by the Specified Addressing Mode
PMMU	— The MC68851
(operand)	— The Contents of the Referenced Location of Register
#xxx or #data	— Immediate Data Located with the Instruction is the Operand

A.3 INDIVIDUAL INSTRUCTION DESCRIPTIONS

The individual instruction descriptions are shown on the following pages.

PBcc

Branch on PMMU Condition
(Privileged Instruction)

PBcc

Operation: If Supervisor state
 then if cc true
  then PC + d → PC
 else trap

Assembler Syntax: PBcc.⟨size⟩⟨label⟩

Attributes: Size = (Word, Long)

Description: If the specified PMMU condition is met, execution continues at location (PC) + displacement. The displacement is a two's complement integer which counts the relative distance in bytes. The value in the PC is the address of the displacement word(s). The displacement may be either 16 or 32 bits.

The condition specifier "cc" may specify the following conditions:

BS	B set	000000	BC	B clear	000001
LS	L set	000010	LC	L clear	000011
SS	S set	000100	SC	S clear	000101
AS	A set	000110	AC	A clear	000111
WS	W set	001000	WC	W clear	001001
IS	I set	001010	IC	I clear	001011
GS	G set	001100	GC	G clear	001101
CS	C set	001110	CC	C clear	001111

PSR: Not affected.

Instruction Format:

15	14	13	12	11	10	9	8	7	6	5	4	3	2	1	0
1	1	1	1	0	0	0	0	1	Size			MC68851 Condition			
16-Bit Displacement, or Most Significant Word of 32-Bit Displacement															
Least Significant Word of 32-Bit Displacement (If Needed)															

Instruction Fields:
 Size field — specifies the size of the displacement.
  0 — the displacement is 16 bits.
  1 — the displacement is 32 bits.
 MC68851 Condition field — Specifies the coprocessor condition to be tested. This field is passed to the MC68851, which provides directives to the main processor for processing this instruction.
 Word Displacement field — The shortest displacement form for MC68851 branches is 16 bits.
 Long Word Displacement Field — Allows a displacement larger than 16 bits.

PDBcc

**Test, Decrement, and Branch
(Privileged Instruction)**

PDBcc

Operation: If supervisor state
    then If cc false
        then (Dn−1 → Dn; If Dn⟨ ⟩ −1 then PC + d → PC)
        else no operation
    else trap

**Assembler
Syntax:** PDBcc Dn, ⟨label⟩

Attributes: Size = (Word)

Description: This instruction is a looping primitive of three parameters: an MC68851 condition, a counter (an MC68020 data register), and a 16-bit displacement. The instruction first test the condition to determine if the termination condition for the loop has been met, and if so, the main processor proceeds to execute the next instruction in the instruction stream. If the termination condition is not true, the low order 16 bits of the counter register are decremented by one. If the result is −1, execution continues at the location specified by the current value of the PC plus the sign extended 16-bit displacement. The value of the PC used in the branch address calculation is the address of the PDBcc instruction plus two.

The condition specifier "cc" may specify the following conditions:

BS	B set	000000
LS	L set	000010
SS	S set	000100
AS	A set	000110
WS	W set	001000
IS	I set	001010
GS	G set	001100
CS	C set	001110

BC	B clear	000001
LC	L clear	000011
SC	S clear	000101
AC	A clear	000111
WC	W clear	001001
IC	I clear	001011
GC	G clear	001101
CC	C clear	001111

PSR: Not affected.

Instruction Format:

15	14	13	12	11	10	9	8	7	6	5	4	3	2	1	0
1	1	1	1	0	0	0	0	0	1	0	0	1	Count Register		
0	0	0	0	0	0	0	0	0	0	MC68851 Condition					
16-Bit Displacement															

PDBcc

**Test, Decrement, and Branch
(Privileged Instruction)**

PDBcc

Instruction Fields:

Register field — Specifies the data register in the main processor to be used as the counter.

MC68851 Condition field — Specifies the MC68851 condition to be tested. This field is passed to the MC68851, which provides directives to the main processor for processing this instruction.

Displacement field — Specifies the distance of the branch (in bytes).

PFLUSH
PFLUSHA
PFLUSHS

Invalidate Entries in the ATC
(Privileged Instruction)

Operation: If Supervisor state
then ATC Entries for Destination Address are Invalidated
else trap

Assembler Syntax:
PFLUSHA
PFLUSH ⟨fc⟩,#⟨mask⟩
PFLUSHS ⟨fc⟩,#⟨mask⟩
PFLUSH ⟨fc⟩,#⟨mask⟩,⟨ea⟩
PFLUSHS ⟨fc⟩,#⟨mask⟩,⟨ea⟩

Attributes: Unsigned

Description: PFLUSHA invalidates all entries in the ATC.

PFLUSH invalidates a set of ATC entries whose function code bits satisfy the relation: (ATC function code bits and ⟨mask⟩) = (⟨fc⟩ and ⟨mask⟩). With an additional effective address argument, PFLUSH invalidates a set of ATC entries whose function code satisfies the relation above, and whose effective address field matches the corresponding bits of the evaluated effective address argument. In both of these cases, ATC entries whose SG bit is set will not be invalidated unless the PFLUSHS is specified.

The function code for this operation may be specified to be:
1. Immediate — the function code is specified as four bits in the command word.
2. Data Register — the function code is contained in the lower four bits in the MC68020 data register specified in the instruction.
3. Source Function Code Register — the function code is contained in the source function code (SFC) register in the CPU. Since the SFC of the MC68020 has only three implemented bits, only function codes $0 through $7 can be specified in this manner.
4. Destination Function Code Register — the function code is contained in the destination function code (DFC) register in the CPU. Since the DFC of the MC68020 has only three implemented bits, only function codes $0 through $7 can be specified in this manner.

PSR: Not affected.

Instruction Format:

15	14	13	12	11	10	9	8	7	6	5	4	3	2	1	0
1	1	1	1	0	0	0	0	0	0	Effective Address Mode			Register		
0	0	1	Mode			0	Mask			FC					

PFLUSH
PFLUSHA
PFLUSHS

PFLUSH
PFLUSHA
PFLUSHS

Invalidate Entries in the ATC
(Privileged Instruction)

Instruction Fields:
   Effective Address field — Specifies an address whose page descriptor is to be flushed from (invalidated) the ATC. Only control alterable addressing modes are allowed as shown:

Addr. Mode	Mode	Register
Dn	—	—
An	—	—
(An)	010	reg number:An
(An)+	—	—
−(An)	—	—
(d_{16},An)	101	reg number:An
(d_8,An,Xn)	110	reg number:An
(bd,An,Xn)	110	reg number:An
([bd,An,Xn],od)	110	reg number:An
([bd,An],Xn,od)	110	reg number:An

Addr. Mode	Mode	Register
(xxx).W	111	000
(xxx).L	111	001
#⟨data⟩	—	—
(d_{16},PC)	—	—
(d_8,PC,Xn)	—	—
(bd,PC,Xn)	—	—
([bd,PC,Xn],od)	—	—
([bd,PC],Xn,od)	—	—

Note that the effective address field must provide the MC68851 with the effective address of the entry to be flushed from the ATC, not the effective address describing where the PFLUSH operand is located. For example, in order to flush the ATC entry corresponding to a logical address that is temporarily stored on the top of the system stack, the instruction 'PFLUSH [(SP)]' must be used since 'PFLUSH (SP)' would invalidate the ATC entry mapping the system stack (i.e., the effective address passed to the MC68851 is the effective address of the system stack, not the effective address formed by the operand located on the top of the stack).

Mode field — Specifies how the ATC is to be flushed.
   001 — Flush all entries
   100 — Flush by Function Code only
   101 — Flush by Function Code including Shared entries
   110 — Flush by Function Code and Effective Address
   111 — Flush by Function Code and Effective Address including Shared entries

Mask field — Indicates which bits are significant in the function code compare. A zero indicates that the bit position is not significant, a one indicates that the bit position is significant. If mode = 001 (flush all entries), mask must be 0000.

FC field — Function code of address to load. If mode = 001 (flush all entries), function code must be 00000
   Otherwise:
      1DDDD — Function code is specified as four bits DDDD
      01RRR — Function code is contained in CPU data register RRR
      00000 — Function code is contained in CPU SFC register
      00001 — Function code is contained in CPU DFC register

PFLUSHR

**Invalidate ATC and RPT Entries
(Privileged Instruction)**

PFLUSHR

Operation: If Supervisor state
then the RPT entry (if any) matching the root pointer specified by ⟨ea⟩ and corresponding ATC entries are invalidated
else trap

**Assembler
Syntax:** PFLUSHR ⟨ea⟩

Attributes: Unsized

Description: The double long word pointed to by ⟨ea⟩ is taken to be a previously used value of the CRP register. The RPT entry matching this CRP (if any) is flushed, and all ATC entries loaded with this value of CRP (except for those that are globally shared) are invalidated. If no entry in the RPT matches the operand of this instruction, then no action is taken.

If the supervisor root pointer is not in use, the operating system should not issue the PFLUSHR command to destroy a task identified by the current CRP. It should wait until the CPR has been loaded with the root pointer identifying the next task until using the PFLUSHR instruction.

Instruction Format:

15	14	13	12	11	10	9	8	7	6	5	4	3	2	1	0
1	1	1	1	0	0	0	0	0	0	\multicolumn{3}{c}{Effective Address Mode}		\multicolumn{3}{c}{Register}		
1	0	1	0	0	0	0	0	0	0	0	0	0	0	0	0

Instruction Fields:

Effective Address field — Specifies the address of a previous value of the CRP register. Only memory addressing modes are allowed as shown:

Addr. Mode	Mode	Register
Dn	—	—
An	—	—
(An)	010	reg number:An
(An)+	011	reg number:An
−(An)	100	reg number:An
(d_{16},An)	101	reg number:An
(d_8,An,Xn)	110	reg number:An
(bd,An,Xn)	110	reg number:An
([bd,An,Xn],od)	110	reg number:An
([bd,An],Xn,od)	110	reg number:An

Addr. Mode	Mode	Register
(xxx).W	111	000
(xxx).L	111	001
#⟨data⟩	111	100
(d_{16},PC)	111	010
(d_9,PC,Xn)	111	011
(bd,PC,Xn)	111	011
([bd,PC,Xn],od)	111	011
([bd,PC],Xn,od)	111	011

Note that the effective address usage of this instruction is different than that of other PFLUSH variants.

PLOAD

Load an Entry into the ATC
(Privileged Instruction)

PLOAD

Operation: If Supervisor state
then search translation table and make ATC entry for effective address
else trap

Assembler Syntax: PLOADR ⟨function code⟩,⟨ea⟩
PLOADW ⟨function code⟩,⟨ea⟩

Attributes: Unsized

Description: The translation table is searched for a translation for the specified effective address. If one is found, it is flushed from the ATC and an entry is made in the ATC as if a bus master had run a bus cycle. Used and modified bits in the table are updated as part of the table search. The MC68851 ignores the logical bus arbitration signals during the flush and load phase at the end of this instruction preventing the possibility of an entry temporarily disappearing from the ATC and causing a spurious table search.

This instruction will cause a PMMU illegal operation exception (vector $39) if the E bit of the TC register is clear.

The function code for this operation may be specified to be:
1. Immediate — the function code is specified as four bits in the command word.
2. Data Register — the function code is contained in the lower four bits in the MC68020 data register specified in the instruction.
3. Source Function Code — the function code is contained in the source function code (SFC) register in the CPU. Since the SFC of the MC68020 has only three implemented bits, only function codes $0 through $7 can be specified in this manner.
4. Destination Function Code Register — the function code is contained in the destination function code (DFC) register in the CPU. Since the DFC of the MC68020 has only three implemented bits, only function codes $0 through $7 can be specified in this manner.

The effective address field specifies the logical address whose translation is to be loaded.

PLOADR causes U bits in the translation tables to be updated as if a read access had taken place. PLOADW causes U and M bits in the translation tables to be updated as if a write access had taken place.

PSR: Not affected.

Instruction Format:

15	14	13	12	11	10	9	8	7	6	5	4	3	2	1	0
1	1	1	1	0	0	0	0	0	\multicolumn{2}{c}{}	\multicolumn{3}{c}{Effective Address Mode}	\multicolumn{3}{c}{Register}
0	0	1	0	0	0	R/W̄	0	0	0	0	\multicolumn{4}{c}{FC}

PLOAD

**Load an Entry into the ATC
(Privileged Instruction)**

PLOAD

Instruction Fields:
Effective Address field — Specifies the logical address whose translation is to be loaded into the ATC. Only control alterable addressing modes are allows as shown:

Addr. Mode	Mode	Register	Addr. Mode	Mode	Register
Dn	—	—	(xxx).W	111	000
An	—	—	(xxx).L	111	001
(An)	010	reg number:An	#⟨data⟩	—	—
(An)+	—	—			
-(An)	—	—			
(d_{16},An)	101	reg number:An	(d_{16},PC)	—	—
(d_8,An,Xn)	110	reg number:An	(d_8,PC,Xn)	—	—
(bd,An,Xn)	110	reg number:An	(bd,PC,Xn)	—	—
([bd,An,Xn],od)	110	reg number:An	([bd,PC,Xn],od)	—	—
([bd,An],Xn,od)	110	reg number:An	([bd,PC],Xn,od)	—	—

Note that the effective address field must provide the MC68851 with the effective address of the entry to be loaded into the ATC, not the effective address describing where the PLOAD operand is located. For example, in order to load an ATC entry to map a logical address that is temporarily stored on the system stack, the instruction PLOAD [(SP)] must be used since PLOAD (SP) would load an ATC entry mapping the system stack (i.e., the effective address passed to the MC68851 is the effective address of the system stack, not the effective address formed by the operand located on the top of the stack).

R/$\overline{\text{W}}$ field — Specifies whether the tables should be updated for a read or a write
    1 — Read
    0 — Write

FC field — Function code of address to load
    1DDDD — Function code is specified as four bits DDDD
    01RRR — Function code is contained in CPU data register RRR
    00000 — Function code is contained in CPU SFC register
    00001 — Function code is contained in CPU DFC register

PMOVE

Move PMMU Register
(Privileged Instruction)

PMOVE

Operation: If Supervisor state
then MC68851 Register ♦ Destination or Source ♦ MC68851 Register
else trap

Assembler Syntax: PMOVE ⟨PMMU Register⟩,⟨ea⟩
PMOVE ⟨ea⟩,⟨PMMU Register⟩

Attributes: Size = (Byte, Word, Long, Double Long)

Description: The contents of the MC68851 register is copied to the address specified by ⟨ea⟩, or the data at ⟨ea⟩ is copied into the MC68851 register.

PMOVE is a double long (eight byte) operation for the following registers: CRP, SRP, DRP.

PMOVE is a long (four byte) operation for the following register: TC.

PMOVE is a word (two byte) operation for the following registers: BAC, BAD, AC, PSR, PCSR.

PMOVE is a byte (one byte) operation for the following registers: CAL, VAL, SCC.

This instruction has side effects when data is read into certain registers. These effects are:
- CRP — Causes the internal root pointer table to be searched for the new value. If a matching value is not found, an entry in the root pointer table is selected for replacement and all ATC entries associated with the replaced entry are invalidated.
- SRP — Cause all entries in the ATC that were formed with the SRP (even globally shared entries) to be invalidated.
- DRP — Causes all entries in the ATC that were formed with the DRP (even globally shared entries) to be invalidated.
- TC — If data written to the TC register attempts to set the E bit (and the E bit is currently clear), a consistency check is performed on the IS, TIA, TIB, TIC, TID, and PS fields.

PSR: Not affected unless the PSR is written to by the instruction.

Instruction Format 1 (PMOVE to/from TC, CRP, DRP, SRP, CAL, VAL, SCC, AC):

15	14	13	12	11	10	9	8	7	6	5	4	3	2	1	0
1	1	1	1	0	0	0	0	0	0	\multicolumn{3}{c}{Effective Address Mode}			\multicolumn{3}{c}{Register}		
0	1	0	\multicolumn{3}{c}{P Reg}			R/W̄	0	0	0	0	0	0	0	0

PMOVE

Move PMMU Register
(Privileged Instruction)

PMOVE

Instruction Fields:

Effective Address field — for memory to register transfers, any addressing mode is allowed as shown:

Addr. Mode	Mode	Register	Addr. Mode	Mode	Register
Dn*	000	reg number:Dn	(xxx).W	111	000
An*	001	reg number:An	(xxx).L	111	011
(An)	010	reg number:An	#⟨data⟩	111	100
(An)+	011	reg number:An			
−(An)	100	reg number:An			
(d_{16},An)	101	reg number:An	(d_{16},PC)	111	010
(d_8,An,Xn)	110	reg number:An	(d_8,PC,Xn)	111	011
(bd,An,Xn)	110	reg number:An	(bd,PC,Xn)	111	011
([bd,An,Xn],od)	110	reg number:An	([bd,PC,Xn],od)	111	011
([bd,An],Xn,od)	110	reg number:An	([bd,PC],Xn,od)	111	011

*PMOVE to CRP, SRP, DRP not allowed with these modes.

For register to memory transfers, only alterable addressing modes are allowed as shown:

Addr. Mode	Mode	Register	Addr. Mode	Mode	Register
Dn*	000	reg number:Dn	(xxx).W	111	000
An*	001	reg number:An	(xxx).L	111	001
(An)	010	reg number:An	#⟨data⟩	—	—
(An)+	011	reg number:An			
−(An)	100	reg number:An			
(d_{16},An)	101	reg number:An	(d_{16},PC)	—	—
(d_8,An,Xn)	110	reg number:An	(d_8,PC,Xn)	—	—
(bd,An,Xn)	110	reg number:An	(bd,PC,Xn)	—	—
([bd,An,Xn],od)	110	reg number:An	([bd,PC,Xn],od)	—	—
([bd,An],Xn,od)	110	reg number:An	([bd,PC],Xn,od)	—	—

*PMOVE from CRP, SRP, DRP not allowed with these modes.

Register field — Specifies the MC68851 register.
   000 — TC
   001 — DRP
   010 — SRP
   011 — CRP
   100 — CAL
   101 — VAL
   110 — SCC
   111 — AC

PMOVE

**Move PMMU Register
(Privileged Instruction)**

PMOVE

R/W field — specifies the direction of transfer
   0 — Transfer ⟨ea⟩ to MC68851 register
   1 — Transfer MC68851 register to ⟨ea⟩

Instruction Format 2 (PMOVE to/from BADx, BACx):

15	14	13	12	11	10	9	8	7	6	5	4	3	2	1	0
1	1	1	1	0	0	0	0	0	0	\multicolumn{2}{c}{Effective Address Mode}		\multicolumn{2}{c}{Register}	
0	1	1	\multicolumn{3}{c}{P Reg}		R/W	0	0	0	0	\multicolumn{3}{c}{Num}		0	0

Instruction Fields:
   Effective Address field — Same as above.

   P Register field — Specifies the type of MC68851 register.
      100 — BAD
      101 — BAC

   R/W field — Specifies the direction of transfer
      0 — Transfer ⟨ea⟩ to MC68851 register
      1 — Transfer MC68851 register to ⟨ea⟩

   Num field — Specifies the number of the BACx or BADx register to be used

Instruction Format 3 (PMOVE to/from PSR, from PCSR):

15	14	13	12	11	10	9	8	7	6	5	4	3	2	1	0
1	1	1	1	0	0	0	0	0	0	Effective Address Mode			Register		
0	1	1	P Reg			R/W	0	0	0	0	0	0	0	0	0

Instruction Fields:
   Effective Address field — Same as above.

   P Register field — Specifies the MC68851 register.
      000 — PSR
      001 — PCSR

   R/W field — Specifies direction of transfer
      0 — Transfer ⟨ea⟩ to MC68851 register
      1 — Transfer MC68851 register to ⟨ea⟩ (must be one to access PCSR using this format)

PRESTORE   PMMU Restore Function   PRESTORE
(Privileged Instruction)

Operation: If Supervisor state
                  then MC68851 State Frame ♦ Internal State, Programmer Registers
                  else trap

Assembler Syntax: Unsized, Privileged

Description: The MC68851 aborts execution of any operation it was performing, and a new internal state and programmer registers are loaded from the state frame located at the effective address. The first word at the specified address is the format word of the state frame, which specifies the size of the frame and the revision number of the MC68851 that created it. The MC68020 will write the first word to the MC68851 restore coprocessor interface register to initiate the restore operation and then read the response coprocessor interface register to verify that the MC68851 recognizes the format as valid. If the format word is invalid for this MC68851 (either because the size of the frame is not recognized, or the revision number does not match the revision of this MC68851), then the MC68020 is instructed to take a format exception and the MC68851 returns to the idle state with its user visible registers unchanged. If the format word is valid, the appropriate state frame is loaded, starting at the specified location and up through higher addresses.

The PRESTORE instruction restores the non-user visible state of the MC68851 as well as the PSR, CRP, SRP, CAL, VAL, and SCC registers fo the user programming model. In addition, if any breakpoints are enabled, all BACx and BADx registers are restored.

This instruction is the inverse of the PSAVE instruction.

The current implementation of the MC68851 supports four state sizes. Refer to **6.2.7.3 STATE FORMATS** for more information on the format of these states.

- **NULL:**   This state frame is four bytes long, with a format word of $0. A PRESTORE with this size state frame places the MC68851 in the idle state with no coprocessor or module operations in progress.
- **IDLE:**   This state frame is 36 ($24) bytes long. A PRESTORE with this size state frame causes the MC68851 to place itself in an idle state with no coprocessor operations in progress, and no breakpoints enabled. A module operation may or may not be in progress. The minimal set of MC68851 registers are restored by this state frame.
- **MID-COPROCESSOR:**   This state frame is 44 ($2C) bytes long. A PRESTORE with this size frame restores the MC68851 to a state with a coprocessor operation in progress, and no breakpoints enabled.
- **BREAKPOINTS ENABLED:**   This state frame is 76 ($4C) bytes long. A PRESTORE with this size state frame restores all of the breakpoint registers, along with other state. A coprocessor operation may or may not be in progress.

PSR: Set according to restored data.

PRESTORE

**PMMU Restore Function
(Privileged Instruction)**

PRESTORE

Instruction Format:

15	14	13	12	11	10	9	8	7	6	5	4	3	2	1	0
1	1	1	1	0	0	0	1	0	1	\multicolumn{3}{c}{Effective Address Mode}			Register

Instruction Fields:

Effective Address field — Specifies the destination location. Only control or postincrement addressing modes are allowed as shown:

Addr. Mode	Mode	Register
Dn	—	—
An	—	—
(An)	010	reg number:An
(An)+	011	reg number:An
−(An)	—	—
(d_{16},An)	101	reg number:An
(d_8,An,Xn)	110	reg number:An
(bd,An,Xn)	110	reg number:An
([bd,An,Xn],od)	110	reg number:An
([bd,An],Xn,od)	110	reg number:An

Addr. Mode	Mode	Register
(xxx).W	111	000
(xxx).L	111	001
#⟨data⟩	—	—
(d_{16},16)	111	010
(d_8,PC,Xn)	111	011
(bd,PC,Xn)	111	011
([bd,PC,Xn],od)	111	011
([bd,PC],Xn,od)	111	011

PSAVE

**PMMU Save Function
(Privileged Instruction)**

PSAVE

Operation: If Supervisor state
then MC68851 Internal State, Programmer Registers ▶ State Frame
else trap

**Assembler
Syntax:** PSAVE ⟨ea⟩

Attributes: Unsized, Privileged

Description: The MC68851 suspends execution of any operation that it was performing and saves its internal state and certain programmer registers in a state frame located at the effective address. The registers copied are: PSR, CRP, SRP, CAL, VAL, and SCC. In addition, if any breakpoints are enabled, all BAC and BAD registers are copied. After the save operation, the MC68851 is in an idle state waiting for another operation to be requested. Programmer registers are not changed.

The state frame format saved by the MC68851 depends on its state at the time of the PSAVE operation. In the current implementation, three format frames are possible. For detailed information on the format of these frames, refer to **6.2.7.3 STATE FORMATS**.

IDLE: This state frame is 36 ($24) bytes long. A PSAVE of this size state frame indicates that the MC68851 was in an idle state with no coprocessor operations in progress, and no breakpoints enabled. A module call operation may or may not have been in progress when this state frame was saved.

MID-COPROCESSOR: This state frame is 44 ($2C) bytes long. A PSAVE of this size frame indicates that the MC68851 was in a state with a coprocessor or module call operation in progress, and no breakpoints enabled.

BREAKPOINTS ENABLED: This state frame is 76 ($4C) bytes long. A PSAVE of this size state frame indicates that one or more breakpoints were enabled. A coprocessor or module call operation may or may not have been in progress.

PSR: Not affected.

Instruction Format:

15	14	13	12	11	10	9	8	7	6	5	4	3	2	1	0
1	1	1	1	0	0	0	1	0	0	\multicolumn{3}{c}{Effective Address Mode}			\multicolumn{3}{c}{Register}		

PSAVE

**PMMU Save Function
(Privileged Instruction)**

PSAVE

Instruction Fields:
    Effective Address field — Specifies the destination location. Only control of predecrement addressing modes are allows as shown:

Addr. Mode	Mode	Register	Addr. Mode	Mode	Register
Dn	—	—	(xxx).W	111	000
An	—	—	(xxx).L	111	001
(An)	010	reg number:An	#⟨data⟩	—	—
(An)+	—	—			
−(An)	100	reg number:An			
(d_{16},An)	101	reg number:An	(d_{16},PC)	—	—
(d_8,An,Xn)	110	reg number:An	(d_8,PC,Xn)	—	—
(bd,An,Xn)	110	reg number:An	(bd,PC,Xn)	—	—
([bd,An,Xn],od)	110	reg number:An	([bd,PC,Xn],od)	—	—
([bd,An],Xn,od)	110	reg number:An	([bd,PC],Xn,od)	—	—

PScc

**Set on PMMU Condition
(Privileged Instruction)**

PScc

Operation: If Supervisor state
    then if cc true
        then 1s ♦ Destination
        else 0s ♦ Destination
    else trap

**Assembler
Syntax:** PScc ⟨ea⟩

Attributes: Size = (Byte)

Description: The specified MC68851 condition code is tested; if the condition is true, the byte specified by the effective address is set to TRUE (all ones), otherwise that byte is set to FALSE (all zeros).

The condition code specifier "cc" may specify the following conditions:

BS	B set	000000
LS	L set	000010
SS	S set	000100
AS	A set	00110
WS	W set	001000
IS	I set	001010
GS	G set	001100
CS	C set	001110

BC	B clear	000001
LC	L clear	000011
SC	S clear	000101
AC	A clear	000111
WC	W clear	001001
IC	I clear	001011
GC	G clear	001101
CC	C clear	001111

PSR: Not affected.

Instruction Format:

15	14	13	12	11	10	9	8	7	6	5	4	3	2	1	0
1	1	1	1	0	0	0	0	0	1	Effective Address Mode			Register		
0	0	0	0	0	0	0	0	0	0	MC68851 Condition					

PScc

**Set on PMMU Condition
(Privileged Instruction)**

PScc

Instruction Fields:

Effective Address field — Specifies the destination location. Only data alterable addressing modes are allows as shown:

Addr. Mode	Mode	Register	Addr. Mode	Mode	Register
Dn	000	reg number:Dn	(xxx).W	111	000
An	—	—	(xxx).L	111	001
(An)	010	reg number:An	#⟨data⟩	—	—
(An)+	011	reg number:An			
−(An)	100	reg number:An			
(d_{16},An)	101	reg number:An	(d_{16},PC)	—	—
(d_8,An,Xn)	110	reg number:An	(d_8,PC,Xn)	—	—
(bd,An,Xn)	110	reg number:An	(bd,PC,Xn)	—	—
([bd,An,Xn],od)	110	reg number:An	([bd,PC,Xn],od)	—	—
([bd,An],Xn,od)	110	reg number:An	([bd,PC],Xn,od)	—	—

MC688541 Condition field — Specifies the coprocessor condition to be tested. This field is passed to the MC68851, which provides directives to the main processor for processing this instruction.

PTEST Get Information About Logical Address PTEST
(Privileged Instruction)

Operation: If Supervisor state
  then Information about Logical Address ▶ PSTATUS
  else trap

Assembler Syntax:
PTESTR ⟨function code⟩,⟨ea⟩,#⟨level⟩[,An]
PTESTW ⟨function code⟩,⟨ea⟩,#⟨level⟩[,An]

Attributes: Unsized

Description: If the E bit of the TC register is set, information about the logical address specified by ⟨fc⟩ and ⟨ea⟩ is placed in the PSTATUS register. If the E bit of the TC register is clear this instruction will cause a PMMU Illegal Operation Exception (vector $39).

The function code for this operation may be specified to be:
1. Immediate — the function code is specified as four bits in the command word.
2. Data Register — the function code is contained in the lower four bits in the MC68020 data register specified in the instruction.
3. Source Function Code Register — the function code is contained in the source function code (SFC) register in the CPU. Since the SFC of the MC68020 has only three implemented bits, only function codes $0 through $7 can be specified in this manner.
4. Destination Function Code Register — the function code is contained in the destination function code (DFC) register in the CPU. Since the DFC of the MC68020 has only three implemented bits, only function codes $0 through $7 can be specified in this manner.

The effective address field specifies the logical address to be tested.

The ⟨level⟩ parameter specifies the depth to which the translation table is to be searched. A value of zero specifies a search of the ATC only. Values one through seven cause the ATC to be ignored and specify the maximum number of descriptors to fetch. Note that finding an ATC entry with ⟨level⟩ set to zero may result in a different value in the PSR register than forcing a table search. Only the I, W, G, M, and C bits of the PSR register are always the same in both cases.

Either PTESTR or PTESTW must be specified. The two instructions differ in the setting of the A bit of the PSR (refer to **6.1.10.4 ACCESS LEVEL VIOLATION**). For systems where access levels are not in use, either PTESTR or PTESTW may be used. U and M bits in the translation table are not modified by this instruction.

If an address register parameter is specified, the physical address of the last descriptor successfully fetched is loaded into the address register. A descriptor is 'successfully' fetched if, and only if, all portions of the descriptor can be read by the MC68851 without abnormal termination of the bus cycle. If the DT field of the root pointer used indicates 'page descirptor', the returned address is $0.

The PTEST instruction continues searching the translation tables until the requested level is reached or until a condition occurs that makes further searching impossible (i.e., a DT field set to 'invalid', a limit violation, or a bus error from memory). The information in the PSR register reflects the accumulated values.

PTEST Get Information About Logical Address PTEST
(Privileged Instruction)

PSR Register: Set as follows:

- **B** Set if a bus error was received during a decriptor fetch, or if, ⟨level⟩ = 0 and no entry was found in the ATC. Cleared otherwise.
- **L** Set if the limit field of a long descriptor was exceeded. Cleared otherwise.
- **S** Set if a long descriptor indicated supervisor-only access and the ⟨fc⟩ parameter did not have bit [2] set. Cleared otherwise.
- **A** If PTESTR was specified, set if the RAL field of a long descirptor would deny access. If PTESTW was specified, set if a WAL field of a long descriptor would deny access. Cleared otherwise.
- **W** Set if the WP bit of a descriptor was set, or if a WAL field of a long descriptor would deny access.
- **I** Set if a valid translation was not available. Cleared otherwise.
- **M** If the tested address is found in the ATC, then set to the value of the M bit in the ATC. If the tested address is found in the translation table, set if the M bit of the page descriptor is set, and cleared otherwise.
- **G** If the tested address is found in the ATC, then set to the value of the G bit in the ATC. If the tested address is found in the translation table, set if the G bit of the page descriptor is set, and cleared otherwise.
- **C** Set if the address is globally shared. Cleared otherwise.
- **N** Set to the number of levels searched. A value of zero indicates an early termination of the table search in the root pointer (DT = 'page descriptor') if the level specification was not zero. If the level specification was zero, N is always set to zero.

Instruction Format:

15	14	13	12	11	10	9	8	7	6	5	4	3	2	1	0
1	1	1	1	0	0	0	0	0	0	Effective Address Mode			Register		
1	0	0	Level			R/$\overline{W}$		A Reg			FC			

Instruction Fields:

Effective Address field — Specifies the logical address about which information is requested. Only control alterable addressing modes are allows as shown:

Addr. Mode	Mode	Register	Addr. Mode	Mode	Register
Dn	—	—	(xxx).W	111	000
An	—	—	(xxx).L	111	001
(An)	010	reg number:An	#⟨data⟩	—	—
(An)+	—	—			
-(An)	—	—			
(d_{16},An)	101	reg number:An	(d_{16},PC)	—	—
(d_8,An,Xn)	110	reg number:An	(d_8,PC,Xn)	—	—
(bd,An,Xn)	110	reg number:An	(bd,PC,Xn)	—	—
([bd,An,Xn],od)	110	reg number:An	([bd,PC,Xn],od)	—	—
([bd,An],Xn,od)	110	reg number:An	([bd,PC],Xn,od)	—	—

PTEST Get Information About Logical Address PTEST
(Privileged Instruction)

Note that the effective address field must provide the MC68851 with the effective address of the logical address to be tested, not the effective address describing where the PTEST operand is located. For example, in order to test a logical address that is temporarily stored on the system stack, the instruction PTEST [(SP)] must be used since PTEST (SP) would test the mapping of the system stack (i.e., the effective address passed to the MC68851 is the effective address of the system stack, not the effective address formed by the operand located on the top of the stack.

Level — Specifies the depth to which the translation table should be searched.

R/$\overline{W}$ field — Specifies whether the A bit should be updated for a read or a write.
   1 — Read
   0 — Write

Areg — Specifies the address register in which to load the last descriptor address.
   0xxx — Do not return the last descriptor address to an address register.
   1RRR — Return the last descriptor address to address register RRR.

FC field — Function code of address to load.
   1DDDD — Function code is specified as four bits DDDD.
   01RRR — Function code is contained in CPU data register RRR.
   00000 — Function code is contained in CPU SFC register.
   00001 — Function code is contained in CPU DFC register.

PTRAPcc

**Trap on PMMU Condition
(Privileged Instruction)**

PTRAPcc

Operation: If Supervisor state
    then if cc true then trap
    else trap

**Assembler
Syntax:**
PTRAPcc
PTRAPcc.W   #⟨data⟩
PTRAPcc.L   #⟨data⟩

Attributes: Unsized or Size = (Word, Long)

Description: If the selected MC68851 condition is true, the processor initiates exception processing. The vector number is generated to reference the cpTRAPcc exception vector, the stacked program counter is the address of the next instruction. If the selected condition is not true, no operation is performed, and execution continues with the next instruction. The immediate data operand is placed in the next word(s) following the MC68851 condition and is available for user definition for use within the trap handler. Following the condition word may be a user-defined data operand specified as immediate data, to be used by the trap handler.

The condition specifier "cc" may specify the following conditions:

BS	B set	000000	BC	B clear	000001
LS	L set	000010	LC	L clear	000011
SS	S set	000100	SC	S clear	000101
AS	A set	000110	AC	A clear	000111
WS	W set	001000	WC	W clear	001001
IS	I set	001010	IC	I clear	001011
GS	G set	001100	GC	G clear	001101
CS	C set	001110	CC	C clear	001111

PSR: Not affected.

Instruction Format:

15	14	13	12	11	10	9	8	7	6	5	4	3	2	1	0
1	1	1	1	0	0	0	0	0	1	1	1	1	\multicolumn{3}{c}{Op-Mode}
0	0	0	0	0	0	0	0	0	0	\multicolumn{6}{c}{MC68851 Condition}
\multicolumn{16}{c}{16-Bit Operand or Most Significant Word of 32-Bit Operand (If Needed)}
\multicolumn{16}{c}{Least Significant Word of 32-Bit Operand (If Needed)}

PTRAPcc   Trap on PMMU Condition   PTRAPcc
(Privileged Instruction)

Instruction Fields:

Op-Mode Field — Selects the instruction form.
- 010 — Instruction is followed by one operand word.
- 011 — Instruction is followed by two opearnd words.
- 100 — Instruction has no following operand words.

MC68851 Condition field — Specifies the coprocessor condition to be tested. This field is passed to the MC68851, which provides directives to the main processor for processing this instruction.

PVALID

**Validate a Pointer
(Privileged Instruction)**

PVALID

Operation: If (source AL bits) > (destination AL bits) then Trap

Assembler Syntax: PVALID VAL,⟨ea⟩
PVALID An,⟨ea⟩

Attributes: Size = (Long)

Description: The upper bits of the source (VAL or An) are compared with the upper bits of the destination ⟨ea⟩. The number of bits compared is defined by the ALC field of the AC register. If the upper bits of the source are numerically greater than (less privileged than) the destination they cause an MMU access level exception. Otherwise, execution continues with the next instruction. If the MC field of the AC register is zero, then this instruction always causes a PMMU access level exception.

PSR: Not affected.

Instruction Format 1 (VAL Contains Access Level to Test Against):

15	14	13	12	11	10	9	8	7	6	5	4	3	2	1	0
1	1	1	1	0	0	0	0	0	0	\multicolumn{3}{c}{Effective Address Mode}		\multicolumn{3}{c}{Register}		
0	0	1	0	1	0	0	0	0	0	0	0	0	0	0	0

Instruction Fields:
Effective Address field — Specifies the logical address to be evaluated and compared against the VAL register. Only control alterable addressing modes are allowed as shown:

Addr. Mode	Mode	Register
Dn	—	—
An	—	—
(An)	010	reg number:An
(An)+	—	—
-(An)	—	—
(d$_{16}$,An)	101	reg number:An
(d$_8$,An,Xn)	110	reg number:An
(bd,An,Xn)	110	reg number:An
([bd,An,Xn],od)	110	reg number:An
([bd,An],Xn,od)	110	reg number:An

Addr Mode	Mode	Register
(xxx).W	111	000
(xxx).L	111	001
#⟨data⟩	—	—
(d$_{16}$,PC)	—	—
(d$_8$,PC,Xn)	—	—
(bd,PC,Xn)	—	—
([bd,PC,Xn],od)	—	—
([bd,PC],Xn,od)	—	—

PVALID

Validate a Pointer
(Privileged Instruction)

PVALID

Instruction Format 2 (Main Processor Register Contains Access Level to Test Against):

15	14	13	12	11	10	9	8	7	6	5	4	3	2	1	0
1	1	1	1	0	0	0	0	0	0	Effective Address Mode			Register		
0	0	1	0	1	1	0	0	0	0	0	0	0	Reg		

Instruction Fields:

Effective Address field — Specifies the logical address to be evaluated and compared against the specified main processor address register. Only control alterable addressing modes are allowed as shown:

Addr. Mode	Mode	Register
Dn	—	—
An	—	—
(An)	010	reg number:An
(An)+	—	—
–(An)	—	—
(d_{16},An)	101	reg number:An
(d_8,An,Xn)	110	reg number:An
(bd,An,Xn)	110	reg number:An
([bd,An,Xn],od)	110	reg number:An
([bd,An],Xn,od)	110	reg number:An

Addr. Mode	Mode	Register
(xxx).W	111	000
(xxx).L	111	001
#⟨data⟩	—	—
(d_{16},PC)	—	—
(d_8,PC,Xn)	—	—
(bd,PC,Xn)	—	—
([bd,PC,Xn],od)	—	—
([bd,PC],Xn,od)	—	—

Note that the effective address field must provide the MC68851 with the effective address of the logical address to be validated, not the effective address describing where the PVALID operand is located. For example, in order to validate a logical address that is temporarily stored on the system stack, the instruction PVALID VAL,[(SP)] must be used since PVLAID VAL,(SP) would validate the mapping on the system stack (i.e., the effective address passed to the MC68851 is the effective address of the system stack, not the effective address formed by the operand located on the top of the stack).

Reg field — Specifies the main processor address register to be used in the compare.

A.4 INSTRUCTION FORMAT DIAGRAMS

The instruction formats are summarized below.

PBcc

15	14	13	12	11	10	9	8	7	6	5	4	3	2	1	0
1	1	1	1	0	0	0	0	1	Size	MC68851 Condition					
16-Bit Displacement, or Most Significant Word of 32-Bit Displacement																
Least Significant Word of 32-Bit Displacement (If Needed)																

PDBcc

15	14	13	12	11	10	9	8	7	6	5	4	3	2	1	0
1	1	1	1	0	0	0	0	0	1	0	0	1	Count Register		
0	0	0	0	0	0	0	0	0	0	MC68851 Condition					
16-Bit Displacement																

PFLUSH

15	14	13	12	11	10	9	8	7	6	5	4	3	2	1	0
1	1	1	1	0	0	0	0	0	0	Effective Address Mode			Register		
0	0	1	Mode			0	Mask			FC				

PFLUSHR

15	14	13	12	11	10	9	8	7	6	5	4	3	2	1	0
1	1	1	1	0	0	0	0	0	0	Effective Address Mode			Register		
1	0	1	0	0	0	0	0	0	0	0	0	0	0	0	0

PLOAD

15	14	13	12	11	10	9	8	7	6	5	4	3	2	1	0
1	1	1	1	0	0	0	0	0	0	Effective Address Mode			Register		
0	0	1	0	0	0	R/$\overline{W}$	0	0	0	0	FC				

PMOVE (FORMAT 1)

15	14	13	12	11	10	9	8	7	6	5	4	3	2	1	0
1	1	1	1	0	0	0	0	0	0	\multicolumn{3}{c}{Effective Address Mode}			Register
0	1	0	\multicolumn{3}{c}{P Reg}	R/W̄	0	0	0	0	0	0	0	0	0

(Row 1: bits 5–3 = Effective Address Mode, bits 2–0 = Register)

PMOVE (FORMAT 2)

15	14	13	12	11	10	9	8	7	6	5	4	3	2	1	0
1	1	1	1	0	0	0	0	0	0	Effective Address Mode			Register		
0	1	1	P Reg			R/W̄	0	0	0	0	Num			0	0

PMOVE (FORMAT 3)

15	14	13	12	11	10	9	8	7	6	5	4	3	2	1	0
1	1	1	1	0	0	0	0	0	0	Effective Address Mode			Register		
0	1	1	P Reg			R/W̄	0	0	0	0	0	0	0	0	0

PRESTORE

15	14	13	12	11	10	9	8	7	6	5	4	3	2	1	0
1	1	1	1	0	0	0	1	0	1	Effective Address Mode			Register		

PSAVE

15	14	13	12	11	10	9	8	7	6	5	4	3	2	1	0
1	1	1	1	0	0	0	1	0	0	Effective Address Mode			Register		

PScc

15	14	13	12	11	10	9	8	7	6	5	4	3	2	1	0
1	1	1	1	0	0	0	0	0	1	Effective Address Mode			Register		
0	0	0	0	0	0	0	0	0	0	\multicolumn{6}{c}{MC68851 Condition}					

PTEST

15	14	13	12	11	10	9	8	7	6	5	4	3	2	1	0
1	1	1	1	0	0	0	0	0	0	\multicolumn{3}{c}{Effective Address Mode}			\multicolumn{3}{c}{Register}		
1	0	0	\multicolumn{3}{c}{Level}			R/$\overline{W}$	\multicolumn{3}{c}{A Reg}			\multicolumn{3}{c}{FC}		

PTRAPcc

15	14	13	12	11	10	9	8	7	6	5	4	3	2	1	0
1	1	1	1	0	0	0	0	0	1	1	1	1	\multicolumn{3}{c}{Op-Mode}		
0	0	0	0	0	0	0	0	0	0	\multicolumn{6}{c}{MC68851 Condition}					
\multicolumn{16}{c}{16-Bit Operand or Most Significant Word of 32-Bit Operand (If Needed)}															
\multicolumn{16}{c}{Least Significant Word of 32-Bit Operand (If Needed)}															

PVALID (FORMAT 1)

15	14	13	12	11	10	9	8	7	6	5	4	3	2	1	0
1	1	1	1	0	0	0	0	0	0	\multicolumn{3}{c}{Effective Address Mode}			\multicolumn{3}{c}{Register}		
0	0	1	0	1	0	0	0	0	0	0	0	0	0	0	0

PVALID (FORMAT 2)

15	14	13	12	11	10	9	8	7	6	5	4	3	2	1	0
1	1	1	1	0	0	0	0	0	0	\multicolumn{3}{c}{Effective Address Mode}			\multicolumn{3}{c}{Register}		
0	0	1	0	1	1	0	0	0	0	0	0	0	\multicolumn{3}{c}{Reg}		

APPENDIX B
HARDWARE CONSIDERATIONS

This appendix discusses several aspects of the MC68851 that can simplify the task of the system hardware designer.

B.1 SIMPLE SYSTEM CONFIGURATION

In this context, 'simple system' refers to a system composed of the MC68020, MC68851, and any number of explicitly addressed physical address space devices (up to 2^n devices, where n is the number of physical address bits used). This system may include alternate physical bus masters but, unless control signals shared between the logical and the physical buses are buffered, concurrent logical and physical bus activity is not allowed. This system may be considered to be a 'minimum configuration' since it includes only the circuitry required to support basic MC68851 operations.

Figure B-1 illustrates the implementation of a simple system showing the connections between the MC68020, MC68851, and the physical address space devices. In this figure, several areas of the circuitry are labeled alphabetically to point out devices discussed below.

The circuitry in (A) provides a decode and strobe generation for CPU space accesses as discussed in **4.2.3.5 TRANSLATION OF CPU SPACE ACCESSES**. The active low output of this logic is used to validate CPU space accesses. If coprocessors reside in the physical address space of the system, address bits [13–15] and [16–19] (logical or physical) must be further decoded to select an individual coprocessor or to signal an interrupt acknowledge (refer to **SECTION 9 COPROCESSOR INTERFACE**). If no coprocessors reside in the physical address space, the output of (A) can be used as an interrupt acknowledge signal without further decode.

The inclusion or exclusion of latch (B) is dependent on the required hold time for the low-order address bits of a particular system. During an address translation the MC68851 drives the high-order physical address bits (PA8–PA31) and can guarantee a minimum hold time for these outputs from the negation of $\overline{PAS}$. However, the MC68851 does not drive the low-order, shared address bits (A0–A7) during a translation and thus cannot provide a hold time relative to $\overline{PAS}$. The logical master drives these signals and specifies a hold time from the negation of its own address strobe ($\overline{LAS}$). Since $\overline{PAS}$ is negated some time after $\overline{LAS}$ (as given by AC specification #118) it is possible that insufficient hold time may be provided. When $\overline{LAS}$ is negated, the low-order address bits are latched and held until $\overline{LAS}$ is again driven low during the next bus cycle.

The data and address buffering (C) is typically required in a system in order to provide increased current drive capability for a large number of physical address space devices. In systems that do not load these buses in excess of the specified maximums, (C) may be excluded. Note, however, that increased noise immunity and a reduction in transient current requirements for the MC68851 can be obtained by reducing the capacitive loading on the physical address and data buses and, therefore, sufficient buffering of these buses is highly recommended.

Logic block (D) contains the address decode, memory timing signal generation, and other various system dependent devices (for example, watchdog timers, parity generator/checkers, . . ., etc.) that are required by the system. This block also contains buffering for any of the bus control

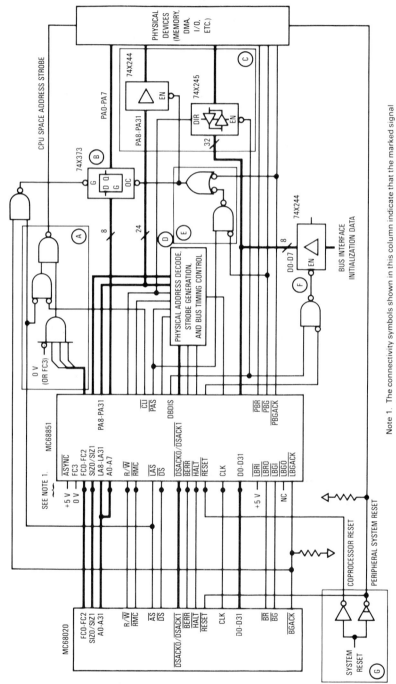

Figure B-1. Example Simple MC68020/MC68851 Hardware Configuration

signals that are heavily loaded. Additionally, (D) includes buffering for any control signals that may be driven by an alternate physical bus master since gaining control of the physical bus through arbitration does not imply that control signals shared between the CPU and the MC68851 will be in the high-impedance state (i.e., they may be driven by the CPU since it is not affected by physical bus arbitration).

The two gates marked (E) in the diagram are used to place buffers (B) and (C) in the high-impedance state when an alternate physical bus master is active on the low-impedance (output) side of these buffers. When the MC68851 completes a bus cycle and the physical bus grant ($\overline{PBG}$) output indicates that an alternate master will take control of the bus before the MC68851 performs another cycle, these gates place the buffers in the high-impedance state and maintain this state as long as $\overline{PBGACK}$ is asserted. If no alternate physical bus master is present in the system, (E) is not required and the output of the buffers can always remain in the low-impedance state. It is possible for an alternate physical master to share the buffers for the high-order physical addresses (PA8–PA31) since these lines are placed in the high-impedance state as a result of arbitration for the physical bus, in which case the buffers can permanently remain in the low-impedance state. However, direct (unbuffered) sharing of the low-order address, data, and control signal buses by an alternate physical master is not allowed unless some provision is made to force the logical master to also relinquish control of the bus in response to physical bus arbitration (for example, arbitrating for both the logical and physical buses simultaneously).

Circuit (F) is used to gate configuration information into the MC68851 during reset as described in **4.1.2 Bus Interface Initialization**. This buffer is allowed to drive the MC68851 only during reset and only after the MC68851 is properly powered-up and asserts the DBDIS signal. Both $\overline{RESET}$ and DBDIS must be used to control the impedance of this buffer in order to avoid bus contention between (F) and any other data bus buffers during reset. Note that this buffer is required only if a reset configuration other than the default configuration is necessary.

Finally, circuit (G) is presented to illustrate the recommended means of distributing the $\overline{RESET}$ signal throughout a system. Since a coprocessor provides an integral part of the system programming model (and state), it is necessary to reset the coprocessor when, and only when, the CPU itself is reset and not when the $\overline{RESET}$ signal is driven by the CPU during a reset instruction. Additionally, resetting the MC68851 disables the translation, breakpoint, and access level mechanisms; this is not typically desirable during instruction execution.

B.2 ALTERNATE LOGICAL BUS MASTERS

An example of the inclusion of a logical address space DMA controller is presented in Figure B-2. In this example, an MC68442 dual-channel DMA controller with a 32-bit address bus is configured to provide low-latency 8- or 16-bit transfers. In Figure B-2, logic and buffering described previously is included but has been reduced to blocks to simplify discussion of additional circuitry.

Circuit (H), shown in detail in Figure B-3, demultiplexes the address/data outputs of the MC68442 and also provides the multiplex control and routing required to allow the 16-bit data bus of the MC68442 to interface to the 32-bit system bus. When an even word address (A1 = 0) is accessed by the MC68442, the multiplex logic routes the high-order (even) word of the system data bus to the MC68442 shared address/data bus. Similarly, when an odd word address is accessed (A1 = 1) the low-order (odd) word of the system data bus is routed to the MC68442. Although the additional hardware required to provide 8-bit single-address transfers is not shown in this figure, it can be included easily (refer to Motorola publication ADI-1002 *MC68440 Dual-Channel Direct Memory Access Controller*).

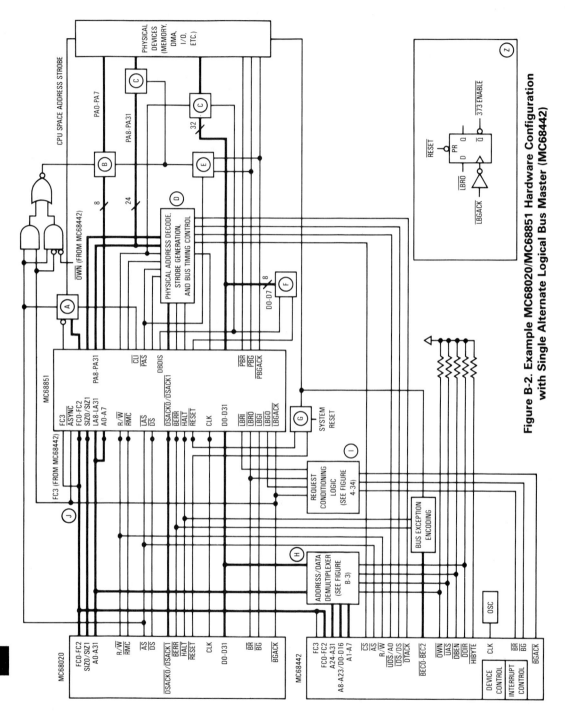

Figure B-2. Example MC68020/MC68851 Hardware Configuration with Single Alternate Logical Bus Master (MC68442)

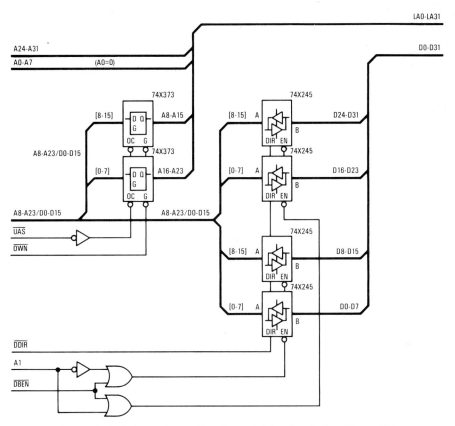

Figure B-3. Address/Data Bus Demultiplex Logic for Figure B-2

Circuit (I) provides the bus request conditioning logic as described in **4.4.1.1 ALTERNATE MASTER REQUESTING THE LOGICAL BUS** and prevents deadlocks of the logical bus should the MC68851 be required to perform a table search operation from the DMA controller. In a system incorporating multiple alternate logical masters, similar circuitry to perform this same function must be included.

Circuit (J) demonstrates the use of the asynchronous control input ($\overline{ASYNC}$). When the alternate logical master asserts $\overline{LBGACK}$ indicating that it is going to perform bus activity, $\overline{ASYNC}$ is asserted to indicate that the master does not present the same bus timings as the MC68020. Note that this circuit also drives $\overline{ASYNC}$ low when the MC68851 is performing table search operations. However, $\overline{ASYNC}$ is monitored only during address translation and accesses to the MC68851 register set and is ignored during table search operations.

The only other major modifications required to include an alternate logical master are to the physical address space strobe generation and bus timing control circuitry (D). Since the bus control signals for the MC68442 are different than those of the MC68020 and MC68851, some provision must be made to incorporate these signals. Additionally, any control signals not driven by the alternate master (e.g., $\overline{RMC}$ and $\overline{DS}$) must be held inactive with resistive pullups while the CPU signal buses are in the high-impedance state.

Note that the control circuitry for (B) is modified to account for the presence of the MC68442. If an alternate logical bus master is employed that does not present an $\overline{\text{OWN}}$ signal, a control circuit as shown in (Z) should be used.

It is important to note that, while the inclusion of DMA hardware potentially provides for low-latency response to external events, a DMA controller generating logical addresses may not provide satisfactory response time unless certain conventions are adhered to by the software controlling the DMA setup. First, both the source and destination of the transfers should physically reside in the system (i.e., both should be currently allocated to and reside in the physical address space and neither can be removed until the DMA operation is complete). Second, translation descriptors for both the source and destination operands should be pre-loaded into the MC68851 address translation cache using the PLOAD instruction. Third, the translation descriptors should be locked into the ATC to prevent their removal by the ATC replacement mechanism. Finally, the descriptors locked into the ATC by previous DMA operations should be flushed from the ATC in order to ensure that enough descriptors remain free to provide sufficient ATC performance for other tasks.

B.3 LOGICAL ADDRESS SPACE DEVICES

Hardware devices are normally located in and accessed via the system's physical address space. However, certain devices may reside in the logical address space and be accessed using only logical address information.

The general class of device that qualifies for this type of organization is one that is accessed via one of the address spaces that are unmapped by the MC68851. An 'unmapped' address space is one for which the MC68851 always provides a unity mapping (i.e., the physical address is always equal to the logical address) and does not enforce any protection checking on the accesses in this address space. Additionally, accesses via an unmapped address space are passed directly through the MC68851 and thus do not require any intervention from the ATC (i.e., translation descriptors for these accesses are neither created nor maintained). The only address space that is unmapped by the MC68851 is the CPU space (FC = 7).

It is possible to create other address spaces that have a unity mapping by setting the descriptor type field of a root pointer register to 'page descriptor' (refer to **SECTION 5 ADDRESS TRANSLATION**). However, as opposed to the 'unmapped' address spaces mentioned above, accesses to other 'unity-mapped' address spaces are always monitored by the MC68851 protection mechanism and do involve the creation and maintenance of ATC entries although the entries (with one-to-one mappings) may be created by the MC68851 without reference to the external translation tables.

B.3.1 Logical Address Space Coprocessors

The MC68851 response to CPU space accesses differs from accesses to other address spaces in that the accesses are always allowed (i.e., are never terminated by the MC68851 except for accesses to the MC68851 register set) and the $\overline{\text{CLI}}$ signal, instead of the physical address strobe ($\overline{\text{PAS}}$), is used to validate these accesses on the phsyical address bus. Since the logical address is always equal to the physical address, the logical address can be used equivalently to access devices residing in these address spaces. Using the logical address provides a performance benefit in that accesses are not subject to the translation overhead of the MC68851 and, with sufficient buffering, also allows accesses to the logical address space coprocessor to be performed while the physical bus is being used by an alternate physical bus master.

Devices residing in the logical address space are accessed using only information from the logical buses (address and control). The only further provisions that must be made are to block propagation of the cycle to physical address space devices by forcing the CPU space address strobe to remain negated and to ensure that transceivers on the system data bus do not conflict with the bus drivers of the logical address space device.

Figure B-4 illustrates the simplest method by which the MC68881 can be included in the logical address space of an MC68020/MC68851 system. The chip-select for the MC68881 (L) is decoded directly from the logical address bus and the bus control strobes of the MC68020 are connected directly to the corresponding MC68881 signals. In this example, the MC68881 is accessed using Cp-ID $2 (A15/A14/A13 = 010). The gate (K) is used to block propagation of the CPU space address strobe to other devices when the MC68881 is accessed. Circuit (M) isolates the local data bus from the external bus transceivers by forcing the transceivers into the high-impedance state unless either the physical or CPU space address strobe is asserted.

B.3.2 Other Logical Address Space Devices

A more restricted class of devices can be considered that consists of those devices that are accessed via an address space with a unity mapping. In these cases, the same general criteria remain valid as discussed above but, additionally, the hardware designer must take into account the possible MC68851 responses to accesses in these address spaces. Since there is no provision for preventing the MC68851 from monitoring all logical bus activity on a cycle-by-cycle basis (i.e., the synchronous timing specifications do not allow for intervening logic between the CPU and the MC68851), any device that is accessed in a logical address space other than the CPU space must be able to correctly respond to MC68851 bus control signals (bus error or relinquish and retry).

The above requirement does not, in general, place any constraints on synchronous logical devices since the MC68851 provides sufficiently fast assertion of the bus control strobes to properly terminate any MC68020 bus cycle. However, due to extra synchronization delays, the MC68851 may not be able to correctly terminate a minimum-period bus cycle executed by an asynchronous logical bus master.

As an example of the application of logical address space devices, consider an operating system that runs all supervisor code with a unity mapping. For this type of operation, the MC68851 supervisor root pointer register is initialized with a value of $0000020100000000 (zero base offset, page descriptor, globally shared) and the SRE bit is set in the translation control register (the SRP is used to translate all supervisor references). This setup provides unity mapping of all supervisor references.

As above, since the physical address is always equal to the logical address, the logical address can be used equivalently to access devices during supervisor bus cycles. The hardware considerations are similar to those of placing a coprocessor on the logical bus: the selection of the logical device (for example, ROM, RAM, . . ., etc.) is based on a decode of the logical address information, and this decode is used to block propagation of the cycle to the physical address space ($\overline{PAS}$ must be blocked in this case).

The primary difference between the two cases is that the MC658851 does monitor all accesses in this case and the logical address space is sub-divided into logical pages each of which must have a translation descriptor resident in the MC68851 ATC in order to be referenced. Otherwise, the MC68851 issues a relinquish and retry ($\overline{BERR}$, $\overline{HALT}$, and $\overline{LBRO}$) and internally generates a translation descriptor with a unity mapping for the referenced page (the relinquish and retry is issued to allow the MC68851 time to create the ATC entry).

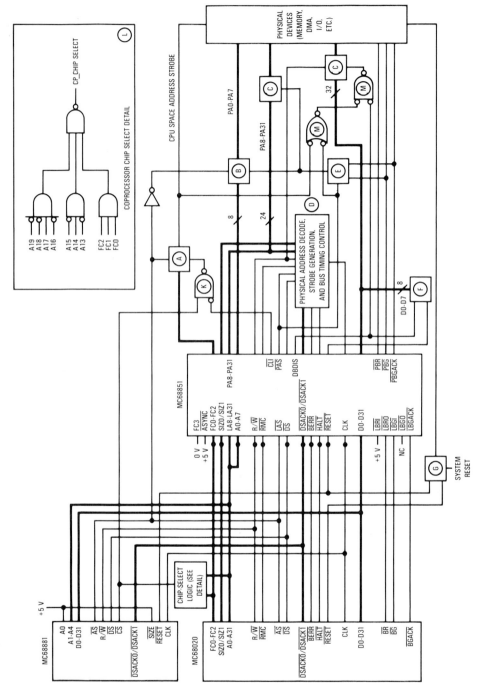

Figure B-4. Example MC68020/MC68851 Hardware Configuration with Logical Address Space Device (MC68881 FPCP)

B.4 ACCESS TIME COMPUTATIONS

The following paragraphs discuss the various timing parameters that are useful in determining critical paths when designing interfaces between the logical bus master, the MC68851, and memory devices.

B.4.1 CPU-to-Memory Access Time Computations

The paths that are typically critical in any memory interface are illustrated and defined in Figure B-5.

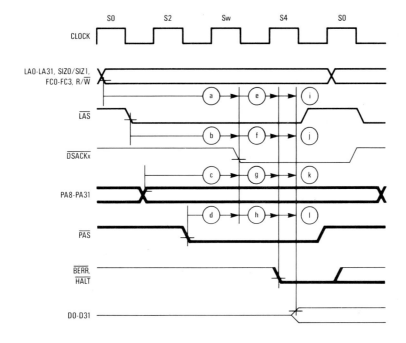

Paramater	Description	Symbol	Equation
a	Logical Address Valid to DSACKx Asserted	t_{LAVDL}	B-1
b	Logical Address Strobe Asserted to DSACKx Asserted	t_{LSADL}	B-2
c	Physical Address Valid to DSACKx Asserted	t_{PAVDL}	B-3
d	Physical Address Strobe Asserted to DSACKx Asserted	t_{PSADL}	B-4
e	Logical Address Valid to BERR/HALT Asserted (Late Termination)	t_{LAVBHL}	B-5
f	Logical Address Strobe Asserted to BERR/HALT Asserted	t_{LSABHL}	B-6
g	Physical Address Valid to BERR/HALT Asserted	t_{PAVBHL}	B-7
h	Physical Address Strobe Asserted to BERR/HALT Asserted	t_{PSABHL}	B-8
i	Logical Address Valid to Data Valid	t_{LAVDV}	B-9
j	Logical Address Strobe Asserted to Data Valid	t_{LSADV}	B-10
k	Physical Address Valid to Data Valid	t_{PAVDV}	B-11
l	Physical Address Strobe Asserted to Data Valid	t_{PSADV}	B-12

Figure B-5. Access Time Computation Diagram

The type of device that is being interfaced to the bus master determines exactly which of the paths is most critical. In general, the strobe asserted to $\overline{DSACKx}$ asserted path is most critical for very fast devices since little time is available between the assertion of the strobe and the point at which $\overline{DSACKx}$ must be asserted to terminate the bus cycle. The address-to-data paths are typically the critical paths for static devices since there is no penalty for initiating a cycle to these devices and later validating that access with the appropriate bus control signal ($\overline{LAS}$ or $\overline{PAS}$). Conversely, the address strobe-to-data valid path is usually most critical for dynamic devices since the cycle must be validated before an access can be initiated. For devices that signal termination of a bus cycle before data has been validated (e.g., error detection and correction hardware) in order to improve performance, the critical path may be from the address or strobes to the assertion of $\overline{BERR}$ (or $\overline{BERR}$ and $\overline{HALT}$). Finally, the use of the logical or physical assertion delays is usually governed by whether the device resides on the logical or physical bus.

For the case of a synchronous master, the equations for determining the address times presented in Figure B-5 are shown in Table B-1.

Table B-1. CPU-to-Memory Access Time Equations

$$t_{LAVDL} = t_{CYC} + t_{CH} - t_{CHAV} - t_{AIST} + n \cdot t_{CYC} \quad (1)$$
$$t_{LSADL} = t_{CYC} - t_{CLSA} - t_{AIST} + n \cdot t_{CYC} \quad (2)$$
$$t_{PAVDL} = t_{CYC} + t_{CH} - t_{CHAV} - t_{LAVPAV} - t_{AIST} + n \cdot t_{CYC} \quad (3)$$
$$t_{PSADL} = n \cdot t_{CYC} - t_{CLPSL} - t_{AIST} \quad (4)$$

$$t_{LAVBHL} = 2 \cdot t_{CYC} + t_{CH} - t_{CHAV} - t_{BELCL} + n \cdot t_{CYC} \quad (5)$$
$$t_{LSABHL} = 2 \cdot t_{CYC} - t_{CLSA} - t_{BELCL} + n \cdot t_{CYC} \quad (6)$$
$$t_{PAVBHL} = 2 \cdot t_{CYC} + t_{CH} - t_{CHAV} - t_{LAVPAV} - t_{BELCL} + n \cdot t_{CYC} \quad (7)$$
$$t_{PSABHL} = t_{CYC} - t_{CLPSL} - t_{BELCL} + n \cdot t_{CYC} \quad (8)$$

$$t_{LAVDV} = 2 \cdot t_{CYC} + t_{CH} - t_{CHAV} - t_{DICL} + n \cdot t_{CYC} \quad (9)$$
$$t_{LSADV} = 2 \cdot t_{CYC} - t_{CLSA} - t_{DICL} + n \cdot t_{CYC} \quad (10)$$
$$t_{PAVDV} = 2 \cdot t_{CYC} + t_{CH} - t_{CHAV} - t_{LAVPAV} - t_{DICL} + n \cdot t_{CYC} \quad (11)$$
$$t_{PSADV} = t_{CYC} - t_{CLPSL} - t_{DICL} + n \cdot t_{CYC} \quad (12)$$

Where:

t_{CYC}	= The Clock Period	(MC68851 – #1)
t_{CH}	= The Clock High Time	(MC68851 – #3)
t_{CHAV}	= The Clock High to Address Valid Delay	(MC68020 – #6)
t_{AIST}	= The Asynchronous Input Setup Time	(MC68020 – #47A)
t_{CLSA}	= The Clock Low to Strobe Low Delay	(MC68020 – #9)
t_{LAVPAV}	= The Logical Address to Physical Address Translation Time	(MC68851 – #95)
t_{CLPSL}	= The Clock Low to $\overline{PAS}$ Low Assertion Delay	(MC68851 – #115)
t_{BELCL}	= The $\overline{BERR}/\overline{HALT}$ to Clock Low Setup Time	(MC68020 – #27A)
t_{DICL}	= The Data-In to Clock Low Setup Time	(MC68020 – #27)
n	= The Number of Wait States	

Example access time calculations for an MC68020 and an MC68851 operating synchronously at 16.67 MHz are shown in Table B-2.

The access times for an asynchronous logical master can be calculated in a fashion similar to the above case for synchronous masters. However, because the logical strobe to physical strobe assertion delay is non-deterministic (dependent on whether or not setup times are met) in the general, asynchronous case, the exact equations for the access times depends on the particular asynchronous master.

Table B-2. Example CPU-to-Memory Access Time Calculations
(MC68020 and MC68851 at 16.67 MHz, t_{CH} = 30 ns, Zero and One Wait State)

			n = 0	n = 1	
t_{LAVDL}	= 60 + 30 − 30 − 5 + n • 60	=	55 ns	115 ns	(1)
t_{LSADL}	= 60 − 30 − 5 + n • 60	=	25 ns	85 ns	(2)
t_{PAVDL}	= 60 + 30 − 30 − 45 − 5 + n • 60	=	10 ns	70 ns	(3)
t_{PSADL}	= 0 − 25 − 5 + n • 60	=	—	30 ns	(4)
t_{LAVBHL}	= 120 + 30 − 30 − 20 + n • 60	=	100 ns	160 ns	(5)
t_{LSABHL}	= 120 − 30 − 20 + n • 60	=	70 ns	130 ns	(6)
t_{PAVBHL}	= 120 + 30 − 30 − 45 − 20 + n • 60	=	55 ns	115 ns	(7)
t_{PSABHL}	= 60 − 25 − 20 + n • 60	=	15 ns	75 ns	(8)
t_{LAVDV}	= 120 + 30 − 30 − 5 + n • 60	=	115 ns	175 ns	(9)
t_{LSADV}	= 120 − 30 − 5 + n • 60	=	85 ns	145 ns	
t_{PAVDV}	= 120 + 30 − 30 − 45 − 5 + n • 60	=	70 ns	130 ns	(11)
t_{PSADV}	= 60 − 25 − 5 + n • 60	=	30 ns	90 ns	(12)

B.4.2 MC68851-to-Memory Access Time Computations

Similar to the access paths evaluated above, the access times for MC68851 initiated-bus cycles during table search operations can be calculated. As shown in Figure B-6, there are six parameters that are of interest in determining the critical paths to memory. Table B-3 provides the equations required to calculate the MC68851-to-memory access times and Table B-4 illustrates example calculations for these equations.

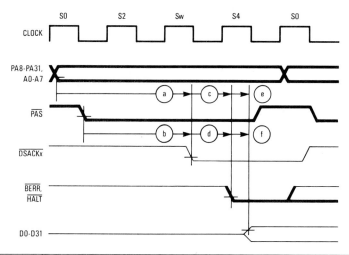

Paramater	Description	Symbol	Equation
a	Physical Address Valid to $\overline{DSACKx}$ Asserted	t_{PAVDL}	B-13
b	Physical Address Strobe Asserted to $\overline{DSACKx}$ Asserted	t_{PSADL}	B-14
c	Physical Address Valid to $\overline{BERR}/\overline{HALT}$ Asserted	t_{PAVBHL}	B-15
d	Physical Address Strobe Asserted to $\overline{BERR}/\overline{HALT}$ Asserted	t_{PSABHL}	B-16
e	Physical Address Valid to Data Valid	t_{PAVDV}	B-17
f	Physical Address Strobe Asserted to Data Valid	t_{PSADV}	B-18

Figure B-6. Access Time Computation Diagram — MC68851 Initiated Accesses

Table B-3. MC68851-to-Memory Access Time Equations

$$t_{PAVDL} = t_{CYC} + t_{CH} - t_{CHAV} - t_{AIST} + n \cdot t_{CYC} \quad (13)$$
$$t_{PSADL} = - t_{CLSA} - t_{AIST} + n \cdot t_{CYC} \quad (14)$$
$$t_{PAVBHL} = 2 \cdot t_{CYC} + t_{CH} - t_{CHAV} - t_{BELCL} + n \cdot t_{CYC} \quad (15)$$
$$t_{PSABHL} = 2 \cdot t_{CYC} - t_{CLSA} - t_{BELCL} + n \cdot t_{CYC} \quad (16)$$
$$t_{PAVDV} = 2 \cdot t_{CYC} + t_{CH} - t_{CHAV} - t_{DICL} + n \cdot t_{CYC} \quad (17)$$
$$t_{PSADV} = 2 \cdot t_{CYC} - t_{CLSA} - t_{DICL} + n \cdot t_{CYC} \quad (18)$$

Where:

t_{CYC}	= The Clock Period	(MC68851 – #1)
t_{CH}	= The Clock High Time	(MC68851 – #3)
t_{CHAV}	= The Clock High to Physical Address Valid Delay	(MC68851 – #6)
t_{AIST}	= The Asynchronous Input Setup Time	(MC68851 – #47A)
t_{CLSA}	= The Clock Low to $\overline{PAS}$ Low Delay	(MC68851 – #9)
t_{BELCL}	= The $\overline{BERR}/\overline{HALT}$ to Clock Low Setup Time	(MC68851 – #27A)
t_{DICL}	= The Data-In to Clock Low Setup Time	(MC68851 – #27)
n	= The Number of Wait States	

Table B-4. Example MC68851-to-Memory Access Time Calculations
(MC68851 at 16.67 MHz, t_{CH} = 30 ns, Zero and One Wait State)

			n = 0	n = 1	
t_{PAVDL}	= 60 + 30 – 30 – 5 + n • 60	=	55 ns	115 ns	(13)
t_{PSADL}	= 60 – 25 – 5 + n • 60	=	30 ns	90 ns	(14)
t_{PAVBHL}	= 120 + 30 – 30 – 20 + n • 60	=	100 ns	160 ns	(15)
t_{PSABHL}	= 120 – 25 – 20 + n • 60	=	75 ns	135 ns	(16)
t_{PAVDV}	= 120 + 30 – 30 – 5 + n • 60	=	115 ns	175 ns	(17)
t_{PSADV}	= 120 – 25 – 5 + n • 60	=	90 ns	150 ns	(18)

B.5 EXTERNAL CACHES

In order to provide lower average access times to memory, many systems implement caches local to the main processor to store recently used instructions and/or data. With reference to the MC68851, the primary decisions in determining a particular cache architecture are whether to place the cache in the logical or the physical address space and whether the cache accesses are terminated early (before the cache look-up is complete) or only after validation.

The MC68020 late $\overline{BERR}/\overline{HALT}$ facility allows an external device to signal completion of a bus cycle by asserting $\overline{DSACKx}$ and later (approximately one clock period) aborting or retrying that cycle if an error condition is detected. As one critical access path in many memory structures is asserting $\overline{DSACKx}$ in sufficient time to avoid additional wait states, the late termination capability allows the memory controller to terminate a bus cycle before data has been validated with the expectation that the data will be valid before it is latched by the processor. If the data validation fails, the memory controller can then abort ($\overline{BERR}$) or retry ($\overline{BERR}/\overline{HALT}$) the cycle. This technqiue is useful in memory error detection schemes where the cycle can be terminated as soon as data becomes available and the error checking can take place during the period between the signaling of termination of the cycle and the latching of data by the processor with a late retry or abort signaled upon error indication. Likewise, this technique can be used in cache implementations where the cache tag validation cannot be completed before termination of the cycle must be signaled but can be completed before late termination must be indicated.

The major consideration that must be evaluated in choosing whether or not to utilize late cycle termination is the overhead involved in retrying a bus cycle after the cycle has missed in the cache. The minimum penalty is the three clock periods required to retry the cycle, assuming that the bus control strobes ($\overline{BERR}$ and $\overline{HALT}$) are negated soon enough after the completion of the aborted cycle that the next cycle can begin immediately. In evaluating this overhead, the projected cache miss rate determines the percentage of cycles that must be retried. Additionally, the degree of parallelism in the system should be considered. If, after a cache miss, it is possible to continue the memory cycle to main memory while the processor is retrying the cycle, it is possible to avoid some, or all, of the performance penalty associated with late termination (although the control circuitry required becomes more complex).

The logical versus physical decision should be based on several design considerations. As shown by the access time calculations in Table B-2, for the same performance on a cycle-by-cycle basis (as measured by the number of wait states), use of logical information provides significantly more access time for performing the tag lookup, compare and cycle termination than is available with physical address information. Thus, for the same cycle-by-cycle performance, the logical cache can utilize slower, lower-cost components; or, with the increased access time available, can tolerate increased buffering delays and hence, construct a larger cache. Additionally, in systems that employ physical address space DMA controllers, a logical cache significantly reduces the physical bus bandwidth requirements of the processor and thus can reduce the performance degradation associated with multiple bus masters sharing a common bus.

The primary benefit of a physical cache over a logical cache is the ability to easily maintain entries for multiple tasks simultaneously and the removal of the requirement to flush the cache on each context switch. Since each task in a system may have its own unique mapping of the logical address space, a logical cache (except as described below) must be flushed of all entries whenever the logical-to-physical mapping of the system changes as occurs during a context switch. Since there is only a single physical address space, this problem does not occur with a physical cache as all references to a particular operand must utilize the same physical address. However, the intended cache size should be evaluated when considering the utility of allowing mutliple tasks to maintain cache entries. If the cache size is relatively small, and the time between context switches is large, each task will tend to fill the cache and to remove all entries created during the execution of previous tasks. Conversely, if the cache size is relatively large and the period between context switches is relatively small, the cache may provide an efficient sharing of entries.

The MC68851 provides the system designer with the ability to construct a logical cache that maintains entries for multiple tasks simultaneously by using the task alias of the MC68851. To implement this type of logical cache, the current value of the task alias is stored in the tag field of each entry loaded into the cache. The current task alias is also stored in a hardware register and is compared, during each bus cycle, against the value stored in the tag array. Only entries that are associated with the current task alias generate valid cache hits. In order to maintain cache consistency, the TA field of the MC68851 PCSR is checked after each write to the CRP register, and if the MC68851 indicates that entries with the current task alias have been flushed, then the logical cache is also flushed of entries with that task alias.

B.5.1 Logical Cache Implementation

An example organization of a logical data cache is shown in Figure B-7. As with the coprocessor example discussed in **B.3.1 Logical Address Space Coprocessors**, the cache uses only logical address information to identify an element in its tag or data stores.

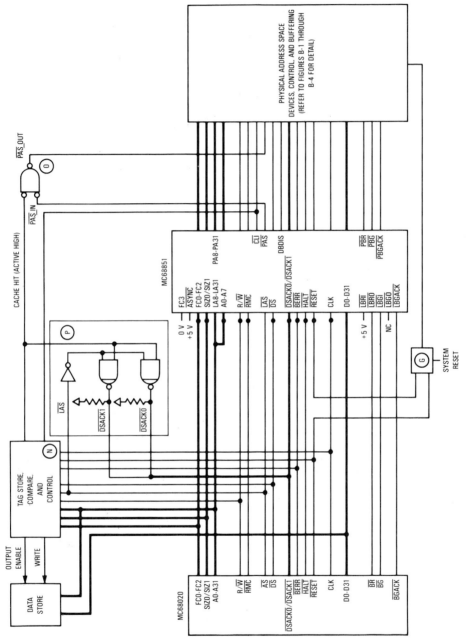

Figure B-7. Example MC68020/MC68851 Hardware Configuration with Logical Data Cache

When a bus cycle is initiated, a cache lookup begins in parallel with address translation by the MC68851. This is done in order to reduce the penalty for cache misses by overlapping the MC68851 translation time with the cache lookup. With this organization, the cache timing controller does not terminate a bus cycle until the cache has had sufficient time to validate the access as a 'hit' or a 'miss'. When a 'hit' decision is made, the cache controller asserts the $\overline{\text{DSACKx}}$ signals and also blocks propagation of the physical address strobe (O). If the cache decision cannot be completed before $\overline{\text{PAS}}$ would normally be asserted by the MC68851, some provision must be made to delay the propagation of $\overline{\text{PAS}}$ until the decision is valid. Otherwise, spurious assertions of the $\overline{\text{PAS}}$ signal are likely to occur.

The cache control circuit (N) contains all logic required to clear or create cache entries. Also contained in (N) is the decision logic required to determine whether a hit or miss has occurred and the timing logic that is required to prevent propagation of the 'hit' signal until the lookup and compare circuitry has had sufficient time to generate a valid decision. The critical path in the design of this cache is from the output of valid address by the CPU to the assertion of $\overline{\text{DSACKx}}$ by the cache controller (equation B-1). After the decision has been made that a cache-hit has occurred, the hit signal propagates through a single level of open-collector logic (P) to drive the $\overline{\text{DSACKx}}$ signals (assuming that the cache is always organized as a 32-bit port). Operating at 16.67 MHz, 55 nanoseconds are available from the presentation of valid address by the CPU to the assertion of $\overline{\text{DSACKx}}$ by the cache controller while 115 nanoseconds are available from valid address to data valid at the processor inputs.

If the access times cannot be met due to the particular cache architecture, size, cost, or other consideration, the system designer may chose to utilize an early termination approach, as discussed above, that increases the decision time available to the cache controller by making the critical path from address valid to $\overline{\text{BERR}}/\overline{\text{HALT}}$ low (Equation B-5). The only required changes to the cache structure shown in Figure B-7 is to the cycle termination logic (P). Figure B-8 shows an example circuit that could replace (P) to provide the early-termination/late-retry function.

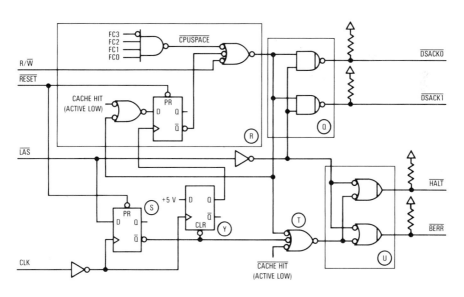

Figure B-8. Example Early-Termination Control Circuit

Normally, as soon as $\overline{\text{LAS}}$ is asserted, circuit (Q) immediately asserts the $\overline{\text{DSACKx}}$ signals to terminate the bus cycle assuming that the cache will produce a valid 'hit' later in the cycle. Circuit (R) prevents the early termination from occurring from those cycles that access operands that are non-cacheable or had missed in the cache on the previous cycle (and have already been retried). In this example, (R) prevents early termination of all CPU space accesses, all write cycles (assuming a write through cache is implemented), and all cycles that missed in the cache on the previous cycle and were not accesses to non-cacheable locations. The flip-flop (Y) latches the termination condition of the current bus cycle at the falling edge of bus state S4 to be used during the next cycle. Other conditions to suppress early termination may be included as required by a particular system but propagation delays must be carefully considered in order that the output of (R) be valid when $\overline{\text{LAS}}$ is asserted in order to avoid spurious assertions of the $\overline{\text{DSACKx}}$ signals. Alternately, $\overline{\text{LAS}}$ could be delayed to allow more time for address decode but the combination of these signals must be valid before the $\overline{\text{DSACKx}}$ signals are sampled (see Equation 4-2).

The late-termination timing chain is formed by the flip-flop (S) and gate (T). After the falling edge of bus state S2, the first clock edge on which $\overline{\text{BERR}}$ or $\overline{\text{HALT}}$ is sampled, the $\overline{Q}$ output of (S) is driven high to enable the late cycle termination by (T). If the current cycle is accessing a cacheable location, as determined by the output of (R), a cache hit has not occurred, and the $\overline{Q}$ output of (S) is high, then the $\overline{\text{BERR}}$ and $\overline{\text{HALT}}$ signals are driven low (U).

Note that the logic depicted in Figure B-8 is designed to support a cache operating with no wait states. A provision for generating wait states may be included by placing additional timing stages in (S) to delay propagation of this output by the required number of clock periods.

In order to minimize the potential for delays in retrying a bus cycle, the negation path of the bus error and halt signals should be carefully controlled. Light capacitive loading of these signal lines as well as use of a properly sized pullup resistor for the open-collector drivers, or some equivalent method, is recommended.

The available cache tag lookup, compare, and logic delay (T and U) time for this implementation is given by Equation 4-5 (100 nanoseconds at 16.67 MHz).

A further design consideration for implementation of an early termination cache controller is the response of the controller to bus cycles that satisfy the MC68851 conditions for signaling either a bus error or a relinquish and retry. The cache controller must allow the MC68851 to correctly terminate those bus cycles. The controller depicted in Figure B-8 allows the processor to accept a relinquish and retry from the MC68851 on the first bus cycle of any access and to accept a bus error from the MC68851 on the first cycle of an access that hits in the logical cache or on the retry of an access that misses in the logical cache (the bus error asserted by the MC68851 is initially masked by the retry signaled by the cache controller).

Finally, the system designer should consider the response of the physical memory controller to accesses that miss in the logical cache (and hit in the MC68851 ATC) and are retried by the CPU. During a retry operation, and in the absence of arbitration for the logical bus, the MC68020 continuously drives the address bus with the address that caused the retry to be signaled. Likewise, as long as the logical master is continuously driving the logical address bus, the MC68851 continuously drives the physical address bus with the logical-to-physical mapping corresponding to the logical address (provided that there is no arbitration for the physical bus). This presents the designer with the opportunity to utilize this information in order to continue (or initiate) the access in the physical address space (by latching the state of the $\overline{\text{PAS}}$ signal during the initial bus cycle and holding it asserted for the duration of the retry) and thus decreasing the overhead associated with retrying the cycle.

B.5.2 Physical Cache Implementation

The general design considerations for a physical address space cache are similar to those of a logical cache except that the primary control signal is the physical address strobe ($\overline{PAS}$).

Figure B-9 illustrates a block diagram of a physical cache similar to the logical cache shown in Figure B-7. The major differences in the two implementations is the removal of the function code signals from the cache tag compare circuitry (X) (they do not provide meaningful address information in the physical address space) and the use of $\overline{PAS}$ to condition the termination of bus cycles instead of $\overline{LAS}$ (V).

Similar to the case discussed for the logical cache, the 'cache hit' signal must be conditioned by timing control logic to prevent assertion of the hit signal before the tag compare circuitry has had adequate time to generate a valid decision. Otherwise, spurious assertions of the conditioned $\overline{PAS}$ signal at (W) are likely to occur. For this cache configuration, the critical path is from the presentation of valid physical address to the assertion of $\overline{DSACKx}$ by the cache controller. This time is given by Equation B-3 (70 nanoseconds at 16.67 MHZ with one wait state).

In general, a physical cache does not exhibit as high a degree of parallelism of activity as does a logical cache since the tag lookup and compare for a physical cache does not begin until the address translation has been completed by the MC68851 (while the logical cache performs these two activities simultaneously). However, certain cache implementations can regain this parallelism if the size of the cache is equal to or less than the physical page size.

With a physical address space of 2^m bytes and a page size of 2^n bytes, $m-n$ bits of the physical address are used to uniquely identify one of 2^{m-n} pages and n bits are used as an index within the page. The n index bits are not translated by the MC68851 and, if the size of the physical address space cache (or the size of the sets in the cache for a semi-associative cache) is equal to or less than the page size, these n bits can be routed directly from the CPU to the cache, allowing the index into the tag array to occur simultaneously with the address translation. Immediately upon completion of the address translation, the physical address can be compared against the tag(s) to determine whether or not the required entry is contained in the cache. This type of implementation removes the tag retrieval time from the critical decision path and provides a potential performance benefit or cost reduction.

Identical to the case discussed for the early-termination of logical cache accesses, the same technique shown in Figure B-8 can be used with a physical cache in order to change the critical path from the address valid to $\overline{DSACKx}$ asserted to address valid to $\overline{BERR}/\overline{HALT}$ asserted. In this case the critical path time is given by Equation B-7 (55 nanoseconds at 16.67 MHz, no wait states).

The design considerations discussed previously concerning bus cycle retry control are equally valid for both logical and physical caches.

B.5.3 A Note on "Instruction-Only" Cache Implementations

In some cases, particularly in multi-processing systems where cache coherence is a concern, it is desirable to store only instruction operands since they are not considered to be alterable and, hence, do not contribute to the coherence problem. In general, this is not feasible with the M68000 architecture since the M68000 Family processors do not provide a clear distinction between instruction fetches and data accesses to the program space.

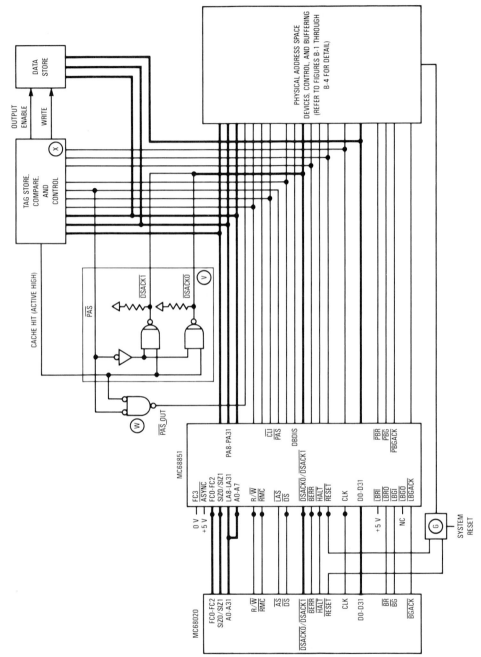

Figure B-9. Example MC68020/MC68851 Hardware Configuration with Physical Data Cache

The ability to generate program counter (PC) relative data accesses makes distinguishing between data accesses and instruction fetches impossible. For example, consider the instruction:
    MOVE.L   8(PC),D0

This instruction uses an offset of eight bytes from the program counter to access a data operand in the program space (i.e., the function code used for the operand read cycle is either one or five, indicating one of the program spaces) and loads it into data register D0. An "instruction-only" cache would load this operand into the cache creating the potential that another processor might modify this data in the main memory and cause the cached value to become inconsistent (which may not be detectable by the cache controller).

The only method by which a true instruction-only cache can be implemented is to disallow all forms of PC relative data addressing, requiring that all code generators for the system and all ported software not use that addressing mode.

B.6 POWER AND GROUND CONSIDERATIONS

The MC68851 is fabricated in Motorola's advanced HCMOS processor, contains approximately 145,000 transistors, and is capable of operating at clock frequencies of 16.67 MHz. While the use of CMOS for a device containing such a large number of transistors allows significantly reduced power consumption in comparison to an equivalent NMOS device, the high clock speed makes the characteristics of power supplied to the part quite important. The power supply must be able to supply large amounts of instantaneous current when the MC68851 performs certain operations, and it must remain within the rated specifications at all times. In order to meet these requirements, more detailed attention must be given to the power supply connection to the MC68851 than is required for NMOS devices that operate at slower clock rates.

In order to supply a solid power supply interface, eight V_{CC} pins and eight GND pins are provided. This allows three V_{CC} and GND pins to supply the power for the physical address bus, three V_{CC} and GND pins to supply the data bus, while the remaining two V_{CC} and GND pins are used by the internal logic, the logical address input buffers, and the clock generation circuitry. Table B-5 lists the V_{CC} and GND pin assignments.

Table B-5. V_{CC} and GND Pin Assignments

Pin Group	V_{CC}	GND
Physical Address	D5, G2, J4	E4, G3, K5
Logical Address, Internal Logic	M7	L7
D0–D31	E10, 0G12, K9	D9, G11, J10
Internal Logic, Clocks	B7	C7

In order to reduce the amount of noise in the power supplied to the MC68851 and to provide for instantaneous current requirements, common capacitive decoupling techniques should be observed. While there is no recommended layout for this capacitive decoupling, it is essential that the inductance between these devices and the MC68851 be minimized in order to provide sufficiently fast response time to satisfy momentary current demands and to maintain a constant supply voltage. It is suggested that a combination of low, middle, and high frequency, high quality capacitors be placed as close to the MC68851 as possible (for example, a set of 10 microfarad, 0.1 microfarad, and 330 picofarad capacitors in parallel provides filtering for most frequencies prevalent in a digital system). These decoupling techniques should also be observed for other VLSI devices in the system.

In addition to the capacitive decoupling of the power supply, care must be taken to ensure a low-impendace connection between all MC68851 V_{CC} and GND pins and the system power supply planes. Failure to provide connections of sufficient quality between the MC68851 power supply pins and the system supplies will result in increased assertion delays for external signals, decreased voltage noise margins, and potential faults in internal logic.

B.7 TEST EQUIPMENT CONSIDERATIONS

A final factor that system designers should consider when observing the operation of the MC68851 in a system is that appropriate test equipment must be used in order to avoid adversely affecting the operation of the MC68851 by altering critical system characteristics (for example, load capcitance on signal lines and buses).

Low-capacitance oscilloscope and logic analyzer probes should be used when observing signals that exhibit fast rise and fall times or that have loads approaching the specified maximums.

When using invasive test equipment (for example, logic analyzer probes that are placed between the MC68851 and the system under test), care must be taken to minimize the capacitive loading of signal lines and buses and also to minimize the addition of inductance between the power and ground pins of the MC68851 and the system power supply.

APPENDIX C
SOFTWARE CONSIDERATIONS

This appendix provides a discussion of several considerations for operating system programmers using the MC68851. This Appendix assumes that the reader is familiar with the MC68851 as discussed in previous sections of this manual and is also familiar with the MC68020.

C.1 CONTEXT SAVE AND RESTORE CONSIDERATIONS

The state of the MC68851 can be saved using the PSAVE and PRESTORE instructions. These instructions save/restore the internal state of the MC68851 and the state of the coprocessor interface, the breakpoint registers (if any are enabled), and the MC68851 root pointer registers.

In the general case, all exception handlers that can modify the state of the MC68851, or can pass program execution control to a routine that can alter the MC68851 state, must save the state of the MC68851 prior to performing any MC68851 instruction and must restore the saved state before returning program control to the routine that generated the exception. If this protocol is not followed, it is possible to permanently lose the state of an MC68851 instruction that has been temporarily suspended (for example, has experienced a page fault) resulting in a nonrecoverable error. Additionally, performing the state save and restore obviates operating system maintenance of the breakpoint and root pointer (SRP and CRP) registers during context switch operations.

To summarize, there are three major reasons for saving the state of the MC68851:
- To prevent losing the state of faulted MC68851 coprocessor instructions (applies to all exception handlers that may be invoked during coprocessor communication and that may cause execution of an MC68851 instruction),
- To maintain breakpoints that have been setup for a user task (applies only to context switch operations), and
- To maintain CRP and SRP registers associated with a particular user task (applies only to context switch operations).

In certain system implementations, the requirement for performing the save and restore operations can be removed. This is possible if, and only if, constructs of the operating system prevent the possibility of abnormal termination of any MC68851 instruction (for example, an instruction aborted by a bus error or a protocol violation) and the operating system also explicitly maintains breakpoints set up for user tasks during context switch operations.

The potential for having MC68851 instructions aborted due to a bus error can be avoided if the operating system ensures that several constraints are followed. First, the code containing the MC68851 instructions must be completely resident in memory prior to execution in order to prevent multi-word instructions that cross page boundaries from being partially paged out. Second, the operating system either must not page out its system tables and stacks (i.e., the memory areas containing data operands to be loaded into the MC68851) or must validate the residence of these areas prior to use. Third, the operating system must not attempt to write to write-protected areas while executing MC68851 instructions as this results in the assertion of the bus error signal by the MC68851. Finally, while the above constraints prevent the operating system from causing faults during execution of MC68851 instructions, some provision must be made to account for faults generated by execution of the PVALID instruction in the user mode. If module operations are allowed (bit [7] of AC register set), the PSAVE and PRESTORE instructions must be used as described above. If module operations are not enabled, execution of the PVALID instruction by a user task is terminated by an access violation exception. However, the MC68851 does not signal this exception until after the 'evaluate and transfer effective address' primitive has been issued which makes it possible for a page fault to occur during execution of this instruction. The operating system can perform one of several actions to circumvent this situation, it can prevent all code generators from generating the PVALID opcode, or it can treat faults of the PVALID instruction in the user mode as access violations resulting in a fatal termination of the user task that attempted execution of the instruction. Alternately, the operating system could allow module operations (MC bit of AC register set and the ALC field clear), thus making all PVALID instructions legal (i.e., no traps will be generated).

C.2 LOGICAL DMA CONSIDERATIONS

When employing a DMA controller that generates logical addresses, there are several factors that the operating system programmer should consider in order to optimize DMA performance.

C.2.1 Use of the L and SG Bits

In applications requiring very fast response time from the logical DMA device, it is necessary for the translation descriptors that map the source and destination of the DMA operation be preloaded into the MC68851 ATC prior to initiation of the channel operation. The MC68851 PLOAD instruction provides an easy means for these entries to be loaded. Additionally, these entries should be locked into the ATC to prevent removal by the MC68851 replacement algorithms. This can be accomplished by setting the L and SG bits in the descriptors that map the channel operation. Setting the L bit prevents removal of the entry by the ATC replacement circuitry and setting the SG bit prevents removal of the entry by the RPT replacement algorithm (refer to **5.2 ADDRESS TRANSLATION CACHE**). Finally, in order to maintain maximum performance of the MC68851 ATC, the operating system must take care to explicitly flush locked entries from the ATC after a channel operation is complete by using the PFLUSHS instruction. Otherwise, it is very likely that locked entries will predominate in the ATC leaving only a small number of entries available for mapping of other activities.

The 'shared globally' attribute can be assigned to a single page or to a contiguous logical address range while the 'locked' attribute can be assigned only at the page level.

C.2.2 Mapping of DMA Activities

The DMA root pointer is used to map address translations whenever the MC68851 observes a high level (logical one) on the FC3 input. In this manner, the translation tables for DMA activity may be maintained separately from, and selectively intermixed with, those of user and supervisor tasks for the CPU.

As an example of the use of the DRP register, consider a system using four channels of logical DMA with each channel assigned its own 16 megabyte virtual address space. The top level of the DMA translation tree (indexed by the function codes) is used to distinguish between user and supervisor activities (there is no distinction between program and data spaces in this example). When a process issues an I/O request to a channel, the upper portion of the DMA translation tree corresponding to the selected channel can simply point to the translation table of the requester and the data transfer can begin with minimal overhead.

To further develop this example, consider a situation in which a DMA operation is requested by a process that wishes to transfer 20,000 bytes from an I/O device with a starting virtual address of $1000 in the requester's buffer. Channel two of the DMA controller, occupying the DMA virtual slot from 16 to 32 megabytes, is currently idle and is selected for the operation. The operating system alters the portion of the translation tree corresponding to the channel two's virtual slot to simply point to the same tables that map the first 16 megabytes of the requester's memory. This causes memory references generated by channel two to be identical to those generated by the requester but having a 16 megabyte offset, allowing each DMA channel to, in effect, have is own mapping. Thus, channel two will be instructed to transfer 20,000 bytes starting at address $10010000 and the physical memory will be that of the requester's buffer. In order to perform this operation, the I/O handler of the operating system only needs to set up one (or a small number) of pointers in the top level DMA translation table.

C.3 CALLM/RTM PROGRAMMING EXAMPLE

The following paragraphs provide a simple example of the CALLM and RTM instructions when utilizing the access level control interface (CALLM type one).

In this example a user task operating at access level three (four access levels in use) calls a sorting routine that operates at access level one (a type one call). The stack change control register is set to $FF indicating that stack pointers must be changed before any change in access level can occur during a module call.

The sort module requires three parameters to be passed on the stack below the module stack frame: the starting address of the list to be sorted, the number of items in the list, and the length of each item. Prior to executing the module call, the calling routine pushes these arguments onto the stack and, after completion of the sort operation, the three parameters are returned to the calling routine. The location of the list is not altered and the called module does not require its own data area (the module data area field of the module descriptor is not used).

The module descriptor location is specified by the label 'SORT' and the module entry word is specified by the label 'SORT_IT'. The following code illustrates how the module call could be accomplished.

```
*******************************************************************************
* THIS CODE PROVIDES AN EXAMPLE USAGE OF THE MC68020/MC68851 MODULE CALL
* OPERATIONS.
*          ENTRY: CAL = $3
*                 VAL = $3
*                 SCC = $FF
*                 MODULE DESCR "SORT": OPT = 0
*                                      TYPE = 1
*                                      ACCESS LEVEL = 1
*                                      ENTRY WORD POINTER = SORT_IT
*                                      DATA AREA POINTER = XX
*                                      MODULE STACK POINTER = NEW_STACK
*                 MODULE ENTRY WORD = $F000
*                 SP = $10000
*                 PC = $40000
*******************************************************************************
```

```
* USER TASK IS PREPARING FOR THE MODULE CALL
          PEA    LIST                PUSH LIST ADDRESS ONTO THE STACK (1)
          MOVE.L LIST_LEN,-(SP)      PUT NBR OF LIST ENTRIES ON THE STACK
   (2)
          MOVE.L ITEM_LEN,-(SP)      PUT NBR OF BYTES/ITEM ON THE STACK
   (3)

          CALLM  12,SORT             PASS 12 BYTES TO MODULE "SORT" (4)
*THE CALL IS COMPLETE AND THE ROUTINE PROCEEDS WITH THE NEXT INSTRUCTION
          ADDI.L #12,SP              THROW AWAY OLD PARAMETERS (5)
```

```
*********************************************************************************
     THE FOLLOWING IS A FRAGMENT SECTION OF THE CALLED MODULE "SORT_IT"
*********************************************************************************
SORT_IT DC.L    $F000                THIS IS THE MODULE ENTRY WORD
        PVALID  VAL,([20,SP])        VALIDATE THE LIST POINTER
          .                          PERFORM THE SORT OPERATION
          .
          .
        RTM     A7                   RETURN TO CALLING ROUTINE (6)
```

NOTES FOR EXAMPLE EXECUTION:

    (1) SP ← SP - 4

    (2) SP ← SP - 4

    (3) SP ← SP - 4

    (4) SP ← SP - $18
      VAL ← $3
      CAL ← $1
      PC ← SORT_IT + 2

    (5) SP ← SP + 12

    (6) SP ← SP + $18
      VAL ← $3
      CAL ← $3
      PC ← RET

C.4 MULTIPROCESSING CONSIDERATIONS

The following paragraphs discuss several aspects of multiprocessing pertaining to the use of the MC68851.

C.4.1 Sharing of Translation Table Structures

In a multiprocessing environment it may be desirable to have two or more processing elements (processor and memory management unit pair) share the same translation tables. The protocol employed by the MC68851 when searching translation tables (refer to **4.3.2.3 READ-MODIFY-WRITE CYCLE**) allows multiple MC68851s to share the same table structure and prevents the devices from potentially corrupting status information maintained in the tables (used and modified indicators). However, it is possible to cause loss of coherency between the MC68851 ATC and the translation tables in physical memory if a remote bus master (other than an MC68851) is allowed to access and modify the translation tables.

In order to avoid problems with ATC coherence, any time that any alteration is made to the translation tables utilized by the MC68851 (whether by local or remote master), the ATC of all MC68851s sharing that table must be explicitly flushed of the mapping that was altered.

C.4.2 Globally Shared Data Areas

The MC68851 'cache inhibit' function allows multiprocessing systems to share data (read/write) areas among several different processing elements without causing coherency problems with local data caches.

When the operating system allocates an area of shared data, the descriptor mapping that area in each translation table (if there are more than one) should have its CI bit set to indicate to local hardware that the data associated with that particular address is non-cacheable. When the MC68851 observes an access to the shared area, the $\overline{\text{CLI}}$ (cache load inhibit) signal is asserted and local caches can be forced to allow the access to proceed to the main store.

C.4.3 Remote Manipulation of MC68851

In multiprocessing systems, it is not uncommon for a remote master (or even an alternate logical master) to require access to the instruction processing capabilities of an MC68851 for which it is not the main processor. For example, if the remote master has altered an entry in a shared table structure, then the master must instruct all MC68851s sharing this table structure to flush the corresponding entry from their ATCs.

Care must be exercised in the design of this type of system if multiple devices are capable of accessing the MC68851 via the coprocessor, access level control, or breakpoint interfaces. For such systems, there are two primary restrictions. First, all interleaved communications must be bounded by PSAVE and PRESTORE instructions. Second, the PSAVE and PRESTORE instructions themselves may not be interleaved and, thus, some other form of interprocessor communication must exist to properly synchronize these instructions. Note that, for the case of the coprocessor interface alone, adhering to the second criterion for all MC68851 instructions (rather than just the context save and restore instructions) removes the requirement for the first restriction. Thus, if the breakpoint and access level control interfaces are not in use, then synchronizing coprocessor interface accesses by multiple processors to instruction boundaries provides sufficient protection to avoid spurious processor/coprocessor protocol violations.

In order to prevent the operations by a remote master from causing a protocol violation (refer to **6.3.2.2 PROTOCOL VIOLATION**), some external means for synchronization of instructions must be enforced. Synchronizing accesses to the MC68851 on instruction boundaries is one simple way to implement this function. For example, associated with each MC68851 there can be a 'PMMU__Busy' flag in shared memory. Prior to execution of any MC68851 instruction, the CPU (whether remote or local) must check this flag to ensure that the MC68851 is not currently processing an instruction. If the flag is set, the CPU waits until it is clear. If the flag is clear, the CPU sets the flag, performs the MC68851 instruction, and then clears the flag indicating that the MC68851 is now available. One example of this protocol is as follows:

```
P_INSTR   TAS      PMMU_BUSY    TEST THE FLAG, SET IF CLEAR
          BNE.S    P_INSTR      IF WAS SET, TRY AGAIN
          PFLUSH   ⟨ea⟩         DO THE INSTRUCTION
          CLR.B    PMMU_BUSY
```

By ensuring that all MC68851 instructions are enveloped by a synchronizing protocol, the operating system can guarantee that spurious processor/coprocessor communication errors do not occur.

Additionally, operating system designers should give consideration to sequences of MC68851 instructions that must operate uninterrupted. For example, if a logical cache utilizes the task alias maintained by the MC68851, then a change of root pointers (via a PMOVE xxx,CRP) is usually followed by a read of the cache status register (with a PMOVE PCSR,xxx) to obtain the next task alias. This type of system should force both PMOVE instructions to operate without interruption in order that the task alias not be altered by some alternate master between the update of the root pointer register and the read of the task alias. The following code sequence could be used to protect these instructions:

```
P_INSTR   TAS      PMMU_BUSY    TEST THE FLAG, SET IF CLEAR
          BNE.S    P_INSTR      IF WAS SET, TRY AGAIN
          PMOVE    ⟨ea⟩,CRP     UPDATE CPU ROOT POINTER
          PMOVE    PCSR,⟨ea⟩    GET THE NEW TASK ALIAS
                                UPDATE TA OF LOGICAL CACHE AND FLUSH
                                IF NEEDED
          CLR.B    PMMU_BUSY    RESET THE FLAG
```

C.5 DEFINING AND USING PAGE TABLES IN AN OPERATING SYSTEM

There are numerous factors to consider when determining how the MC68851 is to be used by an operating system. The MC68851 provides the system programmer with great flexibility such that the O.S. can be optimized for a particular system implementation. Some of the important issues are presented in the example implementation of an MC68851 system described in **C.6 EXAMPLE MC68851 PAGING SYSTEM IMPLEMENTATION**.

C.5.1 CPU and Supervisor Root Pointer Registers

The decision whether to use both the supervisor and the CPU root pointers or only the CPU root pointer is dependent on the complexity of the memory layout by the O.S. If the supervisor root pointer is not used, then the tables pointed to be all CPU root pointers must also map all supervisor references.

The function of separating supervisor and user translation tables can be realized by using both the supervisor and CPU root pointers or, alternately, by using the CPU root pointer alone with a function code lookup as the first index into the translation tables. With proper structuring of the translation tables, both of these methods can provide the same functionality although there are separate advantages for both approaches.

Using the CPU root pointer together with function code lookup separates supervisor and user accesses at the first (highest) level of the translation tree and allows a different supervisor/user mapping for each task in the system. Alternately, the entries in the function code table corresponding to the supervisor spaces for each task can all point to the same tables thus providing a common mapping for all supervisor references.

If the mapping of the supervisor address space is identical for all tasks, then the supervisor root pointer can be used in conjunction with the CPU root pointer to provide a more simple and efficient way to describe the mapping. Using this method, the function code lookup is suppressed (unless distinct mappings are required for the program and data spaces) and user and supervisor accesses are separated at the root pointer level of the translation tables. This allows a single translation table to be defined that maps all supervisor accesses without maintaining a large number of pointers in the translation tables for each task.

Note that the use of the 'shared globally' attribute (refer to **6.1.1.3 SHARED GLOBALLY (SG)**) can significantly effect the performance of the MC68851 ATC for both cases described above.

C.5.2 Task Memory Map Definition

The MC68851 provides several different means by which the supervisor can access the user address space. The M68000 Family MOVES (move space) instruction can be used by the supervisor to access any user address regardless of how the virtual space is partitioned. Some systems may wish to give each user task the image of a complete virtual memory map ranging from zero to 4 gigabytes. Indeed, for operating systems that run other operating systems in a virtual machine environment, this must be done since the full addressing range must be accurately emulated for the subordinate O.S.

On the other hand, the extremely wide address space of the M68000 Family easily allows for each individual or all user tasks to appear within the same memory space as the O.S. itself. This can be done in several ways and one of these methods is chosen for the comprehensive example presented later. One advantage to sharing a common address space is that the O.S. has direct access to user data items since they may appear as part of the supervisor address space. Another advantage in providing a shared virtual space is the ease with which code can be shared. Common routines such as file I/O handlers and arithmetic conversion packages could be written reentrently and restricted to read-only access from all tasks in the system. Another advantage to the system-wide sharing of selected code and data areas is the fact that translation table entries can indicate this shared status and once these entries are loaded into the ATC, the MC68851 automatically uses the same entries for all tasks in the system.

The simplest example of a shared virtual space system is that in which each user and supervisor process is given a unique virtual address range within a single large virtual space ranging from 0 to 4 gigabytes. In other words, there is only one linear virtual address space in the system with all processes running somewhere in that space. This requires only a single translation table for the entire system, but individual tables could be assigned for each task, if desired. The advantage of a common table is that the O.S. has easy and immediate access to any item owned by any task in the system without having to modify the root pointer register. Otherwise, only the currently active task is immediately accessible (although this may be totally adequate). Task switching requires only updating of the user program and user data pointers in the highest level translation table indexed by the function code so that tasks can have access only to their own data. The advantages with this basic scheme are the simplicity of table management and the ease of sharing common items (for example, shared items would all have the same virtual address for all tasks in the system). Operating systems that do not require a great deal of complexity in memory management facilities, such as real-time systems, might find this scheme ideal.

The next logical step towards increased O.S. complexity, with shared user and supervisor virtual memory maps, is to keep the supervisor addresses separate as before, but to give each and every user task its own use of the rest of the virtual space. For example, each user task could have the virtual memory space from zero to 512 megabytes and the O.S. would occupy the remainder of the space with its program and data residing at virtual addresses from 512 megabytes up to 4 gigabytes. This example requires that each user task have its own set of translation tables, although the supervisor root pointer may or may not be used depending on whether the user tables also map the supervisor. Similar to the previous example, when this approach is used the user would not see the O.S. extension to its space unless the O.S. desired it or wanted to share common routines. The advantages of this scheme is that a much larger virtual space is available for any one user task and no 'virtual fragmentation' problems will ever develop. The disadvantage of this approach is a slightly more complex table management. Also, the fact that the O.S. has direct access only to the current user task.

In order to demonstrate that there are very few absolute rules when using the MC68851, re-examine the last statement above. As a general case it is true, however, that a capable O.S. designed may actually allow the supervisor to 'see' each user task space as a distinct portion of its own supervisor map. This can be accomplished by use of the tremendously large M68000 Family linear addressing space and, similar to the DMA scheme discussed in **C.2.2 Mapping of DMA Activities**, cross mapping address space. If each user task is limited to a 16-megabyte virtual space and the supervisor only requires a 16-megabyte space of its own, then there are 256 such spaces that can be simultaneously mapped. The supervisor translation table could 'see' each of these spaces within its own and, by using the indexed addressing mode with a register that contains the proper 16-megabyte constant for a particular task, the supervisor can readily use addresses of that task. The constant used as index provides a supervisor-to-user virtual address conversion. With a little imagination, the flexibility of the MC68851 can be used to provide some very sophisticated functions.

The most complex systems (including those implementing virtual machine capability) support complete virtual address separation between the supervisor and all user tasks or even between individual supervisor tasks running in the same O.S. This scenario has each task, whether supervisor or user, seeing its own virtual memory space starting at 0 and going up to 4 gigabytes. The M68000 Family separation of program and data space via the function code mechanism may be further exploited to provide a 4-gigabyte space for program code and another 4-gigabyte space for data for all supervisor and user tasks. Distinct CPU and supervisor root pointers would most likely be used in this case since there is no sharing between the various spaces. The O.S. would exclusively use the MOVES instruction to interact with the user space. The advantages of this implementation are the maximum availability of the virtual space (required for virtual machine implementations) and a complete logical separation of addresses (i.e., supervisor as well as user programs need not be concerned with unavailable 'holes' in the virtual address space that effect such things as program linkage conventions). The disadvantages of this approach are the more complex table management and more restrictive accesses to other address spaces.

In deciding how task memory spaces are to be arranged, the hierarchical protection mechanism must be considered. The MC68020 and the MC68851 provide an extension to the normal user mode of execution that allows partitioning of code and data into eight distinct access levels. Instructions for module call and return (CALLM and RTM) are provided that allow a lower privilege level routine to call a higher level routine. Each level is nested outside of the other higher levels such that all items owned by one level are available to routines at the higher levels. To accomplish this all virtual addresses must be distinct for each and every task and data item.

The hierarchical protection mechanism is discussed in detail in **SECTION 7 PROTECTION** and in **C.3 CALLM/RTM PROGRAMMING EXAMPLE**.

C.5.3 MC68851 Features and Their Impact on Table Definition

There are several features provided by the MC68851 that impact table definition and these are usually considered after the method for describing task memory maps has been decided. However, for a few systems, these features may make a significant impact on the major mapping decision and so should be included in that analysis.

C.5.3.1 NUMBER OF TABLE LEVELS.
The MC68851 provides the ability to use from zero to five levels of indexing for the translation tables. Zero levels imply that, for the root pointer signalling early termination, the virtual address is taken to be the literal physical address (plus a constant offset, if any). The primary use of this function is in systems that need to provide for limit checks on the ranges of physical addresses generated.

Single level tables are appropriate for systems that either support large page sizes or require only limited amounts of virtual memory space. For systems that are primarily numerically intensive (i.e., primarily involved in arithmetic manipulations as oppposed to data movement operations), where the overhead of virtual managed page faults and paging I/O must be minimized, a single level table with 32K page sizes may be the best choice. Such a system can map a 16-megabyte virtual address space with just 2K bytes of page table space. Additionally, the 64 entries maintained in the MC68851 ATC directly map 2 megabytes of active virtual memory space. With this wide range of mapped address space, MC68851 table search time becomes increasingly insignificant.

At another extreme, consider a single-user business system that only needs to provide for a virtual address space of 2 megabytes. In this case, a 512-byte page size might be quite appropriate, especially since this exactly matches the standard block size formats of several Winchester hard disk file systems. A page table that completely maps the entire 2 megabytes is only 16K bytes in size, and the ATC entries directly map 32K of virtual space at any one time. For both this and the example discussed above, the page tables are so small that they would be permanently allocated in the supporting O.S. data areas and thus would incur no management or swapping overhead.

Two level translation tables provide a lower page level to map the ranges as described in the previous two examples and, in addition, provide a second level of direction at the higher level. For example, in a system using 32K-byte pages and 512-entry page tables, the upper level translation table contains 256 entries (1K bytes for the pointer table) and each of the entries at the upper level maps a 16-megabyte region of the virtual address space. The real advantage of this type of approach for a large 'number-crunching' system is that it allows the O.S. designer to make a trade-off between page size and table size. The system designer may choose to go to a smaller page size to more accurately fit the block sizes on available I/O devices, yet keep the tables manageable. At the same time, the designer must also consider the performance penalty associated with smaller page sizes due to higher frequency of descriptor faults (and resultant table search time) and increased paging I/O. The MC68851 allows the designer to strike a balance rather than forcing only one page size and table structure on the system architecture.

Three level translation tables are useful when the operating system makes heavy use of shared memory spaces and/or shared page tables. Sophisticated systems very frequently need to share translation tables or program and data areas pointed to at the page table level. The fact that a table entry can point to another translation table used by a different task enables efficient sharing. The discussion presented in **6.1.2 Task Memory Map Definition** concerning sharing the virtual memory of a task with DMA or supervisor space provides one example of a system in which table sharing is implemented. The direct access by the supervisor or user address spaces is another case.

Some artificial ingelligence (AI) systems have the characteristic that a very large virtual address space is required and yet only small fragments of memory are normally allocated among these widely differing addresses. The fragmentation occurs because very complex and recursive actions are performed on lists of data that require sophisticated pointers and linked lists to be constantly allocated and freed in the memory map. The fragmentation indicates that a small page size should be used so that large amounts of real physical memory pages are not wasted. However, the need for a large virtual map when coupled to small pages produces relatively large translation table requirements. For example, the page table alone to map 4 gigabytes of virtual address space with 256 byte pages (the smallest that the MC68851 will support) would be 64 megabytes in size! By going to a three or four level table structure, the amount of actual translation table entries required would be drastically reduced. One reason for this compression is the limit function allowed on table entries (refer to **C.5.3.4 LIMIT FIELDS**). The above factors, combined with the fact that the tables themselves can be paged, provides a reasonable tradeoff in table management overhead.

C.5.3.2 INITIAL SHIFT COUNT. The IS field of the translation control (TC) register is primarily used to strip off the high-order bits of logical addresses when the hierarchical protection mechanism is in use since the upper one to three bits determine a protection level instead of a true address (although these bits can be used to provide both). Another use of the IS field is to decrease the size requirement for translation tables if it is known that a full 32 bits of virtual address space is not needed. This is particularly true in systems that could save space by leaving out the extra address lines in a board design. However, it is recommended that such a system still translate the full 32-bit logical address and set up the root pointers such that the limit fields are used to restrict all addresses to the maximum value desired. In this way, if any large (illegal) addresses are generated, they can be properly faulted.

C.5.3.3 LOCKING ENTRIES IN THE ATC. By setting the lock bit (L) in a page descriptor, the O.S. can insure that, once loaded, the descriptor remains in the ATC and any access to that page will never require a table search (assuming that the SG bit is also set). This can be very important for real-time systems that must guarantee minimum latency for I/O exception handlers or other special-purpose code that must be executed without delay. Another example where locked descriptors are useful is where an extremely high-speed DMA-type transfer is to be executed that cannot afford any interruption caused by a table search.

With 64 descriptor entries in the MC68851 ATC, a few can be allocated for less critical entries than discussed above, but locking them can greatly improve system efficiency. For example, by default an O.S. may decide to 'lock down' the entries to its primary exception routines. Or, if there is a table or area of memory that is widely accessed for one reason or another, then it may have a descriptor locked in the ATC as well.

C.5.3.4 LIMIT FIELDS. The fact that the MC68851 allows lower level tables to be only partially present provides for considerable flexibility and memory savings by the O.S. When a limit field is used in a descriptor, the next lower table may have its high- or low-order portions deleted (i.e., non-resident or unallocated) since the limit values can apply to either a maximum or minimum value for the table index at the next level. This saves considerable memory for table storage for most operating systems since seldom are the maximum number of virtual pages possible allocated to a task.

For example, consider an O.S. using a page size of 4K running numerous small tasks, each averaging 80K bytes in size. A 20-entry page table is required to map each task. This means that only 80 bytes are required for the task's page table entries if the upper level tables utilize the limit feature. Without the limit feature, such an O.S. running only ten such tasks would require 40K bytes of space just for the page tables! If the limit feature is used, however, a total of only 800 bytes of page table entries are required.

The decrease in memory required for translation table storage when using limit fields is especially significant for artificial intelligence applications where a massive virtual memory map is usually required. As the virtual space grows, each page table need only be as large as the number of entries being used within it. And, as each higher level table grows, it need only be expanded by the size of the entries being used within it, facilitating the use of three and four level tables that would otherwise be difficult to manage.

C.5.3.5 PAGE TABLES AT OTHER THAN THE LOWEST THREE LEVEL. When the MC68851 encounters an early page descriptor in a table search, this descriptor maps an entire block of pages as a consecutive reference (a contiguous virtual address range). For example, consider an O.S. that has a 32K byte area reserved for special supervisor I/O peripheral devices. This area can be mapped using a single upper level descriptor saving translation table space and table search overhead. Note that the limit fields mentioned previously can also be used such that the block of pages referenced can be less than the total of the virtual space represented by descriptors at that level of the translation tree. Note also that multiple ATC entries may be created for a single descriptor with it's DT field set to 'page descriptor' if that descriptor maps a range of pages.

Additionally, there is another way that early page descriptors can be used to impact the system memory model. Since such descriptors map contiguous blocks of memory, they can be matched one-for-one to all program and data blocks or segments in the environment. Thus each program and data segment can be treated as a block of contiguous memory mapped by a single descriptor with each block being relocatable (via the logical-to-physical base address in the descriptor). This scheme is useful in systems where tasks consist of only one or a few sequential blocks of memory. The blocks could be swapped as a complete group, and the O.S. memory map could treat the entire address space within these blocks as a uniform virtual space common to all tasks. This requires only one translation table for the whole system. In effect, instead of a two-level translation table, only the upper level is present and, by use of the limit fields and early page descriptors, complete segments of memory are mapped.

C.5.3.6 INDIRECT DESCRIPTORS. If, at the page descriptor level, the descriptor type of an entry indicates a pointer instead of a page descriptor, this is treated as an additional memory indirection to the primary page descriptor. It is in this fashion that page descriptors for common program and data areas used by several tasks in the system are made 'common'. An access by any task to a shared common page automatically insures that only the primary used bit (U) is set and any write to a common page also sets one and only one modified (M) bit. Thus, the O.S. need only peruse the primary descriptors when dealing with page swapping heuristics. If this page descriptor sharing was not permitted, the O.S. would face a formidable undertaking in determining shared page status. In essence, the O.S. would have to scan most or all of the page tables of all tasks sharing the common pages before it could determine the used or modified status of any such pages.

The MC68851 affords yet another shared memory efficiency. Recalling that, for system-wide common program and data areas, the MC68851 can cache non-task-specific translation entries with the 'shared globally' (SG) attribute. This indicates that the logical-to-physical address translation for a particular address range is identical for all tasks in the system and thus only a single descriptor for each page in this range need to be kept in the ATC.

C.5.3.7 UNUSED DESCRIPTOR BITS. For almost all descriptor types there are bits that are never used by the MC68851 that can be used for any purpose by the O.S. Additionally, when the descriptor is set to a type of 'invalid', all but two bits can be used by the O.S. A very common example is the use of the address field of a non-resident (paged-out) page to hold the disk block address of the page image. Then, the next time a task faults on the page, the supervisor has ready access to the disk location.

One important O.S. use of the unused bits of a valid page entry (resident page) is for determining page residency status, be it frequency of use or time since last use. Since a paging O.S. must occasionally 'steal' pages from one task for use by another, it is prudent to try to take pages whose removal will have the least impact on system efficiency. Pages taken first would, of course, be real page frames that are not in use by any other task. The next group would be pages that have aged the most time since their last use. If a page has the modified (M) bit set then, before it is re-used, its image must be written to a paging store on auxiliary memory. Thus, when stealing pages, it is usually better to take a write-protected page or a page that has not been modified since it can be re-used without delay.

One way for an O.S. to determine the 'age' of a page is for the O.S. to periodically go through the page tables (for example, once every 10 seconds) and increment a few of the unused bits kept as an age clock. If the page has been referenced since the last 'tick' then the bits are reset. Otherwise, once a page descirptor's bits overflow, that page could be put on a special queue indicating that it is ripe for removal when another page is required by the system. Some operating systems may have several such queues with one queue, for example, containing pointers to unused page frames, the next to unmodified (write-protected) pages, . . ., etc.

The O.S. designer has great leeway in deciding the page reclamation heuristics. One operating system may simply scan the page tables starting at the lowest priority task and 'steal' aged pages as they are found. Another may keep a system-wide list of all page frames as they are used and then simply scan starting at the oldest and steal aged pages as they are encountered. A sophsiticated system may keep a special 'working set' model of the active pages for each individual task such that it can swap in and out complete blocks of pages en-mass with a single I/O operation. Page reclamation heuristics can have a dramatic impact on limiting the page faulting overhead of a very heavily used multi-user system.

C.6 EXAMPLE MC68851 PAGING SYSTEM IMPLEMENTATION

In order to illustrate some of the MC68851 features useful for operating systems a sample design of one such implementation is developed in the following paragraphs. This example demonstrates several features in order that potential variations of the design can be easily understood. In particular, by illustrating the algorithms to allocate a block of memory for a task, the basic code for the memory management services of an O.S. can be derived. The MC68851 access level protection mechanism is not used in this example.

Assume that the target system requires execution of predominantly numerically intensive processing tasks, and towards that end, the ability to map a large virtual memroy task space is required. Average tasks do not need more than 16 megabytes of memory, but occasionally a larger virtual space is needed — up to a maximum of 496 megabytes. In order to minimize thrashing and translation table searches, a relatively large page size of 8K bytes is used. The larger page size allows a smaller number of descriptors to map a larger area of virtual space and, for any given amount of CPU time, results in fewer derscriptor misses in the ATC (and therefore fewer MC68851 table searches). Of course, with larger pages, the paging I/O will be transferring larger blocks of data (equal to the page size) and, at times, only a fraction of a page may be actually used by the task. However, having performed preliminary software model simulations it has been found that for the type of processing required for this example system, 8K pages provide the optimum performance.

For this system, although very large tasks may occasionally be run, the average task is a compiler or text editor that only requires 192K of memory. Thus, only 24 short page descriptors (96 bytes) are required to map the average task. This allows the operating system to take advantage of a unique MC68851 feature (limit fields) that allows sub-tables to reside at the start of any 16-byte boundary and take no more room than required. Because of this, the translation tables are very small and the O.S. does not need to be concerned with the paging of table areas (i.e., they are small enough to be completely resident in physical memory).

The paging hardware of many computer systems requires that pointers to lower-level tables always point to a page boundary, meaning that each of those tables must occupy at least a complete page. However, with the MC68851, the O.S. can provide table storage with an address granularity of 16 bytes and any memory obtained in this manner can be used for memory management tables. The savings in memory utilization are dramatic since, instead of needing 80K of page tables for 10 average tasks (10 tasks times the 8K minimal page table size), only 960 byte (10 times 96 bytes) is needed. Of course, there may be some fragmentation in allocating the ten small blocks, but that is insignificant to the 80K byte otherwise required (this 80K does not take into account the memory used by tables at higher levels). If each level of a two-level tree required a minimum of one page then the ten average tasks would require a minimum of 160K bytes of table area.

The translation tree for the example system consists of an upper and a lower table level. The upper level is a fixed table with 32 entries, with each of these entries consisting of a long descriptor optionally pointing to a lower level page table. Each lower-level table maps up to 16 megabytes of the virtual address space. Since the upper level table is so small, it is convenient to let it reside entirely in the main control block of the task. When a new task is dispatched, the MC68851 CRP register is loaded with a pointer to the upper level table corresponding to that task. Each lower level page table consists of from 0 to 2048 short-format page descriptors. The first level entries use limit fields to determine the size of each page table. Thus, the average task of 192K usually has only one entry of its upper-level table valid for user access and this entry points to a lower-level table with an average size of 96 bytes. Tasks that require over 16 megabytes of memory have more than one of the high-level table entries in use for user memory.

One type of memory allocation that the O.S. must control is that for physical memory (a page frame) to hold a virtual memory page. The entire physical memory available in a system is divided into page size pieces or frames. A system with 4 megabytes of real memory could therefore be divided into 512 8K frames and could theoretically hold 512 pages of active virtual memory at any one time. Usually though, parts of the O.S. such as the exception handlers, kernel code, and the O.S. private memory pool are permanently resident and non-pageable. Only the remaining frames can be considered to be available for holding virtual pages.

An O.S. keeps a linked list of all free unallocated frames. This is simple since a free frame can contain the pointer within itself to the next free frame on the list. Therefore, when a page frame needs to be allocated, the first one on the list is taken (all frames being treated alike). The function **GetFrame** is now defined, and later expanded, as the O.S. primitive that returns the physical real address of a free frame. If there are no free frames, **GetFrame** obtains one by stealing one from another task. **GetFrame** first looks for an unmodified frame to steal, since these can be stolen without waiting for them to be written back to an external storage device that holds all non-resident virtual page images (normally called the paging device or backing store). If no unmodified pages are available, a frame must be stolen that must be swapped out before it is returned. It is assumed that **GetFrame** can wait on behalf of the caller and let other tasks execute until a frame is free to be passed back.

Next, the second type of physical memory management (that used to allocate and free supervisor pieces of work memory) is developed. **GetReal** and **ReturnReal** are the routines to request and return supervisor memory utilizing physical (non-virtual) addresses. The allocation routine must return pieces of memory with addresses on a boundary of at least modulo 16 due to the fact that all MC68851 tables must start on such an offset. Usually, supervisor work memory is parcelled out in minimum chunks of some multiple bytes in order to fight fragmentation problems.

The above routines handle the allocation of physical memory. The next development for the example system is to handle allocation of virtual memory for all tasks. The first step in this process is to determine the system's view of the virtual memory map of a task and how such memory is to be accounted for since there must be some way of keeping track of which virtual memory addresses are free to be assigned to the task. Each system hardware design has two views — the physical map view and the virtual map view. The physical view represents actual physical addresses of all hardware components (64K boot/diagnostic ROM, 64K I/O area, 1 megabyte of RAM) in the system and is as follows:

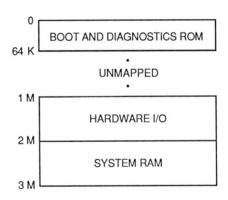

The virtual memory map is what all programs see after the MC68851 has been initialized and it is as follows:

Note that user programs can only 'see' virtual addresses starting at 16 megabytes and higher. This is the area where the code, data and stack areas for the user tasks are allocated in virtual memory. Supervisor programs 'see' the entire virtual map that directly accesses the I/O ports as well as the entire physical memory at untranslated addresses (in other words, the tables are set up such that virtual addresses equal physical addresses for the supervisor between 1 and 3 megabytes). This 'folding' of the physical space into the virtual space allows for greatly simplified operation when the physical addresses must be handled (such as with page frames). Note that the folding does not necessarily keep the virtual addresses the same as the physical. For example, the boot/diagnostic ROM at physical address zero could easily appear in the virtual address space starting at three megabytes. However, any external bus masters or circuitry (such as breakpoint registers) resident on the physical side of the bus must be provided with physical addresses (reintroducing the overhead of O.S. code handling address translation).

Low Memory

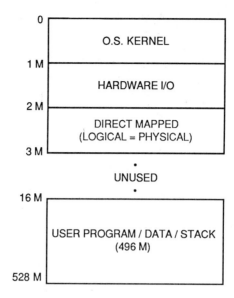

An additional advantage of the virtual mapping presented in this example is that all addresses are unique between the supervisor and user maps and thus all supervisor routines can directly access any user area with no restrictions as to instructions or addressing modes. The separate maps at first suggest that two MC68851 root pointers be used, one for the supervisor map and one for the user map. However, a closer look shows that the supervisor must be provided with access to the user translation tables for proper access of user data items. With separate root pointers, the supervisor table structure must be linked to that of the user. This can be done but only at the expense of forcing an extra level of table lookup (such as including the function code lookup).

Instead, a simpler scheme is used for this example. The CPU root pointer alone is used, however, and the first entry of the upper level table (representing the first 16 megabytes of the virtual map — the supervisor portion) for each task (each task having its own translation tree) points to the same lower level table. This common lower table indicates supervisor-only access and maps the entire virtual O.S., and physical I/O and real memory areas. Also, each entry in the common table is marked as 'globally shared' so that task switches do not invalidate any ATC-resident descriptors used by the O.S. This scheme conveniently avoids the requirement for extra lookup levels or pointer manipulations during a task switch to furnish correct access across the user/supervisor boundary. The only overhead is the simple setting of the first upper-level table entry to point to the common page table of the supervisor whenever the translation tree for a new task is created.

Returning to the problem of how to account for the virtual memory areas that have been assigned to a user task, the technique used is to simply let the existing translation tables for the task be the indication of what virtual memory has already been assigned. In other words, if a valid table entry exists for a given virtual address (page), then that 8K of virtual memory has been allocated. Certainly, if tasks continuously obtain and free virtual memory space during their lifetimes this would be inefficient due to the 8K granularity and some other scheme would be used (such as the creation of auxiliary tables to indicate virtual space availability). The allocation scheme used here provides only 'chunks' of memory in multiples of the page size (8K) but, the tasks in this system rarely, if at all, request any extensions to their memory space and when they do it is for large chunks, so this scheme suffices. Note that this is similar to most kinds of applications and utilities running in the UNIX™ environment.

The O.S. primitive **GetVirtual** is now defined which is passed a block size, in bytes, and returns the virtual address of the new block for the task. **GetVirtual** first checks to insure the request isn't too large. It then starts scanning the translation tables looking for a virtual 'hole' big enough to hold the block requested. if none is found, an attempt is made to 'grow' the page table to its maximum size. Still, if no virtual space is found, an error is returned. If virtual space for the block is found, the new page entries are set to virgin status ('page invalid but allocated') so that when the pages are first used, a page fault is generated. This indicates to the O.S. that no page images exist on backing store to be read in (most page faults do require that a page image be read from the backing store). Only a page frame would need to be allocated for that page entry and the task can then be continued with the now present page in place.

When **SwapinPage** is called, it points to the MC68851 table entry that contains the disk address of the page to be read in and restored. After reading in the page (and before returning), the routine replaces the disk address with the physical page address and sets the appropriate flags so that the entry is immediately ready for use by the MC68851.

Although this example provides many of the functions required by an O.S., a complete operating system must have a complement function for each of the routines mentioned to perform the opposite action. These routines usually perform the same steps but in reverse order and meaning. **GetVirtual** would have a **ReturnVirtual** and **SwapinPage** would have the partner **SwapOutPage**. These counterparts are easily derived since they normally perform identical steps but in reverse order.

A loose high-level language syntax is used for the code presented in subsequent descriptions and many liberties are taken to enhance readability. For example, return status values are assigned descriptive strings instead of a binary value as would be the normal. Since loops that scan tables have obvious subscripts these are abbreviated to empty brackets []. For example:
    for Upper_Table_Index = 1 to 31 do
        if Upper_Table [Upper_Table_Index]. Status = Invalid then . . .
the second line becomes:
        if Upper_Table_Index []. Status = Invalid then . . .
Flag operations are assumed to be system-defined and may imply more complex operations than simple bit manipulations. For example, the page table status of 'invalid_virgin' can be implemented with the MC68851 page table entry DT field indicating 'invalid' and a software flag bit showing that it is allocated but not swapped out (has never been used).

The virtual address for the example system is sub-divided as follows:

```
         31                                        0
         xxxu uuuu llll llll lllo oooo oooo oooo
```

    3 bits x = ignored
    5 bits u = upper level table index — [maps 32 long table entries]
    11 bits l = lower level table index — [maps 2048 short page entries]
    13 bits o = page offset

The translation table structure for the system is described as follows:
  CRP ♦ upper level table area in task control block of 32 long pointers

  [0] ♦ lower level table common to all tasks and mapping all O.S. areas (first four megabytes of virtual space). This common table is 512 short page entries in size (2K bytes).
  [1] ♦ lower level table for first 16 megabytes of user program/data/stack area.
  [2] ♦ lower level table for second 16 megabytes of user program/data/stack area.
  •
  •
  •
  [31] ♦ lower level table for last 16 megabytes (of 496 total) of user program/data/stack area.

C.6.1 O.S. Allocation Modules for Example System

The following paragraphs detail the routine '**Vallocate**' which is the central module and is used by all user programs to obtain memory. The required memory size in bytes is an input parameter for **Vallocate**. Status information and the user's virtual address to the start of the area (if the allocation was successful) are the outputs.

The code for **Vallocate** is simplified in that the amount of memory returned is always a multiple of the system page size and blocks are never allocated across 16-megabyte boundaries. The first restriction could be removed if a control structure that subdivides pages was implemented but care would have to be taken since the user could corrupt such structures if they resided within the allocated pages themselves. The second restriction could be circumvented by adding code that keeps track of consecutive free blocks found when scanning the low level tables (each block representing 16 megabytes of address space). Once the total area is found, each block is allocated in order returning only the address of the first (lowest) block).

The 32 upper-level table entries are long pointer types and each represent 16 megabytes of virtual space. They are either '**Invalid**' meaning they have no lower page tables or '**Allocated**' meaning they do have lower tables and that the limit field indicates how large these tables are. The first entry always exists since, by convention, it maps the supervisor address space and is always restricted to supervisor-only references. The first entry is never touched by this routine. The 31 entries after that are available for user space allocation.

Note that a routine similar to this could be written that grows or linearly extends a previously allocated memory block. Since the M68000 supports stack notions, the O.S. can allocate the top of memory (the thirty-second upper level table entry) as a stack and always grow it in the reverse direction. Such a system can support multiple large stacks by allocating each at a different upper level (16 megabyte) boundary and setting software flags indicating that it is a stack that grows downward.

The logic of **Vallocate** is as follows:
1) Validate the request and find number of pages required.
2) Scan each upper table entry's lower page tables (where they exist) looking for an unallocated group of pages large enough.
3) If no space found, see if the lower table is less than its maximum size and if the block can be allocated by expanding it at the end.
4) If still no space found, use the next free upper table entry and initialize its new lower level page table to allocate the block here.
5) Set allocated page entries to indicate virgin status (not swapped out, allocated, and invalid).
6) Return status and virtual address (if OK).

The procedure is defined as follows:

Vallocate (SizeInBytes, VirtualAddressReturned, Status);

/* The following are global to all routines   */

/* Symbolically define the upper level pointer table   */

Declare Upper_Table[32] Record of
        Status=(unallocated, allocated),   /* lower table here or not   */
        Limit_Field=(0 to 4k),   /* limit for lower page table   */
        Pointer;   /*address of lower page table if allocated   */

/* Symbolically define the lower level page table   */

Declare Lower_Table[0 to Limit_Field] Record of
        Status=(invalid_unallocated,   /*not allocated to User   */
                invalid_paged_out,   /*allocated but paged out   */
                invalid_virgin,   /*allocated but not yet used   */
                valid_in_memory),   /*allocated and in memory   */
        Pointer;   /*physical address or disk address of page */

Declare Upper_Table_Index, Lower_Level_Index;   /*table indexes   */

Declare NumPages;   /* number of pages required to hold request */

Status = "Out of virtual Memory";   /* default result status to this error   */

if SizeInBytes > 16 megabytes then exit **Vallocate**;

NumPages = (SizeInBytes+PageSize-1)/PageSize;   /* Pages needed   */

/* Scan User eligible page tables   */

for Upper_Table_Index = 1 to 31 do
    If Upper_Table[].Status = allocated then call **SearchPageTable**;
    If Status = "OK" then Exit **Vallocate**;
    end;

/* Block not found so find upper level entry unallocated and call **SearchPageTable** that will 'expand' */
/* the null table to hold the block.   */

for Upper_Table_Index = 1 to 31
    If Upper_Table[].Status = unallocated then call **SearchPageTable**;

/* No more virtual space, exit leaving Status = "out of virtual memory"   */

exit **Vallocate**;

    Procedure **SearchPageTable**;

/* Scan table pointed to by upper level index to see if it can hold the block. If not, see if it can be   */
/* be expanded.   If successful then set flags in the page entries, set status to "OK" and return   */
/* User's virtual address   */

    Declare Maxfound;   /* Count of consecutive free blocks found   */

```
Maxfound = 0;
For Lower_Level_Index = 0 to Upper_Table[].Limit_Field

            /* count consecutive free pages until Maxfound met or not           */
            If Lower_Table[].Status = invalid_unallocated then do
                    Maxfound = Maxfound+1;
                    if Maxfound >= NumPages then do
                    /* Go Back and Allocate Found Pages                          */

                            /* Found! Now flag the page entries, update the MC68851 and  */
                            /* return the User's virtual address                         */
                            while (Maxfound > 0) do
                                    Lower_Table[].Status = invalid_virgin;
                                    Lower_Level_Index = Lower_Level_Index-1;
                                    Decrement Maxfound;
                            end;

                            Status = "OK";
                            VirtualAddressReturned =
                                    Upper_Level_Index*16Meg +
                                    Lower_Level_Index*8k;
                            exit SearchPageTables;
                    end;
            end;

    /* allocated page hit so start counting from zero again                      */
    else Maxfound = 0;

    /* If we get here there was not enough room.  See if we can expand the page table to hold the
    new block                                                                    */
    /* If so grow it and set the new page entries as virgin                       */

    If Upper_Table[].Limit + NumPages < 4k then do
            NewLimit = Upper_Table[].Limit + NumPages;

            /* We can grow the page table! First get area for new table          */
            Call GetReal(4*NewLimit, NewPageTable);

            /* Now copy the first part of the old table into the new             */
            (pointer use indicated by "->" symbol)
            for Lower_Table_Index = 0 to Upper_Table[].Limit
                    NewPageTable->Lower_Table[] = Lower_Table[]

            /* Return the old table and install the new table pointer            */
            Call ReturnReal(4*Upper_Table[].Limit, Upper_Table[].Pointer);

            Upper_Table[].Pointer = NewPageTable;

            /* Set returned virtual address and load it replacing the old        */
            VirtualAddressReturned = Upper_Level_Index*16Meg + Lower_Level_Index*8k;

            /* Set all the new entries at the end to virgin status               */
            While (Lower_Table_Index < NewLimit) do
                    Lower_Table_Index = Lower_Table_Index + 1;
                    Lower_Table[].Status = invalid_virgin;
            end;
            /* Set OK status and return with it                                  */
            Status = "OK";
            exit SearchPageTables;
    end;

    /* cannot expand the table.  return with status unchanged (failed)           */
    end SearchPageTables;
```

C.6.2 O.S. Paging System Bus Error Handler Example

The most critical part of an O.S. supporting demand-paged memory is the page-fault handling portion of the supervisor program. The major activity of this handler is to determine the validity of the page fault and perform necessary processing. The MC68851 PTEST instruction provides the facility for investigating the cause of a bus fault by reflecting the status of an address in the PSR register (refer to **6.1.8 PMMU Status Register (PSR)**).

The PTEST instruction may signal that no error was detected for the tested address indicating that the system most likely had a true bus error (for example, a transient memory failure occurred) and it is up to the O.S. to handle this case.

The table search performed by the MC68851 during the PTEST instruction may cause a bus error implying that the MC68851 tables are not properly setup or main memory has had a failure (either transient or permanent).

Three types of return status from the PTEST instruction: 'supervisor violation', 'access level violation', and 'write protected' usually indicate that the interrupt task has attempted to access an area of the virtual space that is not a legal part of the address space of the task. The O.S. usually recovers from such an error by terminating (aborting) the task.

The 'invalid' status indicates that a page fault has indeed occurred. The O.S., at this point, must decide more specifically what the page fault means. If the 'limit violation' bit is also set, this indicates that there was no descriptor representing the faulted address (since it was outside of the tables representing the valid virtual space). In this O.S. example system, encountering an 'limited violation' error forces the task to terminate since it is trying to access beyond the allocated portion of one of the existing lower page tables. However, other operating systems may very well take this to mean an implicit request for more memory, praticularly if the memory reference is considered to be within a stack area.

If the limit violation bit is not set, then there is a descriptor that had its DT type set to 'invalid'. Again, it is up to O.S. conventions, but typically the descriptor will contain software flags indicating further disposition. The example O.S. first checks to see if the invalid descriptor was in the upper or lower level of tables. If the descriptor is in the upper table then it was a long pointer descriptor that was unallocated on behalf of the task and this indicates that the address used is a non-existent virtual address and that the task should be terminated. If the invalid descriptor was a page descriptor then software flags further indicate what action should be taken by the O.S.

One of the indications provided by the 'invalid' page descriptor is an unallocated page. This is yet another method of indicating that the address was invalid for the task. Next, it could be an allocated but virgin page which means it has been assigned to the task but has not yet been accessed. Note that if this is a read request, the O.S., may still consider this invalid since it would be abnormal for a task to access virgin memory with a read of data that has an unknown value. The duties for the O.S. in this case are to find a physical page frame and assign it to the task for use. Some systems may automatically clear (zero) virgin pages when they are first used and, in this case, it may be valid to let the first access to such pages be a read instead of a write.

The software flags can also indicate that the page is allocated but paged-out and residing on an external storage medium (such as a disk). In this case, not only must the O.S. find a page frame, but it must read in the page (swap it in) before returning to the interrupted task. Finally, software flags may indicate unique handling such as treating the memory in the page as a virtual I/O device area for virtual machine simulation.

The fetching of a physical page frame to hold the virtual page for a task may seem like an obvious and simple operation. However, what happens if there are no idle physical memory frames left to assign? The answer is that one must be found and stolen from another (or the same) task. The task from which it is stolen must have its translation table page entry altered to reflect that it is now missing (invalid) and swapped out. Typically, in the entry, there is a pointer left in place of the old physical address that indicates where the old page image resides in external storage.

The method by which an O.S. selects a page to 'steal' is very dependent on the particular system implementation. A very simple system may simply 'steal' a page from the lowest priority task. More advanced systems attempt to keep track of page frame aging; they try to keep track of which frames have been idle (not used) the longest time. This can be done in a variety of ways. One method to 'age' pages is to dedicate some software-reserved bits in the page entries as an aging counter. Every so often (say once every five or ten seconds), the O.S. can run through all page tables and, by examining the U (used) bits, increment those entries that have not been used. When entries reach the maximum count or overflow they can be remembered by building a queue of pointers to them. The queue can then be used by the routine **GetFrame** when there are no free page frames available.

Some systems may even keep more than one queue. It is obvious that once a page of memory that is read-only (no task can write to it) is swapped out (copied) to external memory then that external image always represents the data in the virtual page. Therefore, if that page is in memory and stolen for use by another task, it does not need to be written out before it is taken. An operating system that supports read-only page swaps can have a queue with just read-only pages that are more efficient to steal.

The design of page stealing heuristics is more of an art than a craft and depends widely on the nature of the tasks in execution and other dynamics of a system such as I/O activity. Consideration can be given to task priority, read-only page status, working-set determinations, number of tasks executing, thrashing level, and other factors.

The code presented below is much more general than **Vallocate** since it relies on several O.S.-dependent items. The variable pointer **VictimTask** is assumed to point to a table from the task that is having a page stolen. This must be done since it cannot be assumed that the control block layout or method of searching and finding other tasks in an operating system is known. Another simplification is the ignoring of the function code value and read/write status of the address given to the bus error procedure since they don't effect the basic logic of the program.

```
/* Paging Bus Error Handler for example O.S.                                          */

Procedure BusErrorHandler (BusErrAddress);

/* Global Variables to all code                                                       */

Declare TableEntry;                     /*Pointer returned by PTEST instruction       */
                                        /* pointing to the lowest level entry in the  */
                                        /* translation tables.                        */

/* Use MC68851 PTEST instruction to get fault status and table entry                  */
case PTEST (BusErrAddress,TableEntry) of

        /* Bus Error - translation table is invalid or memory hardware problems.  Terminate the task.   */
        B: AbortTask("Invalid table or memory hardware error");

        /* Supervisor Violation - task tried accessing restricted memory              */
        S: AbortTask("Attempted access of Supervisor-only memory");

        /* Access Level Violation - task tried accessing higher privilege level.  Note that for our example */
        /* O.S. this should never occur.                                              */
        A: AbortTask("Attempted access of higher privileged memory");

        /* Write Protected - tried writing into read-only memory                      */
        W: AbortTask("Attempted write into read-only memory");

        /* Limit Violation - tried accessing unmapped virtual space.  This happens in our example */
        /* O.S. when accessing within a 16 megabyte segment in User memory beyond what is */
        /* currently allocated for the lower page table as determined by the upper level limit field. */
        L: AbortTask("Invalid address");

        /* Invalid - pointer indicates invalid.  Must determine status.               */
        I: begin

                /* If upper level entry then that 16 Meg chunk of the virtual space is unallocated */
                /* and has no page tables.                                            */
                If TableEntry is upper level then AbortTask("Invalid address");

                /* We are at a page table entry.  Look at software flags.             */

                /* If this page unallocated to the User then abort task               */
                If EntryStatus=invalid_unallocated then
                        AbortTask("Invalid Address");

                /* If this page is virgin then assign to it a physical frame          */
                if EntryStatus = invalid_virgin then do
                        GetFrame(TableEntry);           /* address returned in entry  */
                        PLOAD (BusErrAddress);          /* update MC68851 entry       */
                        exit BusErrorHandler;           /* done so continue task      */
                        end do;

                /* If this page is swapped out then read it back in                   */
                if EntryStatus = invalid_swapped_out then do
                        /* first get a frame to hold the new page                     */
                        DiskAddress = TableEntry.Pointer;   /* disk location          */

                        GetFrame(TableEntry);           /* address returned in entry  */
```

```
                /* Now read in the virtual page image                          */
                call SwapPageIn(TableEntry,DiskAddress);
                PLOAD (BusErrAddress);          /* update MC68851 entry         */
                exit BusErrorHandler;           /* done so continue task        */
                end do;

        end begin;

            /* No MC68851 status bits on. Must be memory malfunction or RMW cycle with no  */
            /*ATC entry                                                                    */
Otherwise:  If Stack_Frame shows RMW instruction (SSW) then
                    /*ATC did not have descriptor loaded and MC68851 cannot    */
                    /*search tables to load it. Explicitly load it and allow the task to   */
                    /*continue normally                                          */

                Begin
                    PLOAD (BusErrAddress); /*update ATC                         */
                    exit BusErrorHandler;    /*done so re-execute instruction   */
                    end Begin

            Else: AbortTask ("Memory Malfunction");

    end case;
```

Procedure GetFrame(FrameTableEntry);
    /* This module returns the address of a physical frame in the passed table entry. It obtains one   */
    /* from the free frame list. If none there, it scans a queue pointing to pages that have been   */
    /* recorded as having aged by not being accessed frequently. It first tries to find a read-only   */
    /* page in the queue but if none, it returns the first (oldest) entry after swapping the page out */
    /* to disk and altering the translation tables of the owning task. If nothing in the queue it waits */
    /* for some other task to free a frame by terminating or deallocating memory   */

Restart:
    if Free_Frame_Queue NOT null then
        Dequeue first entry and return its value.

    if Aged_Frame_Queue NOT null then begin

        /* First try to find a read-only page   */
        If scanning finds read-only page then use and dequeue it
          else dequeue the first entry (which is the oldest);

        Find owning task and the frame's current page entry;

        /* Invalidate owning task's page   */
        PFLUSH (User_Space,VictimTask.VirtualAddress);

        /* If modified page, swap it out. SwapPageOut either gives control to other tasks   */
        /* during the I/O or copies the page returning immediately.   */
        If modified then call SwapPageOut(VictimTask.TableEntry);
        /* Disk address now in Victim's page entry   */

        /* Now set the old task's page status and return the frame   */
        VictimTask.TableEntry.Status = invalid_swapped_out;
        return physical frame value;
        end do;

    /* At this point we can use some other stealing method but we just wait until another task frees */
    /* a frame by terminating or freeing memory.   */
    call wait (Free_Frame);
    go to Restart;

    end **GetFrame**;

Procedure **SwapPageIn (SwapinTableEntry,DiskAddress);**
    /* This procedure takes the disk address and reads the page from the paging external media   */
    /* into the physical address residing in the table entry pointer.   */
    end **SwapPageIn**;

Procedure **SwapPageOut(SwapoutTableEntry);**
    /* This procedure performs output on the external paging device and then replaces the   */
    /* physical page frame address in the page entry pointer field with the disk address of the   */
    /* block holding the image of the page.   */
    end **SwapPageOut**;

Procedure **AbortTask(TerminationMsg);**
    /* This procedure terminates the current task and issues a diagnostic message.   */
    end **AbortTask**;

end **BusErrorHandler**;

1	Introduction
2	Overview of System Operation
3	Signal Description
4	Bus Operation Description
5	Address Translation
6	Instruction Set Processor
7	Protection
8	Breakpoints
9	Coprocessor Interface
10	Access Level Control Interface
11	Operation Timings
12	Electrical Specifications
13	Ordering Information and Mechanical Data
A	Instruction Set
B	Hardware Considerations
C	Software Considerations

NOTES

NOTES

NOTES